PLATO

Republic

The Focus Philosophical Library

PLATO
Republic

Translation, Glossary, and Introductory Essay

Joe Sachs
ST. JOHN'S COLLEGE, ANNAPOLIS

with an Afterword by John White

focus Publishing
R. Pullins Company
PO Box 369
Newburyport, MA 01950
www.pullins.com

Plato Republic
© 2007 by Joe Sachs

Focus Publishing/R. Pullins Company
PO Box 369
Newburyport, MA 01950
www.pullins.com

ISBN 13: 978-1-58510-261-7
Also available as PDF eBook (978-1-58510-383-6)

Printed in the United States of America

15 14 13 12 11 10 9 8 7 6 5

1012TS

CONTENTS

INTRODUCTION

If a large random group of people were asked to name an important work of philosophy, the answer given most often would probably be Plato's *Republic*. Why it merits such distinction is something fewer people might venture to say. Those whose acquaintance with the book is primarily second-hand, guided by a lecturer or by books about it, could be excused for being puzzled about its enduring power. It is said to be a portrait of an "ideal state," but one that no actual government has ever tried to put into practice, and it is said to contain a statement of a famous philosophic "theory," but one it would be hard to find anyone who believed in. What, then, makes it more than a strange relic of obsolete thinking? The answer is easily found by anyone who ignores the masses of learned explanations that surround the *Republic*, and simply plunges into reading it. There has rarely been a book that so successfully grabs a reader and stirs spirited responses.

A number of philosophers over the centuries have written dialogues. That means, in most cases, that they have written arguments and counterarguments, and put them in the mouths of imaginary speakers. Plato went about it the opposite way. He wrote imagined conversations among people whom, for the most part, he knew, and made those conversations rise to the level of philosophic discussion. Plato did not treat philosophy as something that could be delivered or presented or even imitated in a written work. He knew that there is no way to encounter philosophy except from the inside, and he wrote with the purpose of stimulating, provoking, and inspiring the experience of it. He himself had been strongly affected by listening to the conversations Socrates used to have in public, and he made Socrates the primary speaker in most of his dialogues. Even in those dialogues in which Socrates is not present, or says little, a Platonic dialogue is always an imitation of Socrates. Plato made the things he wrote as substitute encounters with Socrates: not depictions of such encounters for us to watch, but evocations of them for us to experience. So great can be the power of imitative fiction that Plato successfully sets in motion philosophic activity every time a reader gives him the slightest chance.

A chance to respond to Plato's imitation of Socrates does not depend on being favorably disposed to their words in advance, or even on approaching the dialogues with an open mind. Since the dialogues teach no doctrine, an antagonistic response is as effective as any other kind in making a reader a more active thinker. Within the *Republic*, Socrates is challenged in Book I by a hostile and angry opponent, and then again in Book II by two friendly but determined young men who think he hasn't given that opponent anything like an adequate answer. All three, and a few other characters who get hooked along the way, have one thing in common: they all put aside everything else they intended to do for many hours, and become absorbed in a conversation about philosophic topics and about philosophy itself. The only person present who is immune to it all is a very old man, intent on preparations for his death. The rest of the characters in the dialogue are a lot like us, a diverse array of people who pick up the *Republic*, and for one reason or another can't put it down.

The *Republic* depicts people with different interests and desires being brought together into a shared activity freely chosen by each; this is a reflection not only of our situation as readers of it, but also of its primary theme. The dramatic situation in a Platonic dialogue is never mere literary ornamentation for a set of arguments, but always in some way shows the reader the way to an answer to the question discussed in it. The question that sets in motion the whole discussion in the *Republic* is, what is justice? That question receives a succession of formal answers, but none of them reveals as much about what justice is as does the human interaction we witness. In the dialogue, one person pressures a second person into joining him and his friends to help them kill a little time, a third person leaves the gathering to pursue his own business, a fourth person tries to break up the discussion as soon as it begins to get somewhere, and a fifth and sixth person insist on imposing their concerns on the group, but with the adroit management of the situation by one of their number, they become a harmonious partnership in an extended activity that in some way satisfies them all. If we can say what makes the *Republic* possible as a living event, an understanding of what justice is cannot be far away.

The one adroit member of the group who manages to pull them all together is of course Socrates. The *Republic* is one of Plato's longest dialogues, and it is in some ways all Socrates. Every word of it is given to us through Socrates' narration, and no other dialogue is so packed with his opinions, his imagination, and his ways of looking at things. At the same time, though, no dialogue so emphatically presents a partnership in learning. Most dialogues of Plato resemble one or more aspects of Book I of the *Republic*, in which someone is brought to realize he understands less than he thought he did, someone else is provoked to anger, a few others begin to be curious, and the end comes with a question sharpened and unresolved. In the *Republic*, we are given three more books in which a couple of intelligent listeners initiate a dialogue about the original dialogue, and then six more books in which all those still present commit themselves to remain involved, and state a consensus about how the discussion should proceed. The beginning of Book V is presented as something like a constitutional convention in which those assembled unanimously and explicitly associate themselves into a community and choose a leader. So the *Republic* is simultaneously an extended portrait of Socrates and a concentrated representation of all humankind.

The political community referred to in the dialogue's traditional title is most explicitly the imagined city discussed at length in it, designed to make justice evident, but that title takes on additional meaning when one sees that it applies also to the group of people assembled for the discussion. Each of those communities is a willing combination of ruler and ruled, brought together not by force or by practical necessity but for the sake of improving the lives of all concerned. But one of the most striking facts about the city is the presence in it of an ambiguous class of people who are somehow both rulers and ruled, and somehow neither. The guardians of the city are the middle part that makes the whole partnership possible. They display neither the private desires and interests of the population at large, nor the ultimate directing judgment that rules the city. They willingly sacrifice the former and acquiesce in the latter because they find the fulfillment of their spirited natures in holding together a healthy community. Like the city, the assembled group in the *Republic* has a middle part that makes it possible for it to be more than a two-way encounter between Socrates and others, a mere Book I, and to become a stable whole. That middle part consists of the two young men, Glaucon and Adeimantus, who happen to be brothers of Plato.

Glaucon and Adeimantus show in Book II of the dialogue that they are capable thinkers and self-starters. Both are marvelously articulate, and each has already thought through questions about justice and injustice that go far beyond most people's unreflective opinions. But each is aware of his own inability to resolve the questions that seem to him to be most in need of resolution. They see the need for some trustworthy clarification of the goals of human life, but they have sufficient respect for their own powers of judgment to know that none of the things they've ever heard argued or praised, by parents, poets, politicians, or philosophers, gives them a satisfactory account of what makes life good. Between them they provide a critique of Socrates' arguments in Book I, and between them they sustain the lengthy discussion with him that their critique demands. They recognize the need for Socrates' leadership, and they supply the energy and effort to make that leadership effective for their friends as well. They are the middle part of the partnership that lets it be one and not many.

This threefold structure of ruling and ruled parts, bound into unity by a middle part, is the dominant image of the *Republic*. It is present not only in the large community discussed and the small community that discusses it, but ultimately in another community that makes up each one of us. The dialogue discusses political topics, but all for the sake of seeing more clearly the interior composition of a single human being. The political themes of the dialogue have their purpose in an analogy to the human soul that finds in it the original three-part structure that is the source of all the rest. We may be accustomed to think of ourselves as a combination of head and heart, or of reason and desire. But how could a twofold entity become one human being? One part could overpower the other or even destroy it, or each could sometimes win and sometimes lose in an ongoing power struggle. The *Republic* presents the possibility that the many conflicting aims and desires within us can compose their differences in the same way a community of people can, because there is a middle part in us capable of playing the unifying role.

The three-part soul, in which spiritedness permits reason to rule, and not squelch, desire, makes possible a life in which everything in us can be in harmony and can fulfill its cravings without depriving any of the other parts of satisfaction. This arrangement is the basis of the answer Socrates finds in the *Republic* to the question of what justice is, and the result it can produce is what he calls happiness. As an outline sketch, this proposal may be more useful than anything comparable to it as an aid to thinking about the goals of human life. But it is not a theory. In the sketchy form in which I have stated it here, it is in fact just short of useless. It gains its utility when it is fleshed out by the living activity of a reader of the *Republic*, built into a whole by thinking and imagination, and given life by application to examples in and out of the dialogue. But a reader may be unwilling to try out such a way of looking at things, just because it speaks of us as having souls. This is not a popular way of thinking these days. A difficulty of this sort brings a reader to a crucial turning point. To suspend one's own opinions for a while can open the door to philosophy; to balk at entering into thoughts that are not familiar and comfortable can make philosophy impossible.

As a reader nears that particular fork in the road, when the parts of the soul are being spoken of in Book IV, one thing he might happen to recall is a passage near the beginning of Book I (329B-D) in which the old man Cephalus reports on an unexpected benefit of old age. Once sexual and other desires have slackened, he had said, someone can finally be at peace, if he happens to have an orderly disposition. But what is it in him that is left at peace when the desires die down? What components go into an orderly disposition, and how are they disposed? If Cephalus is talking about an imaginable human experience, it might be convenient to think of it as reflecting the relation among the parts of someone's soul. Whether "soul" is really the best word to use can be left as a topic for another day. A certain courtesy and civility toward others, the kind of attitude without which conversation is impossible, is sufficient to let us entertain the idea of a soul while Socrates and others speak of it, and a self-interested desire to understand something inherently interesting makes it worth a try. For a good and alert reader, one who thought in Book I that there was something wrong with the way Cephalus was thinking about his life, the idea of the three-part soul may already be paying off by suggesting that Cephalus himself was a spiritless man, a two-part soul. In his younger days, he was by his own report a slave of his desires. Having lived long enough for those desires to atrophy, he comes before us as a fragment of a human being, as though he were nothing but a head, which is what his name happens to mean.

This sort of word-play with someone's name is something Plato is fond of, but it is of no importance. At best it adds a little confirmation to a connection or interpretation a reader has come up with on the basis of better evidence. What is more important is that there are no loose ends in a Platonic dialogue. If a character enters and leaves, whatever he had to say will be connected with themes that emerge in the main body of the discussion. Cephalus claims to enjoy philosophic conversation, but he has no time for it and no curiosity about it, and no spiritedness is aroused in him when his own opinions are shown to be inadequate. He lives outside the city of Athens, and places himself outside the community of learning that spontaneously forms in his own house. Something seems to have been lacking in his makeup or at least in his education. The idea of the three-part soul offers a chance to think more fully and deeply about him. A reader who avails himself of that chance is well launched on the road toward a more examined life, and the particular assumption that human beings have souls is not what matters most about that examination, nor even a part of it that can't be discarded later if a reason to do so comes along. What that reader has done is not adopt a theory, but follow some distance along a dialectical path.

Now the three-part soul is not the only thing the *Republic* gives us to think about, and Cephalus is not the only example it gives us to apply that thought to, but the process that Socrates calls dialectic is the heart of everything that goes on in that or any other Platonic dialogue. Dialogue as a form of writing and dialectic as a way of thinking are, in Plato's handling of them, inseparable. In this dialogue, dialectic becomes an explicit topic in Book VI, and large claims are made about it. What Socrates is talking about, though, has been in front of us all along, and he has even given a simple description of it in Book I. At 348A-B, he recommends a way of handling his disagreement with Thrasymachus. He says the two of them could take turns making speeches, each refuting the other point by point, and let the others serve as a jury to decide who got the better of whom in the argument. What he prefers, though, is that they start with something they agree about, and see how it bears on the question under discussion. In that way, he says, each of them would be a juror and an advocate at the same time. This reflects a preference for the attitude involved in discussion rather than debate, and the Greek word for dialectic is made out of the verb that means to engage in conversation. A debater treats the other speaker as someone who can only be right if he himself is wrong, whom he must defeat at all costs. In a conversation, though, we generally have the decency to accept the things another person says, at least temporarily and tentatively. If we disagree, and take the matter seriously, we might say "if that's true, doesn't such-and-such follow?" or "doesn't that depend on assuming so-and-so?" At such a point dialectic has begun, and the give-and-take that ensues is nothing like the back-and-forth of a debate.

The difference is that the dialectical interchange is taking place within the thinking of each participant, as well as between them. By adopting the double role of judge and advocate at the same time, each of them detaches himself from his own opinions in order to examine them. But those opinions are not just propositions up for debate, but things one also sees good reason to believe. All our powers can be involved in dialectic; a spirited attachment to one's own opinions can be opposed by a desire to understand things better, and some sort of insight into evidence must come into play to move things forward. If the discussion is pressed back through deeper and deeper assumptions, presuppositions one never knew one was relying on can come to sight. And if the inquiry doesn't break off at that stage but continues, Socrates claims (533C-D), it becomes possible to discover the difference between opinion and knowledge, and to advance toward the latter. That discovery is also the beginning of philosophy, and it is what Socrates refers to at one important moment as a turning around of the whole soul (518C-D). This turning is said to be possible for someone who has emerged from a cave in which he, like all of us, has been imprisoned. The cave analogy is perhaps the best known passage in the *Republic*, and it bears more than one good interpretation. In one of them, emergence from the cave into the sunlight can represent the condition of someone who has not realized that all his thinking has relied on opinion, at the moment when he discovers by experience that knowledge is possible.

The dual perspective involved in dialectical thinking is a bringing together in one activity of the ways of seeing represented as in and out of the cave. This same duality is also at the heart of a characteristic way of speaking Socrates was famous for: his irony. Students beginning to read Plato often misinterpret this irony as sarcasm, but its purpose is never to belittle another person. Typically, it takes the form of a mock fear of his own ignorance and someone else's wisdom. An instance of this at 336D-337A infuriates Thrasymachus. Protestations like those of Socrates, while some might find them annoying, can be insulting only to someone who refuses to acknowledge any ignorance of his own. Socratic irony can always be taken as an invitation to inquire. Someone who refuses that invitation may well be so locked into one way of looking at things that one could imagine his head as held rigidly in one position by shackles. In Plato's *Apology*, his depiction of the speech Socrates gave when he was on trial for his life, Socrates describes his own condition by saying (22D) "I was aware that I know nothing." The knowledge of ignorance is the theme of all Socratic irony. It became a common saying in the more paradoxical form reported by Diogenes Laertius in his *Lives of the Philosophers* (II, 32): "he used to say...that he knew nothing except just that (*auto touto*)." But Socrates had no interest in logical puzzles. The assertion that he *knows* that he does not know is Socrates' provocative way of declaring a permanent commitment to philosophy, a willingness always to return to the moment of discovery when one first experiences the insight that opinion is not knowledge, and discerns that this insight is not just one more opinion.

The purpose of Socrates' irony is never to mock someone while praising him in words, but to spark a response in which the listener cannot remain in a passive relation to his own opinions. If that listener is roused even to defend those opinions, or to figure out what's wrong with Socrates' formulation, he can become actively engaged in seeing evidence in a way that will stand before him as a contrast to his ordinary reliance on opinion. Knowing is understood by Socrates as the living activity of insight, for which the Greek word is *noêsis*. The cave analogy at the beginning of Book VII is the companion to a mathematical image at the end of Book VI that likens the powers of the soul to the segments of a line divided in a certain repeated ratio. The highest power is first called dialectic, then insight, and finally knowledge. Commentators will tell you that the divided line image presents "Plato's theory of forms," but the passage itself (510E-511A) introduces the notion of forms, the invisible looks of intelligible things seen directly in live thinking, as a criticism of the sort of thinking embodied in theories. A theory is unable to step off above its own assumptions. The divided line offers the possibility that we can and should strive to do just that, and that nothing less is genuinely philosophic. Socrates uses his irony to goad, and his images to beckon, others toward that highest thinking that leaves its familiar certainties behind and relies on nothing but the power it has in the moment of its exercise to assess truth.

In the image of the divided line, the power of knowing is a fourth proportional. If we are given the ratio of two magnitudes a:b and a third magnitude c, a fourth magnitude is there to be found if we make the effort. Socrates tells us that genuine knowing is related to the sort of understanding involved in theories as a visible tree is related to its reflection in a pond. The crucial component of this complex image is the power at the bottom of the line, the way of seeing by which we recognize an image as an image. If your back is to the tree, you can still tell that what you are looking at is its image, and imagine the tree itself. Similarly, the divided line suggests, there is an intellectual imagination that assures us there are intelligible things themselves that stand behind and above anything we may reason about on the basis of assumptions.

The divided line is an image about images, in the middle of a dialogue full of images. One of the things that most of all gives the *Republic* its characteristic flavor is its profusion of images of all kinds. At various points in the dialogue (such as 435D and 506E), Socrates emphasizes that a precise account of the things under discussion would have to go by a longer and harder road, but that a lot can still be gained by the use of images. In fact an image has the advantage over a theory in that one can more easily be reminded that it is not knowledge but only a dialectical step toward knowing. And Socrates repeatedly reminds Glaucon and Adeimantus, when they become too convinced of things they ought to be examining critically, not to be so sure that they've really found the best plan for education (416B-C), that the city they've designed is really the best (450C), or that the soul really has three parts (612A). One of the words used most frequently in the *Republic* is *oiomai*, translated here almost always as "I imagine" as another constant reminder that everything made intelligible in the dialogue is offered first to the imagination, and is thought through, and into, only by those willing to make their own efforts to ascend through the stages of the divided line.

The topic that occupies the largest part of the dialogue is the arrangement of laws and other provisions that would make the best political community. Whether Socrates is making serious practical proposals is much disputed by readers. Socrates himself at different times seems to argue both sides of that question (as at 450C, 540D, 592B), but one might have to distinguish features of the city that could and would improve political life from those meant only to be thought about. And at one point Socrates draws back from his own seriousness, calling the whole discussion playful (536C), but he goes on to argue that the best learning always begins as play, in which the learner's own powers become spontaneously active. Practicality and seriousness may be best served by free-ranging discussion that places no possibilities off-limits. Readers who fiercely disagree about whether any sort of slavery is being condoned, or whether a general censorship is being imposed beyond the early education of one part of the population, may be doing exactly what Socrates hopes for, on matters that the text itself will not settle in any unambiguous way. But no matter what one makes of the political content of the dialogue, discussion of it is always serving another purpose, in which the design of the city is not the ultimate topic but an image of it. The organization of a city is introduced (368C-369A) as something to be looked at, for the sake of seeing more clearly how justice might be present in a single human being. The design of the city as the image of a soul may require assumptions unnecessary or inappropriate to a city considered on its own terms.

In particular, the governing principle for the city designed in the *Republic* is that it must have the greatest possible unity (423B, 462A-B). But Aristotle, discussing Socrates' city in Book II, Chapter 2 of his *Politics*, argues that the unity appropriate to a city is not simply unity as such, and that too great a unity can destroy a city. This is often spoken of as a "refutation of Plato," but anyone who has gotten the hang of the dialectical style of the dialogues can see that Aristotle may simply be following a path that Socrates has opened up. Socrates explicitly says in 462C that he is designing his city to be most like a single human being. This may have the double benefit of revealing in one image the multiplicity that needs to be harmonized in each of us and the limits to the possible unity in any association we might have with others. That is, the analogy is equally revealing both where it applies and where it breaks down. Socrates has given to our imaginations a city for us to see and think about, not to take literally as a political program. His imaginary city is on the borderline between the soul and political life, a vantage point from which we are invited to try to understand them both. We need to interpret the city ourselves, to make any such understanding our own, and we can try out interpreting it on various assumptions. The variety of interpretations, and any inherent difficulties in each of them, are discrepancies that call forth the activity of intellect and can disclose to us some of our own unexamined opinions. The dialectical motion that results is not merely a substitution of one opinion for another, but an advance to opinions that are more well-grounded in insight.

There are those who think the arguments Socrates makes in this or any dialogue can be detached from their contexts and refuted. Such readers fail to grasp the nature of dialectic not only as it animates the text but also as it enhances their own engagement with the text. They may think that philosophy is logical analysis. If they confine themselves to the third segment of the divided line, their disdain for the images in its lowest part denies them any chance to achieve the kind of seeing that belongs to its highest part. When people speak of arguments in Platonic dialogues as fallacious, they rarely allege any errors in reasoning. What they turn out to mean in virtually all cases is that there is some assumption governing the conclusion that is either untrue or unnecessary. Such an assumption may be an opinion of the person Socrates is talking to. The whole point of Socrates' approach to discussion is to explore such assumptions by exposing them, tracing conclusions to which they lead, and following them back to higher assumptions. Sometimes assumptions are introduced by Socrates, not because he is unaware of them or endorsing them, but because they clarify connections and reveal choices that confront the other person. In all these cases it is the listener or reader who is invited to find the flaws or choose the way forward, but this is not a contest, a chess match in which someone is challenged to show how smart he is. The challenge is a much deeper one, in which logical moves play a role but are the least important of the things that are at stake. Socrates is always offering help, in the form of images, by means of which another person can begin to see more possibilities and open up his thinking. And for the reader, Plato too offers the image of the people engaged in the dialogue, and invites us to see something in what they are doing or failing to do that might let us advance beyond them.

A small example of the sort of thing Socrates does with images can be found at 375D-E. He and Glaucon appear to be at a loss to find a type of human character that is at once high-spirited and gentle, until Socrates suggests that they might find an image of it in dogs. By nature, dogs get angry at strangers but they treat people they know with affection. They must be lovers of learning, Socrates concludes, so maybe philosophically inclined human beings would be similarly spirited and gentle. Now as a piece of reasoning this is obvious nonsense, but true conclusions can follow from false premises, and in any case the ensuing discussion about how to educate people to be both spirited and gentle leaves aside both the analogy to dogs and anything purportedly derived from it. Why then does Socrates make this detour through an image that seems useless if not destructive to the argument? References to dogs crop up a number of times in the rest of the dialogue, and the memory of Socrates' earlier abortive analogy may serve some purpose for a reader who found it puzzling or annoying at first. It seems to do just that for Glaucon at 440D, where Socrates praises him for getting hold of a conception in thought by taking to heart what was first in his imagination. It begins to emerge there that the spirited part of the soul is not just another irrational element in us like desire, but also rational to the extent that it can listen to and be persuaded by reason. Perhaps too, spirited but gentle souls need not be philosophic, but capable of recognizing and following the lead of those who are. The whole arrangement and significance of the three-part city and soul gains new depth for someone who is willing to work with the material left behind in his imagination by a faulty analogy, and that work will be all the more effective to the extent that it is his own. What Socrates has offered is not an answer or a theory or a doctrine, but a question, a suggestion, and an image, all of which tend to awaken our own powers.

Another example of a small image left behind early in the dialogue is Socrates' brief reference in 351C to a gang of thieves. It is offered as a picture of the way injustice divides a group of people against itself, so that even an unjust purpose can be accomplished in common only by those who practice justice among themselves. Socrates generalizes this into a suggestion that justice, if one should ever come to understand it, would be what unites people. And since he goes on to ask about injustice within a single human being, we are left with the possibility that justice may be the power that makes any whole made of parts be capable of acting as one thing rather than many. Much later in the dialogue, when the three-part soul is connected with the four cardinal virtues of human character, justice seems to be an unnecessary remnant, and the formulations arrived at about it may not be very satisfying. A reader who has the gang-of-thieves picture in the back of his mind has something to work with to carry his understanding forward. But am I right to call this an image or picture at all? Is it not just one of a number of thinkable situations into which justice and injustice can be inserted as variables? There is certainly no development of it, and no sensory detail is used to make it vivid. But there is some confirmation in the text that it is intended to be used not just as something posited for analysis but as a reflection and likeness of things other than itself. Thrasymachus agrees to allow Socrates' suggestion that justice unites people, not because he is persuaded of it but "so I won't be at odds with you." We are witnessing, in our imaginations, an interaction of people that looks a lot like the thing being discussed, even though it has nothing to do with thieves. If a connection is made, it will originate not in sorting through logical alternatives but in paying attention to the promptings of our lowly faculty of picturing things.

The image of the dog mentioned above is similarly short on imaginative detail, but Socrates explicitly calls it an image. Most of the images in the dialogue lack the elaboration of the cave analogy early in Book VII, or the myth of Er late in Book X, or Glaucon's story early in Book II of Gyges' ancestor who gained a magical power to become invisible whenever he pleased. But it is probably true that everything brought up to be thought about in the dialogue is connected with or embedded in something meant to engage the imagination first. Much of the dialogue is concerned with criticizing imitative poetry. It is a common observation that the *Republic* is itself a work of imitative poetry, and that Plato cannot therefore be serious about such criticism. But we might understand better what Plato is doing with his imitation if we look at what he shows us Socrates doing with his images. Every one of Socrates' images is meant to lead beyond itself. The philosopher-dog and the gang of thieves are not offered to us for any inherent interest they might have. They engage our imaginations in order to take us beyond imagination altogether. They are like the example of the last three fingers on a hand that Socrates gives in 523A-E, to illustrate that the sense of sight sometimes blends contradictory attributes, and can arouse us to go beyond sight to insight. Only the intellect can resolve the discrepancies that sight first brings to our attention. People sometimes dismiss the example of the fingers by saying that large and small are only relative terms, not realizing that they have thereby proved Socrates' point, since the word "relative" refers to nothing visible, but only to something intelligible. The senses contribute to philosophic reflection wherever they reveal inconsistencies that they themselves cannot resolve. In such cases we are compelled to climb the divided line, at least partway. This seems to me also to be what distinguishes Socratic image-making from the poetic imitations he questions. Every image Socrates gives us cries out for interpretation. None tempts us to remain absorbed in it as an end in itself.

Perhaps the most memorable image in the *Republic* is the cave analogy, but it remains with us not because of any beauty in its depiction but because it stimulates so rich and endless a process of interpretation. It does not overwhelm us with a sense that all questioning must recede in deference to its power. It is an image we are forever climbing out of, into a realm free of images. The three great images that come before us in the middle of the *Republic*—the sun, the line, and the cave—are on three different steps of the divided line. The sun is a direct sensory image of something belonging to its second segment. The divided line itself is a mathematical image belonging to the third. The cave analogy is an image of shadows, of artifacts, and of the turn toward the sensory originals above and behind them, the motion that takes place within the first segment. The three are all tied together, and this emphasizes that there is an absent fourth, a segment in which there can be no images. But the abundant material for thinking our way forward that the three images provide, separately and in all their interconnections, makes them step off the page into a dialectic in which we are already enacting the kind of thinking that Socrates assigns to the fourth level. For a reader who accepts the invitation to interpret its images, the *Republic* is an immersion into a philosophic education.

But the act of interpreting the divided line discloses nothing in it that implies a motion in only one direction. If an image achieves its purpose when it is replaced by an understanding free of images, the insight one may gain into intelligible things reciprocally calls out for confirmation by an application to examples in the imagination. If justice is giving back what one takes, what about weapons belonging to someone who has gone temporarily insane? This downward turn to the imagination at 331C begins a process that does not lose clarity or intelligibility but gains, deepens, and enhances them. The imagination is not left behind as a lower and lesser faculty, but is the mediating power that draws all our experience into one whole. The divided line is given first as undivided, continuous and one, and the ratios between its parts are all symmetrical, pointing upward no more than downward. The most striking mathematical implication of the divided line, to which attention is called in the notes to 511A and 534A, is that its second and third segments are equal in magnitude. That in turn makes either of them a mean proportional between the top and bottom segments, and that suggests that it may be the same power of the soul that appears in the visible realm as trust in the senses, and in the intelligible realm as reasoning based on assumptions. If this way of playing with the image has anything to it, the four segments of the divided line may after all be only three, and that would give us yet another three-part structure with a middle part that looks both upward and downward.

The cluster of images in which the divided line is central can now be seen as all about the reciprocal relations of higher and lower parts in ordered wholes. The sun shines on everything under it, not only as a source of illumination but as a source of growth. But what might be the most controversial passage in the dialogue is the discussion of the return of the philosopher to the cave (519C-520E). If the example of returning weapons to their rightful owner when he's out of his mind begins a process of refining one's thinking about justice, that process must culminate in a reader's reaction to the necessity for the philosopher to return to an active role in a political community. The analogy to the soul does not remove the need to understand the return in terms of human interactions as well as within the interior life of anyone who has tasted a contemplative life. Glaucon is persuaded that he was wrong to see the demands of community life as an injustice to the philosopher, but Socrates' argument leaves open the possibility that such obligations are not present outside the best city. But we have an example in front of us in Socrates himself of a philosopher living in a less-than-best city. The first word of the *Republic* means "I went down," and the fact that Socrates spends so many hours down in the Piraeus means that he has chosen that as a better use of his time than anything he might have done back up in Athens. He refuses to be kept down below when Polemarchus merely insists on it from his own desire; he pretends to be tempted by the chance to see a torch race on horses when Adeimantus uses that to rekindle the curiosity that had brought him down from town in the first place; what finally tips the scales and persuades him to stay (328B) is Glaucon's joining the others in a consensus that they should stay. From the moment a group of people draws together into a whole with a common interest, Socrates is persuaded to join the community, even if his purpose is to steer it toward a more worthwhile activity than the one it has in view.

The Piraeus, soon to be torch-lit not only for a horse race but also for an all-night party, turns out in retrospect to be the first image in the *Republic* that invites us to reflect on the possible uses that can be made of a life shared with others unlike oneself. The last such image is the myth that concludes the dialogue, in which all the souls that have been journeying through the heavens and under the earth, with the exception of a few who are incurably depraved, meet again in friendship in a meadow (614E) a few days' march from the center of the cosmos, where everyone present has the chance to return to earth with a good and satisfying life. For each of them, that life is a result of choice, and their choices take place within sight of the shaft of light that extends from above throughout all the heavens and earth. Still, some of the souls make poor choices, relying on habits rather than on reflection. Their choices are influenced by all their experiences, and not always with all the clarity of sight of which each is capable. One may imagine, though, that the conversations they've shared so recently with one another about those experiences would make some of those choices better than they might otherwise have been, and thus make life on earth better and more civilized for them all.

The torchlight that represents so much of earthly life is only a half-light, that obscures as well as illumines. Only sunlight would be bright enough to illumine everything in visible range, and only at noon is it high enough to minimize all the shadows it also produces. But our nature as human beings does not seem to be fitted to dwell always in the noonday sun. Socrates, on the day he recounts in the *Republic*, chooses to spend the torch-lit hours in conversation in the Piraeus. When he tells Glaucon that justice brings the philosopher back into the cave (520B), he argues that, in the best city, the philosopher owes a debt to the city in return for the education it gave him. But we have already read the first six books of the dialogue by that point, and we know that the understanding of justice as paying debts has long since been left behind (331D). It made sense to the calculating soul of Cephalus, and nothing in him was roused to follow when the conversation moved on. His more spirited son Polemarchus was attracted by the idea that justice means helping friends and hurting enemies (332D), but that claim too soon lost its persuasiveness (335E). The democratic soul of Thrasymachus was positive that acting out of justice always means sacrificing one's own interests to those of someone stronger (343C), but that view was at least neutralized by the end of Book I. Socrates himself eventually formulates what justice is in the cryptic phrase "doing what's properly one's own" (433B), but this is only after he has earlier made the point that recognizing a virtue such as justice depends on seeing the accord of a state of human character with a certain state of harmony in oneself (401D-402D), not on any accordance between an action and a definition. The image of Socrates, not arguing with opponents but conversing with friends, seems meant to allow us to bring justice to sight. The *Republic* also gives us abundant material to work with in order to think through what we might be seeing, and to come to an understanding of what it might have to do with happiness. In order to achieve that seeing, that thinking, and that understanding, we too must join the conversation.

* * *

But why should the English-speaking world be subjected to yet another version of the *Republic*? Over the past forty years or so, I have read the dialogue all the way through in translation at least a dozen times. Whatever new translation I have read from time to time, I have always returned to that of Allan Bloom as by far the most accurate available. I have no serious complaints about Bloom's translation, but the mere fact that it has held the field since 1968 is reason enough to try to discover whether a worthy alternative to it can be provided. I don't seek to emulate Thrasymachus, who thinks an intelligent person would want to outdo any artful piece of work by someone else, but it is at least true that I don't share Bloom's preoccupations, and the different choices I have made may foster some new thought and discussion about an inexhaustible book. I depart a bit farther than Bloom does from the 19th century diction enshrined forever in such reference works as the lexicons of Liddell and Scott and the commentary of James Adam, without moving all the way into current colloquial speech. That sort of attempt to hit a moving target can never simply be a success. "You're a damned shyster," Raymond Larson's version of a remark at 340D, no more captures the exact tone and content of the original than "Do you play the sycophant with me, my good sir?" would; it merely changes the manner of its obsolescence. Plato's characters can be kept recognizably human and natural, speaking neither the English one might have heard in the rooms of an Oxbridge don in 1905, nor the sort one would find in barrooms, or chat rooms, in 2005.

Like Bloom, I have tried to respect the text as written. I have no desire to revise the author's style to suit my own tastes, as Cornford did in 1941, or to recast a recollected conversation into the format of dramatic imitation, as C. D. C. Reeve's 2004 version does. Reeve cites as a precedent for his liberties the character Eucleides, whom Plato presents as the transcriber of the conversation in the *Theaetetus*. But Eucleides was a slightly comic figure, used as a way of highlighting the opinion discussed in the first half of that dialogue that everything is in flux, never gathered up for contemplation in the act of recollection. Other defects of a dramatic as opposed to a narrative presentation are explicitly discussed in the *Republic*. Clearly such choices by Plato are not thoughtless or incidental, but intrinsic parts of intelligent and artful work, and if any author's judgment is worthy of respect, this author's is. But the example Bloom cites as a model translator is not one I would care to imitate either. William of Moerbeke translated the works of Aristotle on the assumption that Greek of the 4th century BC was a coded form of his own 13th century AD Latin, and could be transposed into it by a simple one-to-one substitution of prefix for prefix, root for root, and ending for ending. If that assumption is false, and no word in any natural language has the same range of meaning as any one word in another, then that sort of literalism has to sacrifice accuracy much of the time. Bloom, of course, is never guilty of such a foolish consistency, but I am less likely than he to regard a Greek word as too important to be allowed to vary with its context. Plato's Greek is conversational, and words that others have taken in fixed senses always have a certain fluidity in his dialogues, as Socrates leads those around him, and us, to see more and more in them. To sacrifice the way in which both Plato and Socrates shift various aspects of meaning to the foreground may produce a literal translation, but it cannot be considered accurate translation.

One matter of fact that provides an occasion for a new round of translations of the *Republic* is the availability since 2003 of a newly edited version in the Oxford Classical Texts series. This is not a seismic shift, but it does produce a slight resettling of the ground beneath our feet. S. R. Slings has no major new discoveries to work from, but he reports consultation of an extensive array of evidence, including papyrus manuscripts and ancient translations into Middle Eastern languages. John Burnet's Oxford text was kept in print for a century, but he and James Adam of Cambridge had many small disagreements based on their opinions of the relative trustworthiness of the various medieval manuscript traditions. I hereby declare that (with the two exceptions noted in 454B and 556E) I have trusted Slings's scholarship to resolve all such discrepancies better than I could, but in fact most of the textual points in dispute are so small that they will be invisible to the reader within the inevitable differences among translations. To give one random example typical of many, at 370B where the text Bloom worked from has the word *práxei*, accented as a verb in the future, he translates it with the phrase "for the accomplishment," while the text I used has *prâxin*, accented as a noun in the accusative, which I translate "in practice"; Reeve, basing his translation on the same text I used, leaves the word out of his English version altogether.

This volume contains a number of features designed to help the reader contend with the length and complexity of the dialogue. At the beginning of each of its ten books there is a listing of the main shifts among the principal speakers, identified by ranges of Stephanus numbers; these run from 327A to 621D, page numbers and page divisions from a 16th-century Greek edition of Plato's works, now used universally as a standard pagination, and included here in the margins. Boldface type is used to mark the entrance into the discussion of a new speaker who will be talking with Socrates for an extended time, so you can always look back to the last boldface name, or to the list at the beginning of that book, to remind you who "he" is. There is also a brief prefatory note at the beginning of each book to summarize the content and flow of the discussion, and there are footnotes throughout. The latter serve various purposes, primarily to identify references and to mention anything I've learned over the years that has been particularly helpful to my reading of the dialogue. You shouldn't take my word for any interpretation contained in these comments; I encourage you to use such notes for what they're worth and dismiss them whenever your own thinking supersedes them. The glossary provides comments on some of the most important words used in the dialogue, when their exact meanings cannot easily be gathered from their uses in context; it may be worthwhile to read through the glossary before reading the dialogue. The index does not aspire to comprehensiveness in any respect; it has the more modest purpose of providing a sufficient array of signposts to help you find your way around among the various regions of the dialogue. Entries in the index are to the Stephanus pages within the text, or, when followed by the letter n, to the footnotes to them. The afterword is intended to balance the general discussion of the dialogue in this introduction with an example of a sustained exploration of a single major theme. An effort has been made throughout to choose all this supplementary material with a light touch, aimed at that happy medium which may assist an intelligent reading without overwhelming it.

* * *

I first heard the *Republic* lectured about, in a class called Phil. 1 or something of the sort, when I was a freshman at Oberlin College in 1963. As for the content of that lecture, the kindest thing I can say is that the lecturer was dutifully performing a task for which his talents did not suit him. I had the good fortune the following year to start over as a freshman at St. John's College, where I actually read the dialogue and took part in a number of discussions of it, led by Robert Bart, who knew how to meet a book on its own ground. In those classes, the turning around of the soul was not just an academic topic but an open opportunity. Not long after that, I heard Eva Brann give the splendid lecture "The Music of the Republic." The occasion had a festive character, celebrated, as she walked off the stage, by three students who marched across it in costume suggestive of the Revolutionary War, with fife and drum. And shortly after I had graduated, I heard John White, who was then a graduate student, give a summer lecture that showed me that graduate study could be a way to carry one's own thinking very far and very deep. Eva Brann's lecture was the first version of the essay that is now the title piece of a book published in 2004 by the Paul Dry Press, and John White's lecture on imitation was the forerunner of the essay included here as the afterword to this book. I recommend the former, and offer the latter here, to anyone who wants to get some idea why the *Republic* can be a source of lifelong learning. The breadth of imagination brought to bear by Eva Brann on seeing the dialogue whole, and the intensity of imagination sustained on one major topic in it by John White, show that this is a book that will reward all the powers anyone can summon to the reading of it.

I am grateful to Pamela Kraus, editor of the *St. John's Review*, for permission to reprint John White's piece, which appeared in an earlier version in that journal's 1989-90 double issue on the *Republic* (Vol. XXXIX, Nos. 1 and 2). I am grateful also to Emily Kutler who lavished great care on bringing the torch and horses to life, to Robert Abbott who did most of the work on the index (and did so under difficult circumstances), and to Cordell Yee before whom all computer problems disappear. Eric Salem once again gave generously of his time, of which he has little, and his knowledge, of which he has much, by reading through an entire draft of the translation and suggesting countless improvements; an accurate brief description of Eric's character may be found in the dialogue at 487A 2-5. The origin of this translation, in the realm of proximate causes, was a suggestion made by Mitchell Jones to Ron Pullins that the Focus Philosophical Library ought to have the *Republic* on its list. In the realm of deeper causes, what has been most responsible for the possibility of a project such as this is the community of learning at St. John's College; as always, I am particularly grateful to all those who carry on the struggle, against all odds, to keep that small community going, and to keep it small enough to be what it is.

Annapolis, Maryland
Summer, 2006

PLATO
THE REPUBLIC

BOOK I

Note

The only speaker in the dialogue is Socrates. He begins recounting a conversation he had on the occasion of a foreign religious festival that took place just outside Athens. Between the day and night portions of the festivities, a group of young men latches on to Socrates, who could be expected to provide entertaining talk. Polemarchus takes the group to his house, where they meet his father Cephalus, a very old man preoccupied with making amends before his death for any injustices in his life. Socrates asks him what he understands justice to be, and begins to examine the implications of his answer, when Cephalus excuses himself to tend to the practical side of those concerns, leaving his son to discuss them. Before long, Thrasymachus explodes into the conversation. He is a traveling professional teacher, and his antipathy to Socrates might involve some feeling of rivalry, but he has a palpable disgust with any intelligent adult who can entertain the possibility that justice might be in his own interest. It is obvious to Thrasymachus that human life is a competition in which those who are more unjust succeed more, and those who are most unjust can achieve the ultimate in happiness by becoming tyrants. Socrates finds a starting point for an exchange between them in Thrasymachus's pride in his intelligence, and raises the question whether the just or the unjust have a greater resemblance to people skilled in practical arts. By the end of Book I, Thrasymachus has been compelled to back down from some of his certainties, but nothing seems to have been resolved. But the conversation has stirred up questions in two of the younger men, Glaucon and Adeimantus, who happen to be brothers of Plato, and those questions will lead to an inquiry lasting for nine more books.

327A   **Socrates:** I went down yesterday to Piraeus[1] with Glaucon, Ariston's son, to pray to the goddess, wanting at the same time also to see the way they were going to hold the festival, since they were now conducting it for the first time. The parade of the local residents seemed to me to be beautiful, while the one that the Thracians put

B   on looked no less appropriate. And having prayed and having seen, we went off toward the city. Spotting us from a distance then as we headed home, Polemarchus, Cephalus's son, ordered his slave to run and order us to wait for him. And grabbing me from behind by my cloak, the slave said "Polemarchus orders you to wait." And I turned around and asked him where the man himself was. "He's coming along from behind," he said. "Just wait." "Certainly we'll wait" said Glaucon.

C   And a little later Polemarchus came, and also Adeimantus, Glaucon's brother, and Niceratus, Nicias's son, and some others, apparently from the parade.

Then Polemarchus said "Socrates, you folks seem to me to be heading toward the city as though you're going away."

"That's not bad seeming," I said.

"Do you see us," he said, "how many of us there are?"

"How could I not?"

"Then either get stronger than they are," he said, "or stay right here."

"But isn't something still left," I said, "that we persuade you that you ought to let us go?"

"And do you have the power," he said, "to persuade people who don't listen?"

"Not at all," said Glaucon.

"Then consider us people who aren't going to listen."

328A   And Adeimantus said "Don't you know that there will be a torch race at nightfall on horses for the goddess?"

---

1   The port of Athens, some distance from the main city, was called, then as now, *the* Piraeus. Socrates' omission of the article is unusual. Eva Brann (in *The Music of the Republic*, Paul Dry Books, 2004, pp. 117-118) argues that it suggests a journey to the Land Beyond, a place of the dead (or at least shades and shadows), an image that fits in with the descent conjured up by the dialogue's beginning. The port area was a place of commerce, where resident alien merchants like Cephalus (a native of Syracuse in Sicily) could live and where foreign religious practices could be imported. It was legendary in antiquity that Plato had lavished great care on the composition of this first sentence.

"On horses?" I said. "That's something new. While they hold torches will they pass them to one another in a relay race on horses? Or how do you mean it?"

"That way," said Polemarchus. "And they're also going to have an all-night party that will be worth seeing. We're going to rouse ourselves up after dinner and see the all-night party, and we'll be with many of the young people at it and talk with them. Just stay and don't do anything else."

And Glaucon said "It seems to be something one has got to stay for."

"Well, if it seems good,² " I said, "that's what one ought to do."

So we went to Polemarchus's house, and caught up there with Lysias and Euthydemus, Polemarchus's brothers, as well as Thrasymachus the Chalcedonian, Charmantides the Paeanian, and Cleitophon, Aristonymus's son. And Polemarchus's father Cephalus was also inside. He seemed to me to be very old, for I was seeing him after some interval of time. He was sitting, crowned with wreaths, on a sort of headrest seat, for he had just been sacrificing in the inner courtyard. So we sat down by him, since some seats were set up there in a circle.

Seeing me then, **Cephalus** greeted me right away and said "Socrates, you don't often come down to the Piraeus to visit us, but you ought to. For if I still had the power to travel easily to the city, there would be no need for you to come here, since we would come to you. But now you ought to come here more often. You can be sure that just as much as the other pleasures, the ones that depend on the body, are withering away in me, that's how much the desires and pleasures having to do with talk are growing. Don't fail then to do this; spend time with these youngsters but also come visit us here regularly as you would your friends and your very own kin."

"Really, Cephalus," I said, "I enjoy talking with those who are very old very much, for it seems to me one ought to learn from them, as from those who have gone before us down a certain road which we too no doubt will need to travel, about what sort of road it is, rough and hard or easy and readily traversable. And from you especially I would be glad to learn how this looks to you, since you are just now at that point in life which the poets say is 'on the doorstep out of old age,' whether it is a hard part of life or how you report it."

"By Zeus, Socrates," he said, "I'll tell you what it looks like, at least to me. For often some of us get together who are of just about the same age, keeping the old proverb going. Now most of us complain when we're together, yearning for the pleasures in youth and reminiscing

B

C

D

E

329A

---

2   The "good" is implied in the word "seems" when it is used alone to indicate a decision, such as a resolution of a political assembly. The playful language of arrest, compulsion, and refusal to listen to reason is here replaced by a phrase suggesting consensus or compromise, and this phrase will recur through the dialogue.

B

about sexual indulgences and about drinking binges and feasts, and certain other matters that are involved in those sorts of things, and they get irritable as though they'd been deprived of some great things and as though they'd lived well then but now weren't even living. And some also bewail the way the old are treated like dirt by their families, and they sing a lament on this theme about all the troubles old age has been responsible for to them. But, Socrates, they don't seem to me to be blaming what is responsible. For if this were the responsible thing, I too would have suffered these same things on account of old age, as would everyone else who had come to this point in life. But as it is, I have met up before with others too who were not in this condition,

C

especially when I was nearby the poet Sophocles when he was asked by someone, 'Hey Sophocles, how are you doing with sex? Can you still be with a woman?' And he said 'Hush, fellow. I escaped it most happily indeed, as if I had run away from some raging savage master.' He seemed to me then to be speaking well, and no less so now. For in every way a great peace and freedom from such things comes to pass in

D

old age. When the desires stop straining and slacken, Sophocles' words come to pass in every way, and it is a release from very many insane masters. But in regard to these things and also those that have to do with families, there is one particular cause: not old age, Socrates, but the dispositions of the people. For if they are orderly and peaceable, even old age is a burden within bounds. But if they aren't, Socrates, both old age and youth turn out hard for such a person."

E

And I felt admiration for him for saying these things, and wanting him to say more, I said, to nudge him on, "Cephalus, I imagine when you say these things most people don't accept them from you but regard you as bearing old age easily not on account of your disposition but because you possess great wealth, for they say that rich people have many consolations."

"You're telling the truth," he said. "They don't accept them. And they have a point, though not as much of one as they imagine. Instead, the saying of Themistocles holds well. To a Seriphian who was insult-

330A

ing him and saying that he was well regarded not on his own account but on account of his city, he replied that neither he himself, if he were a Seriphian, nor that man, if he were an Athenian, would have become notable. And for those who are not rich, and bear old age with difficulty, the same statement holds well, that a decent person would not bear old age very easily at all with poverty, but neither would someone who is not decent, even though he were rich, ever come to be at peace with himself."

"But Cephalus," I said, "did you inherit the greater part of what you possess or acquire it?"

B

"What sort of acquisition did I make, Socrates?" he said. "One that makes me a sort of mean as a moneymaker between my grandfather and my father. For my grandfather and namesake, having inherited pretty nearly as much wealth as I now possess, made it many times as much, but my father Lysanias made it even less than it is now. But I'm satisfied if I leave these boys not less but some little amount more than I inherited."

"The reason I asked, really," I said, "is that you seemed to me not to have a very strong love of money, and this is the way people are, for the most part, who didn't acquire it themselves, while those who did acquire it cling to it twice as lovingly as the others. As poets love their own poems and fathers love their children, in just this way moneymakers too take their money seriously as their own work, as well as for its use the same way other people do. So they are hard even to be around, since they are not willing to praise anything other than their riches."

"You're telling the truth," he said.

"Very much so," I said. "But tell me this much more: what do you suppose is the greatest good you've enjoyed from possessing your great wealth?"

"Something," he said, "that I probably won't persuade many people of when I say it. You can be sure, Socrates," he went on, "that when someone is close to imagining that he is coming to the end, fear and care come into him about things that didn't enter his thoughts before. For the stories that are told about the things in Hades' realm, about how the one who committed injustice here must pay the penalty there, stories he scoffed at up to that time, now twist his soul with a fear that they are true. And he—either from the weakness of old age or since he discerns something more of the things there, being already closer to them—becomes filled with suspicion and terror, and he totals up his account to that time and examines whether he has done any injustice to anyone. Now one who finds many injustices of his own in his life even wakes up often from sleep in terror, the way children do, and he lives in expectation of evil. But to one who is conscious of no injustice in himself, a pleasant and good hope is always present to nourish his old age, as Pindar puts it. For truly gracefully, Socrates, does he say this, that for one who lives out his life in a just and holy way,

> Sweet it gathers in him at heart,
> Nurturing and nourishing his old age,
> Hope that most surely steers
> The much-twisting purposes of mortals.

So well he says it—wonderfully so—how very much so! And it's for this very thing that I for my part hold the possession of money to be of its greatest worth, not for every man but for a decent and orderly one. For not having cheated or lied to anyone even unwillingly, and for not departing for there in fear, owing any sacrifices to a god or money to a human being, in great part the possession of money makes a contribution. And it does have many other uses, but setting one thing against another, I for my part would put down to this, for a man with any sense, Socrates, the greatest use for riches."

C "Wholly beautiful are the things you're saying, Cephalus," I said. "But about this very thing, justice, shall we simply claim in this way that it is truth and giving back anything one takes from anyone? Or is it possible to do these very things sometimes justly and sometimes unjustly? I mean, for instance, this sort of thing: surely everyone would say, if someone were to receive weapons from a friend, a man of sound mind, and he kept demanding them back when out of his mind, that one ought not to give back things of that sort, and that anyone who gave them back would not be just, and neither would anyone who was willing to tell all the truth to a person in that condition."

D "You're right," he said.

"Then this is not the definition of justice, to tell the truth and give back what one takes."

"It most certainly is, Socrates," said **Polemarchus**, breaking in, "at least if one ought to believe Simonides at all."

"Indeed," said Cephalus, "and I hand over the discussion to you folks, since I need to take care of the sacrifices now."

"So I'm heir to a share in what's yours?" said Polemarchus.

"Quite so," he said with a laugh, and as he did he went off to the sacrifices.

E "So tell me," I said, "heir to a share in the discussion, what do you say that Simonides says that speaks rightly about justice?"

" That it's just," he said, "to give what's owed to each person, and in saying this he seems to me to put it beautifully."

"And surely," I said, "it's not an easy thing to disbelieve a Simonides, since he is a wise and godlike man; however, whatever it is that he means by this, you no doubt know, Polemarchus, but I'm ignorant of it. For it's obvious that he doesn't mean this, the thing that we were talking about just now, giving anything that's been entrusted to him back to anyone whatsoever when, not being of sound mind,

332A he demands it. And yet this that he entrusted to someone is certainly owed him, isn't it?"

"Yes."

"But it is not by any means to be given back at a time when someone not of sound mind demands it?"

"True," he said.

"So it's likely that Simonides means something other than this sort of thing in saying that the giving of what's owed is just."

"He sure does, by Zeus," he said, "for he assumes that friends owe it to friends to do something good and nothing bad."

"I understand," I said, "that whoever gives back to someone gold
B that's been entrusted to him does not give what's owed if the giving and the getting would be harmful and the people getting it back

and giving it back are friends—isn't this what you say Simonides means?"

"Very much so."

"Then what? Is one to give back to enemies whatever happens to be owed them?"

"Absolutely," he said, "just what's owed them, and I suppose that what's owed from an enemy to an enemy is the very thing that's fitting, something bad."

"Then it's likely," I said, "that Simonides was being cryptic, in a   C
poetic way, about what would be just. For as it appears, he thought that it would be just to give each person what's fitting, but he used the word 'owed.'"

"What else could you think?" he said.

"For Zeus' sake," I said, "if someone then asked him, 'Simonides, by giving what that's owed and fitting to what does an art get called medical?' what do you suppose he'd say in reply?"

"It's clear," he said: "drugs and also foods and drinks to bodies."

"And by giving what that's owed and fitting to what does an art get called culinary?"

"Seasonings to delicacies."   D

"Okay; now by giving what to what would an art be called justice?"

"If it needs to follow along with the things said before, Socrates," he said, "by giving benefits and damage to friends and enemies."

"Then does he mean that doing good to one's friends and harm to one's enemies is justice?"

"It seems so to me."

"So who has the most power to do good to sick friends and harm to sick enemies in regard to disease and health?"

"A doctor."

"And who to those aboard ships in regard to danger at sea?"   E

"A helmsman."

"And what about someone who's just? In what action and with regard to what work does he have the most power to benefit friends and damage enemies?"

"In going to war and taking a side in battle, it seems to me."

"Okay. Now to those who aren't sick, my friend Polemarchus, a doctor is useless."

"True."

"And so is a helmsman to those who aren't aboard ships."

"Yes."

"Then is it also the case that someone who's just is useless to those who are not fighting a war?"

"That doesn't seem so to me at all."

"Then justice is useful also in peacetime?"   333A

"It's useful."

"And farming too, or not?"

"Yes."

"For obtaining crops?"

"Yes."

"And surely leatherworking too?"

"Yes."

"For obtaining shoes, I suppose you'd say?"

"Certainly."

"So then what? For using or obtaining what in peacetime would you say justice is useful?"

"For contracts, Socrates."

"And by contracts do you mean partnerships, or something else?"

"Partnerships, of course."

B   "So then is a just person a good and useful partner in the placement of checkers, or a skilled checker player?"

"A skilled checker player."

"And for the placement of bricks and stones, is a just person a more useful and better partner than a housebuilder?"

"By no means."

"But then for what sort of partnership is a just person a better partner than a housebuilder and a harpist, in the way a harpist is better than a just person for strumming?"

"For what has to do with money, it seems to me."

C   "Except perhaps, Polemarchus, for using money, when the money is needed for a share in buying or selling a horse; and then, as I imagine, it's the horse expert, isn't it?"

"So it appears."

"And surely when it's for a ship, it's the shipbuilder or helmsman?"

"It seems like it."

"Then when there is a need to use silver or gold in common, for what purpose *is* a just person more useful than anyone else?"

"When they need to be entrusted to someone and kept safe, Socrates."

"So do you mean when there is no need to use them but they are lying around?"

"Certainly."

D   "Therefore it's when money is useless that justice is useful for it?"

"That's liable to be so."

"And when a pruning knife needs to be guarded, justice is useful in common as well as in private, but when it needs to be used what's useful is skill at tending vines?"

"So it appears."

"And will you claim about a shield and a lyre that when they need to be guarded and not used, justice is useful, but when they need to be used, what are useful are the arts of soldiering and music?"

"Necessarily so."

"And about all other things, that justice is useless in the use of each of them but useful in the uselessness?"

"That's liable to be so."

"Well then, my friend, justice would not be a very serious thing if it's useful just exactly for useless things. And let's consider this point: the person who's cleverest at hitting someone in a fight, whether in boxing or any other kind—isn't he also cleverest at guarding against it?"

E

"Very much so."

"Then too, whoever is clever at guarding against disease—isn't he also cleverest at going undetected when causing it?"

"It seems so to me."

"And surely the same person is a good guardian of an army who is also good at getting to know the enemies' deliberations and other actions by stealth?"

334A

"Very much so."

"Then whatever someone is a clever guardian of, of this he's also a clever thief."

"It seems that way."

"So if someone who's just is clever at guarding silver, he's also clever at stealing it."

"That's the way the argument is pointing, at any rate," he said.

"Then it looks like the just person has shown up as a certain kind of thief, and you're liable to have learned this from Homer, since he's fond of Autolycus, Odysseus's grandfather on his mother's side, and says he 'excelled all men at stealing and swearing false oaths.' It's likely then, according to you and to Homer and to Simonides, that justice is a certain skill at thievery, though for the benefit of one's friends and harm to one's enemies. Isn't that the way you meant it?"

B

"No, by Zeus," he said, "but I no longer know what I meant. This, though, still seems right to me, that justice is benefiting one's friends and harming one's enemies."

"And by friends do you mean those who seem trustworthy to each person, or those who are trustworthy, even if they don't seem to be, and likewise with enemies?"

C

"It's likely," he said, "that one loves those one regards as trustworthy and hates those one regards as worthless."

"And don't people make mistakes about this, so that many people seem trustworthy to them without being so, and many the other way around?"

"They make mistakes."

"And to them, good people are enemies and bad people are friends?"

"Certainly."

"But is it still a just thing for these people to benefit the worthless and harm the good?"

"It appears so."

D "But surely the good are just and not the sort to do injustice?"

"True."

"So according to your statement it's just to do harm to those who do nothing unjust."

"There's no way that's true, Socrates," he said. "It's likely to be the statement that's worthless."

"Then it's unjust people," I said, "that it's just to harm, and just people that it's just to benefit?"

"This statement appears to be more beautiful than that other."

"Then for many, Polemarchus, all those people who make mis-
E takes, it will turn out to be just to harm their friends, since they have worthless ones, and benefit their enemies, if they're good. And so we'll be saying the very opposite of what we claimed Simonides meant."

"That's much the way it turns out," he said. "But let's change it around. For we're liable to have put friend and enemy in a way that's not right."

"By putting them how, Polemarchus?"

"That the one who seems trustworthy is a friend."

"And now," I said, "how shall we change it around?"

"That the one who both seems and is trustworthy," he said, "is a
335A friend, but the one who seems so but isn't trustworthy seems to be but isn't a friend. And putting it the same way about the enemy."

"So it looks like one who's good, by this statement, will be a friend, and one who's worthless will be an enemy."

"Yes."

"So you're ordering us to put an addendum on what's just, com-
pared to the way we were first speaking of it, when we said that it's just to do good to a friend and harm to an enemy, and now in addition to this to say it this way: that it's just to do good to a friend who *is* good and to harm an enemy who's bad?"

B "Entirely so," he said, "and that way seems to me to say it beautifully."

"Does it therefore belong to a just man," I said, "to do harm even to any human being at all?"

"Very much so," he said; "by all means he needs to do harm to those who are both worthless people and enemies."

"And when horses are harmed, do they become better or worse?"

"Worse."

"In regard to the virtue of dogs or to that of horses?"

"In regard to that of horses."

"So also, when dogs are harmed, they become worse in regard to the virtue of dogs but not to that of horses?"

"Necessarily."

"But as for human beings, shall we not say the same thing, my companion, that when they're harmed they become worse in regard to human virtue?"   C

"Very much so."

"But isn't justice human virtue?"

"This too is necessary."

"And therefore, my friend, those human beings who are harmed necessarily become more unjust."

"It looks likely."

"Well now, do musicians have the power to make people unmusical by means of music?"

"They're powerless to."

"But are skilled horsemen able to make people inept at riding by means of horsemanship?"

"It can't be."

"But then are those who are just able to make people unjust by means of justice? And, putting it all together, are the good able to make people bad by means of virtue?"   D

"They're powerless to."

"For it's not the work of heat, I presume, to cool anything, but of its opposite."

"Yes."

"Nor of dryness to moisten anything, but of its opposite."

"Certainly."

"Nor, then, of what's good to harm anything, but of its opposite."

"So it appears."

"And one who's just is good?"

"Certainly."

"Then it's not the work of the just person to do harm, Polemarchus, either to a friend or to anyone else, but of his opposite, the unjust person."

"You seem to me to be speaking the truth absolutely, Socrates,"   E
he said.

"Then if someone claims it's just to give what's owed to each person, and this carries the meaning for him that harm is owed from the just man to his enemies, but benefit to his friends, the one saying these things was not wise, since he wasn't telling the truth. For it has become obvious to us that it is never just to harm anyone."

"I go along with that," he said.

"Then we'll go into battle," I said, "you and I in partnership, if anyone claims that Simonides or Bias or Pittacus or any of the other wise and blessed men has said that."

"I for my part am ready," he said, "to be your partner in the battle."[3]

336A "But do you know," I said, "whose way of speaking it seems to me to be, to claim that it's a just thing to benefit friends and harm enemies?"

"Whose?" he said.

"I suppose it to be the statement of Periander or Perdiccas or Xerxes or Ismenias the Theban, or some other rich man who imagines he has great power."

"What you say is most true," he said.

"Well then," I said, "since it has come to light that this is neither justice nor a just thing, what else should one claim they are?"

B And when **Thrasymachus** many times, even while we were in the middle of our conversation, was making motions to take over the argument, he was prevented by those sitting by him, who wanted to hear the argument out. But when we paused as I said this, he could no longer keep still, but having gathered himself to spring like a wild animal, he launched himself at us as if to tear us to pieces. Both I and Polemarchus were quaking in fear, and he, snarling into our midst, **C** said: "What drivel are you people full of now, Socrates? And why do you act like idiots kowtowing to each other? But if you truly want to know what's just, don't merely ask and then, as befits someone with a passion for honor, cross-examine whenever anybody answers, knowing that it's easier to ask than to answer, but also answer yourself and **D** tell what you claim the just thing is. And don't give me any of that about how it's the needful or the beneficial or the profitable or the gainful or the advantageous, but tell me clearly and precisely what you mean, since I won't stand for it if you talk in such empty words."

And I was flabbergasted when I heard this, and was afraid as I looked at him, and it seemed to me that if I had not seen him before he saw me I would have been struck dumb.[4] But as it was, just as he was beginning to be driven wild by the argument I looked at him first, **E** and so I was able to answer him, and said, trembling a little, "Don't be rough on us, Thrasymachus. If we're mistaken in any point in the examination of the argument, I and this fellow here, you can be assured that we're going astray unwillingly. For don't even imagine, when, if we were looking for gold, we wouldn't be willing to kowtow to each other in the search and ruin our chances of finding it, that when we're looking for justice, a thing more valuable than much gold,

---

3   This playful remark is a reversal for Polemarchus not only in his opinion but in his attitude, since he began the action of the dialogue by insisting on imposing his will on Socrates.

4   This alludes to an ancient legend about wolves.

we'd be so senseless as to defer to each other and not be as serious as possible about bringing it to light. Don't so much as imagine that, friend. But I imagine we don't have the power to find it. So it's much 337A more fitting anyway for us to be pitied by you clever people instead of being roughed up."

And hearing this, he burst out laughing with great scorn and said "Oh Heracles, this is that routine irony[5] of Socrates. I knew about this, and I kept telling these people before that you wouldn't be willing to answer, but you'd be ironic and do everything else but answer if anyone asked you anything."

"That's because you're wise, Thrasymachus," I said, "so you know very well that if you asked anyone how much twelve is, and in asking B demanded of him in advance, 'don't give me any of that, fellow, about how twelve is two times six or three times four or six times two or four times three, since I won't stand for such drivel from you,' it was clear to you, I imagine, that no one could answer someone who interrogated him that way. But if he said to you, 'Thrasymachus, how do you mean it? That I must give none of the answers you prohibited in advance? Not even, you strange fellow, if it happens to be one of these, but instead I have to say something other than the truth? Or how do C you mean it?' What would you say to him about that?"

"Oh sure," he said, "as if this was like that."

"Nothing prevents it," I said. "But then even if it isn't like it, but appears to be to someone who is asked such a question, do you imagine he'll any the less answer the question the way it appears to him, whether we forbid it or not?"

"So what else," he said; "are you going to do the same thing? Are you going to give any of those answers I banned?"

"I wouldn't be surprised," I said, "if it seemed that way to me when I had examined it."

"Then what if I show you a different answer about justice," he D said, "beyond all these, better than they are? What penalty would you think you deserve to suffer?"

"What other penalty," I said, "than the one it's fitting for someone who doesn't have knowledge to suffer? And it's fitting, no doubt, for him to learn from someone who has knowledge. So I think I too deserve to suffer this penalty."

"You're amusing," he said, "but in addition to learning, pay a penalty in money too."

"Okay, whenever I get any," I said.

"He's got it," said Glaucon. "So as far as money's concerned, Thrasymachus, speak up, since all of us will chip in for Socrates."

---

5   The Greek word refers only to the gracious self-deprecating way of speaking that was a specialty of Socrates. It would not be applied to Thrasymachus's own scornful sarcasm.

E

"I imagine you will," he said, "so Socrates can go on with his usual routine: he won't answer but when somebody else answers he'll grab hold of his statement and cross-examine him."

"Most skillful one," I said, "how could anyone give an answer who in the first place doesn't know and doesn't claim to know, and then too, even if he supposes something about these things, would be banned from saying what he believes by no inconsiderable man?

338A   So it's more like it for you to speak, since you do claim to know and to have something to say. So don't do anything else but gratify me by answering, and don't be grudging about teaching Glaucon here as well as the others."

And when I'd said these things, Glaucon and the others kept begging him not to do otherwise. And Thrasymachus was obviously longing to speak in order to be well thought of, believing that he had an answer of overwhelming beauty. But he made a pretense of bat-

B   tling eagerly for me to be the one that answered. But making an end of this, he gave way, and then said, "This is the wisdom of Socrates; he himself is not willing to teach, but he goes around learning from others and doesn't even pay them any gratitude."

"In saying that I learn from others," I said, "you tell the truth, Thrasymachus, but when you claim that I don't pay for it in full with gratitude, you lie, for I pay all that is in my power. I have the power only to show appreciation, since I don't have money. And how eagerly I do this, if anyone seems to me to speak well, you'll know very well

C   right away when you answer, for I imagine you'll speak well."

"Then listen," he said. "I assert that what's just is nothing other than what's advantageous to the stronger. So why don't you show appreciation? But you won't be willing to."

"First I need to understand what you mean," I said, "since now I don't yet know. You claim that what's advantageous to the stronger is just. Now whatever do you mean by this, Thrasymachus? For I'm sure you're not saying this sort of thing: that if Polydamas the no-holds-barred wrestler is stronger than we are, and bull's meat is advanta-

D   geous to him for his body, this food would also be advantageous, and at the same time just, for us who are weaker than he is."

"You're nauseating, Socrates," he said, "and you grab hold of the statement in the way that you can do it the most damage."

"Not at all, most excellent man," I said, "just say more clearly what you mean."

"So you don't know," he said, "that some cities are run tyranni-cally, some democratically, and some aristocratically?"

"How could I not?"

"And so this prevails in strength in each city, the ruling part?"

"Certainly."

E   "And each ruling power sets up laws for the advantage of itself, a democracy setting up democratic ones, a tyranny tyrannical ones,

and the others likewise. And having set them up, they declare that this, what's advantageous for them, is just for those who are ruled, and they chastise someone who transgresses it as a lawbreaker and a person doing injustice. So this, you most skillful one, is what I'm saying, that the same thing is just in all cities, what's advantageous to   339A the established ruling power. And this surely prevails in strength, so the conclusion, for someone who reasons correctly, is that the same thing is just everywhere, what's advantageous to the stronger."

"Now," I said, "I understand what you mean. But whether it's true or not, I'll try to learn. So you too answer that the advantageous is just, Thrasymachus, even though you made a prohibition for me that I could not give this answer, though there is added to it 'for the   B stronger.'"

"A small addendum, no doubt," he said.

"It's not clear yet whether it's a big one. But it is clear that whether you're speaking the truth needs to be examined. For since you're saying and I'm agreeing that what's just is something advantageous, but you're making an addition and claiming it to be that of the stronger, while I don't know that, it needs to be examined."

"So examine it," he said.

"That will be done," I said. "Now tell me, do you not claim, though, that it's also just to obey the rulers?"

"I do."

"And are the rulers in each city infallible, or the sort of people   C who also make mistakes?"

"By all means," he said, "they're surely the sort of people who also make mistakes."

"So when they try to set up laws, they set up some correctly and certain others incorrectly?"

"I certainly imagine so."

"Then to set them up correctly is to set up laws that are advantageous to themselves, and incorrectly, disadvantageous ones? Or how do you mean it?"

"That's the way."

"But whatever they set up needs to be done by those who are ruled, and this is what is just?"

"How could it be otherwise?"

"Then according to your statement, not only is it just to do what's   D advantageous to the stronger, but also to do the opposite, what's disadvantageous."

"What do you mean?" he said.

"What you mean, it seems to me; but let's examine it better. Wasn't it agreed that when the rulers command those who are ruled to do certain things they're sometimes completely mistaken about what's best for themselves, but what the rulers command is just for those who are ruled to do? Wasn't this agreed?"

"I certainly imagine so," he said.

E   "Well then," I said, "imagine also that it was agreed by you that doing what's disadvantageous for those who rule and are stronger is just, whenever the rulers unwillingly command things that are bad for themselves, while you claim that for the others to do those things which they commanded is just. So then, most wise Thrasymachus, doesn't it turn out necessarily in exactly this way, that it's just to do the opposite of what you say? For what's disadvantageous to the stronger is without doubt commanded to the weaker to do."

340A   "By Zeus, yes, Socrates," said Polemarchus, "most clearly so."

"If you're going to be a witness for him," Cleitophon interjected.

"And what need is there for a witness? Thrasymachus himself agrees that the rulers sometimes command things that are bad for themselves, and that for the others to do these things is just."

"That's because Thrasymachus set it down, Polemarchus, that doing what's ordered by the rulers is just."

"Because he also set it down, Cleitophon, that what's advanta-
B   geous to the stronger is just. And having set down both these things, he agreed next that sometimes the stronger order things that are disadvantageous to themselves for those who are weaker and ruled to do. And from these agreements what's advantageous to the stronger would be no more just than what's disadvantageous."

"But," said Cleitophon, "he meant that the advantage of the stronger is what the stronger believes is advantageous to himself; this is what needs to be done by the weaker, and he set this down as what's just."

"But he didn't say it that way," said Polemarchus.

C   "It makes no difference, Polemarchus," I said, "but if Thrasymachus says it this way now, let's accept it this way from him. And tell me, Thrasymachus, was this what you wanted to say the just is, what seems to the stronger to be the advantage of the stronger, whether it might be advantageous or not? Shall we say you mean it that way?"

"That least of all," he said. "Do you imagine that I call someone who makes a mistake stronger when he's making a mistake?"

"I did imagine that you were saying that," I said, "when you agreed
D   that the rulers are not infallible but are even completely mistaken about some things."

"That's because you're a liar who misrepresents things in arguments, Socrates. To start with, do *you* call someone who's completely mistaken about sick people a doctor on account of that very thing he's mistaken about? Or call someone skilled at arithmetic who makes a mistake in doing arithmetic, at the time when he's making it, on account of this mistake? I imagine instead that we talk that way in a manner of speaking, saying that the doctor made a mistake, or the one skilled at arithmetic made a mistake, or the grammarian. But I assume
E   that each of these, to the extent that this is what we address him as,

never makes a mistake, so that in precise speech, since you too are precise in speech, no skilled worker makes a mistake. For it's by being deficient in knowledge that the one who makes a mistake makes it, in respect to which he is not a skilled worker. So no one who's a skilled worker or wise or a ruler makes a mistake at the time when he is a ruler, though everyone would say that the doctor made a mistake or the ruler made a mistake. Take it then that I too was answering you just now in that sort of way. But the most precise way of speaking is exactly this, that the one who rules, to the extent that he is a ruler, does not make mistakes, and in not making a mistake he sets up what is best for himself, and this needs to be done by the one who is ruled. And so I say the very thing I've been saying from the beginning is just, to do what's advantageous to the stronger."

341A

"Okay, Thrasymachus," I said. "I seem to you to misrepresent things by lying?"

"Very much so," he said.

"Because you imagine that I asked the question the way I did out of a plot to do you harm in the argument?"

"I know that very well," he said. "And it's not going to do you any good, because you couldn't do me any harm without it being noticed, and without being unnoticed you wouldn't have the power to do violence with the argument."

B

"I wouldn't even try, blessed one," I said. "But in order that this sort of thing doesn't happen to us again, distinguish the way you mean someone who rules and is stronger, whether it's the one who is so called or the one in precise speech whom you just now mentioned, for whose advantage, since he's stronger, it will be just for the weaker to act."

"The one who's a ruler in the most precise speech," he said. "Do harm to that and misrepresent it by lies if you have any power to—I ask for no mercy from you—but you won't be able to."

C

"Do you imagine," I said, "that I'm crazy enough to try to shave a lion or misrepresent Thrasymachus by lies?"

"You certainly tried just now," he said, "but you were a zero even at that."

"That's enough of this sort or thing," I said. "But tell me, the doctor in precise speech that you were just now talking about, is he a moneymaker or a healer of the sick? And speak about the one who *is* a doctor."

"A healer of the sick," he said.

"And what about a helmsman? Is the one who's a helmsman in the correct way a ruler of sailors or a sailor?"

"A ruler of sailors."

D

"I assume there's no need to take into account that he does sail in the ship, and no need for him to be called a sailor, since it's not on account of sailing that he's called a helmsman, but on account of his art and his ruling position among the sailors."

"That's true," he said.

"Then for each of the latter there's something advantageous?"

"Certainly."

"And isn't art by its nature for this," I said, "for seeking and providing what's advantageous in each case?"

"For that," he said.

"Then is there any advantage for each of the arts other than to be as complete as possible?"

E   "In what sense are you asking this?"

"In the same sense," I said, "as, if you were to ask me whether it's sufficient for a body to be a body or whether it needs something extra, I'd say 'Absolutely it needs something extra, and it's for that reason that the medical art has now been discovered, because a body is inadequate and isn't sufficient to itself to be the sort of thing it is. So it's for this reason, in order that it might provide the things that are advantageous for the body, that the art was devised.' Would I seem to you to be speaking correctly in saying this," I said, "or not?"

342A   "It's correct," he said.

"What then? Is the medical art itself—or any other art—inadequate, and is it the case that it has need of some extra virtue? Just as eyes need sight and ears need hearing and for these reasons there is need of some art applied to them that will consider and provide what's advantageous for these things, is there then in the art itself some inadequacy in it too, and a need for each art to have another art that will consider what's advantageous for *it*, and for the one that will consider that to have another art in turn of that kind, and this is

B   unending? Or will it consider what's advantageous for itself? Or is there no additional need either for it or for any other art to consider what's advantageous for its inadequacy, because there is no inadequacy or mistake present in any art, nor is it appropriate for an art to look out for the advantage of anything other than that with which the art is concerned, but it itself is without defect and without impurity since it is correct as long as each is the whole precise art that it is. Consider it in that precise speech now: is that the way it is, or is it some other way?"

"That way," he said, "as it appears."

C   "So then," I said, "the medical art considers what's advantageous not for the medical art but for a body."

"Yes," he said.

"And horsemanship considers what's advantageous not for horsemanship but for horses, and neither does any other art consider what's advantageous for itself, since there's no extra need for that, but for that with which the art is concerned."

"So it appears," he said.

"But surely, Thrasymachus, the arts rule over and have power over that with which they're concerned."

He went along with that too, very grudgingly.

"Then no sort of knowledge considers or commands what's advantageous for the stronger, but what's advantageous for what's weaker and ruled by it."

D

He finally agreed with this too, though he tried to make a fight about it, and when he agreed I said, "So does anything else follow except that no doctor, to the extent he is a doctor, considers or commands what's advantageous for a doctor, but instead for someone who's sick? For it was agreed that the doctor is precisely a ruler of bodies but not a moneymaker. Or was that not agreed?"

He said so.

"Then the helmsman too was agreed to be precisely a ruler of sailors but not a sailor?"

E

"It was agreed."

"Then this sort of helmsman and ruler at any rate will not consider and command what's advantageous for a helmsman, but what's advantageous for the sailor who's ruled."

He said so, grudgingly.

"Therefore, Thrasymachus," I said, "neither will anyone else in any ruling position, to the extent he is a ruler, consider or command what's advantageous for himself, but what's advantageous for whatever is ruled, for which he himself is a skilled workman, and looking toward that, and to what's advantageous and appropriate for that, he both says and does everything that he says and does."

Now when we were at this point in the argument, and it was obvious to everyone that the statement about what's just had turned around into its opposite, Thrasymachus, instead of replying, said "Tell me, Socrates, do you have someone nursing you?"

343A

"What?" I said. "Shouldn't you give an answer rather than asking things like that?"

"Well," he said, "she must not be noticing your snotty nose because she's not wiping it when you need her to, if it's her fault you can't tell a sheep from a shepherd."

"Because of what in particular?" I said.

"Because you imagine that shepherds or cattlemen consider the good of the sheep or cattle and fatten them up and take care of them looking to anything other than the good of their bosses and of themselves, and so you also believe that the rulers in cities, the ones who truly are rulers, think about those who are ruled in any other way than someone would treat sheep, and that they consider anything, day and night, other than this: how they themselves are going to benefit. And you're so far off about what's just and justice and what's unjust and injustice that you don't know that justice and what's just are in fact someone else's good, what's advantageous for the person who's

B

C

stronger and a ruler, and one's own harm for the person who obeys and is subservient; injustice is the opposite, and rules over those who are truly simpletons and just people, while the ones who are ruled do what's advantageous for the person who's stronger and make him happy by serving him, but themselves not in any way whatsoever.

D

"It needs to be looked at this way, most simple-minded Socrates: a just man has less than an unjust one in every situation. First, in contracts with each other, where the one sort is partnered with the other, nowhere would you find that the one who's just had more in the breaking up of the partnership than the unjust one—only less. Next, in things related to the city, whenever there are any taxes, the one who's just pays more tax on an equal amount of property,

E

the other less, and whenever there are allotments, the former gains nothing, the latter a lot. Also, whenever each of the two holds some ruling office it goes without saying for the one who's just, that even if he has no other loss, his household circumstances get into a sorry state from lack of attention, while, on account of being just, he gets no benefit from the public treasury, and on top of that he gets the antagonism of his family and acquaintances when he isn't willing to do them any services contrary to what's just. And for the one who's unjust, it goes without saying that everything is the opposite of this

344A

—I mean the person I was just now talking about, the one who has the power to get a lot more than his due. So consider this person if you want to judge by how much more what's unjust is to his private advantage than what's just.

"You'll understand this most easily of all if you go up to the most complete injustice, which makes the one who does the injustice the most happy and the ones the injustice is done to the most miserable if they aren't willing to be unjust too. And this is tyranny, which, by both furtiveness and force, takes away what belongs to others, both the sacred and the profane, both the private and the public, not little by little but all at one swoop. When anyone who does injustice in a

B

single portion of that doesn't go undetected, he is punished and has the greatest disgrace—impious men, hijackers, home invaders, cheats, and thieves are names given to those who do the injustice involved in parts of that sort of evildoing—but when someone, in addition to stealing the citizens' money, steals the men themselves and makes

C

slaves of them, instead of these disgraceful names he's called happy and blessed, not only by the citizens but by everyone else who hears that his injustice has been total injustice. Those who condemn injustice condemn it not because they're afraid of doing unjust things but because they're afraid of suffering them.

"This is the way, Socrates, that injustice, when it comes on the scene with sufficient strength, is stronger, more free, and more overpowering than justice, and the way that what's just is exactly what I was saying from the beginning, what's advantageous to the stronger, while what's unjust is profitable and advantageous to oneself."

When he'd said these things, Thrasymachus had it in mind to go away, just like a bath attendant who had sloshed a lot of speech into our ears all at once. But those who were present didn't let him go but forced him to stay and submit to a discussion of the things he'd said. And I too myself begged him very strongly and said "Thrasymachus, you supernatural being, what sort of speech have you flung at us, that you have it in mind to go away before teaching us adequately or learning whether it's that way or some other? Or do you imagine it's a small matter to try to determine the course of a lifetime, by which each of us who leads it would live the most profitable life?"

"Do I imagine it's any different?" said Thrasymachus.

"You seemed to," I said, "or else not to be bothered at all about us, or have any concern whether we'll live worse or better lives for being ignorant of what you claim to know. But, good fellow, be willing to display it to us too —it certainly won't be a bad deposit to your account that you did a good deed for us, so many as we are—because I'm telling you that for my part I'm not persuaded, nor do I suppose that injustice is more of a gain than justice, not even if one gives it its own way and doesn't hinder it from doing what it wants. But, good fellow, let someone be unjust, and let him have the power to do injustice either by going undetected or by fighting his way through; he still doesn't persuade me that that's more of a gain than justice. Now perhaps some other one of us, and not I alone, has gotten this impression, so persuade us, blessed one, in an adequate way, that we aren't being counseled correctly when we hold justice at a greater value than injustice."

"And how," he said, "am I going to persuade you? If you're not persuaded by the things I was saying just now, what more am I going to do for you? Or shall I bring the argument and spoon-feed it into your soul?"

"By Zeus," I said, "not that—not you. But first, stick by whatever you say, or if you change them make the change openly and don't mislead us. But you see what you're doing now, Thrasymachus—because we still need to examine the things you said before—that after first defining the true doctor, you later supposed there was no longer a need to be on guard in a precise way about the true shepherd, but imagined that, to the extent that he is a shepherd, he fattens up his sheep, not looking toward what's best for the sheep, but, like someone at a banquet about to be feasted, toward a good meal, or else toward turning a profit, like a moneymaker instead of a shepherd. But surely nothing is of concern to the art of shepherding other than how it's going to provide what's best for that over which it's appointed—since it's no doubt sufficiently provided for that the things pertaining to the art itself will be best so long as it lacks nothing of being the art of shepherding. That's why I supposed just now that it was necessary for us to agree that every ruling office, to the extent that it is a ruling office, considers what's best for no other thing than the one that's ruled over and cared for, in both political and private rule. And do you imagine that the rulers in cities, the ones who truly are rulers, rule willingly?"

"I don't imagine it, by Zeus," he said, "I know it well."

"Then what about the other kinds of rule, Thrasymachus?" I said. "Don't you realize that no one willingly desires to rule, but people demand wages on the grounds that there won't be any benefit to them from their ruling but only to the ones that are ruled? Because tell me this much: don't we claim, no doubt, that each of the arts is different in each case in this respect, in having a different power? And so that we may get to a conclusion, blessed one, don't answer contrary to your opinion,"

"They are indeed different in that respect," he said.

"Then does each of these also furnish us with some benefit that's particular to it and not shared by them all, such as health with the medical art, safety in sailing with helmsmanship, and so on with the others?"

"Certainly."

"So then wages too with the wage-earning art? Because that's *its* power—or do you call the medical art and helmsmanship the same? Or if in fact you want to distinguish them with precision, as you set down for our principle, even if someone becomes healthy as a helmsman, because it's advantageous to him to sail on the sea, do you any the more on that account call his skill the medical art?"

"Of course not," he said.

"Nor, I imagine, do you call the wage-earning art medical, even if someone earning wages gets healthy?"

"Of course not."

"And what about the medical art—even if someone who heals someone earns wages do you call his skill the wage-earning art?"

"No," he said.

"Didn't we agree that the benefit of each art is particular to it?"

"So be it," he said.

"Therefore it's clear that whatever sort of benefit all skilled workmen benefit by in common, they get that benefit from using in addition something that's the same, shared by them in common."

"It seems like it," he said.

"Then we're saying that the wages the skilled workmen gain for their benefit come to them from their additional use of the wage-earning art."

He said so grudgingly.

"Therefore it's not from his own art that this benefit, that of getting wages, belongs to each of them, but if one is required to consider it

wage earning is separate art

with precision, the medical art produces health and the mercenary art wages, and the housebuilding art produces a house and the mercenary art following along with it produces wages, and it's this way with all the other arts—each works at its own work and benefits that over which its work is appointed. And if there were no wages attached to it, is there any benefit that the workman would get from his art?"

"It doesn't appear so," he said.

"And does he produce a benefit even on an occasion when he does his work for free?"

"I imagine so."

"Then, Thrasymachus, this is already obvious, that no art nor any ruling function provides for its own benefit, but, the very thing we've been saying for so long, it both provides for and commands the benefit of the one ruled, considering the benefit of that weaker one and not that of the stronger. So it's for these reasons, Thrasymachus my friend, that I was also saying just now that no one willingly desires to rule and deal with straightening out other people's troubles, but people demand wages because the one who's going to do a beautiful job by art never does what's best for himself or commands it when he's commanding in accord with his art, but only for the one ruled, on account of which, as is only fitting, there need to be wages for those who are going to be willing to rule, either money, or honor, or a penalty if one does not rule."

"How do you mean that, Socrates," said **Glaucon**. "I recognize the two sorts of wages, but I don't understand what you mean by the penalty and how you've declared it to be in the class of wages."

"Then you don't understand the wages of the best people," I said, "on account of which the most decent ones rule, when they're willing to rule. Or don't you know that people are said to be passionate for honor and money as a reproach, and it is one?"

"I do," he said.

"So," I said, "that's why good people aren't willing to rule for the sake of either money or honor. They don't want to be called mercenary if they openly get wages for the ruling office, or thieves if they secretly take money from the office themselves. And they don't rule for the sake of honor either, since they aren't passionate for honor. So there needs to be a necessity attached to it for them, and a penalty, if they're going to be willing to rule; that's liable to be where it comes from that it's considered shameful to go willingly to rule rather than to await necessity. And the greatest sort of penalty is to be ruled by someone less worthy, if one is not oneself willing to rule. It's on account of fearing this that decent people appear to me to rule, when they do rule, and then they go to rule not as though they were heading for something good or as though they were going to have any enjoyment in it, but as though to something necessary, since they have no one better than or similar to themselves to entrust

E

347A

B

C

D

it to. Because, if a city of good men were to come into being, they'd be liable to have a fight over not ruling just as people do now over ruling, and it would become obvious there that the person who is a true ruler in his being is not of such a nature as to consider what's advantageous for himself rather than for the one ruled. So everyone with any discernment[6] would choose to be benefited by someone else rather than to have the trouble of benefiting someone else. On this

E point, then, I by no means go along with Thrasymachus that what's just is what's advantageous for the stronger. But we'll examine this some other time, for what Thrasymachus is saying now seems to me to be much more important, when he claims that the life of someone who's unjust is more powerful than that of someone who's just. Now you, Glaucon," I said, "which way do you choose? And which claim seems to you to be more truly spoken?"

"To me, the one that says the life of the one who's just is more profitable."

348A "Even though you heard all the good things Thrasymachus went through just now," I said, "about that of the one who's unjust?"

"Because I heard them," he said, "but I'm not persuaded."

"Then do you want us to persuade him, if it's in our power to discover a way, that he's not speaking the truth?"

"How could I not want it?" he said.

"Well now," I said, "if we're to address him by spreading out one statement in exchange for another along the length of his speech, about all the good things being just includes, and he'd reply in turn,

B and we with another speech, it will be necessary to count up the good points each of us makes in each speech and measure how good they are, and by that time we'll need some sort of jury of people to judge it. But if, as we were doing just now, we examine the question based on things we agree with each other about, we ourselves will be jurors and advocates at the same time."[7]

"Very much so," he said.

"Whichever way you please, then," I said.

"The latter," he said.

"Come now, **Thrasymachus**," I said, "answer us from the beginning. Do you claim that complete injustice is more profitable than justice when it's complete?"

C "I claim it very much so," he said, "and I've said why."

---

6   This is a key word for understanding how Socrates gets under Thrasymachus's skin. If the long preceding argument seems merely verbal or logical in a petty way, the reader may be neglecting the possibility that Socrates has discerned Thrasymachus's strongest motive as a desire to be seen as one of those discerning ones who can see beyond popular beliefs.

7   This sentence is a good brief description of what Socrates means by dialectic. It is useful to remember this when that word comes to be used in exalted ways, for instance in 511B or 533C-D.

"Well then, how do you speak about them in this respect? I presume you call one of the pair virtue and the other vice?"

"How could it be otherwise?"

"So you call justice virtue and injustice vice?"

"Yeah, right, you most amusing fellow," he said, "since I also say that injustice is profitable and justice isn't."

"What then?"

"The opposite," he said.

"Justice is vice?"

"No, just very well bred simplemindedness."

"Then do you call injustice bad character?"   D

"No," he said, "just good judgment."

"And do unjust people seem to you, Thrasymachus, to be intelligent and good?"

"If they're able to be completely unjust," he said, "and have the power to bring cities and throngs of people under their control. But you probably imagine I'm talking about pickpockets. Now things like that are profitable too," he said, "so long as one goes undetected—they're just not worthy of mention compared to what I was talking about just now."

"On that point," I said, "I'm not unaware of what you want to say,   E
but I did wonder about this one, whether you place injustice in the class of virtue and wisdom, and justice among their opposites."

"That's exactly the way I place them."

"This is already something harder, my companion," I said, "and it's no longer easy to have anything one could say about it. For if you placed injustice as being profitable, but still agreed, the way some others do,[8] that it's vice and shameful, we'd have something to say by speaking in accordance with the things customarily believed, but now you're obviously going to claim that it's both beautiful and strong, and   349A
you'll add to it all the other things that we attribute to what's just, since you even had the nerve to place it among virtue and wisdom."

"Your premonition is very true," he said.

"But still," I said, "one mustn't shrink from going through the argument to examine it, so long as I get the impression that you're saying exactly what you think. For you seem to me now, Thrasymachus, without pretense and not joking, but stating what seems to you about the truth."

"What difference does it make to you," he said, "whether it seems that way to me or not? Aren't you just cross-examining the argument?"

"No difference," I said. "But try to answer this further question for   B
me in addition to those: does it seem to you that a just person wants to have more of anything than another just person?"

---

8   One such person is Polus in Plato's *Gorgias* (474C).

"By no means," he said, "since then he wouldn't be the refined simpleton I just said he is."

"What then? Would he want to go beyond a just action?"

"Not that either," he said.

"And would he consider it appropriate to get more than the unjust person and regard that as just, or would he not?"

"He'd regard it as just and consider it appropriate," he said, "but he wouldn't have the power to."

C

"But I'm not asking you that," I said, "but whether someone who's just would not consider it appropriate or even want to have more than a just person, while he would consider it so and want that in relation to an unjust person."

"That's the way it is," he said.

"And what then about someone who's unjust? Would he consider it appropriate to go beyond a just person and a just action?"

"How could he not," he said, "since he considers it appropriate to have more than everybody?"

"Then will someone who's unjust also go beyond an unjust human being and an unjust action, and will he compete to get the most of everything himself?"

"That's it."

"So should we say this," I said, "that someone who's just does

D

not go beyond one who's like him but one who's unlike him, while someone who's unjust goes beyond both one who's like him and one who's unlike him?"

"You've said it best," he said.

"And is someone who's unjust intelligent and good," I said, "while someone who's just is neither one?"

"This too is well said," he said.

"So then," I said, "someone who's unjust is like one who's intelligent and one who's good, while someone who's just is not like them?"

"How's he not going to be like people of that sort," he said, "when he's that sort of person, while the other is not like them?"

"Beautiful. Then each of them is the sort of person that each is like?"

"What else are they going to be?" he said.

E

"Fine, Thrasymachus. Now do you call one person musical and another unmusical?"

"I do."

"Which is intelligent and which ignorant?"

"The one who's musical is surely intelligent, and the unmusical one ignorant."

"Then in those respects in which one is intelligent, one is good, and in those respects in which one is ignorant one is bad?"

"Yes."

"And what about someone who's medical? Isn't it the same way?"

"The same."

"So does it seem to you, most excellent one, that any musical man who's tuning a lyre desires to go beyond a musical man in stretching and loosening the strings and considers it appropriate to have more?"

"Not to me."

"Then what? Beyond one who's unmusical?"

"Necessarily so," he said.

"And what about someone who's medical? About food and drink would he want in any way to go beyond either a medical man or a medical action?"

350A

"Surely not."

"But beyond an unmedical one?"

"Yes."

"Then see whether it seems to you that for any kind of knowledge and ignorance, anyone whatever who has knowledge desires to take or do or say more than another person with knowledge would, and not do or say the same things as someone like himself in the same action."

"Well, maybe it's necessary for it to be that way," he said.

"And then what about someone who lacks knowledge? Wouldn't he go beyond both someone with knowledge and someone without it alike?"

B

"Maybe."

"And someone who has knowledge is wise?"

"I'd say so."

"And someone who's wise is good?"

"I'd say so."

"Therefore someone who's good and wise won't desire to go beyond someone like himself, but beyond someone who's unlike and the opposite of himself."

"It looks like it."

"But someone who's bad and stupid desires to go beyond both the one who's like him and the one who's opposite."

"So it appears."

"Now then, Thrasymachus," I said, "according to us, someone who's unjust goes beyond both the one who's unlike him and the one who's like him? Weren't you saying that?"

"I was," he said.

"And someone who's just won't go beyond the one who's like him, but beyond the one who's unlike him?"

C

"Yes."

"Therefore," I said, "someone who's just is like one who's wise and good, and someone who's unjust is like one who's bad and stupid."

"They're liable to be."

"But surely we also agreed that each of the two is the sort of person that each would be like."

"We did agree on that."

"Therefore the just person has been brought to light by us as being good and wise, and the unjust person as being stupid and bad."

D   Now Thrasymachus did agree to all these things, though not as easily as I'm telling it now, but being dragged along and grudging it, after sweating a prodigious amount, seeing as how it was also summer. And then I saw something I had never seen before: Thrasymachus blushing. So when we had come to agreement that justice is virtue and wisdom, and injustice vice and stupidity, I said "Okay, let this be the way it now stands according to us, but we were also claiming that injustice is something strong. Or don't you remember, Thrasymachus?"

"I remember," he said, "but what you're saying now isn't good enough for me, and I have something to say about it. But if I were to say

E   it, I know well that you'd claim I was speaking rhetorically. So either let me speak as much as I want or, if you want to ask questions, ask them, and I'll treat you the way people do old women when they're telling stories, and tell you 'okay,' and nod my head or shake it."

"Don't by any means do that contrary to your own opinion," I said.

"Just to please you," he said, "seeing as how you won't let me speak. What else do you want?"

"Nothing, by Zeus," I said; "but if you're going to do that, do it, and I'll ask questions."

"Ask away."

"Well, I'm asking this, the very thing I asked just now, so that

351A   we might go through an orderly examination of the argument about exactly what sort of thing justice is in relation to injustice. For it was said, surely, that injustice would be a more powerful and stronger thing than justice, but now," I said, "if justice is in fact wisdom and virtue, it will easily be brought to light, I imagine, as a stronger thing than injustice, seeing as how injustice is stupidity. No one could any longer be ignorant of that. But, Thrasymachus, I don't wish for it to be

B   considered so simply, but in something like the following way: would you claim that a city is unjust that tries to enslave other cities unjustly, and has made slaves of them, and holds them in slavery to itself?"

"How could it be otherwise?" he said. "And the best city will do this the most, since it is also the most completely unjust."

"I understand," I said, "that this was your argument, but I'm considering this about it: will the city that becomes master of a city hold this power without justice, or is it necessary for it to hold it with justice?"

"If, as you were saying just now, justice is wisdom," he said, "with   C
justice. But if it's the way I was saying, with injustice."

"I very much admire, Thrasymachus," I said, "the fact that you
aren't just nodding or shaking your head but also answering very
beautifully."

"Well, I'm doing it to humor you," he said.

"And you're doing it well. Now just humor me this much more
and tell me, do you believe that either a city or an army or pirates
or thieves or any other group that embarks on anything in common
unjustly will have the power to accomplish it if they behave unjustly
toward one another?"

"Not at all," he said.

"And what if they don't behave unjustly? Won't they accomplish   D
more?"

"Very much so."

"For surely, Thrasymachus, injustice causes factions and hatreds
and fights among one another, while justice causes like-mindedness
and friendship. Isn't that so?"

"So be it," he said, "so I won't be at odds with you."[9]

"And you're behaving very well, most excellent fellow. But tell
me this: if that's the work of injustice, to bring in hatred wherever
it's present, won't it also, when it comes in among the free as well as
the enslaved, make them hate each other and form factions and be   E
powerless to act in common with one another?"

"Certainly."

"Then what if it comes to be present in two people? Won't they
be at odds and hate and be enemies of one another as well as of those
who are just?"

"They will be," he said.

"Then, you surprising fellow, if injustice comes to be present in
one person, will it lose its power completely, or still have it to no less
extent?"

"Let it have it to no less extent," he said.

"Then does it come to light as having some such power as this, in
that in which it comes to be present, whether a particular city, a race of
people, an army, or anything else whatsoever, that first of all injustice   352A
makes it powerless to act with itself on account of being in factions
and at odds, then also makes it be an enemy to itself and everything
opposed to it and to what is just? Isn't that the way it is?"

"Certainly."

"So even when it's present in one person, I assume, it will do these
very same things that are its workings by its nature: first it will make
him powerless to act, being at faction and not of one mind himself

---

9   Thrasymachus, in spite of himself, is enacting what the conversation is about. At 498D,
Socrates will say that he and Thrasymachus have become friends. This may or may not be a
step in that direction.

with himself, and then an enemy both to himself and to those who are just. Right?"

"Yes."

"And, my friend, the gods too are just?"

B   "So be it."

"Therefore, Thrasymachus, someone who's unjust will also be an enemy to the gods, but someone who's just will be a friend."

"Gorge yourself on the argument fearlessly," he said. "I won't oppose you anyway, so that I won't be hateful to these people here."

"Come on then," I said, "and fill up what's left of the feasting for me by answering just as you are now. Because those who are just have come to light as wiser and better and more empowered to act, while

C   those who are unjust are not able to act in any way with each other, but in fact we aren't speaking the whole truth when we claim that people who are unjust ever yet acted vigorously in common with one another in anything, since they couldn't have kept their hands off each other if they were completely unjust, but it's clear that there was a certain justice in them which made them not do injustice to each other, at least at the same time they were also doing it to those they were doing it to. It was by means of this justice that they acted in whatever respects they did act, and they embarked on their unjust deeds as semi-vicious people, since those who are all-vicious and completely

D   unjust are also completely powerless to act. Now I understand that these things are so, and not the way you set them down at first. But whether those who are just also live better and are happier than those who are unjust, the very thing we proposed to consider later, needs to be considered. And now, as it seems to me at least, they do appear to from the things we've said. Nevertheless, it needs to be examined still better, since the discussion is not about some random thing, but about the way one ought to live."

"So examine it," he said.

"I'm examining it," I said, "and tell me, does it seem to you that

E   there is a certain work that belongs to a horse?"

"To me, yes."

"And would you set this down as the work of a horse or of anything else whatever—what one could do only, or best, with it?"

"I don't understand," he said.

"Try it this way: is there anything else you could see with except eyes?"

"Surely not."

"What then; could you hear with anything except ears?"

"Not at all."

"Then do we justly claim that these things are their work?"

"Certainly."

353A   "What about this? Could you cut off a branch from a vine with a dagger or a carving knife or with many other things?"

"How could I not?"

"But with none of these, I imagine, so beautifully as with a pruning knife that's worked up for this use?"

"True."

"Then shall we not set this down as the work of this thing?"

"We certainly shall."

"So now I assume you'd understand better what I was asking just now, when I inquired whether the work of each thing wouldn't be that which only it accomplishes, or which it, compared to other things, accomplishes most beautifully."

"I do understand," he said, "and it does seem to me that this is the work of each thing."

"Okay," I said, "and then does it seem to you that there's a virtue for each thing that has some work attached to it? Let's go back to the same examples: we claim there's some work that belongs to eyes?"

"There is."

"So is there also a virtue that belongs to eyes?"

"A virtue too."

"What next? Was there a work belonging to ears?"

"Yes."

"Then a virtue too?"

"A virtue too."

"What then about everything else? Isn't it that way?"

"It's that way."

"Keep on. Could eyes ever accomplish their own work beautifully if they didn't have their own particular virtue but vice instead of the virtue?"

"How could they?" he said. "You no doubt mean blindness instead of sight."

"Whatever virtue belongs to them," I said, "since I'm not yet asking about that, but whether with the particular virtue that pertains to their work they're going to do the work they do well, but do it badly with the vice."

"On this point," he said, "you're telling the truth."

"So then ears too, when deprived of their virtue, will accomplish their work badly?"

"Certainly."

"And will we put everything else too into the same statement?"

"It seems that way to me."

"Come then, after these things, consider this one. Is there any work belonging to a soul that you couldn't perform with any single other thing there is? Like this, for instance—managing and ruling and deliberating and everything like that—is there anything other than a soul to which we could justly attribute them and claim that they belong to that in particular?"

"Nothing else."

"And next, what about living? Won't we claim that it's work belonging to a soul?"

"Especially that," he said.

"Then do we also claim there's some virtue belonging to a soul?"

"We claim that."

E   "So, Thrasymachus, will a soul ever accomplish its work well if it's deprived of its own particular virtue, or is that out of its power?"

"Out of its power."

"Therefore it's necessary for a bad soul to rule and manage things badly and for a good one to do all these things well."

"Necessary."

"And haven't we granted that justice is virtue of soul and injustice vice?"

"We've granted it."

"Therefore the just soul and the just man will live well and the unjust badly."

"So it appears," he said, "according to your argument."

354A   "But surely someone who lives well is blessed and happy and someone who doesn't is the opposite."

"How not?"

"Therefore someone who's just is happy and someone who's unjust is miserable."

"So be it," he said.

"But surely it's not being miserable that's profitable, but being happy."

"How not?"

"Therefore, blessed Thrasymachus, injustice is never more profitable than justice."

"So, Socrates," he said, "let these things be your feast in the festivities for Bendis."

"It's thanks to you, Thrasymachus," I said, "since you have become gentle and stopped being savage toward me. I haven't feasted myself
B   beautifully, though, but that's on account of myself and not you. Just as greedy eaters are always taking a bite of what's carried past them, grabbing at it before they've enjoyed the previous dish in full measure, I too seem to myself to be like that. Before finding the thing we were considering first—what in the world the just thing is—I let go of that to start looking around it to see whether it's vice and stupidity or wisdom and virtue. And when in turn an argument fell my way later that injustice is more profitable than justice, I couldn't hold back from going after this one and away from that one. And so
C   it has come to pass that now I know nothing from the conversation, because when I don't know what the just thing is, I'm hardly going to know whether it happens to be a virtue or not, or whether someone who has it is unhappy or happy."

BOOK II

Note

In this book Socrates begins the project of finding the justice in a human soul by first looking for it in a nascent city. The city is understood to be the natural form of a self-sufficient political community. The development of it considered here is not an imagined history, but an attempt to uncover the deepest causes that are always at work. As Thrasymachus became a test case in Book I for the possibility of human co-operation, Glaucon and Adeimantus in Book II are examples of the raw human materials out of which a good community might be made. Thrasymachus was compared to a wolf, a lion, or a snake in need of taming or charming. Plato's two brothers are reflected in the images of well born and well bred puppies or young horses whose eager spiritedness needs to be given direction. The search for the best city is quickly transformed into a search for the best education.

Now when I said these things, I imagined I'd be released from discussion, but as it seems, it was just a prologue. For **Glaucon** is always most courageous in confronting everything, and in particular he wouldn't stand for Thrasymachus's giving up, but said "Socrates, do you want to seem to have persuaded us or truly persuade us that in every way it's better to be just than unjust?"

"If it would be up to me," I said, "I'd choose truly."

"Then you're not doing what you want. For tell me, does it seem to you there's a certain kind of good that we'd take hold of not because we desire its consequences, but to embrace it itself for its own sake, such as enjoyment and any of the pleasures that are harmless and from which nothing comes into the succeeding time other than to enjoy having them?"

"It seems to me," I said, "that there is such a thing."

"Then what about the kind that we love both itself for its own sake and for the things that come from it, such as thinking and seeing and being healthy? For presumably we embrace such things for both reasons."

"Yes," I said.

"And do you see a third form of good," he said, "in which there's gymnastic exercise, and being given medical treatment when sick, and giving medical treatment, as well as the rest of moneymaking activity? Because we'd say these are burdensome, but for our benefit, and we

D wouldn't take hold of them for their own sake, but we do for the sake of wages and of all the other things that come from them."

"There is also this third kind," I said, "but what about it?"

"In which of these kinds," he said, "do you put justice?"

358A "I imagine in the most beautiful kind," I said, "which must be loved both for itself and for the things that come from it by someone who's going to be blessedly happy."

"Well it doesn't seem that way to most people," he said, "but to belong to the burdensome kind that ought to be pursued for the sake of the wages and reputation that come from opinion, but ought to be avoided itself on its own account as being something difficult."

"I know it seems that way," I said, "and a while ago it was condemned by Thrasymachus as being that sort of thing, while injustice was praised, but, as it seems, I'm a slow learner."

B "Come then," he said, "and listen to me, if the same things still seem true to you, because Thrasymachus appears to me to have been charmed by you like a snake, sooner than he needed to be. But to my way of thinking, no demonstration has taken place yet about either one, since I desire to hear what each of them is and what power it has itself by itself when it's present in the soul, and to say goodbye to the wages and the things that come from them.

"So I'm going to do it this way, if that seems good to you too: I'll

C revive Thrasymachus's argument, and I'll say first what sort of thing people claim justice is and where they say it comes from, and second that everyone who pursues it pursues it unwillingly as something necessary but not good, and third that they do it fittingly since the life of someone who's unjust is much better than that of someone who's just—as *they* say, since it doesn't seem that way to me at all, Socrates, though I'm stumped as my ears are talked deaf when I listen to Thra-

D symachus and tens of thousands of other people, while I haven't yet heard the argument on behalf of justice, that it's better than injustice, from anyone in the way I want it. I want to hear it itself by itself praised, and I assume that I'd hear this most of all from you.

"That's why I'll strain myself to speak in praise of the unjust life, and as I speak I'll point out to you in what way I want to hear you in turn condemn injustice and praise justice. But see if what I'm saying is to your liking."

"Most of all," I said, "for what would anyone who has any sense

E enjoy more to talk about and hear about repeatedly?"

"You're speaking most beautifully," he said. "Listen then to what I said I'd talk about first, what sort of thing justice is and where it comes from. People claim that doing injustice is by its nature good and suffering injustice is bad, but that suffering injustice crosses over farther into bad than doing injustice does into good, so that when people both do injustice to and suffer it from each other and get a taste of both,

359A it seems profitable to the ones who don't have the power to avoid the latter and choose the former to make a contract with each other neither to do injustice nor suffer it. And from then on they begin to set up laws and agreements among themselves and to name what's commanded by the law both lawful and just, and so this is the origin and being of justice, being in the middle between what is best, if one could do injustice and not pay a penalty, and what is worst, if one were powerless to take revenge when suffering injustice. What's just, being at a mean between these two things, is something to be content with not as something good, but as something honored out of weakness at doing injustice, since someone with the power to do it and who was truly a man would never make a contract with anyone neither to do nor suffer injustice. He'd be insane.

B

"So, Socrates, it's the nature of justice to be this and of this sort, and these are the sorts of things it comes from by its nature, as the argument goes. The fact that those who pursue it pursue it unwillingly from a lack of power to do injustice, we might perceive most clearly if we were to do something like this in our thinking: by giving to each of them, the just and the unjust, freedom to do whatever he wants, we could then follow along and see where his desire will lead each one. Then we could catch the just person in the act of going the same route as the unjust one because of greed for more, which is what every nature, by its nature, seeks as good, though it's forcibly pulled aside by law to respect for equality.

C

"The sort of freedom I'm talking about would be most possible if the sort of power ever came to them that people say came to the ancestor of Gyges the Lydian. They say he was a shepherd working as a hired servant to the one who then ruled Lydia, when a big storm came up and an earthquake broke open the earth, and there was a chasm in the place where he was pasturing the sheep. Seeing it and marveling, he went down and saw other marvels people tell legends about as well as a bronze horse, hollowed out, that had windows in it, and when he stooped down to look through them he saw a dead body inside that appeared bigger than a human being. And this body had on it nothing else but a gold ring around its finger, which he took off and went away.

D

E

"And when the customary gathering of the shepherds came along, so that they could report each month to the king about his flocks, he too came and had on the ring. Then while he was sitting with the others, he happened to turn the stone setting of the ring around toward himself into the inside of his hand, and when this happened he became invisible to those sitting beside him, and they talked about him as though he'd gone away. He marveled, and running his hand over the ring again he twisted the stone setting outward, and when he had twisted it he became visible. And reflecting on this, he tried out whether the ring had this power in it, and it turned out that way for him, to become invisible when he twisted the stone setting in

360A

B

and visible when he twisted it out. Perceiving this, he immediately arranged to become one of the messengers attending the king, and went and seduced the king's wife, and with her attacked and killed the king and took possession of his reign.

"Now if there were a pair of rings of that sort, and a just person put on one while an unjust person put on the other, it would seem that there could be no one so inflexible that he'd stand firm in his justice and have the fortitude to hold back and not lay a hand on things belonging to others, when he was free to take what he wanted from

C

the marketplace, and to go into houses and have sex with anyone he wanted, and to kill and set loose from chains everyone he wanted, and to do everything he could when he was the equal of a god among human beings. And in acting this way, he would do nothing different from the other, but both would go the same route.

"And surely someone could claim this is a great proof that no one is just willingly, but only when forced to be, on the grounds that it is not for his private good, since wherever each one imagines he'll be

D

able to do injustice he does injustice. Because every man assumes that injustice is much more profitable to him privately than justice, and the one saying the things involved in this sort of argument will claim that he's assuming the truth, because if anyone got hold of such freedom and was never willing to do injustice or lay a hand on things belonging to others, he'd seem to be utterly miserable to those who observed it, and utterly senseless as well, though they'd praise him to each other's faces, lying to one another from fear of suffering injustice.

"So that's the way that part goes. But as for the choice itself of the

E

life of the people we're talking about, we'll be able to decide it correctly if we set the most just person opposite the most unjust; if we don't, we won't be able to. What then is the way of opposing them? This: we'll take nothing away either from the injustice of the unjust person or from the justice of the just person, but set out each as complete in his own pursuit. First, then, let the unjust one do as clever workmen do; a top helmsman, for instance, or doctor, distinguishes clearly between

361A

what's impossible in his art and what's possible, and attempts the latter while letting the former go, and if he still slips up in any way, he's competent to set himself right again. So too, let the unjust person, attempting his injustices in the correct way, go undetected, if he's going to be surpassingly unjust. Someone who gets caught must be considered a sorry specimen, since the ultimate injustice is to seem just when one is not.

"So one must grant the completely unjust person the most complete injustice,[10] and not take anything away but allow him, while doing

10   Note that Glaucon's completely unjust person is the third version so far. At 344A, Thrasymachus identified complete injustice with tyranny, which had no need for concealment, but in 352C-D, Socrates concluded that complete injustice would be an inability to do anything, being always at odds with itself.

the greatest injustices, to secure for himself the greatest reputation for justice; and if thereafter he slips up in anything, one must allow him to have the power to set himself right again, and to be competent both to speak so as to persuade if he's denounced for any of his injustices, and to use force for everything that needs force, by means of courage and strength as well as a provision of friends and wealth. And having set him up as this sort, let's stand the just person beside him in our argument, a man simple and well bred, wishing not to seem but be good, as Aeschylus puts it.[11]

"So one must take away the seeming, for if he's going to seem to be just there'll be honors and presents for him as one seeming that way. Then it would be unclear whether he would be that way for the sake of what's just or for the sake of the presents and honors. So he must be stripped bare of everything except justice and made to be situated in a way opposite to the one before, for while he does nothing unjust, let him have a reputation for the greatest injustice, in order that he might be put to the acid test for justice: its not being softened by bad reputation and the things that come from that. Let him go unchanged until death, seeming to be unjust throughout life while being just, so that when both people have come to the ultimate point, one of justice and the other of injustice, it can be decided which of the pair is happier."

"Ayayay, Glaucon my friend," I said, "how relentlessly you scrub each of them pure, like a statue, for the decision between the two men."

"As much as is in my power," he said, "and now that the two are that way, there's nothing difficult any more, as I imagine, about going on through in telling the sort of life that's in store for each of them. So it must be said, and if in fact it's said too crudely, don't imagine I'm saying it, Socrates, but the people who praise injustice in preference to justice.

"They'll say this: that situated the way he is, the just person will be beaten with whips, stretched on the rack, bound in chains, have both eyes burned out, and as an end after suffering every evil he'll be hacked in pieces, and know that one ought to wish not to be but seem just. And therefore the lines of Aeschylus would be much more correct to speak about the unjust person, since they'll claim that the one who is unjust in his being, inasmuch as he's pursuing a thing in contact with truth and not living with a view to opinion, wishing not to seem but be unjust

> Gathers in the fruit cultivated deep in his heart
> From the place where wise counsels breed.

B

C

D

E

362A

B

---

11   A reference to Amphiaraus in the *Seven against Thebes* (line 592). Glaucon quotes the two following lines shortly below.

In the first place, he rules in his city as one who seems to be just; next, he takes a wife from wherever he wants, and gives a daughter to whomever he wants; he contracts to go in partnership with whomever he wishes; and besides benefiting from all these things, he gains by not being squeamish about doing injustice. So when he goes into competition both in private and in public, he overcomes his enemies and comes out with more, and since he has more he is rich

C   and does good to his friends and damages his enemies. And to the gods he makes sacrifices in an adequate way and dedicates offerings in a magnificent way, and does much better service to the gods, and to the human beings it pleases him to, than the just person does, so that in all likelihood it's more suitable for him, rather than the just person, to be dearer to the gods.

"In that way, Socrates, they claim that, on the part of both gods and human beings, a better life is provided for the unjust person than for the just."

D   When Glaucon had said these things, I had something in mind to say in response to them, but his brother **Adeimantus** said "You surely don't imagine at all, Socrates, that what has to do with the argument has been sufficiently stated?"

"But why?" I said.

"The very thing that most needed to be stated was not mentioned," he said.

"Well," I said, "the saying goes 'a brother should be beside a man,' and so you too, if this one here is leaving anything out, should come to his defense. And yet, even the things said by him are sufficient to pin

E   me to the mat and make me powerless to give any aid to justice."

And he said "You don't mean that at all, so just listen to these things too. Because it's necessary for us also to go through the arguments opposite to the ones he stated, that praise justice and condemn injustice, in order for the thing that Glaucon seems to me to want to say to be clearer.

363A   "Certainly fathers tell their sons that one ought to be just, as all those who are in charge of anyone do, and exhort them, not by praising it, justice, but the good opinions that result from it, in order that ruling offices and marriages and all the things Glaucon went through just now should come as a result of that opinion to someone who seems to be just, things that belong to the just person as a result of his being well thought of.

"And these people go farther with the things they say come from opinions, for by throwing in the favorable opinions from the gods they have a bounty of good things to tell of for those who are pious,

B   which they, like the noble Hesiod and Homer, claim the gods give them. The one says that for the just the gods make

> Oak trees bear acorns aloft and honeybees in their midst,
> And fleecy sheep go heavy laden with wool,[12]

and many other good things annexed to these. And the other says just about the same thing too, how

> For some blameless, god-fearing king, who   C
> Upholds righteousness, the black earth bears
> Wheat and barley and trees laden with fruit, and
> Sheep bear young without fail, and the sea yields fish.

"And Musaeus and his son give the just more childish goods than these, for in their verse they bring them to Hades' realm and recline them on couches, crowned with wreaths, and set up a drinking party   D
for the pious, and make them go through all time from then on drunk, considering the most beautiful reward for virtue to be perpetual drunkenness. And others stretch out the wages paid by the gods still more distantly than these, since they claim children's children and a race are left down the generations by one who's pious and faithful to his oaths.

"So with these things and others of the sort they extol justice, but those who are impious and unjust, on the other hand, they bury in some sort of muck in Hades, or force them to carry water in a strainer, and while they're still living they bring them bad reputations. The   E
same punishments Glaucon went through for just people reputed to be unjust, they say are the punishments for unjust people, and they have no others.

"So this is their praise and blame for each sort. And on top of these things, Socrates, consider next another form of speaking about justice and injustice used both ordinarily and by poets. From one mouth they   364A
all sing the hymn that moderation and justice are beautiful but hard and burdensome while intemperance and injustice are sweet and easy to fall into one's grasp, and ugly only by opinion and law. They say that for the most part unjust actions are more profitable than just ones, and they're willing readily in public as well as private to congratulate dishonest people who are rich, or have other sorts of power, on their happiness, and to give them honor, but to slight and disregard those   B
who might be in any way weak or poor, while granting that they're better people than the others.

"But of all these things they say, the ones that are most to be wondered at are said about the gods and virtue, that after all, the gods also allot misfortunes and a bad life to many good people, and an opposite

---

12   From Hesiod's *Works and Days*, parts of lines 232-234. Note that the last line suggests a partial reply to Thrasymachus's earlier claim about shepherds (343B-C), since an economy dependent on sheep herding benefits primarily from a commodity the removal of which benefits the sheep as well. Socrates will quietly reinforce this point in 370D-E. Glaucon's quotation of Aeschylus just above seems to have roused Adeimantus's competitive spirit. His next quotation is from Bk. XIX of the *Odyssey*, lines 109 and 111-113.

destiny to people of the opposite sort. Beggars and fortune-tellers who go to the doors of the rich persuade them that they have a power from the gods at their disposal, made available through sacrifices and

C   incantations, and if there has been any injustice on his part or that of his ancestors, it can be atoned for with pleasures and feasts, or if he desires to ruin some enemy with little cost, a just person the same as an unjust one, he can do him damage by means of certain supplications and binding spells with which they, as they claim, persuade the gods to do their service.

"And as witnesses to all these things they say about vice, those who attribute an effortlessness to it bring forward poets to say how

D   Vices in droves are chosen lightly.
            Smooth is the road and it dwells very near.
            But the gods have put sweat in the way of virtue,[13]

and a long, rough, steep road. And those who say the gods are swayed by human beings call Homer as a witness, because he too said

E   Even the gods themselves are moved by prayer,
            And with sacrifices and gentle vows
            Humans turn them from wrath by libations and burnt offerings
            As they pray, when anyone transgresses and sins.

And they produce a racket of noise out of the books of Musaeus and Orpheus, descendants, they claim, of the Moon and the Muses, by whose prescriptions they keep busy with sacrifices, persuading not only private persons but even cities that, for those still living, there is

365A absolution and purification from injustices by means of sacrifices and festive pleasures, and there are even rites for those who die, which they call mysteries, that absolve us from the evils hereafter, while terrible ones await those who've made no sacrifices.

"Socrates, my friend," he said, "when all these things of such a kind and in such quantity are said about virtue and vice, the sort of esteem in which human beings and gods hold them, what do we imagine it does to the souls of young people who hear them, all those with good natures and equal to the task, as if they were floating above all the things that are said in order to gather from them what sort of person

B   to be and how to make one's way through life so that one might go through it the best possible way? From what seems likely, that person would speak to himself as Pindar wrote, 'Is it by justice or by crooked tricks that I make the wall rise higher' so as to fortify myself to live my life? For the things that are said claim there's no benefit for me to be just if I don't also seem to be, but obvious burdens and penalties, while they describe a divine-sounding life for an unjust person

C   provided with a reputation for justice. So, since, as those who're wise show me, 'the seeming overpowers even the truth' and is what

---

13   Hesiod, *Works and Days*, 287-289. The lines of Homer quoted next are from *Iliad* IX, 497 and 499-501.

governs happiness, one should turn completely to that. It's necessary for me to draw a two-dimensional illusion of virtue in a circle around myself as a front and a show, but drag along behind it the cunning and many-sided fox of the most wise Archilochus.[14]

"'But,' someone says, 'it's not easy always to go undetected in being evil.' Well, we'll tell him that no other great thing falls into one's lap either, but still, if we're going to be happy, this is the direction we've got to go, where the tracks of the argument take us. To go undetected, we'll band together in conspiracies and secret brotherhoods, and there are teachers of persuasion who impart, for money, skill at speaking to assemblies and law courts, by means of which we'll use persuasion about some things, but we'll use force about others, so as to get more than our share of things without paying the penalty.

"'But no power can escape the notice of the gods, or use force on them.' So, if there are no gods, or nothing among human things is of concern to them, why should we even be concerned about escaping their notice? And if there are gods and they are concerned, we certainly don't know about them and haven't heard anything about them from anyplace other than the laws and the poets who gave their genealogies, and these are the very ones who say they're the sort to be swayed when persuasion is applied through 'sacrifices and gentle vows' and dedicated offerings; one has to believe them either on both counts or neither. So if they're to be believed, one should do injustice and offer sacrifices out of the things unjustly acquired. Because by being just, we'll only be unpunished by the gods, and we'll be rejecting the gains from injustice, but by being unjust, we'll have the gains, and by praying when we transgress and sin, we'll get off unpunished by persuading them.

"'But we'll pay the penalty in Hades for the things we did unjustly here, either ourselves or our children's children.' 'But friend,' the one who's doing the calculation will say, 'the mystery rites too have great power, as well as the gods who give absolution from sin, as the greatest cities tell us, and so do the children of the gods who've become poets and prophets, who give us the revelation that this is how these things are.'

"By what argument, then, could we still choose justice in preference to the greatest injustice? If we get hold of the latter with a deceitful outward show, we'll achieve our purpose with both gods and humans while we're living and when we're dead, according to the word declared by most people and also by the top people. Out of all that's said, Socrates, what contrivance could there be for anyone to be willing to respect justice, anyone who has any power of soul, body, money, or family, and not instead laugh when he hears it praised? So

D

E

366A

B

C

---

14   A poet from whom we have some fragments of fables about the fox, including a cryptic line usually translated as "The fox knows many little things but the hedgehog knows one big thing."

surely, if anyone can demonstrate that what we've said is false, and has discerned adequately that justice is best, he no doubt has great sympathy for those who are unjust and isn't angry at them, since he knows that unless someone scorns doing injustice out of a god given

D   nature, or refrains from it because he's gained knowledge, no one else is willingly just, but from lack of courage or from old age or some other weakness someone condemns injustice because he's powerless to do it. It's clear this is so, since the first person of that sort who comes into any power is the first to do injustice, to the extent he's able.

"And there is nothing else responsible for all these things than that very thing that set in motion all this argument directed at you by this fellow and me, Socrates, and moved us to say 'You strange man, of all

E   of you who claim to be admirers of justice, starting from the heroes at the beginning whose sayings are left to us, down to people nowadays, no one has ever yet condemned injustice or praised justice other than for reputations and honors and presents that come from them. But each one of them itself, with its own power when it's present in the soul of the person who has it, and unnoticed by gods or humans, no one has ever yet, in poetry or in ordinary speech, gone over thoroughly in an adequate discussion how the one is the greatest of all the evils

367A   a soul has within itself, and justice is the greatest good. Because if it had been explained that way from the beginning by all of you, and you had persuaded us from our youth, we wouldn't be guarding one another against doing injustice, but instead each of us ourselves would be his own best guardian, fearing that by doing injustice he'd be sharing living quarters with the greatest evil.'

"These are the things, Socrates, and perhaps even still more things than these, that Thrasymachus and no doubt some other person might say about justice and injustice, twisting the power of the two around

B   in a vulgar way as it seems to me. But I, since I have no need to hide anything from you, am straining myself to state it to the utmost of my power, longing to hear the opposite from you. So don't just show us by your argument that justice is more powerful than injustice, but what each of them itself, by itself, does to the person who has it so that the one is bad and the other good. And take away the reputations, as Glaucon urged, because if you don't take the true ones away from each of them and attach the false ones, we'll say you're not praising

C   justice but its seeming, and not condemning injustice but its seeming, and that you're exhorting us to be unjust without being detected, and agreeing with Thrasymachus that what's just is someone else's good, what's advantageous to the stronger, while what's unjust is advantageous and profitable to oneself, but disadvantageous to the weaker.

"So since you agreed that justice is one of the greatest goods, which are worth possessing both for the sake of the things that come from them and, much more, themselves for themselves, like seeing, hearing, thinking, being healthy, and all the other good things that are true-

born from their own nature and not from opinion, praise justice for   D
this very thing, what it itself by itself does to help the one who has it
and injustice does to harm him. But leave wages and reputations for
others to praise, since I could stand for others to praise justice and
condemn injustice in that way, singing their praises and delivering
their abuse about them for reputations and wages, but not from you,
unless you were to insist on it, because you've gone through all your
life examining nothing other than this. So don't just show us by your   E
argument that justice is more powerful than injustice, but also what
each of them itself, by itself, does to the person who has it, whether
or not he goes unnoticed by gods and humans, so that the one is good
and the other bad."

And as I listened, though I had always admired the nature of
Glaucon and Adeimantus, I was completely delighted then and said,   368A
"The way Glaucon's lover saluted you, children of that man,[15] wasn't
bad, when you had won a good reputation at the battle at Megara,
and he made the beginning of his poem call you

> Children of Ariston, godlike progeny of an illustrious man.

To me, dear friends, that seems to be well put, since you've experienced something godlike if you haven't been persuaded that injustice
is better than justice, though you have the power to speak that way
on behalf of it. And you seem to me truly not persuaded, but I gather   B
this from other indications of your disposition, since from your arguments I'd distrust you. But to the degree that I trust you more, I'm that
much more stumped as to how I can be of use, and I have no way to
help out, since I seem to myself to be powerless. A sign of this for me
is that I imagined what I said to Thrasymachus demonstrated that
justice is better than injustice, but you didn't let my argument stand.
But neither is there any way for me not to help out, since I'm afraid
that it would be irreverent to be standing by while justice is being   C
defamed and not help out as long as I'm still breathing and have the
power to utter a sound. So what has the most force is for me to come
to its defense in whatever way is in my power."

Then Glaucon and the others begged me in every way to help out
and not give up the argument, but to track down what each of them is
and what the truth is about the sort of benefit that goes with the two
of them. So I said exactly what seemed to me the case: "The inquiry
we're setting ourselves to is no inconsiderable thing, but for someone

---

15   Looking ahead to the line quoted, "that man" would mean that eminent man who is your
father, and whose name means "best," but looking back to the way Glaucon and Adeimantus
have taken up the argument, they are also figuratively "children" of Thrasymachus, inheriting
his position in much the way Polemarchus was heir to Cephalus's in 331D. Glaucon's lover would
have been an older man, established in life and probably married. Sexual attachments between
such men and those in early manhood were not only respectable but fashionable among the
aristocracy in much of Greece at the time. A conventional view of this practice may be found
in a speech in Plato's *Symposium*, 180C-185E.

D   sharp-sighted, as it appears to me. So since we aren't clever," I said, "the sort of inquiry for us to make about it seems to me exactly like this: if someone had ordered people who were not very sharp-sighted to read small print from a distance, and then it occurred to someone that maybe the same letters are also somewhere else, both bigger and on something bigger, it would plainly be a godsend, I assume, to read those first and examine the smaller ones by that means, if they were exactly the same."

E   "Certainly," Adeimantus said, "but Socrates, what have you spotted in the inquiry about justice that's of that sort?"

"I'll tell you," I said. "There's justice, we claim, of one man, and there's presumably also justice of a whole city?"

"Certainly," he said.

"Isn't a city a bigger thing than one man?"

"It's bigger," he said.

"Then maybe more justice would be present in the bigger thing,
369A   and it would be easier to understand it clearly. So if you people want to, we'll inquire first what sort of thing it is in cities, and then we'll examine it by that means also in each one of the people, examining the likeness of the bigger in the look of the smaller."

"You seem to me to be saying something beautiful," he said.

"Then if we were to look at a city as it comes into being in speech," I said, "would we see the justice and injustice that belong to it coming into being as well?"

"Probably so," he said.

B   "And then, once it has come into being, is there a hope of seeing what we're looking for more readily?"

"Very much so."

"Does it seem good, then, that we should try to accomplish this? Because I imagine it's not a small task, so you people consider it."

"It's been considered," Adeimantus said. "Don't do anything else."

"Okay," I said. "A city, as I imagine, comes into being because it happens that each of us is not self-sufficient, but needs many things. Or do you imagine a city is founded from any other origin?"

"None at all," he said.

"So then when one person associates with another for one use,
C   and with another for another use, since they need many things, and many people assemble in one dwelling place as partners and helpers, to this community we give the name city, don't we?"

"Certainly."

"And they share things one with another, if they give or take shares of anything, because each supposes it to be better for himself?"

"Certainly."

"Come then," I said, "and let's make a city from the beginning in our speech. And it seems like what will make it will be our need."

"What else could it be?"

"But surely the first and greatest of needs is the provision of food   D
for the sake of being and living."

"Absolutely."

"And second is the need for a dwelling place, and third for clothes
and such things."

"That's so."

"Well then," I said, "how big a city will be sufficient to provide
this much? Is it anything else than one person as a farmer, another a
housebuilder, and some other a weaver? Or shall we add to it a leatherworker or someone who attends to something else for the body?"

"Certainly."

"And the city that's most necessary anyway would consist of four
or five men."   E

"So it appears."

"And then what? Should each one of these put in his own work
for them all in common, with the farmer, say, who is one, providing food for four and spending four times the time and effort in the
provision of food for the others too to share, or paying no attention
to that, make a fourth part of this food for himself alone in a fourth   370A
part of the time and devote one of the other three to providing for a
house, another to a cloak, and the other to shoes, and not have the
trouble of sharing things with others but do himself, by himself, the
things that are for himself?"

And Adeimantus said, "Probably, Socrates, the first way would
be easier than that one."

"And by Zeus, there's nothing strange about that," I said. "For I'm
thinking too myself, now that you mention it, that in the first place,   B
each of us doesn't grow up to be entirely like each, but differing in
nature, with a different person in practice growing toward a different
sort of work. Or doesn't it seem that way to you?"

"It does to me."

"Then what? Would someone do a more beautiful job who, being
one, worked at many arts, or when one person works at one art?"

"When one person works at one art," he said.

"And I assume this too is clear, that if anyone lets the critical
moment in any work go by, it's ruined."

"That's clear."

"Because I don't imagine the thing that's being done is willing to
wait for the leisure of the person who's doing it, but it's necessary   C
for the one doing it to keep on the track of the thing he's doing, not
when the turn comes for a sideline."

"That's necessary."

"So as a result of these things, everything comes about in more
quantity, as more beautiful, and with more ease when one person does
one thing in accord with his nature and at the right moment, being
free from responsibility for everything else."

"Absolutely so."

"So there's need for more than four citizens, Adeimantus, for the provisions we were talking about, since the farmer himself, as seems likely, won't make his own plow, if it's going to be beautifully made, or his pickax, or any of the other tools for farming. And neither will the housebuilder, and there's need of many things for that, and likewise with the weaver and the leatherworker."

"That's true."

"So with carpenters and metalworkers and many such particular kinds of craftsmen coming in as partners in our little city, they'll make it a big one."

"Very much so."

"But it still wouldn't be a very big one if we add cattlemen and shepherds to them, and other herdsmen, so that the farmers would have oxen for plowing, and the housebuilders along with the farmers could use teams of animals for hauling, and the weavers and leatherworkers could use hides and wool."

"It wouldn't be a small city either," he said, "when it had all these."

"But still," I said, "even to situate the city itself in the sort of place in which it won't need imported goods is just about impossible."

"It's impossible."

"Therefore there's still a further need for other people too who'll bring it what it needs from another city."

"There'll be a need."

"And if the courier goes empty-handed, carrying nothing those people need from whom ours will get the things for their own use, he'll leave empty-handed, won't he?"

"It seems that way to me."

"Then they'll need to make not only enough things to be suitable for themselves, but also the kinds and quantity of things suitable for those people they need things from."

"They'll need to."

"So our city will need more of the farmers and other craftsmen."

"More indeed."

"And in particular other couriers no doubt, who'll bring in and carry away each kind of thing, and these are commercial traders aren't they?"

"Yes."

"So we'll also need commercial traders."

"Certainly."

"And if the commerce is carried on by sea, there'll be an additional need for many other people gathered together who know the work connected with the sea."

"Very many."

"And how about in the city itself? How are they going to share out with each other the things each sort makes by their work? It was for the sake of this that we even went into partnership and founded the city."

"It's obvious," he said: "by selling and buying."

"So a marketplace will arise out of this for us, and a currency as a conventional medium of exchange?"

"Certainly."

"But if, when the farmer or any other workman has brought any of the things he produces into the marketplace, he doesn't arrive at the same time as those who need to exchange things with him, is he going to stay unemployed at his craft sitting in the marketplace?"

C

"Not at all," he said, "but there are people who, seeing this, take this duty on themselves; in rightly managed cities it's pretty much for the people who are weakest in body and useless for any other work to do. Because there's a need for it, so they stay around the marketplace to give money in exchange to those who need to sell something and to exchange in turn for money with all those who need to buy something."

D

"Therefore," I said, "this useful service makes for the origin of retail tradesmen in the city. Don't we call people retail tradesmen who are set up in the marketplace providing the service of buying and selling, but call those who travel around to cities commercial traders?"

"Certainly."

"And as I imagine, there are still certain other serviceable people, who don't entirely merit sharing in the partnership for things that involve thinking but have sufficient strength of body for labors, so since they sell the use of their strength and call this payment wages, they are called, as I imagine, wage laborers, aren't they?"

E

"Yes."

"And the wage laborers, as seems likely, are the component that fills up the city?"

"It seems that way to me."

"Well then Adeimantus, has our city already grown to be complete?"

"Maybe."

"Then where in it would the justice and the injustice be? And together with which of the things we examined did they come to be present?"

"I have no idea, Socrates," he said, "unless it's somewhere in some usefulness of these people themselves to each other."

372A

"And maybe you're putting it beautifully," I said. "We need to examine it though and not be shy about it. So first, let's consider what style of life people will lead who've been provided for in this way. Will they do otherwise than produce grain and wine and cloaks and shoes? And when they've built houses, by summer they'll work

B
at most things lightly clad and barefoot, but in winter adequately clothed and in shoes. And they'll nourish themselves by preparing cereal from barley and flour from wheat, baking the latter and shaping the former by hand, and when they've set out fine cakes of barley meal and loaves of wheat bread on some sort of straw or clean leaves, reclining on leafy beds spread smooth with yew and myrtle, they and their children will feast themselves, drinking wine to top it off, while crowned with wreaths and singing hymns to the gods, joining with

C
each other pleasurably, and not producing children beyond their means, being cautious about poverty or war."

And **Glaucon** broke in, saying "It looks like you're making your men have a feast without any delicacies."[16]

"That's true," I said. "As you say, I forgot that they'll have delicacies too, salt obviously, as well as olives and cheese, and they'll boil up the sorts of roots and greens that are cooked in country places. And as

D
sweets we'll doubtless set out for them some figs and chickpeas and beans, and at the fire they'll roast myrtle berries and acorns, while sipping wine in moderation. And in this way it's likely that, going through life in peace combined with health and dying in old age, they'll pass on another life of this sort to their offspring."

And he said, "And if you were making provisions for a city of pigs, Socrates, what would you fatten them on besides this?"

"But how should they be provided for, Glaucon?" I said.

"With the very things that are customary," he said. "I assume they'll lie back on couches so they won't get uncomfortable, and take

E
their meals from tables, and have exactly those delicacies and sweets that people do now."

"Okay, I understand," I said. "We're examining, it seems, not just how a city comes into being, but a city that lives in luxury. And maybe that's not a bad way to do it, since by examining that kind of city we might quickly spot the way that justice and injustice take root in cities. Now it seems to me though that the true city is the one we've gone over, just as it's a healthy one. But if you want us also to

373A
look in turn at an infected city, nothing prevents it. For these things, it seems, aren't sufficient for some people, and neither is this way of life, but couches and tables and the other furnishings will be added, and especially delicacies as well as perfumed ointments and incense and harem girls and pastries, and each of these in every variety. And so it's no longer the necessities we were speaking of at first—houses, cloaks, and shoes—that have to be put in place, but painting and multicolored embroidery have to be set in motion, and gold and ivory and all that sort of thing have to be acquired, don't they?"

"Yes," he said.

16   The last word refers to everything other than bread that people eat, but also has the sense of savory or appealing food, and particularly meat. Socrates, playing dumb, replies to the literal meaning.

"Isn't there a need then to make the city bigger again? Because   **B**
that healthy one isn't sufficient any longer, but is already filled with
a mass of things and a throng of people, things that are no longer in
the cities for the sake of necessity, such as all the hunters as well as
the imitators, many of whom are concerned with shapes and colors,
many others with music, and also the poets and their assistants, the
reciters, actors, dancers, theatrical producers, and craftsmen for all
sorts of gear, including makeup for women and everything else. And   **C**
we'll especially need more providers of services, or doesn't it seem
there'll be a need for tutors, wet nurses, nannies, beauticians, barbers,
and also delicacy-makers and chefs? Furthermore, there'll be an extra
need for pig farmers; this job wasn't present in our earlier city because
there was no need for it, but in this one there's the extra need for this
too. And there'll be a need for a great multitude of other fattened
livestock too, if one is going to eat them. Isn't that so?"

"How could it be otherwise?"

"Then won't we be much more in need of doctors when people   **D**
live this way instead of the earlier way?"

"Very much so."

"And doubtless the land that was sufficient then to feed the people
then will now have gone from sufficient to small. Or how do we put
it?"

"That way," he said.

"Then does something have to be cut off by us from our neighbors'
land if we're going to have enough to graze on and plow, and by them
in turn from ours if they too give themselves over to the unlimited
acquisition of money, exceeding the limit of necessities?"   **E**

"That's a great necessity, Socrates," he said.

"So what comes after this, Glaucon, is that we go to war? Or how
will it be?"

"That way," he said.

"And let's say nothing yet, at any rate," I said, "about whether
war accomplishes anything bad or good, but only this much, that we
have discovered in its turn the origin of war, in those things out of
which most of all cities incur evils both in private and in public, when
they do incur them.

"Very much so."

"So, my friend, there's a need for the city to be still bigger, not by
a small amount but by a whole army, which will go out in defense of   **374A**
all their wealth and in defense of the things we were just now talking
about, and do battle with those who come against them."

"Why's that?" he said. "Aren't they themselves sufficient?"

"Not if it was beautifully done," I said, "for you and all of us to
be in agreement when we were shaping the city; surely we agreed,
if you recall, that one person has no power to do a beautiful job at
many arts."

"What you say is true," he said.

B   "Then what?" I said. "Does the contest involved in war not seem to you to require art?"

"Much of it," he said.

"So is there any need to go to more trouble over leatherworking than over warfare?"

"By no means."

"But that's the very reason we prevented the leatherworker from attempting at the same time to be a farmer or a weaver or a housebuilder, but just be a leatherworker, so that the work of leathercraft would be done beautifully for us, and in the same way we gave out

C   one job to one person for each of the others, the job into which each had grown naturally and for which he was going to stay at leisure from the other jobs, working at it throughout life and not letting the critical moments slip by to accomplish it beautifully. But isn't it of the greatest consequence that the things involved in war be accomplished well? Or are they so easy that even some farmer is going to be skilled at warfare at the same time, or a leatherworker or anyone working at any other art whatever, while no one could become sufficiently skillful at playing checkers or dice who didn't practice that very thing from his youth but treated it as a sideline? And someone who picks up a

D   shield or any other weapon or implement of war, on that very day is going to be an adequate combatant in heavy-armor fighting or any other sort of battle that's needed in war, when no other implement that's picked up is going to make anyone a craftsman or fighter or even be usable to someone who hasn't gotten any knowledge about it or been supplied with adequate training?"

"Those implements would be worth a lot," he said.

E   "So then," I said, "to the extent that the work of the guardians is the most important, would it also be in need of the most leisure compared to other pursuits, as well as of the greatest art and care?"

"I certainly imagine so," he said.

"So wouldn't it also need a nature adapted to that very pursuit?"

"How could it not?"

"So it would be our task, likely, if we're going to be capable of it, to pick out which and which sort of natures are adapted to the guarding of the city."

"Ours indeed."

"By Zeus," I said, "it's no light matter we've called down as a curse on ourselves. Still, it's not something to run away from in fear, at least to the extent our power permits."

375A   "Certainly not," he said.

"So do you imagine that for guarding" I said, "there's any difference in nature between a pure bred puppy and a well bred young man?"

"What sort of nature are you talking about?"

"For instance, each of the pair, I suppose, needs to be sharp at perceiving things, nimble at pursuing what it perceives, and also strong, if it needs to fight when it catches something."

"There is certainly a need for all these things," he said.

"And to be courageous too, if it's going to fight well."

"How could it be otherwise?"

"But will a horse or a dog or any other animal whatever that's not spirited be likely to be courageous? Or haven't you noticed how indomitable and invincible spiritedness is, and how, when it's present, every soul is both fearless and unyielding against everything?"[17]

"I've noticed."

"And surely it's obvious what the guardian needs to be like in the things that belong to his body."

"Yes."

"And particularly in what belongs to the soul, that he has to be spirited."

"That too."

"Then how, Glaucon," I said, "when they're that way in their natures, will they not be fierce toward each other and toward the other citizens?"

"By Zeus," he said, "not easily."

"But surely they need to be gentle toward their own people but rough on their enemies, and if they aren't, they won't wait for others to destroy them but do it first themselves."

"True," he said.

"So what will we do?" I said. "Where are we going to find a character[18] that's gentle and high-spirited at the same time? For presumably a gentle nature is opposite to a spirited one."

"So it appears."

"But surely if someone lacks either one of these things, he won't become a good guardian. But these things seem like impossibilities, and so it follows that a good guardian becomes an impossibility."

"It's liable to be that way," he said.

I too was stumped and was thinking over what had been said before, and I said, "Justly are we stumped, my friend, because we've gotten away from the image we were setting up."

"How do you mean that?"

"We didn't notice that there are natures, after all, of the sort we were imagining there aren't, that have these opposites in them."

"But where?"

---

17   The words Socrates uses allude to a saying of Heracleitus (Diels-Kranz fragment 85): "Spiritedness is hard to fight against; whatever it wants to happen, it will pay for with its life."

18   This word (*êthos*) refers to something formed, in part, through choice and discipline; it differs from the word Cephalus used at 329D (*tropos*), translated as disposition, which can be a merely natural inclination. The use of the former word in E below is intentionally incongruous.

E

"One might see it in other animals too, though not least in the one we set beside the guardian for comparison. Because you know, no doubt, about pure bred dogs, that this is their character by nature, to be as gentle as possible with those they're accustomed to and know, but the opposite with those they don't know."

"Certainly I know it."

"Therefore," I said, "this is possible, and it's not against nature for the guardian to be of the sort we're looking for."

"It doesn't seem like it."

"Well then, does it seem to you that there's still a further need for this in the one who'll be fit for guarding, that in addition to being spirited he also needs to be a philosopher by nature?"

376A

"How's that?" he said. "I don't get it."

"You'll notice this too in dogs," I said, "which is also worth wondering at in the beast."

"What sort of thing?"

"That when it sees someone it doesn't know, it gets angry, even when it hasn't been treated badly by that person before, while anyone familiar it welcomes eagerly, even when nothing good has ever been done to it by that one. Or haven't you ever wondered at this?"

"Till this moment," he said, "I haven't paid it any mind at all. That they do this, though, is certainly obvious."

B

"But surely it shows an appealing attribute of its nature and one that's philosophic in a true sense."

"In what way?"

"In that it distinguishes a face as friend or enemy," I said, "by nothing other than the fact that it has learned the one and is ignorant of the other. And indeed, how could it not be a lover of learning when it determines what's its own and what's alien to it by means of understanding and ignorance?"

"There's no way it couldn't," he said.

"But surely," I said, "the love of learning and the love of wisdom are the same thing?"

"They're the same," he said.

"Then shall we have the confidence to posit for a human being too,[19] that if he's going to be at all gentle to his own people and those known to him, he needs to be by nature a lover of wisdom and of learning?"

C

"Let's posit it."

"So someone who's going to be a beautiful and good guardian of our city will be philosophic, spirited, quick, and strong by nature."

"Absolutely so," he said.

---

19   The comparison to the dog, meant about half-seriously, gives no explanation of such a conclusion other than the resemblance. The verb in 375D meaning "set beside for comparison" later came to mean "tell a parable." What is posited is that people who care most about learning and knowing are less at odds with those among whom they live.

"So he'd start out that way. But now in what manner will they be brought up and educated by us? And if we examine it, is there anything that gets us forward toward catching sight of the thing for the sake of which we're examining all this, the manner in which justice and injustice come into being in a city? The point is that we might not allow enough discussion, or we might go through a long one."

And Glaucon's brother said, "For my part, I expect this examination to be one that gets us very far along into that."

"By Zeus, **Adeimantus** my friend," I said, "it's not to be given up then, even if it happens to be overlong."

"Not at all."

"Come then, and just as if they were in a story and we were telling the story and remaining at leisure, let's educate the men in our speech."

"We should do just that."

"So what is the education? Isn't it hard to find a better one than what has been discovered by the passage of much time? And that, presumably, is gymnastic exercise for bodies and music[20] for a soul."

"That's it."

"Won't we start educating them with music before gymnastic exercise?"

"How could we not?"

"And in music," I said, "do you put speeches, or not?"

"I do."

"And of speeches, is there a double form, one true, the other false?"

"Yes."

"Are they to be educated in both, but first in the false?"

"I don't understand how you mean that," he said.

"Don't you understand," I said, "that at first we tell children stories? And this is doubtless, to speak of the whole, something false, but in it there's also something true. But we use stories for children before gymnastic exercises."

"These things are so."

"And that's what I meant, that music is to be taken up before gymnastic exercise."

"That's correct," he said.

"You know, don't you, that the beginning is the most important thing in every work, in other cases too, but especially with anything young and tender? For then most of all each one is molded, and pressed into the shape anyone wants to stamp onto it."

"That's exactly so."

---

20   This word includes our meaning, but within a broad sense that takes in all the arts that refine the sensibilities and civilize a human being. The name comes from attributing these pursuits to the inspiration of the Muses.

"Then shall we so easily permit the children to listen to haphazard stories made up by haphazard people and take into their souls opinions that are on the whole opposite to those we'll imagine they ought to have when they're full grown?"

"Under no circumstances will we permit it."

C   "So the first thing for us to do, as it seems, is to take charge of those who make up the stories, and what they compose that's beautiful is to be accepted, but what isn't is to be rejected. And those that are accepted, we'll persuade the nurses and mothers to tell their children, and mold their souls with stories much more than they massage their bodies with their hands. But most of those they tell now are to be eliminated."

"What sort exactly?" he said.

"In the greater stories," I said, "we'll see the lesser ones, since the greater and the lesser ones need to be of the same stamp and have the same power. Don't you think so?"

D   "I do," he said, "but I have no idea what you mean by the greater ones."

"The ones the pair[21] Hesiod and Homer told us," I said, "and other poets too. They certainly used to tell people false stories they had contrived, and they go on telling them."

"But what sort of stories," he said, "and what in them do you mean to blame?"

"The very thing that one ought to blame first and most of all," I said, "both for other reasons and especially if someone tells a lie in an unbeautiful way."

"What's that?"

E   "When someone in his speech makes a bad likeness of the sorts of beings gods and heroes are, as if a painter painted things not at all resembling the ones he wanted to depict a likeness of."

"It is in fact right to blame things of that sort," he said. "But how do you mean it exactly and what sort of things are you talking about?"

"First of all," I said, "the one who told the greatest lie, and about the greatest beings, didn't tell his lie beautifully,[22] how Uranus carried

378A   on the way Hesiod said he did, and how Cronos in turn got revenge on him. And as for the deeds of Cronos in particular, and the things done to him by his son, even if they were true I wouldn't imagine one should tell them so readily to those who are without judgment and young, but best of all should leave them in silence, or if there were

---

21   This word is not in the Greek, but is used here to approximate the effect of making Hesiod and Homer the subject of a verb not plural but dual in number. These two preeminent poets were responsible between them for most of the prevalent lore about the Greek gods. What Socrates proposes would be a bit like saying that children shouldn't be told any stories from Shakespeare or the Bible.

22   The curious can find the salacious details in Hesiod's *Theogony*, lines 154-210 and 453-506.

any necessity to speak of them, as few people as possible should hear them as secrets not to be repeated, after sacrificing not a suckling pig but some great and scarce offering, in order that they end up with the least people hearing them."

"Indeed," he said, "these passages are hard to take."

"And not to be spoken, Adeimantus," I said, "in our city. Nor   B
should it be said in the hearing of a young person that in doing the extremes of injustice, or in punishing an unjust father by every means, he would be doing nothing to be wondered at, but would do the very same things the first and greatest gods did."

"By Zeus, no," he said, "it doesn't seem to me fit to speak of it either."

"And," I said, "it's absolutely not fit to say that gods make war on gods and plot against them and fight them, since it's not even true, but   C
in any case if there's a need for those who'll guard our city to regard it as most shameful to be at odds with each other easily, far from needing to have stories told and embroidered about battles of gods and giants and many other hostilities of all sorts of gods and heroes toward their families and their own people. But if we're going to persuade them somehow that one citizen would never be at odds with another, and that this is impious, things like that should be said to the children   D
instead right from the start by the old men and old women, and as the children grow older, the poets too need to be required to compose stories in these areas. But the chains put on Hera by her son, and the hurling down of Hephaestus by his father when he was about to defend his mother who was being beaten, and all the battles of gods Homer has made up are not to be allowed into the city, whether they've been made with or without deeper meanings. A young person isn't able to discern what's a deeper meaning and what's not, but what he takes in   E
among his opinions when he's that age tends to become hard to rub off and impossible to change. So on account of this, one probably ought above all to make what they hear first the most beautiful storytelling about virtue that it's possible to hear."

"That does make sense," he said. "But if someone were to ask us next what particular things these are and what stories tell them, what would we say?"

And I said, "Adeimantus, you and I aren't poets at present but   379A
founders of a city. And it's appropriate for founders to know the general outlines along which the poets need to tell stories; if they compose things outside these, they're not to be accepted, but it doesn't belong to the founders themselves to make up stories."

"That's correct," he said. "But that's the very point: what would be the general outlines for talk about the gods?"

"No doubt some such ones as these," I said; "the god, presumably, always needs to be represented as exactly the sort of being he is, whether anyone depicts him in epics, in lyric poetry, or in tragedies."

"He needs to be."

B   "Then certainly the god is good in his very being and needs to be spoken of as such?"

"What else could he be?"

"But surely none of the good things is harmful; or is it?"

"It doesn't seem so to me."

"So does what is not harmful do any harm?"

"Not at all."

"And what does no harm, does it do anything bad at all?"

"Not that either."

"And what does nothing bad, could it even be responsible for anything bad?"

"How could it be?"

"What, then? What's good is beneficial?"

"Yes."

"Therefore it's responsible for things that go well?"

"Yes."

"Therefore what's good isn't responsible for all things, but is responsible for things in a good condition while it's not responsible for things in a bad condition."

C   "That's totally so," he said.

"Nor, therefore," I said, "could the god, since he's good, be responsible for all things, as most people say, but responsible for a few things among human beings and not responsible for many, because there are a lot less good things among us than bad ones. So while no one else should be given the credit for the good things, some other causes need to be sought for the bad ones, but not the god."

"You seem to me to be saying something most true," he said.

"Then it shouldn't be accepted," I said, "either from Homer or

D   from any other poet,[23] if he foolishly makes this mistake about the gods, going astray in saying that two urns

> rest on Zeus's doorstep
> Full of fates, one filled with good, but the other with miseries,
> and for someone to whom Zeus, mixing them, doles out from both urns,
> Sometimes he meets up with bad, sometimes with good,
> but anyone he doesn't mix them for, but gives the second ones pure,
> Him a grinding evil misery drives across the sacred earth,

E

> nor if he says that Zeus serves out to us
> Both the good and the bad that come to pass.

And if anyone says the confounding of the oaths and truces that Pandarus violated was brought about by Athena and Zeus, we won't

---

23   The next three quotations are from Bk. XXIV of the *Iliad*, lines 527-528, 530, and 532, with some slight discrepancies from our texts of Homer in the first and third. The fourth is loosely related to IV, 84 of that poem, the last line of the passage about Athena and Zeus alluded to next, and the allusion to Themis and Zeus refers to the beginning of Bk. XX. The Aeschylus play quoted is not extant.

approve of it, and the young are not to be allowed to hear that strife
and conflict of the gods were the doing of Themis and Zeus, or in
turn, as Aeschylus says, that

> A god engenders the cause in mortals
> When he wants to ruin a house entirely.

And if anyone composes a work about the sufferings of Niobe, like
the one these verses are in, or those of the family of Pelops or the Trojans or anything else of that sort, he's either not to be allowed to say
they're the deeds of a god, or if they are from a god, he needs to find
an explanation for them pretty much like the one we're now seeking.
And he needs to say that the god brings about things that are just and   B
good and the people are helped by being punished, but the poet is not
to be allowed to say that the people who pay the penalty are in misery
and the one doing that to them is a god. If he were to say, though, that
they were in need of punishment because those who are bad are in
misery, and by paying the penalty they are benefited by the god, that is
to be allowed, but as for claiming that a god, who is good, comes to be
responsible for what is bad for anyone, one needs to do battle in every
way for no one to say these things in one's own city, if it's going to be   C
law-abiding, and no one, either younger or older, to hear them told
in stories either in meter or without meter, because if they were said
they would be neither pious things to say nor things of any advantage
to us nor things themselves in harmony with themselves."

"I cast my vote with you for this law," he said, "and it is accepted
by me."

"So this," I said, "would be one of the laws and general outlines
about gods within which those who talk about them will need to
talk and those who write poems will need to write them: the god is
responsible not for all things but for the good."

"And a very satisfactory one it is," he said.

"And what about this for the second one? Do you imagine that the   D
god is a sorcerer and the sort of being that schemes to become visible
in a different look at a different time, sometimes himself fluctuating
and changing his form into many shapes, and other times tricking us
and making that sort of thing seem to happen to him, or that he is
unitary and least of all the sort to move out of his own look?"

"I don't have the ability right now to say how that is," he said.

"Then what about this? Isn't it necessary, if anything could be
displaced from its own look, for it to be changed either by itself or   E
by something else?"

"It's necessary."

"But aren't things that are in the best condition the ones that are
least altered and moved by anything else? For instance a body is
altered by foods and drinks and labors, and every sort of plant by the
heat of the sun and by winds and such things that it undergoes, but
isn't the healthiest and strongest one altered least?"

"How could it be otherwise?"

"And isn't it the most courageous and thoughtful soul that some external experience would disturb and alter the least?"

"Yes."

"And surely for all artificial things too, furniture and houses and clothes, by the same argument the ones with good workmanship and in good condition are the least altered by time and other things that happen to them."

"These things are so."

B   "So everything in a beautiful condition, whether by nature or by art or by both, least admits of change by anything else."

"It looks like that."

"But surely the god and the things that belong to the god are best in every way."

"How could they not be?"

"So in this respect, the god least of all would have many shapes."

"Least indeed."

"But would he himself change and alter himself?"

"It's clear that he would," he said, "if he were altered."

"Then is the change to something better and more beautiful or to something worse and uglier than himself?"

"Necessarily to something worse," he said, "if he is altered. For cer-

C   tainly we're not going to say the god is lacking in beauty or virtue."

"You're speaking most correctly," I said. "And does it seem to you that anyone whatever in this condition, whether among gods or humans, would willingly make himself worse?"

"Impossible," he said.

"Therefore it's impossible too," I said, "for a god to be willing to alter himself, but it looks like, since they are the most beautiful and the best it's possible to be, each of them simply remains always in his own shape."

"That seems entirely necessary to me," he said.

D   "Therefore, most excellent fellow," I said, "let none of the poets tell us that

>Gods looking like strangers from foreign lands,
>Turning into every kind, often come into cities,[24]

and let none lie about Proteus and Thetis, or introduce a transformed Hera in tragedies or in any other poems as a priestess begging on behalf of

>The life-bringing sons of Argos's river Inachus,

E   or tell us the many other lies of that sort they tell. And let the mothers in their turn, when they've been persuaded by these things, not scare their children by telling stories that are bad to tell, about how

---

24   *Odyssey* XVII, 485–486, a reason for treating all strangers well. The following line is thought to be from a lost play of Aeschylus; the river's sons are its tributaries.

certain gods prowl around at night looking like a lot of foreigners of all sorts, so that they won't speak blasphemy against the gods and at the same time make their children more cowardly."

"Let them not indeed," he said.

"But then," I said, "while the gods themselves are the sort that don't change, do they make it seem to us that they appear in all ways by tricking and bewitching us?"

"Maybe," he said.

"What then?" I said. "Would a god be willing to lie in word or deed by putting out a false appearance?"   382A

"I don't know," he said.

"Don't you know," I said, "that all gods and humans hate the true lie, if it's possible to speak that way?"

"How do you mean it," he said.

"This way," I said: "that no one willingly desires to tell a lie to what is presumably most authoritative in himself about the most authoritative things, but fears most of all things to let it get in there."

"I still don't understand now," he said.

"Because you imagine I'm saying something elevated. But I mean   B
that everyone would least of all stand for telling and having told a lie to the soul about the things that *are*, and to be ignorant and to have and hold the lie there, and hates it most in such a case."

"Very much," he said.

"But surely what I was talking about just now would most correctly be called a true lie, and this is the ignorance in the soul of someone who's been lied to, since the lie in words is a sort of imitation of the   C
experience in the soul, an image that comes afterward, and not a completely unmixed lie. Isn't that so?"

"Very much so," he said.

"So a lie in its very being is hated not only by gods but also by human beings."

"It seems so to me," he said.

"So what then about the lie in words? When and to whom is it something useful, so that it doesn't deserve to be hated? Wouldn't it be against enemies and for those calling themselves friends when, on account of insanity or some senselessness they try to do something bad? Then, for the sake of a preventive measure like a medicine it   D
becomes useful. And in the circumstances we were just now talking about, the telling of stories, on account of not knowing where the truth is about ancient things, is it by making the lie as much as possible like the truth that we make it useful?"

"That's very much the way it is," he said.

"So then in which of these cases is a lie useful to the god? Would he lie by making a likeness of ancient things because of not knowing them?"

"That would surely be ridiculous," he said.

"Therefore a god doesn't have it in him to be a lying poet."

"It doesn't seem so to me."

"But would he lie from being afraid of enemies?"

E

"Far from it."

"But because of the senselessness or insanity of his own associates?"

"But no one senseless or insane is a friend of a god," he said.

"Therefore there isn't anything for the sake of which a god would lie."

"There isn't."

"Therefore a divine messenger and a divine being are free of lies in every respect."

"Entirely so," he said.

"Therefore the god is something absolutely straightforward and truthful in deed and word, and doesn't transform himself or trick others by false appearances or by words or by sending signs in either a waking vision or a dream."

383A

"It appears that way to me too now that you speak of it."

"Then do you go along with it," I said, "for this to be a second general outline within which one needs to talk about the gods and compose things about them, that they aren't sorcerers who change themselves and they don't mislead us by lies in word or in deed?"

"I go along with it."

"Then while approving of many other things from Homer, we won't approve of him for this, the sending of the dream by Zeus to Agamemnon,[25] or of this from Aeschylus, when Thetis claims that Apollo, singing at her wedding, dwelt on her blessings in her children,

B

> Who'd suffer no diseases and live long lives.
> He called all my fortunes dear to the gods,
> And sang a hymn of praise that heartened me,
> And I had confidence in Phoebus' divine mouth,
> Filled with the art of prophecy, to be free of lies.
> But he, the very one who sang, the very one there at the feast,
> The very one who told these things, is the very one
> Who killed my son.

C

Whenever anyone says such things about gods we'll be severe and not sponsor a chorus, and not allow teachers to use them for the education of the young, if our guardians are going to be reverent toward the gods and become godlike to the greatest extent possible for a human being."

"I go along completely with these guidelines," he said, "and I would use them as laws."

---

25   *Iliad* II, 1-42. The quotation from Aeschylus is thought to be from the lost play *The Decision of the Arms*. Tragedies were performed in Athens at public festivals, with choruses provided from funds donated by rich citizens but allocated by a government official.

BOOK III

Note

> In the first half of this book, Socrates draws out the consequences of the claim of **Adeimantus** that the choices of young people are heavily influenced by the things they've heard praised or glamorized by poets. In the second half, the examination of early education goes back further, to the harmony and rhythm heard by a child before it is old enough to understand words. Socrates claims that good states of character have a look, recognizable only to those whose souls have absorbed harmonious patterns akin to them. The choice of a path in life may depend less on the prevailing opinions surrounding a child than on the earliest attachments formed by an inner resonance that inspires love for the visible harmony in souls. Glaucon begins to display signs of an education in character himself in response to Socrates' questions. The simple style of life he couldn't stand the look of in the healthy city described in Book II gets his spirited approval in Book III as a choice to reject luxury for the sake of a gymnastic training more serious than that of athletes. The book ends with one more recommendation, for the telling of one "noble lie." Spirited young souls that have been inspired by music to a capacity to recognize virtue, and trained by gymnastic discipline to a capacity for the virtues of courage and moderation, still need to believe in something that attaches them to the land they live in and makes them feel a protective kinship toward those who share it with them.

"As far as gods are concerned, then," I said, "those are some of the things, it seems, that need to be heard and not heard straight from childhood by people who are going to respect both the gods and their parents and not treat their friendship with one another as a small thing." $\quad$ **386A**

"And for my part," he said, "I too assume that the way it appears to us is right."

"And what if they're going to be courageous? Don't they need to be told those things that are of the sort to make them least afraid of death? Or do you think anyone at all could become courageous if he had this terror in him?" $\quad$ **B**

"By Zeus," he said, "I don't."

"What next? Do you imagine that anyone who thinks there's a realm of Hades and terrible things there is going to be unafraid of death and prefer death in battle over defeat and slavery?"

"Not at all."

"So it seems that for these stories too, it's necessary for us to take charge of those who attempt to tell them, and require them not simply

C   to slander the things in Hades's realm the way they do but instead to praise them, on the grounds that they're neither telling the truth nor saying things of benefit to people who'll be warriors."

"It's certainly necessary," he said.

"Then," I said, "we'll delete everything of that sort, starting with this verse,[26]

> I'd rather be a bond-servant to another, tilling the soil
> For a man without land of his own and not much to live on
> Than be lord over all those wasted away among the dead,

and this,

> And the dwelling of the dead would be seen by mortals and
>   immortals,
> Gruesome, rotting things that the very gods abominate,

and

> Ah me! So there is something after all even in Hades' house,
> A soul and a phantom, but no beating heart in it at all,

and this,

> He alone a breathing soul, the rest flitting shades,

and

> And the soul, fluttering out of his limbs, went to Hades,
> Howling at its fate, leaving behind its manhood and strength,

387A   and this,

> Under the ground, like smoke,
> The soul went shrieking,

and

> As when bats in the innermost part of an uncanny cavern
> Fly around shrieking when one falls out of the chain
> Holding onto one another up against the rock,
> So the souls went off together shrieking.

B   And we'll beg Homer and the other poets not to take it hard if we cross out these things and everything of the sort, not because they aren't poetic and pleasant for most people to hear, but the more poetic they are, that much less should they be heard by children and men who need to be free and be more in fear of slavery than of death."

"Absolutely so."

C   "Then too, don't all the terrible and frightening names for these things need to be thrown out, Cocytus and Styx,[27] beneath the earth, withered, and all the other things of this type that are supposed to make everyone who hears them shudder when they're named? Maybe

---

26   The next seven quotations are, in order, *Odyssey* XI, 489-491, *Iliad* XX, 64-65, XXIII, 103-104, *Od.* X, 495, *Il.* XVI, 856-857, XXIII, 100, and *Od.* XXIV, 6-9.

27   River of Shrieking and Abominable River.

they're okay for some other purpose, but we're afraid on behalf of our guardians, that they don't get warmer and softer from that sort of shudder than we need them to be."

"And we're right to be afraid," he said.

"Then they're to be taken away?"

"Yes."

"And a general outline opposite to these is to be followed in speaking and writing?"

"That's clear."

"And therefore we'll take out the complaints and laments of celebrated men?"   D

"That's necessary," he said, "if the earlier things were too."

"Consider then," I said, "whether we'll be taking them out rightly or not. And surely we claim that a decent man will hold that dying is not a terrible thing for a decent man whose comrade he is."

"We do claim that."

"Then he wouldn't wail over him as having suffered something terrible."

"Certainly not."

"But surely we also say this, that such a person is the most self-sufficient, himself for himself, for living well, and to a degree that surpasses others, is least in need of anyone else."   E

"That's true," he said.

"Therefore it's least terrible for him to be deprived of a son or brother, or of money or anything else of the sort."

"Least indeed."

"Then he's also least the sort to wail but bears it in the mildest way when any such misfortune overtakes him."

"Very much so."

"Then we would rightly take away the lamentations of noteworthy men and give them over to women, and not to women of serious stature, and among the men all those of the bad sort would make them,   388A
in order that those we claim to be raising for guarding the land for us wouldn't be able to stand acting like those people."

"That would be right to do," he said.

"So again we'll ask Homer[28] and the other poets not to write of Achilles, son of a goddess

> Lying now on his side, now again
> On his back, and now face down,
>   then standing up and   B
> Darting back and forth, beside himself, on the barren sea beach,

---

28   The next seven displayed quotations are from the *Iliad*: XXIV, 10-11, 12, XVIII, 23-24, XXII, 414-415, XVIII, 54, XXII, 168-169, XVI, 433-434. Some have slight discrepancies from our texts of Homer.

or

> Taking in both hands the grimy ashes
> And pouring them over his head,

or wailing and making so many other laments of the kinds that poet wrote, or of Priam, descended from near the gods, pleading and

> Rolling in dung,
> Calling to each man by name.

C

And still more by far than about these things, we'll beg them not to write of the gods at least lamenting and saying

> Poor wretched me, poor wretched mother of the best man.

But if they do write of the gods that way, let them at least not have the nerve to imitate the greatest of the gods in so unlikely a way as to say

> Oh no! A truly beloved man being chased around the city
> I see with my eyes, and my heart grieves,

and

> Ah me! Sarpedon, dearest of men to me
> Is fated to be struck down by Patroclus, son of Menoetius.

D

Because, dear Adeimantus, if any of our young people would listen to such things seriously, and not laugh them off as things unworthy of being said, he'd hardly regard these things as unworthy of himself, being human, or rebuke himself for them, if it came over him to say or do anything of the sort. Instead, feeling no shame and having no endurance, he'd sing many dirges and lamentations over slight sufferings."

"What you say is most true," he said.

E

"So one ought not to hear them, as the argument just indicated to us; we have to be persuaded by it until someone persuades us that something else is more beautiful."

"Then one ought not to hear them."

"And they ought not to be lovers of laughter either. For just about anytime anyone gives way to a forceful laugh, he's looking for a forceful change from such a thing."

"It seems to me he is," he said.

389A

"Therefore, when anyone writes of human beings worthy to speak of, much less of gods, as being mastered by laughter, it's not to be accepted."

"Much less indeed," he said.

"Then we won't accept this sort of thing about gods from Homer either:

> And uncontrollable laughter broke out among the blessed gods
> As they saw Hephaestus huffing and puffing through the halls.[29]

---

29   *Iliad* I, 599-600.

According to your[30] argument, it's not to be accepted."

"If you want to put it down as mine," he said; "it's certainly not   B
to be accepted."

"But surely truth is also something that needs to be taken seriously. Because if we were speaking rightly just now, and a lie by its very nature is useless to gods, though useful to humans in the form of medicine, it's clear that such a thing needs to be granted to doctors and not handled by laymen."

"That's clear," he said.

"So it's appropriate for the rulers of the city, if for anyone at all, to lie for the benefit of the city as far as either enemies or citizens are concerned, but for everyone else, such a thing is not to be touched. But we'll declare that for a private citizen to lie to the rulers is the   C
same thing, and a greater fault, as for a sick person not to tell the truth about the things happening to his body to a doctor, or someone in training to a trainer, or as for someone who doesn't tell the helmsman the things that *are* about the ship or the sailors concerning the way he or any of his shipmates are doing."

"Most true," he said.

"Then if someone catches anyone else in the city lying,   D

> Any of those who are workmen for the public,
> Prophet or healer of sicknesses or joiner of wood,[31]

he'll punish him for bringing in a practice as subversive and destructive for a city as for a ship."

"If in fact deeds should fulfill one's word," he said.

"What next? Won't there be a need for moderation in our young people?"

"How could there not be?"

"And for the majority of people, aren't such things as these the biggest parts of moderation: being obedient to rulers and being rulers   E
themselves over the pleasures that have to do with drink and sex and with food?"

"It seems so to me."

"So I imagine we'll say that things like these, that Diomedes says in Homer,[32] are said beautifully,

---

30   Why does Socrates say this? Possibly to indicate that he has undertaken the whole project of banning poetry as a dialectical elaboration of the claims made by Adeimantus in Bk. II (especially 365A-B). Or possibly he is just teasing Adeimantus because he enjoys a laugh, even if not a belly-laugh. In any case, those who are confident they know what Socrates, much less Plato, thinks about "censorship" might be advised to be cautious. John White has called attention to the oddity of quoting in public passages one thinks should not be heard. (See "Imitation," Afterword, p. 323.)

31   *Odyssey* XVII, 383-384.

32   This line, *Iliad* IV, 412, begins a passage in which Diomedes demands from an older companion not just obedience to himself but respect for their commander and their fathers, in a stern and gracious speech. The following couplet telescopes III, 8 with IV, 431. The insult quoted next is I, 225.

> Hush, old friend; keep still and obey my word,

as well as those that go along with them,

> The Achaeans went breathing courage,
> In silence, fearing their commanders,

and all the others of that sort."
  "Beautifully."
  "But what about this sort of thing,

> Weighed down with wine, with a dog's eyes and a deer's heart,

390A and the things following this? Is this beautifully said, or all the other childish remarks any private person has made to rulers in prose or verse?"
  "Not beautifully."
  "Because I don't imagine they're fit for young people to hear, at least with a view to moderation, but if they provide some other pleasure that's not at all surprising. Or how does it appear to you?"
  "That way."
  "And what about making the wisest man[33] say that it seems to him to be the most beautiful of all things when

B   tables are overflowing
> With bread and meats, and drawing wine from the bowl,
> The wine steward brings it and pours it in cups;

does it seem to be fit for a young person to hear for his own self-control? Or this,

> The most pitiful thing is to die and meet one's fate by hunger.

Or the way Zeus, when the other gods and humans were asleep and
C he was the only one awake making plans, easily forgot all these things because of a desire for sex, and was so struck by seeing Hera that he wasn't even willing to go into the house but wanted to have sex right there on the ground, saying he wasn't so possessed by desire even

> When they first made love to one another, with their dear
>   parents unaware,

or the chaining together of Ares and Aphrodite by Hephaestus for other acts of that sort."
  "No, by Zeus," he said. "They don't seem fitting to me."
D   "But presumably," I said, "if any acts of endurance in the face of everything are spoken of and performed by noteworthy men, they're to be seen and heard, such as this,[34]

---

33   Odysseus, *Odyssey* IX, 8-10. The next quotation is XII, 342 of that poem, the following one is *Iliad* XVI, parts of 295 and 296, and the Ares-Aphrodite story is in *Od.* VIII, beginning at 266.

34   Odysseus, *Odyssey* XX, 17-18; the word for "humiliating" is literally "dog-like." The next line quoted is thought to be from Hesiod. The three following references to Achilles are to *Iliad* IX, 515-518, XIX, 145-147, 278-281, and XXIV, 592-594.

Striking his chest, he scolded his heart with words: bear up
Heart, you put up with something else even more humiliating
    once.

"Absolutely," he said.
"And it's certainly not acceptable for the men to be bribe takers
or money lovers."   E
"By no means."
"And it's not to be chanted to them that

Gifts persuade gods, gifts persuade awe-inspiring kings,

and Achilles' tutor Phoenix is not to be praised as having spoken in
a level-headed way when he advised him to come to the aid of the
Achaeans because he got gifts, but not to give up his wrath without
gifts. And we won't consider it worthy of Achilles himself, or agree
that he was so money-loving that he took gifts from Agamemnon, or   391A
that he released a dead body when he got a ransom, but otherwise
wasn't willing to."
"It certainly wouldn't be just to praise things like that," he said.
"I'm reluctant, for Homer's sake," I said, "to say that it's also not
pious to allege these things against Achilles, or to believe them when
others say them, or that he said to Apollo[35]

You've thwarted me, Attacker from afar, most malignant of
    all gods;
I'd pay you back, if I had the power,

or that he was defiant toward the river, which was a god, and was   B
ready to fight it, or said in turn about the locks of hair dedicated to
the other river, Spercheius,

I will send my hair for the hero Patroclus to carry,

when Patroclus was a corpse; that he did this is not to be believed.
And as for dragging Hector around the tomb of Patroclus, and cutting
the throats of live captives on his funeral pyre, we'll declare that all
these things are untruly alleged and we won't allow our people to   C
believe that Achilles, who was the son of a goddess and of the very
moderate Peleus, a grandson of Zeus, and was brought up by the very
wise Chiron, was so mixed-up inside that he had a pair of disorders
opposed to one another, the mean-spiritedness that goes with a love
of money and also a haughty disdain for gods and humans."
"You're speaking rightly," he said.
"Then we won't believe this either," I said, "or let it be said that   D
Theseus, a son of Poseidon, and Perithous, a son of Zeus, incited such
terrible rapes, or that any other hero and son of a god would dare to
carry out terrible and unholy deeds of the sort that are now falsely
reported about them, but we'll force the poets either not to claim that

---

35   *Iliad* XXII, 15, 20, followed by XXIII, 151. The two references following that are to XXIV,
14-18 and XXIII, 172-177.

those deeds were theirs or not to claim they were sons of gods, but not to say both or try to persuade our young people that the gods generate evils and that demigods are no better than human beings.

E   It's exactly what we were saying in the earlier cases; these things are neither pious nor true. For surely we demonstrated that it's impossible for evils to come from gods."

"How could it be otherwise?"

"And in fact they're harmful to those who hear them, because everyone will forgive himself for being bad, in the persuasion that, after all, even those dwelling near the gods did and are doing such things,

> Close relatives of Zeus, on Mount Ida's peak,
> Whose altar to ancestral Zeus is in the upper air,
> And in them the blood of divinities is not yet extinct.[36]

392A   For that reason such stories need to be stopped, so they don't give birth to a big encouragement toward vice in our young people."

"Quite right," he said.

"Well then," I said, what form of speeches is still left for us to determine the sorts of things to be said and not said about it? How one ought to speak about gods has been discussed, and about divinities and heroes and the things in Hades' realm."

"Very much so."

"So wouldn't the thing that's left be what has to do with human beings?"

"Clearly."

"But it's not in our power, my friend, to settle this at present."

"How's that?"

"Because I assume we'll say that both poets and prose writers
B   speak badly about human beings in the most important respects, saying that many unjust people are happy and just people miserable, that doing injustice is profitable if one is undetected, and that justice is someone else's good but one's own loss. And we'll forbid them to say such things and command them to sing and tell stories opposite to them. Don't you imagine so?"

"I know it very well," he said.

"Then assuming you agree that I'm speaking rightly, shouldn't I say you've granted what we've been looking for all along?"

C   "You've made a correct assumption," he said.

"And won't the time for us to agree that one needs to make such statements about human beings be the time when we discover what sort of thing justice is, and how, by its nature, it profits the one who has it, whether he seems to be that way or not?"

"Very true," he said.

---

36   Thought to be lines from Aeschylus's lost play *Niobe*.

"Then let that be an end for the things belonging in speeches; but I imagine that what has to do with the style of speech needs to be examined after this, and then both what needs to be said and how it needs to be said will have been completely considered by us."

And Adeimantus said "I don't understand what you mean by this."

"Well," I said, "you need to. Maybe you'll get a better notion of it this way. Isn't everything said by storytellers and poets a narrative that happens to be about things that have been or are or will be?"

"What else?" he said.

"And don't they bring this about either by a simple narration or through one that arises from imitation or by means of both?"

"This too," he said, "I still need to understand more clearly."

"I seem to be a ridiculous teacher," I said, "and an unclear one; so just like people who are incompetent at speaking, I'll try to make clear to you what I mean not as a whole, but by taking out some piece of it. So tell me, do you know the first lines of the *Iliad*, in which the poet says Chryses begs Agamemnon to release his daughter, but the latter is rough on him, and the former, when he doesn't meet with success, appeals to the god about the Achaeans?"

"I do."

"Then you know that up to these verses,[37]

and he beseeched all the Achaeans,
But especially the two sons of Ares, marshals of the people,

the poet himself is speaking and makes no attempt to divert us into thinking a different way, that the one speaking is anyone other than himself. But in the lines after this he speaks as though he himself were Chryses, and tries as hard as he can to make it seem to us that the one speaking is not Homer but the priest, who is an old man. And he wrote pretty much all the rest of his narrative in that way, both about the things that happened in Troy and about those in Ithaca, and the whole *Odyssey*."

"Quite so," he said.

"Then isn't it narration both when he speaks the speeches on each occasion and when he describes things between the speeches?"

"How could it not be?"

"But when anyone is speaking a speech as though he were someone else, won't we say that at that time he makes his style as much as possible like each person he announces as speaking?"

"We'll say that, sure"

"Isn't making oneself like another person, either in voice or in gesture, imitating that person one likens oneself to?"

"Why, yes."

393A

B

C

---

37   *Iliad* I, 15-16.

"So in such a case, it seems, both he and the rest of the poets make their narratives by means of imitation."

"Very much so."

D "But if the poet wouldn't hide himself anywhere, all his poetry and narration would have taken place without imitation. And so that you won't say again that you don't understand, I'll explain how this could come about. When Homer said that Chryses came bringing ransom for his daughter and as one asking favor from the Achaeans, and especially from their kings, if after that he spoke not as though he had become Chryses but still as Homer, you know that it would not be imitation but simple narrative. It would have gone this way: I'll speak without meter, though, since I'm not poetic. When he came,

E the priest prayed for the gods to grant it to them to stay safe as they captured Troy, and for them to free his daughter, accepting the compensation and showing reverence to the god. And when he said these things, the rest of the people approved of them and consented, but Agamemnon was angry, commanding him to leave at once and not come back again, or his staff of authority with its wreaths for the god might not protect him; before being released, he said, his daughter

394A would grow old in Argos with *him*. And he ordered him to go away and not annoy him, in order to get home safe. And the old man was afraid when he heard him, and left in silence, but when he'd retreated from the camp he made many a prayer to Apollo, calling on him by his ceremonial names and reminding him and insisting that he be repaid if he had ever done anything pleasing to him either in building temples or in making sacrificial offerings. So for the sake of these things, he prayed for him to make the Achaeans pay for his tears with

B his arrows. That, my comrade," I said," is the way simple narration without imitation is done."

"I understand," he said.

"Understand, then," I said, "that the opposite of this happens in turn when someone takes out the things in between the poet's speeches and leaves behind the talk back and forth."

"I understand too," he said, "that this is sort of thing that's in tragedies."

"You've assumed it most correctly," I said, "and now I imagine I'm making clear to you what I couldn't before, that, of poetry and

C storytelling, the one sort is wholly done by imitation, just as you say tragedy and comedy are, and another sort by the report of the poet himself, and you'd find it most of all, I suppose, in dithyrambic lyrics. And, in turn, the sort that's done by both means is in epic poetry and many other places, if you understand me."

"I do," he said; "I get what you wanted to say before."

"Now call to mind what we were saying before this, that the things that need to be said have already been described, but how they need to be said is still to be examined."

"I remember."

"This, then, is the very thing I was saying, that we need to agree   D
whether we'll let the poets make their narratives for us by imitating,
or by imitating some things and not others, and what sort of thing
each of those is, or not let them imitate at all."

"I get the impression," he said, "that you're considering whether
we'll admit tragedy and comedy into the city or not."

"Maybe," I said; "but maybe there are also more things than these
to consider. I don't yet know exactly. But as with a wind, where the
argument takes us, we have to go."

"You're saying it beautifully, too," he said.

"Consider this, then, Adeimantus, whether our guardians ought   E
to be adept at imitating or not. Or does this too follow from what
was said before, that each one person could do a beautiful job at one
pursuit, but not at many, and if he were to try it, by taking up many
things he would presumably fail in all cases to be noteworthy?"

"How could that not happen?"

"Then doesn't the same argument apply to imitation, that the
same person doesn't have the power to imitate many things as well
as one thing?"

"No, he doesn't."

"Therefore he's hardly going to work at any of the pursuits worthy   395A
of mention and at the same time imitate many things and be an imitator, since presumably the same people don't even have the power
to imitate well in two sorts of imitation that seem to be close to one
another, such as writing comedy and tragedy. Weren't you just now
calling this pair imitations?"

"I was. And you're telling the truth; the same people don't have
that power."

"And not even to be reciters and actors at the same time either."

"True."

"And really, the same people don't even have the power to be   B
actors in both comedies and tragedies, though all these are imitations,
aren't they?"

"They're imitations."

"And the nature of a human being appears to me, Adeimantus,
to be cut up in pieces even smaller than these, so as to be powerless
to imitate many things beautifully any more than to do those very
things from which the imitations are copied off."

"Very true," he said.

"Therefore, if we're going to maintain our first argument, that
our guardians, giving up all other sorts of craftsmanship, need to be   C
craftsmen of the city's freedom in a completely precise way, and work
at nothing else that doesn't carry over into this, then there would be a
need for them not to do or imitate anything else at all. But if they do
engage in imitation, they'd need to imitate, straight from childhood,

D

what's appropriate for them: people who are courageous, moderate, pious, free, and everything of that sort. But anything fit for slaves, or anything else shameful, they should neither do nor even be clever at imitating, so they don't start to enjoy being those things from imitating them. Or haven't you noticed that imitations, if people persevere long in them from youth, settle into habits and into nature, in both body and voices, and in thinking as well?"

"Very much so," he said.

"So," I said, "we won't permit those we claim to care about, when we need them to become good men, since they are men, to imitate a woman, a young one or an older one, abusing her husband, or feeling rivalry toward the gods and full of big talk because she imagines she's favored by fortune, or caught up in misfortunes and in wailing and moaning, and still less will we want one who's sick or in love or in labor."

E

"Absolutely not," he said.

"And not female slaves or male slaves either, doing all the things that belong to slaves."

"Not that either."

"And not bad men either, as it seems, who are cowards and do things that are opposite to the ones we mentioned just now, insulting and ridiculing each other, using vile language when they're drunk and even when they're sober, and committing all the other offenses in words and deeds towards themselves and others that such people do. And I don't imagine they should get in the habit of making themselves like the insane, in words or in deeds; they need a knowledge of people who are insane and of those who are worthless too, both men and women, but they're not to do or imitate anything that belongs to them."

396A

"Most true," he said.

"What next?" I said. "Are metalworkers or any other craftsmen, or those who ply the oars in galleys or drive the oarsmen on, or anything else having to do with these things to be imitated?"

B

"How could they," he said, "when they're not even allowed to pay any attention to any of those things?"

"Then what about horses whinnying and bulls bellowing and streams gurgling and the sea crashing and thundering and everything else of that sort? Will they imitate those?"

"But they've been forbidden," he said, "either to act insane or make themselves like the insane."

"So," I said, "if I'm understanding what you're saying, there is a certain form of style and narrative in which someone who's a gentleman in his very being would tell a story any time he would need to tell one, and a different form, unlike that one, which someone born and raised in a way opposite to that person would always keep to and in which he would tell a story."

C

"What sorts are they?" he said.

"It seems to me," I said, "that when a level-headed man arrives in a narrative at any speech or action of a good man, he'll be willing to report it as though he himself were that man and not be ashamed of that sort of imitation, especially if he's imitating the good man   D
acting in a safe and sound way, but he'll be willing less often and to a lesser degree if the man is undone by disease or by passions, or else by drunkenness or any other misfortune. But whenever he comes to anyone unworthy of himself, he won't be willing in seriousness to make himself into an image of a worse person, unless it's just briefly when that person's doing something decent; otherwise he'd be ashamed, not being in practice for imitating such things, and at the same time feeling a distaste for molding himself and putting himself into the outlines of worse people, since he has contempt for the very   E
thought of it, unless it's for the sake of playfulness."

"Likely so," he said.

"Then won't he use a narration of the sort we were going through a little while ago in connection with Homer's verses, and won't the style of it be one that has a share of both imitation and the other sort of narrative, but with a small portion of imitation in a long account? Or is there nothing in what I'm saying?"

"There's a lot," he said. "It's necessary for the general guideline for such a public speaker to be of just that sort."

"Then for the one who's not that sort, on the other hand," I said,   397A
"the lower sort of person he is, the more he'll narrate everything and not suppose anything to be unworthy of himself, so that he'll attempt to imitate everything seriously and in front of many people, even the things we were speaking of just now, thunder and noises of winds and hailstorms, axles and pulleys, trumpets and flutes and pipes and sounds of all the instruments, and even the cries of dogs and sheep and birds; won't the whole style of this person be by way of imitation   B
in voices and gestures, or have a little bit of narration in it?"

"That too is necessary," he said.

"Well," I said, "these are the two forms of style I was talking about."

"So they are," he said.

"Of the two, then, the one involves small variations, and if someone gives it a tonal range and rhythm appropriate to its style, won't he come close, if he's speaking correctly, to speaking in the same tone of voice and in one range, since the variations are slight, and especially in some rhythm that's of pretty much the same sort?"

"Exactly so," he said; "that's the way it would be."   C

"And what about the form that belongs to the other? Won't it need the opposite things, all pitches and all rhythms, if it in turn is going to be spoken appropriately, since it involves variations of every shape and sort?"

"That's emphatically the way it would be."

"Well then, don't all poets, and all those who say anything, happen upon one or the other type of style, or one mixed together out of both?"

"Necessarily," he said.

D "What are we going to do, then?" I said. "Will we accept them all into the city, or one of the unmixed, or the mixed?"

"If my opinion wins out," he said, "the unmixed imitator of the decent person."

"But Adeimantus, the mixed sort of imitator is pleasing too, and the one who's opposite to the person you choose is by far the most pleasing to children and their tutors as well as to the great mass of people."

"He is most pleasing."

E "But maybe you'd claim he's not in harmony with our polity,[38] because there's no twofold or manyfold man among us, since each one does one thing."

"No, he's not in harmony."

"And isn't that why it's only in such a city that we'll find a leatherworker who's a leatherworker and not a helmsman on top of his leatherworking, and a farmer who's a farmer and not a judge on top of his farming, and a warrior who's a warrior and not a moneymaker on top of his war making, and the same way with them all?"

"True," he said.

398A "So as it seems, if a man who had the power by wisdom to come to be of every sort, and to imitate all things, were to come into our city, wanting to give a display of himself and his poems, we'd bow down before him as someone holy, wondrous, and pleasing, but we'd say that there's no such man in our city and that it's not divinely sanctioned for one to come among us. And we'd send him off to another city, anointing his head with perfume and crowning him with wool,

B while we ourselves would make use of a more austere and less pleasing poet and storyteller for our benefit, who'd imitate the style of a decent person for us and say what he says within those guidelines that we set up as laws at the beginning, when we set ourselves the task of educating the soldiers."

"That's exactly what we'd do," he said, "if it were up to us."

"So now, my friend," I said, "we're liable to be completely finished with the part of music that has to do with speeches and stories; what's to be said and how it's to be said have been described."

"That's the way it seems to me about it too," he said.

---

38   This is the first use in the *Republic* of the Greek word that is the title of the dialogue (*politeia*). It refers not only to associated group of people but to the form of their association, the arrangement of functions and responsibilities that holds them together. It can apply by extension to the arrangement that constitutes any other whole out of parts. The joining of the word with the notion of harmonizing is no accident.

"After this, then," I said, "isn't the thing that's left what has to do   C
with the style of lyric poetry and songs?"

"Clearly."

"But by now couldn't everyone find what's to be said by us about
what sorts they'd have to be if we're going to be in harmony with the
things we said before?"

And **Glaucon**, laughing, said "Then, Socrates, I'm in danger of
being left out of 'everyone'; at least I'm not sufficiently able at present to contribute anything about the sorts of things we need to say,
though I have a suspicion."

"At any rate, I presume," I said, "that to start with you're sufficiently able to say this, that song is composed of three things, speech,   D
melody, and rhythm."

"Yes," he said, "at least that."

"Then as much of it as is speech is presumably no different from
speech that's not sung in respect to its needing to be spoken within
the same guidelines we were describing just before, and in the same
manner."

"True," he said.

"And surely the melody and rhythm need to follow the speech."

"How could it be otherwise?"

"But we claimed that there was no more need for dirges and lamentations in the speeches."

"No indeed."

"Then what are the dirge-like modes?[39] Tell me, since you're   E
knowledgeable about music."

"Mixolydian," he said, "and taut Lydian, and some of that sort."

"Then don't these need to be eliminated?" I said. "Because they're of
no use even for women, who ought to be decent, much less for men."

"Very much so."

"But surely drunkenness is most inappropriate for guardians, as
well as soft living and laziness."

"How could it be otherwise?"

"So which of the modes are soft and suited to drinking parties?"

"In the Ionian and also Lydian ones," he said, "some varieties are
called relaxed."

"Is it possible, my friend, that you'd use these for warlike men?"   399A

"Not at all," he said; "it's pretty much the Dorian and Phrygian
ones you've got left."

---

39   Musical modes are ways of tuning a melodic scale. The placement of a semitone among
whole tones in a half-octave changes the character of the intervals. The difference between the
major and minor modes of modern music will give some sense of the differences Socrates is
asking about. A tuning would be chosen in accordance with the occasion and purpose of what
was to be played, and on a stringed instrument, a change of mode would result from a tightening
or loosening. The Greek word used technically for "mode" is *harmonia*, translated just above as
"melody" and at 397B as "tonal range"; it originally referred to a joining or fitting in carpentry,
and is used for any fitting together of high and low tones.

"I don't know the modes," I said; "just leave us that mode that would appropriately imitate the sounds and intonations of someone who's courageous in a warlike action and in every sort of work involving force, even when he's had bad luck or when he's heading toward

B   wounds or toward death, or has fallen into some other misfortune, repelling the assaults of chance with a spirit of discipline and endurance. And also leave us another one for him when he's involved in an interaction that's peaceable and not forcible but voluntary, when he's either winning someone over about something he's asking for, whether a god by prayer or a human being by instruction and admonition, or on the contrary when he's submitting himself to someone else who's requesting something by teaching him or changing his mind, while he responds to these things as he thinks fit, not behav-

C   ing arrogantly but acting moderately and in a measured way in all these matters and being content with the outcome. These two modes, a forcible one, a voluntary one, for the unfortunate, for the fortunate, of the moderate, of the courageous, whichever ones most beautifully imitate their sounds—leave us these."

"Well," he said, "you're asking me to leave none other than the ones I just mentioned."

"Therefore," I said, "there'll be no need of many-stringed or all-modal music in our lyric poetry and songs."

"It doesn't appear so to me," he said.

"Therefore we won't maintain craftsmen for three-cornered lutes

D   and Panpipes and all the other instruments that are many-stringed and multi-modal."

"We obviously won't."

"And what about this? Will you admit flute makers or flute players into the city? Isn't the flute the most many-stringed instrument, and aren't the all-modal ones just imitations of the flute?"

"That's clear," he said.

"So," I said, "you've got the lyre and cithara left as useful in the city, and there'd also be some sort of pipe for the herdsmen in the fields."

"That's the way our argument is pointing at any rate," he said.

E   "At least we're not doing anything new, my friend," I said, "in judging Apollo and Apollo's instruments superior to Marsyas[40] and his instruments."

"By Zeus," he said, "we don't look like it to me."

"And by the dog,"[41] I said, "without noticing it, we've been making a city pure again that we just now claimed was living in luxury."

---

40   A satyr who challenged Apollo to a contest. The Muses preferred Apollo's music on the cithara to that of Marsyas on the flute.

41   This is a common oath of Socrates' but was rarely used by others. Eva Brann explains it as an invocation of Hermes (depicted by the Egyptians with a dog's head, as Anubis), used in contexts that associate Socrates with Heracles, the hero who brought a monster up from Hades into the light of day. (See *The Music of the Republic,* pp. 118-119.)

"*We're* moderate, anyway," he said.

"Come then," I said, "let's purify it the rest of the way. Because following on the modes we'd have what concerns rhythm, so we don't chase after intricate ones with every sort of metric feet, but see which rhythms belong to an orderly and courageous life. And once we've seen that, we'll require the foot, as well as the melody, to go with the speech of that sort of life, rather than have the speech follow the foot and melody. It's your job to say which of the rhythms these would be, just as with the modes."

400A

"By Zeus, I just can't tell," he said. "I could say from having seen them that there are three particular forms out of which the metric feet are woven,[42] just as, among tones, there are four that all the modes come from, but which sorts are imitations of what sort of life I can't say."

"Well," I said, "we'll also take counsel with Damon[43] about which are the appropriate feet for slavishness or insolence or insanity or other vices, and what rhythms need to be left for their opposites. I believe I've heard him, unclearly, naming a certain compound 'armored march' rhythm that was dactylic and heroic as well, arranging it I know not how and setting it out as equal on the upbeat and downbeat when it passes into a short or a long syllable; I believe he also named one rhythm iambic and another one trochaic and applied longs and shorts to them. And in some of these I believe he criticized and approved of the ways of pacing the foot no less than the rhythms themselves, or else both together somehow—I can't really tell. But as I was saying, let these things be referred back to Damon, since distinguishing them is no matter for a short discussion. Do you imagine it is?"

B

C

"By Zeus, I sure don't."

"But do you have the power to distinguish them in this respect at least, that what belongs to gracefulness or gracelessness follows a well-proportioned rhythm or a lack of rhythm?"

"How could it not?"

"But what's well-proportioned rhythmically or lacks rhythm goes along, in the one case, with a beautiful style, likening itself to it, or in the other case to an opposite style, and what's well harmonized or lacks harmony works the same way, if indeed rhythm and harmony follow speech, as we were just saying, and speech doesn't follow them."

D

"Certainly," he said, "these things need to follow speech."

"And what about the speech," I said, "and the manner of its style? Don't they go with the character in the soul?"

---

42   These forms are usually taken to be the ratios of syllable lengths within a foot, 2:2, 3:2, and 2:1, where one is a short syllable or half a long syllable. The analogous forms among tones are probably the ratios of string lengths of the principal intervals, the octave (2:1), fifth (3:2), fourth (4:3), and whole tone (9:8).

43   An older contemporary of Socrates, famous as one of the teachers of Pericles.

"How could they not?"

"But the other things go with the style?"

"Yes."

E

"Therefore goodness of speaking, harmoniousness, gracefulness, and rhythmic proportion follow goodness of character, not the mindlessness we condescendingly refer to as good-naturedness, but the thinking that has literally done a beautiful job of building a character that's good."

"Absolutely so," he said.

"Then don't these things need to be pursued everywhere by young people, if they're going to act in ways appropriate to them?"

"They certainly need to be pursued."

401A

"And presumably the art of painting is filled with these attributes, as is all such craftsmanship; weaving and embroidery and architecture are filled with them, and also every sort of workmanship of other furnishings, and in addition the nature of our bodies and that of other growing things. In all these a gracefulness or gracelessness is present. And gracelessness, lack of rhythm, and lack of harmony are in close kinship with bad speaking and bad character, while their opposites are close kin and imitations of the opposite sort, a moderate and good character."

"Totally so," he said.

B

"Then is it only the poets we need to take charge of, requiring them to produce the image of good character in their poems or else not produce poems among us, or do we need to have charge of the other craftsmen as well, and prevent them from producing this bad character, an intemperate, slavish, and graceless one, either in images of animals or in buildings or in any other work of craftsmanship? And shouldn't one who is incapable of this not be allowed to work at his craft among us, so that our guardians won't be nourished on images

C

of vice as though in a bad pasture, each day, little by little, gathering up and feeding on a great deal from many places that will, without their knowing it, build up into some one great evil in their soul? Shouldn't we instead look for those craftsmen who are naturally gifted to seek out the nature of the beautiful and graceful so that the young will draw benefit from everything, as though dwelling in a healthy place[44] where something from the beautiful works around them will strike their sight or their hearing, like a breeze wafting health from auspicious regions, and straight from childhood it will, without their

D

knowing it, draw them into likeness, friendship, and harmony with beautiful speech?"

"Very much so," he said; "they'd be nourished most beautifully in that way."

---

44   A place that provides the benefits found, for example, in the city constructed first in Bk. II. See 372E.

"And isn't it for the sake of these consequences, Glaucon," I said, "that nourishment on music is of supreme importance? Aren't rhythm and harmony infused to the greatest possible extent into the inward part of the soul, and don't they take hold of it most vigorously with the gracefulness they bring, and make it graceful if one nourishes it rightly, or the opposite if one doesn't? And wouldn't the person who'd been nourished as one ought to be in that area also have the most acute perception of things left inadequate and not beautifully crafted or not formed beautifully by nature, and from having a rightful disdain for them, wouldn't he appreciate beautiful things and delight in them, and by admitting them into his soul wouldn't he take nourishment from them and become gentlemanly? And wouldn't the person nourished in that way rightly find fault with ugly things and hate them while he was still young, before having the power to grasp reason, so that when reason comes he'll embrace it most eagerly, recognizing it by a feeling of kinship?"

E

402A

"It seems to me, at any rate," he said, "that nurture on music is for the sake of just such things."

"Then it's just like what has to do with written words," I said; "we were competent with them when the letters, though there are few of them, couldn't elude us in any of the combinations in which they're passed around, and we didn't look down on them in either a small or a large instance as not needing to be noticed, but were eager to recognize them everywhere, because we weren't going to be literate before we had that ability."

B

"True."

"And if images of written words were to show up anywhere, either in water or in mirrors, we won't recognize them, will we, before we know the words themselves? Don't they belong to the same art and endeavor?"

"Absolutely so."

"Before the gods, then, is it the way I'm saying, that we're not going to be musically literate, and neither are those whom we claim need to be educated by us as guardians, before we recognize the look[45] of moderation and of courage and generosity and greatness of manner and all their near kin, and also their opposites, everywhere they pass around us, and notice their presence in the things they're found in, both they themselves and their images, and not look down on them in either small or large instances, but consider them to belong to the same art and endeavor?"

C

---

45   The word is *eidos*, usually translated "form," as at 400a. There the reference was to an intelligible look, the 2:2 ratio, for example, shared by a dactyl and a spondee. Here it refers to the recognizable pattern of a state of character, as grasped immediately by the senses, though the claim seems to be that only someone nourished properly on music when very young would be capable of recognizing it. This passage is one of the primary preparations in the dialogue for the deeply philosophic sense the word *eidos* is given later in the dialogue, beginning at 476A.

"That's a big necessity," he said.

D   "So if beautiful states of character present in someone's soul coincide with something in the look of that person in agreement and harmony with those states of character, sharing the same contours, wouldn't that be a most beautiful sight for someone able to see it?"

"Very much so."

"And surely what is most beautiful most inspires love?"

"How could it not?"

"Then someone really musical, most of all, would love such people, but if someone were lacking in harmony he wouldn't love that person."

"He wouldn't if something was lacking in the soul; if, however, there was some defect in the body, he'd be tolerant enough to accept him willingly."

E   "I understand," I said; "you have, or had, a boy of that sort that you loved, and I go along with what you say. But tell me this: is there anything in common with moderation in extreme pleasure?"

"How could there be?" he said. "It drives someone out of his mind no less than pain does."

"How about with any other virtue?"

403A   "Not at all."

"With what then? Insolence and intemperance?"

"Most of all."

"And can you name a greater and more acute pleasure than the one connected with sex?"

"I can't," he said. "And none that makes one more insane."

"But the right sort of passion of love is to love what's orderly and beautiful in a moderate and musical way?"

"Very much indeed," he said.

"Then nothing insane or akin to intemperance is to be brought into the right sort of love?"

"It's not to be brought into it."

B   "Then that sort of pleasure is not to be brought into it, and the lover and the boys he loves are not to take part in it if they love and are loved in the right way?"

"Certainly not, by Zeus," he said; "it's not to be brought into it, Socrates."

"So it seems likely that, in the city that's being founded, you'll make it a law for a lover to kiss, be with, and touch a boy as he would a son, for enjoyment of what's beautiful, if he persuades him, but to associate in other respects with the boy he's serious about in such a

C   way that they will never seem to be involved together farther than that. Otherwise he'll incur blame for lacking the good taste inspired by music and by an experience of beauty."

"That's how it will be," he said.

"Does it appear to you too," I said, "that our discussion about music stands at an end? It has ended up where it ought to end, anyway; presumably what has to do with music ought to end in what has to do with love of the beautiful."

"I fully agree," he said.

"So after music, the young people are to be brought up on gymnastic exercise."

"Certainly."

"It's necessary in this too for them to be brought up in a definite   D
way from childhood throughout life. The way it is, as I imagine it, is the following, but you consider it too. Now it doesn't appear to me that what's sound in a body by its virtue makes a soul good, but on the contrary, a good soul by *its* virtue allows a body to be the best it can be. How does it appear to you?"

"That way to me as well," he said.

"Then if after giving sufficient care to the power of thinking, we left it to it to figure out precisely the things involving the body, while we guided it as far as the general outlines, in order not to be long-   E
winded, would we be doing rightly?"

"Entirely so."

"Well, we were saying that drunkenness needed to be abstained from by them, since it's surely more permissible for anyone except a guardian to be drunk, not knowing where on earth he is."

"It would be ridiculous," he said, "for a guardian to need a guardian."

"And what about food? These men are athletes in the most important competition, aren't they?"

"Yes."

"Then would the conditioning of those in training among us be   404A
appropriate for these?"

"Maybe."

"But that's a routine that dozes off," I said; "and it's a shaky basis for health. Or don't you see that those athletes drowse their lives away, and if they deviate a little from a prescribed routine, they get sick in big and intense ways?"

"I do see."

"So for athletes fit for war," I said, "there's need for a more advanced kind of training, since they have to be like sleepless dogs and as sharp as possible at seeing and hearing, and, on their campaigns,   B
adjust to many changes of water and other food, and of the sun's heat and storms, without being fastidious about their health."

"It looks that way to me."

"So wouldn't the best gymnastic training be closely kin to the sort of music we were going over a little earlier?"

"How do you mean?"

"A simple and decent sort of gymnastic training, and one especially adapted to the things involved in war."

"In what way, exactly?"

C
"Even from Homer," I said, "one could learn that sort of thing. You know that, in the feasts of the heroes on the campaign, he doesn't feast them with fish, even though they're by the sea at the Hellespont, or with boiled meats either, but only roasted ones, which would be the most readily available to soldiers, since everywhere, one might say, to use the fire itself is easier than to carry around pots."

"Very much so."

"And I don't believe Homer ever made any mention of sauces. Don't even the others in training know this, that it's necessary for a body that's going to be in good shape to abstain from everything like that?"

"And rightly," he said, "both in the knowing and in the abstaining."

D
"Then, my friend, it looks like you aren't recommending a table set in Syracusan style with a Sicilian variety in delicacies if those things seem right to you."

"I don't seem to be."

"Then you also object to a Corinthian girl as a lover for men who're going to keep their bodies in good condition."

"Absolutely so."

"And to what are supposed to be the delights of Athenian pastries?"

"Necessarily."

"Because I imagine if we likened that style of eating and living as a whole to the all-modal style of song- making and to lyric poetry
E
written in all rhythms, we'd be making a correct likeness."

"How could it be otherwise?"

"And doesn't variety engender intemperance there, and disease here, while simplicity in music makes for moderation in souls, and simplicity in gymnastic training makes for health in bodies?"

"Most true," he said.

405A
"And when intemperance and diseases become prevalent in a city, don't a lot of law courts and medical clinics open their doors, and don't the arts of lawyering and doctoring puff themselves up when lots of free men take them with great seriousness?"

"How could that not happen?"

"And will you get any greater indication of a bad and shameful education in a city than its needing top-notch doctors and judges not only for the common people and manual laborers but also for those who pass themselves off as having been brought up in a style fit for
B
someone who's free? Or doesn't it seem shameful and a great indication of being uneducated, for each person, from a lack of his own resources, to be forced to use a justice coming from other people, as though they were his masters and judges?"

"That's the most shameful thing of all," he said.

"Does that really seem to you to be more shameful than this," I said, "when someone not only wastes most of his life in law courts defending and prosecuting, but is even persuaded by his inexperience of beauty to pride himself on that very thing, because he's clever at being unjust and competent at turning all the twists, squirming through all the loopholes until he twists himself crooked to avoid submitting to a just penalty, and this for the sake of small and worthless things, since he's ignorant of how much better and more beautiful it would be to arrange his life so he'd have no need of a drowsy judge?"   C

"No," he said, "this is even more shameful than that was."

"And the need for doctoring," I said, "that's not for wounds or for any of the seasonal illnesses that overtake people, but from lack of exercise and from a style of life of the sort we were going over, because they're filled like a swamp with fluids and gases that force the ingenious followers of Asclepius[46] to make up the names 'bloats' and 'fluxes' for diseases—doesn't that seem shameful?"   D

"Very much so," he said; "and these names for diseases are truly newfangled and absurd."

"And of a sort, I imagine, that weren't around in Asclepius's time," I said. "I take as a sign of this that his sons at Troy, when the wounded Eurypylus was given Pramneian wine to drink, with a lot of barley and grated cheese sprinkled on it, which are considered to be inflammatory, they didn't find fault with the woman who gave it to him to drink or blame Patroclus who was treating him."   E

406A

"Well," he said, "it was a strange potion for someone in that condition."

"Not if you keep in mind," I said, "that this coddling of diseases by the current medical art was not in use by the followers of Asclepius formerly, as people claim, until Herodicus came along. Herodicus, who was an athletic trainer who became sickly, mixed gymnastic exercise with medical treatment, and worried to death, first and foremost, himself, then many others in later times."   B

"In what way, exactly?" he said.

"By making himself die a long death," I said. "Though he paid close attention to his disease, he wasn't able to cure himself, because it was a deadly one, I imagine, so he lived out his life giving himself treatments with no leisure for anything else, worried if he deviated in any way from his habitual routine, and by his wisdom he reached old age in a constant struggle with death."

"A lovely reward he was brought by his art," he said.

---

46   Asclepius was the legendary first doctor, from the generation before the Trojan war, and centuries later doctors used his name as a badge of respectability. His two sons are characters in the *Iliad*. In his next speech, Socrates appears to mix up some details from Book XI of that poem, but they don't affect the point he makes. Pramneian wine was thickened into a sort of broth, perhaps used as a comfort food not unlike our chicken soup.

C   "Of a fitting sort," I said, "for someone who didn't know that it wasn't from ignorance or inexperience of this form of medical treatment that Asclepius didn't reveal it to his offspring, but because he knew that for all people living under good laws, a certain job is assigned to each person in the city, which it's necessary to work at, and no one has leisure to spend his life sick and being treated. Ridiculously, we recognize that in the case of those with trades, but we don't recognize it when it comes to rich people who are supposedly happy."

"How so?" he said.

D   "When a carpenter is sick," I said, "he expects to swallow medicine from the doctor in order to heave up the disease or be purged of it below, or to suffer burning or cutting to get rid of it, but if anyone prescribes a long course of treatment for him, putting cloths on his head and the things that go with them,[47] he says without hesitation that he has no leisure to be sick and that it's not profitable to live that way, keeping one's attention on a disease while neglecting his

E   appointed work. After that, he says goodbye to that sort of doctor, steps back into his accustomed routine, gets healthy, and lives doing the things that belong to him; but if his body isn't adequate to bear up, he's set free from troubles by dying."

"For that sort of person, anyway," he said, "it does seem appropriate to use the medical art that way."

407A   "Is that because he had some work to do," I said, "and if he couldn't do it living was not profitable?"

"Clearly," he said.

"But what we're claiming is that the rich person has no such work appointed to him, which, if he were forced to refrain from it, would make his life not worth living."

"There's not said to be any, at least."

"Don't you listen to Phocylides,"[48] I said, "the way he claims that when someone already has a living, he needs to work at virtue?"

"Before that too, I imagine," he said.

"Let's not fall out with him over that," I said, "but teach ourselves whether this is something the rich person needs to exert himself over

B   and whether life is not worth living for someone when he doesn't make that effort, or whether nursing a disease is an impediment to paying attention to carpentry and the other arts but doesn't impede Phocylides' exhortation."

"Yes it does, by Zeus," he said. "This excessive care for the body that goes beyond gymnastic exercise is just about the most obstructive thing of all. It's a pain for running a household and on military

47   This is perhaps a reference to a practice like one still in use in the mid-20th century, of treating headaches by lying in a darkened room with a damp washcloth on the forehead, with camphor or some other aromatic medicine on the cloth.

48   A writer of moral aphorisms in verse.

service, and for ruling functions in a city that people carry out sitting down."

"But the most important thing is that it also makes it difficult for any sort of learning, reflecting, or studying within oneself, by constantly suspecting some kind of strain or dizziness in the head and claiming that it comes from philosophy, so that, wherever virtue is being practiced and put to that sort of test, nursing diseases is obstructive in every way. It makes someone constantly imagine he's sick and never leave off being in agony about his body."

C

"Very likely," he said.

"So won't we claim it was because Asclepius knew these things that it was for people whose bodies are in a healthy condition by nature and their way of living, but who have some isolated disease in them, that he introduced, for those in this condition, an art of medicine so he could drive out diseases by means of drugs and surgery and prescribe their accustomed routines, so as not to interfere with the life of the city? Won't we claim that for bodies diseased internally throughout, he made no attempt to bleed off a little of this and pour in a little of that according to regimens, to produce a long bad life for a human being, in order for him to beget, in all likelihood, other offspring with such lives, but that he didn't believe he ought to treat someone who lacks the power to live in his established course of life, since it wouldn't be profitable to that person or to his city?"

D

E

"That's a civic-minded Asclepius you're describing," he said.

"Clearly," I said. "And don't you see that, because he was that way, his sons too showed themselves to be good men at the war in Troy and used a medical art like the one I'm describing? Or don't you recall that they treated the wound Pandarus inflicted on Menelaus

408A

By squeezing out the blood and rubbing on soothing salves.[49]

And they didn't prescribe what he ought to drink or eat after that any more than they did for Eurypylus, taking the medicines to be sufficient to heal men who were healthy before their wounds and orderly in their way of living, even if they happened to drink a miscellaneous concoction there on the spot. But for people sickly by nature and intemperate, they believed that living was not profitable for themselves or anyone else, and that it wasn't to these that their art should be applied and they weren't obliged to treat them, even if they were richer than Midas."

B

"Those are very fastidious sons of Asclepius you're describing," he said.

"Fittingly so," I said, "and yet the tragic poets and Pindar, unpersuaded by us, claim that even though Asclepius was the son of Apollo, he was induced by gold to cure a rich man who was already at the

C

---

49   *Iliad* IV, 218, slightly altered by Socrates.

point of death, and that he was struck by a thunderbolt for that reason. But according to what we said before, we aren't persuaded by them of both things, but if he was a god's son, we'll claim, he wasn't out for sordid gain, and if he was out for sordid gain he wasn't a god's son."

"And most rightly on that point," he said. "But what do you say about this, Socrates? Isn't there a need to get good doctors in the city? And these would presumably be especially all those of the sort who've had hands-on experience with the greatest numbers of people both

D   healthy and sick, and the same way that with judges too, the best would be those who've gotten familiar with all sorts of natures."

"I'm talking about good ones," I said, "very much so. But do you know the ones I consider to be of that sort?"

"If you tell me," he said.

"Well, I'll try," I said, "but you asked in the same question about things that aren't alike."

"How so?" he said.

"Doctors," I said, "would get to be the most clever if, starting from childhood, in addition to learning the art, they familiarized themselves

E   with as many bodies as possible that were as sick as possible, and if they themselves got sick with every disease and weren't entirely healthy by nature. That's because it's not with a body, I assume, that they treat a body, since then it wouldn't be possible for those to be or become bad, but they treat a body with a soul, and it's not possible for *it* to treat anything well once it has come to be and is bad."

"That's right," he said.

409A   "But a judge, my friend, rules over a soul with a soul, and it's not acceptable for it to have been brought up from youth among corrupt souls and become familiar with them, and for it to have gone through all sorts of unjust deeds by having committed them, so as to judge the signs of unjust deeds in others acutely from itself, as with diseases in a body. Instead, it needs to have come through without experience of, and unmixed with, bad states of character while it's young, if it's going to judge what's just in a healthy way as a soul with the beauty of goodness.[50] That's why decent people, when young, appear to be

B   simpletons, easily deceived by unjust people, since they have no patterns in themselves of a like nature with corrupt people."

"Exactly," he said; "that's just the experience they have."

"And for just that reason," I said, "a good judge needs to be not young but old, a latecomer to learning about what injustice is like, not from having observed it as a presence at home in his own soul, but from having studied it over a long time as something alien in the

---

50   The last phrase, literally "beautiful and good," was translated at 402A as "gentlemanly." It was a standard phrase used by the Athenian nobility to describe itself. At 396C Socrates begins to speak of being that way "in one's very being" in contrast to the external advantages of one's birth.

souls of other people to discern how it's naturally bad, having made use of knowledge, not his own experience."

"At any rate," he said, "that sort of judge would be the most true-born."   C

"And a good one," I said, "which is what you were asking about. For someone with a good soul is good. But that clever and suspicious person who, having committed many injustices himself, assumes that he's amoral and wise, when he's in the company of those like himself, looks formidable because he's on high alert against them, going by the looks of the patterns in himself. But when he's around good people who are older, he now looks clueless, being distrustful at the wrong   D times and unaware of what a healthy state of character is, since he has no pattern of that sort. But since he meets up with corrupt people more often than with honest ones, he seems to himself and to others to be more wise than stupid."

"That's absolutely true," he said.

"Then it's not that sort of person one needs to look for," I said, "to be a good and wise judge, but the previous one. For vice could never know both virtue and itself, but virtue in an educated nature will in time acquire a knowledge of itself and vice at once. This person comes   E to be wise, as it seems to me, but the bad one doesn't."

"It seems that way to me in common with you," he said.

"Then will you establish by law in the city a medical art of the sort we were talking about, together with this sort of judicial art? They'll care for the bodies and souls of your citizens, those with good natures   410A that is, but for those who lack them, they'll allow all those so lacking in body to die off, and they themselves will put to death those who are of an evil nature in soul and not curable."

"That has at any rate shown itself to be the best way," he said, "for the people themselves that it happens to as well as for the city."

"Then it's clear," I said, "that your young citizens will be guarded against coming into need of the judge's art, being used to that simple sort of music that we claimed gives rise to moderation."

"Certainly," he said.

"And won't someone who's instilled with music get hold of a   B gymnastic art, if he wants one, by following those same tracks, so that he won't need the medical art except as a matter of necessity?"

"It seems that way to me."

"And he'll work hard at the exercises and exertions themselves with an eye toward the spirited side of his nature and to awaken that, rather than looking toward strength, unlike the other sorts of athletes, who arrange their diets and workouts as a means toward bodily power."

"Most rightly," he said.

"So then, Glaucon," I said, "is it also the case that those who instituted educating people by music and gymnastic exercise didn't   C institute them for the purpose that some imagine, to care for the body with one and for the soul with the other?"

"For what instead?" he said.

"They're liable," I said, "to have instituted both for the sake of the soul above all."

"How so?"

"Don't you notice," I said, "how their thinking itself is channeled in those who devote themselves to gymnastic exercise throughout life and have no contact with music? Or in turn in those who are directed the opposite way?"

"What are you referring to?" he said.

D   "To brutality and hardness, and in the other case to softness and tameness," I said.

"I do notice," he said, "that people who avail themselves of unmixed gymnastic exercise come away more brutal than they ought to be, while people who do so with music become softer than what would be the more beautiful thing for them."

"And surely," I said, "what's brutal would be derived from the spirited side of one's nature, and if rightly nurtured it would be courageous, but when it's stretched tighter than it ought to be, it would, likely, become hard and harsh."

"It seems that way to me," he said.

E   "What then? Wouldn't the philosophic nature have what's tame, and if it's relaxed more than it ought to be it would be too soft, but when beautifully nurtured it would be tame and orderly?"

"That's how it is."

"But we claim the guardians need to have this pair of natures both together."

"They do need to."

"Then don't the natures need to be harmonized with one another?"

"Of course."

411A   "And the soul of the person who has them harmonized is moderate and courageous?"

"Entirely."

"But the soul of the unharmonized person is cowardly and brutish?"

"Very much so."

"So when anyone allows music to go completely unchecked and to pour into his soul through his ears, as if through a funnel, the sweet, soft, dirge-like modes we were just talking about, and is continually humming his whole life, enchanted by song, doesn't he first, if he

B   had anything spirited in him, soften it up like iron and make it usable instead of useless and hard? But when he doesn't let up from pouring it on, but is enthralled, the next thing after this is that he's melting and dissolving his spiritedness until he melts it away and it's as if he cuts the guts out of his soul and makes himself a 'soft spearman.'"[51]

"Very much so," he said.

"And if, to start with," I said, "he got a soul lacking in spiritedness by nature, he accomplishes this quickly, but if it's spirited, once he's made his spirit weak, it ends up being volatile, quickly flaring up at small things and quickly snuffed out. Then they've become sharp-tempered and irritable instead of spirited, full of crankiness."

"Totally so."

"Then what about someone who works out a lot at gymnastic exercise and eats very well, but has no contact with music and philosophy? At first, with his body in good condition, doesn't he fill up with proud conceit and spiritedness, and get so that he's more courageous than he is himself?"

"Very much so."

"But what about when he does nothing else and participates in nothing at all in common with any of the Muses? Even if there was any love of learning in his soul, because of not getting a taste of any learning or of the quest for it, or taking part in discourse or anything else belonging to music, doesn't his soul become weak, deaf, and blind, since it's not awakened or nourished and its powers of perception aren't clarified?"

"That's the way of it," he said.

"It's exactly this sort of person, I imagine, who becomes a hater of discourse and devoid of music, and has no use any more for persuasion by speech, but gets his point across about everything by violence and brutality, like a wild animal, and lives in ham-fisted stupidity without grace or rhythm."

"That's absolutely how it is," he said.

"So since, as it seems, there is this pair of things in the soul, I would claim that some god gave human beings two arts, musical and gymnastic, for the spirited and philosophic parts, not for a soul and a body except as a side-effect, but for that pair, so that they might be harmonized with each other by being tightened and loosened to the appropriate degree."

"That does seem likely," he said.

"Therefore, someone who applies to his soul gymnastic exercise that's most beautifully mixed and balanced with music is the one we could most correctly claim is musical and in harmony to complete perfection, much more so than someone who tunes the strings of an instrument to one another."

"Very likely so, Socrates," he said.

"Then won't there also be a need in our city, Glaucon, for someone of this sort always to preside, if the polity is going to be kept secure?"

C

D

E

412A

B

---

51   *Iliad* XVII, 588.

"There will certainly be a need, the greatest one there could be."

"So these would be the general outlines of their education and upbringing. As for their dances, why should anyone go through such things, or their hunting with and without dogs, or their competitions in gymnastic events or on horses? Because it's pretty obvious that they need to be in keeping with those outlines, and it's no longer difficult to figure them out."

"Not *as* difficult," he said.

C "Okay," I said, "what would be the next thing after that for us to distinguish? Wouldn't it be which of these same people will rule and which will be ruled?"

"Sure."

"And it's clear that the older ones should be the rulers and the younger should be ruled?"

"That's clear."

"And that it should be the best among them?"

"That too."

"And aren't the best farmers the ones most adept at farming?"

"Yes."

"But since in this case they need to be the best among the guardians, don't they need to be the most adept at safeguarding the city?"

"Yes."

"So don't they need, to start with, to be intelligent at that as well as capable, and also protective of the city?"

D "That's so."

"But someone would be most protective of that which he happened to love."

"Necessarily."

"And surely someone would love that thing most which he regarded as having the same things advantageous to it as to himself, and believed that when it fared well it followed that he himself fared well, and the other way around when it didn't."

"That's the way it is," he said.

"Therefore the men who need to be selected from among the rest of the guardians are those who appear to us, when we examine the whole course of their lives, as if they most of all would do wholeheartedly whatever they'd regard as advantageous to the city, and who wouldn't be willing in any way to do what was not."

E

"They'd be suited to it," he said.

"It seems to me, then, that they need to be observed in all stages of life to see if they're adept guardians of this way of thinking, and don't drop it when they're bewitched or subjected to force, forgetting their opinion that they ought to do what's best for the city."

"What do you mean by dropping?" he said.

"I'll tell you," I said. "It appears to me that an opinion goes away

413A from one's thinking either willingly or unwillingly. A false one goes away willingly from someone who learns differently, but every true one unwillingly."

"The case of the willing dropping I understand," he said, "but I need to learn about the unwilling case."

"What?" I said. "Don't you too believe human beings are deprived of good things unwillingly but of bad ones willingly? Isn't it a bad thing to think falsely about the truth and a good thing to think truly? Or doesn't believing things that *are* seem to you to be thinking truly?"

"You're certainly speaking rightly," he said, "and it does seem to me that people are unwilling to be deprived of the truth."

"And don't they suffer this by being robbed, bewitched, or over-   B
powered?"

"Now I'm not understanding again," he said.

"I guess I'm speaking like a tragedy,"[52] I said. "By those who are robbed, I mean people who are persuaded to change their minds and people who forget, because from the latter, time, and from the former, speech takes opinions away without their noticing it. Now presumably you understand?"

"Yes."

"And by those who are overpowered I mean people that some grief or pain causes to change their opinions."

"I understand that too," he said, "and you're speaking rightly."

"And I imagine that you too would claim that people are bewitched   C
who change their opinions when they're either entranced by pleasure or in dread of something frightening."

"Yes," he said, "it's likely that everything that fools people is bewitching."

"Then as I was just saying, one needs to find out which of them are the best guardians of the way of thinking they have at their sides, that the thing they always need to do is to do what seems to them to be best for the city. So they need to be observed right from childhood by people who set tasks for them in which someone would be most likely to forget such a thing or be fooled out of it; anyone who remembers it and is hard to fool is to be chosen and anyone who doesn't is to be   D
rejected. Isn't that so?"

"Yes."

"And laborious jobs, painful sufferings, and competitions also need to be set up for them in which these same things are to be observed."

"That's right," he said.

"Thus a contest needs to be made," I said, "for the third form as well, that of bewitchment, and it needs to be watched. The same way

---

52   In fact the metaphors Socrates uses are taken from Gorgias's *Encomium of Helen*, a rhetorical display that exalts the manipulative power of rhetoric in lavish terms.

E

people check out whether colts are frightened when they lead them into noisy commotions, the guardians, when young, need to be taken into some terrifying situations and then quickly shifted into pleasant ones, so as to test them much more than gold is tested in a fire. If someone shows himself hard to bewitch and composed in everything, a good guardian of himself and of the musical style that he learned, keeping himself to a rhythm and harmony well-suited to all these situations, then he's just the sort of person who'd be most valuable both to himself and to a city. And that one among the children and the youths

414A   and the men who is tested and always comes through unscathed is to be appointed as ruler of the city as well as guardian, and honors are to be given to him while he's living and upon his death, when he's allotted the most prized of tombs and other memorials. Anyone not of that sort is to be rejected. It seems to me, Glaucon," I said, "that the selection and appointment of rulers and guardians is something like that, described in outline, not with precision."

"It looks to me too like it would be done some such way," he said.

B

"Isn't it most correct, then, to call these the guardians in the true sense, complete guardians for outside enemies and also for friends inside, so that the latter won't want to do any harm and the former won't have the power to? The young ones that we've been calling guardians up to now, isn't it most correct to call auxiliaries and reinforcements for the decrees of the rulers?"

"It seems that way to me," he said.

"Then could we come up with some contrivance," I said, "from among the lies that come along in case of need, the ones we were

C

talking about just now,[53] some one noble lie told to persuade at best even the rulers themselves, but if not, the rest of the city?"

"What sort of thing?" he said.

"Nothing new," I said, "but something Phoenician[54] that has come into currency in many places before now, since the poets assert it and have made people believe; but it hasn't come into currency in our time and I don't know if it could—it would take a lot of persuading."

"You seem a lot like someone who's reluctant to speak," he said.

---

53   See 382C-D. Some of the things said there about a lie that would be acceptable are that it is about ancient things no one knows the truth of, is fashioned like truth, and is useful as a preventive medicine for unreliable friends.

54   Cadmus, the legendary founder of the Greek city Thebes, came from Phoenicia (the region roughly the same as modern Lebanon). To found the city he had to kill a dragon. A god told him to plant the dragon's teeth, and the first inhabitants of the city sprang up from those seeds. When Socrates says the story was current in many places, he means there were other local legends of races sprung from the ground they now live on, all originally brothers and sisters whose first mother is the land that feeds them and that they defend and love. Some readers have also suspected an allusion to stories Odysseus tells in the *Odyssey*, that either embellish or lie about his past but always contain some deeper truth.

"And I'll seem to you very appropriately reluctant," I said, "when I do speak."

"Speak," he said. "Don't be shy."

"I'll speak, then. And yet I don't know how I'll get up the nerve   D
or find the words to tell it. First I'll try my hand at persuading the rulers themselves and the soldiers, and then also the rest of the city, that, after all, the things we nurtured and educated them on were like dreams; they seemed to be experiencing all those things that seemed to be happening around them, but in truth they themselves were at the time under the soil inside the earth being molded and cultivated, and their weapons and other gear were being crafted, and when they   E were completely formed, the earth, that was their mother, made them spring up. So now, as if the land they dwell in were a mother and nurse, it's up to them to deliberate over it, to defend it if anyone were to attack, and to take thought on behalf of the rest of the citizens as their earthborn siblings."

"It's not without reason," he said, "that you were ashamed for so long to tell the lie."

"It was entirely reasonable," I said. "But all the same, listen to   415A the rest of the story as well. What we'll say in telling them the story is: 'All of you in the city are brothers, but the god, when he molded those of you who are competent to be rulers, mixed gold into them at their formation—that's why they're the most honorable—but all the auxiliaries have silver in them, and there's iron and bronze in the farmers and other skilled workers. So since you're all kin, for the most part you'll produce children like yourselves, but it's possible   B for a silver offspring sometimes to be born from a gold parent, and a gold from a silver, and all the others likewise from one another. So the god exhorts the rulers first and foremost to be good guardians of their children, of nothing more diligently than that, and to keep watch for nothing so diligently as for what they have intermixed in their souls. And if a child of theirs is born with bronze or iron mixed   C in it, they'll by no means give way to pity, but paying it the honor appropriate to its nature, they'll drive it out among the craftsmen or farmers, and if in turn any children are born from those parents with gold or silver mixed in them, they'll honor them and take them up, some to the guardian group, the others to the auxiliary, because there's an oracle foretelling that the city will be destroyed when an iron or bronze guardian has guardianship over it.' So do you have any contrivance to get them to believe this story?"

"There's no way," he said, "at least for these people themselves. There might be one, though, for their sons and the next generation   D and the rest of humanity after that."

"But even that," I said, "would get things going well toward their being more protective of the city and of one another, because I understand pretty well what you mean. And that's that it will carry on the way an oral tradition leads it. But once we've armed these offspring of the earth, let's bring them forth with their rulers in the lead. And when they've come, let them look for the most beautifully situated spot in the city to set up a military camp, from which they could most effectively restrain the people in the city if any of them were unwilling to obey the laws, and defend against those outside it if any enemy, like a wolf, were to attack the flock. And when they've set up the camp and offered sacrifices to those whom they ought, let them make places to sleep. Or how should it be?"

"That way," he said.

"The sort of places that would be adequate to give shelter in both winter and summer?"

"Of course," he said, "because you seem to be talking about dwellings."

"Yes," I said, "dwellings for soldiers anyway, but not for moneymakers."

"How do you mean the one differs from the other?" he said.

"I'll try to tell you," I said. "Because it's surely the most dreadful and shameful of all things for a shepherd to raise dogs as auxiliaries for the flock that are of the sort and brought up in such a way that, from intemperance or hunger or some bad habit of another kind, the dogs themselves try to do harm to the sheep, acting like wolves instead of dogs."

"It is dreadful," he said; "how could it be anything else?"

"Then isn't there a need to be on guard in every way so that our auxiliaries won't do that sort of thing to the citizens, since they're the stronger, becoming like savage masters instead of benevolent allies?"

"There's a need to be on guard," he said.

"And wouldn't they have been provided with the most effective safeguard if they've been beautifully educated in their very being?"

"But surely they have been," he said.

And I said, "That's not something that deserves to be asserted with certainty, Glaucon my friend. What we were saying just now does deserve to be, though, that they need to get the right education, whatever it is, if they're going to what's most important for being tame, both toward themselves and toward those who are guarded by them."

"That's certainly right," he said.

"Now in addition to this education, any sensible person would claim that they need to be provided with dwellings and other property of that sort, whatever it takes for them not to be stopped from being the best possible guardians and not to be tempted to do harm to the citizens."

"And he'll be claiming something true."

"Then see whether they need to live and be housed in some such way as this," I said, "if they're going to be that sort of people. First, no private property that's not completely necessary is to be possessed by any of them. Next, there's to be no house or treasure room belonging to any of them except one that everyone who wants to will enter. Provisions, of all things men need who are moderate and courageous fighters in war, they're to receive at fixed times from the other citizens as recompense[55] for guarding them, of such an amount that they have nothing over and nothing lacking each year. Going regularly to public dining halls, they're to live in common like soldiers in a camp. About gold and silver, it's to be said to them that they have the divine sort from gods always in their souls, and have no further need of the human sort, and that it's not pious to defile their possession of the former by mixing with it the possession of mortal gold, because many impious deeds have occurred over the currency most people use, while the sort they have with them is uncorrupted. And for them alone of those in the city, it's not lawful to handle or touch gold and silver, or even to go under the same roof with them, or wear them as ornaments, or drink out of silver or gold cups.

"And in this way they'd keep themselves and the city safe. But whenever they possess private land and houses and currency, they'll be heads of households and farm owners instead of guardians, and they'll become hostile masters instead of allies of the other citizens, and spend their whole lives hating and being hated, and plotting and being plotted against, fearing those inside the city instead of and much more than the enemies outside it, as they and the rest of the city race onward, already very close to destruction.

"For all these reasons, then," I said, "we'll declare that's the way the guardians need to be provided for in the matter of housing and the rest, and we'll set these things down as laws, won't we?"

"Very much so," said Glaucon.

E

417A

B

---

55 This is the same word translated "wages" earlier, but the details make clear that it is set up here not as a fee for service but as a public provision of the means of living, as Socrates points out in 420A. The soldiers and rulers are not given monetary incentives to perform their jobs but spared the need to think about money.

BOOK IV

Note

Differences between the two brothers become evident in this book. Glaucon had objected to the simple life of the first city described because it seemed an affront to human dignity, but Adeimantus now objects to the severe life led by the guardians of the second city because it goes against conventional opinions about happiness. And while Glaucon had been won over by a positive vision of a disciplined life, Adeimantus is aroused instead against a picture of the self-indulgent lives of people ordinarily considered happy (425E-426B). Once both brothers have wholeheartedly endorsed it, the imaginary city has been "founded." The task of finding the justice in it, in order to see its reflection in the human soul, eventually requires exploring the way in which the soul too is a whole composed of parts. The partitioning must be threefold, to match the city, but the common understanding of moderation as a relation to oneself already indicates that the soul cannot be simply uniform (430E-431B). As with the city, the middle part turns out to be the least obvious, the most interesting, and the only means to bring unity back into the whole. Once the focus has been shifted to the interior life of each human being, the desirability of harmony rather than conflict becomes obvious, and the arguments in favor of injustice appear laughable.

419A   And **Adeimantus**, interrupting, said, "How would you defend yourself against the charge, Socrates, if someone were to claim you aren't making these men very happy at all, and that it's their own doing, since in truth the city belongs to them but they don't enjoy anything good from the city, as others do who own land, build beautiful big houses, get furnishings for them on an appropriate scale, offer the gods private sacrifices, entertain foreign visitors, and especially do what you were just talking about, acquiring gold and silver and everything that's regarded as belonging to people who're going to be blessedly happy? Frankly, he might claim, they look just

420A   like auxiliary forces paid to camp in the city and do nothing other than stand guard."

"Yes," I said, "and at that they're provided with food and don't even get any wages in addition to their rations the way those others do. So it isn't even possible for them to take an outing in private if they want to, or give anything to a lady friend, or spend money in any other direction they might want to, on the sorts of things people who seem to be happy spend their money on. You're leaving these things and scads of others like them out of your indictment."

"Well," he said, "let these things too be included in the charge."

"So you're asking how we'll make our defense?"   B
"Yes."

"We'll find what needs to be said, I imagine," I said, "by going along the same road. For we'll say that there'd be nothing surprising if these people living this way are also the happiest ones,[56] even though that wasn't what we were looking toward when we founded the city, that some one class of people would be exceptionally happy, but that the whole city should be happy to the greatest possible extent. Because we imagined we'd find justice most of all in such a city, and injustice in turn in the worst-managed one, and by looking closely   C
at them we'd judge what we've been seeking all along. So now, as we're imagining it, we're molding a city that's happy as a whole, not taking aside some few people in it to make them that way; and we'll consider the opposite sort of city shortly.

"Now it's just as if, when we were painting a statue, someone who came up complained, saying that we weren't putting the most beautiful paints on the most beautiful parts of the figure, since the eyes, which are the most beautiful part, weren't painted purple   D
but black; we'd think we were making a decent defense if we said 'Strange fellow, don't expect us to have to paint such beautiful eyes that they don't even look like eyes, or the other parts either, but see whether we're making the whole beautiful by giving each of the parts what's appropriate to it.' So now too, don't force us to fasten onto the guardians a type of happiness that will make them anything other than guardians. We also know how to dress farmers in magnificent   E
robes, adorn them with gold, and tell them to work the land at their pleasure, and have the potters lie back in front of the fire, feasting and matching drinks with one another around a circle, having the wheel brought to them for as long as they feel like making pots, and make everyone else blessedly happy in this manner, so the whole city is happy. But don't give us that kind of advice, because, if we're   421A
persuaded by you, the farmer won't be a farmer or the potter a potter, and no one else will hold onto any of the characteristic features out of which a city comes about.

"But for the others the argument is less important, because when people become bad shoemakers and corrupt, and pretend to be something they're not, it's no terrible thing for a city, but when people aren't guardians of the laws and the city but seem to be, you surely see that they utterly destroy a whole city, and also, on the other hand, that they alone are in a position to manage it well and make it happy. So if we're making them guardians in the true sense, who do the least   B
harm of all to the city, while the one who made the charge would make them some sort of gentleman farmers, and, as if they were at a big party and not in a city, happy banqueters, he'd be talking about something other than a city.

---

56   This first clause of Socrates' reply is easily, and too frequently, overlooked.

"What needs to be considered, then, is whether we're instituting the guardians with a view to that, in order for the greatest possible happiness to be brought about in them, or else, with a view toward this for the whole city, it needs to be seen whether it's being brought about there. In the latter case, these auxiliaries and guardians would

C   need to be compelled and persuaded to see to that, so that they'll be the best craftsmen at their own work and all the others will be the same, and once the city is growing all together in that way and is beautifully established, one needs to leave it up to nature to allow each class of people to partake of happiness."

"You seem to me to be speaking beautifully," he said.

"Then will I also seem to you to be speaking in a level-headed way," I said, "in saying something closely akin to this?"

"What in particular?"

"Consider whether these things corrupt the other craftsmen as well, so that they too go bad."

D   "What sort of things are these?"

"Riches," I said, "and poverty."

"How so?"

"Like this. Does it seem to you that a pottery maker who's gotten rich will still be willing to attend to his art?"

"Not at all," he said

"And will he himself become more lazy and careless that he was?"

"Very much."

"So he becomes a worse pottery maker?"

"That too," he said, "much worse."

"And then too, if from poverty he can't even provide himself with tools or any of the other things that go into his art, he'll produce

E   substandard work and he'll train his sons, or any others he trains, to be inferior craftsmen."

"How could he not?"

"From both poverty and riches, then, the works of the art are worse, and the people themselves are worse."

"So it appears."

"So it looks like we've discovered other things that the guardians need to be on guard against in every way, so that they never sneak into the city unnoticed by them."

"What sort of things are these?"

422A   "Riches," I said, "and poverty, since the one brings in luxury, laziness, and upheaval, and the other brings in stinginess and bad workmanship, in addition to upheaval."

"Certainly," he said. "But consider this, Socrates: how will our city be able to wage war when it hasn't acquired any money, especially if it's forced to make war against a big and rich city?"

"It's obvious," I said, "that it would be a harder thing against one, but against two of that sort it would be easier."   B

"How can you say that?" he said.

"First of all," I said, "presumably when it's necessary to do battle, won't they be trained warriors in battle against rich men?"

"Yes, that's right," he said.

"Well then, Adeimantus, doesn't it seem to you that that one boxer prepared for that as beautifully as possible could easily fight with two who were not boxers, and were also rich and fat?"

"Maybe not," he said, "not at the same time, anyway."

"Not even if he had the ability," I said, "to dodge away and continually turn and punch the first one to approach, and if he were to do this often in the sun and stifling heat? Couldn't someone like that handle even more opponents of that sort?"   C

"I take it back," he said; "there'd be nothing surprising about it."

"But don't you imagine rich people have a bigger share of knowledge and experience about boxing than about warfare?"

"I do," he said.

"Therefore in all likelihood our warriors will easily do battle with twice or three times their number."

"I'll go along with you on that," he said, "since you seem to me to be speaking correctly."   D

"And what if they sent a delegation to the other city and told them the truth? They'd say 'we have no use for gold or silver, nor is it even lawful for us, but it is for you; so go to war alongside us and you keep what belongs to the other side.' Do you imagine anyone who heard that would choose to go to war against solid, lean dogs rather than alongside dogs against fat, tender sheep?"

"I think not," he said; "but if the money belonging to the others is gathered together into one city, look out that it doesn't present a danger for the one that isn't rich."

"You're a lucky one," I said, "in that you imagine any other city   E
than one of the sort we're fitting out is worth being called a city."

"But what, then?" he said.

"The others should be addressed in a bigger way," I said, "since each of them is a whole bunch of cities, not a city, as they say in the game.[57] Whatever they are, each of them is two things at war with each other, one made up of the poor, the other of the rich, and in each   423A
of these there are a great many parts; if you treat them as one thing, you'd miss the whole point, but if you treat them as many, and offer to some the property and power of the others, or even those others themselves, you'll always have a lot of allies and few enemies. And as

---

57   This is thought to refer to something like checkers in which a player had to gather a certain number of pieces, a "city," to win.

long as your city is managed moderately in the way it was just organized, it will be the greatest one; I don't mean by being well thought
of, but greatest in fact, even if has only a thousand men who go to war

B   on its behalf. You won't easily find a single city as great as it is among
the Greeks or the barbarians, though many, that are many times its
size, are thought to be. Do you imagine it's any different?"

"No, by Zeus," he said.

"Then wouldn't this be the most beautiful limit for our rulers to
use, for how big in size they ought to make the city, and how much
land to mark out for one that's that size, letting the rest go?"

"What limit is that?" he said.

"This one, I imagine," I said: "for it to grow as far as it can grow
and be willing to be one, that far but not beyond."

C   "That would indeed be beautifully done," he said.

"Then shall we also assign this as another ordinance for the guardians, to be on guard in every way that the city not be small or think
itself great, but something sufficient and one?"

"That's probably a light task we'll be assigning them," he said.

"And here's one even lighter than that," I said. "We made mention
of it in the earlier discussion, saying that if any child of light ability

D   was born among the guardians, he'd need to be sent away to the
others, and if one with serious promise was born among the others,
he'd need to be sent away to the guardians. And this was meant to
make it clear about the rest of the citizens as well, that they need to
bring each one to one job, the one for which he's naturally suited, so
that each of them, by pursuing the one thing that belongs to him, will
become one and not many, and in that way the city as a whole will
grow to be one and not many."

"Sure," he said; "this is a tinier task than the other one."

"Well, my good Adeimantus," I said, "these aren't, as one might

E   think, a lot of big tasks we're assigning them, but they're all light ones
if they safeguard the proverbial one big thing, or rather, instead of
big, sufficient."

"What's that?" he said.

"Their education and upbringing," I said. "Because if, by being
well educated, they become decent men, they'll easily see about all
these things, as well as all the other things we're now leaving out,

424A   the possessing of women, marriages, the procreation of children, that
all these things ought to be done as much as possible by the proverb
'what belongs to friends is shared.'"

"That would be the most correct way," he said.

"And then the polity," I said, "once it's been well set in motion,
goes on growing like a circle, because a sound upbringing and education, when they're maintained, instill good natures, and sound natures,
getting that sort of education in turn, grow up even better than those

before them, in other respects and especially in procreation, the same as among the other animals."

"Very likely," he said.   B

"So then, putting it in few words, this is what those in charge of the city need to hold on to, so that it won't get corrupted without their notice but they'll safeguard it above all: no innovating contrary to the organized plan for gymnastic training and music. But they'll safeguard them as much as they possibly can, alarmed whenever anyone says

> People pay more regard to the newest song,
> Whatever drifts around among the singers,[58]

that often someone might imagine the poet was talking not about   C
new songs but a new style of song, and might approve of that. But one ought not to approve of such a thing or understand the poet in such a way. For changing over to a strange form of music is something one needs to be cautious about as bringing danger into the whole, since nowhere are styles of music changed without changes in political customs of the greatest importance, as Damon[59] says and I'm persuaded."

"Put me down also," said Adeimantus, "among the persuaded."

"So," I said, "it seems that the place the guardians need to build   D
their fortification is here, in music."

"Certainly this sort of undermining of custom easily slips in unnoticed," he said.

"Yes," I said, "as if it fell in the category of amusement and did no harm."

"That's because it doesn't do any," he said, "other than the fact that when it settles in little by little, it flows quietly under the surface into people's characters and habits, and from them comes out stronger into their dealings with one another, and from their interactions it goes on   E
with great recklessness to their customs and polities, Socrates, until it ends up overturning everything in private and public life."

"Really!" I said. "It goes that far?"

"It seems that way to me," he said.

"Then as we were saying at the beginning, don't our children need to be involved right away in a more law-abiding sort of play, since, if the play itself becomes lawless, and the children come to be that way too, it would be impossible for law-abiding serious men to   425A
grow out of them?"

"How could it be otherwise?" he said.

"So whenever, by starting out in a beautiful way at playing, children open themselves up to lawfulness by means of music, then back in the opposite direction from those others, lawfulness follows

---

58   *Odyssey* I, 351-352, slightly altered by Socrates.

59   See 400B-C.

along with them and makes everything grow, setting back on its feet anything in the city that had been knocked down."

"True indeed," he said.

"Then they even rediscover the customary practices that seem to be small things," I said, "all of which their predecessors destroyed."

"What sort?"

B

"This sort: silence of young people in the presence of their elders when it's appropriate, letting them sit and standing up for them, and taking care of parents, as well as haircuts, clothes, shoes, and the appearance of the body generally, and all the other things of that sort. Don't you think so?"

"I do."

"To make them laws, I imagine, is silly, since presumably they don't come about and they wouldn't be maintained by being legislated in words and in writing."

"How could they be?"

"At any rate, Adeimantus," I said, "the direction in which someone

C

gets set in motion by his education is liable to be of a piece with the things that follow it as well. Doesn't like always call forth its like?"

"Certainly."

"And in the final result, I imagine, we'd claim that it turns into a single vigorous whole, either good or the reverse."

"How could it not?" he said.

"For these reasons, then," I said, "I wouldn't attempt to legislate about such things any further."

"That's reasonable," he said.

"And before the gods," I said, "what about the business of the marketplace, having to do with the contracts each sort of people

D

agree to with one another in the market, and, if you like, having to do with engaging the services of skilled workmen, and with slander and insults and seeking legal redress and appointing juries, and the collecting and paying of taxes if any are necessary either in the markets or the ports, and on the whole, any sort of regulation of the markets, town, and harbors—will we have the nerve to legislate anything about these things?"

"It's not worth it," he said, "to dictate to men who are gentlemen,

E

since presumably they'll easily discover a lot of them, all the ones that ought to be legislated about."

"Yes, my friend," I said, "so long as a god grants them the preservation of the laws we went through before."

"And if not," he said, "they'll spend their lives continually setting down a lot of such laws and straightening them out, imagining they'll catch hold of what's best."

"You're saying," I said, "that such people would be living like those who're sick, but from intemperance aren't willing to give up a worthless way of life."

"Very much so."

"And the way they go through life is sure charming; they accom- **426A**
plish nothing with their medical treatments except to make their
diseases more varied and stronger, always hoping that, if only someone would recommend some drug, they'll be healthy on account of
that."

"That's exactly the sort of thing that happens," he said, "with
people who're sick in that way."

"And what about this?" I said. "Isn't it a charming thing about
them that they consider the most hateful thing of all to be someone
who tells them the truth, that until they cease from drunkenness, stuff-
ing themselves, sexual indulgences, and lack of exercise, no drugs,   **B**
burning, or cutting will do them any good, and neither will any sort
of thing they chant or wear around their necks?"

"Not charming at all," he said. "There's nothing charming about
getting angry at someone who's speaking for their benefit."

"You're no fan of such men, it seems," I said.

"No I'm not, by Zeus."

"Then if the city as a whole does that sort of thing, the way we
were just talking about, you won't approve of it either. Or don't they
appear to you to act the same way as these people, all those cities that,
despite being badly governed, warn their citizens against changing the   **C**
city's whole set-up, on penalty of death for anyone who does that? But
whoever ministers to them most pleasingly while they're governed
that way, gratifying and cozying up to them, who anticipates their
wishes and is clever at fulfilling them, will be for that reason a good
man and wise in great matters, and will be honored by them."

"They do seem to me to act the same way," he said, "and I'm no
fan of theirs either by any means."

"And what about those, for their part, who're willing and eager   **D**
to minister to such cities? Don't you marvel at how brave and accom-
modating they are?"

"I do," he said, "except for the ones who are taken in by them
and imagine they really are statesmen because they're praised by
most people."

"You mean you don't sympathize with these men?" I said. "Do you
imagine it's possible for a man who doesn't know how to measure,
when lots of other people of his sort are telling him he's six feet tall,
not to believe what they say about it?"   **E**

"No," he said, "I don't imagine that."

"Then don't be so hard on them, since such people are probably
the most charming ones of all, making laws of the sort we just went
over and correcting them, always imagining they'll find some limit
for wrongdoing in business dealings and the things I was just talk-

ing about, ignorant that it's in fact just like they were cutting off the Hydra's heads."[60]

427A "And certainly," he said, "they're doing nothing else."

"That's why I'd imagine," I said, "that a true lawgiver ought not to trouble himself with such a form of laws or such a form of polity, either in a badly governed or a well governed city, in the one because it's pointless and does no good, and in the other because anybody at all could discover some of them and the rest follow by themselves from the practices mentioned before."

B "Then what legislation would still be left for us?" he said.

And I said, "For us, none; for Apollo at Delphi, though, the greatest, most beautiful, and first pieces of legislation."

"What sort are they?" he said.

"Dedications of temples, sacrifices, and other sorts of worship of the gods, divinities, and heroes, and also burial of the dead and all the things people need to do as service to those in that place for them to be kindly disposed. Because we don't know that sort of thing, and

C if we have any sense we won't be persuaded by anyone else when we're founding a city, and won't use any interpreter other than the ancestral one. For no doubt this god, as the interpreter of such things for all human beings, reveals them from his seat at the center and navel of the earth."

"Beautifully said," he said, "and so it must be done."

D "Then your city, son of Ariston," I said, "should now be founded. So after that, take a look around in it yourself, once you've provided a light from somewhere, and call in your brother and Polemarchus and the others, if in any way we might see wherever its justice might be, and its injustice, and what differentiates the pair from each other, and which of the two someone who's going to be happy ought to get hold of, whether he goes unnoticed or not by all gods and human beings."

"You're talking nonsense," said **Glaucon**. "You took it on yourself

E to search for it because it's irreverent for you not to come to the aid of justice in every way to the limit of your power."

"It's true," I said, "as you remind me, and so it must be done, but you folks need to do your part too."

"Well that's what we'll do," he said.

"Then I hope to find it this way," I said. "I imagine our city, if in fact it's been correctly founded, is completely good."

"Necessarily," he said.

"So it's clear that it's wise and courageous and moderate and just."

"That's clear."

---

60   A mythical sea monster that grew two new heads whenever one was cut off.

what is and what is not

428A

4 opposites

"Then whatever we find in it from among them, the leftover part will be what hasn't been found?"[61]

"Of course."

"Then just as with any other four things, if we were looking for a particular one of them in whatever it was, whenever we recognized that one first that would be good enough for us, but if we recognized the three first, by that very means we would have recognized the thing we're looking for, because it's obvious that it couldn't any longer be anything else than the thing left over."

"You're saying it correctly," he said.

"So for these things too, since they happen to be four, they need to be looked for in the same way?"

"Obviously."

"Well then, the first thing that seems to me to be clearly visible in   B
it is wisdom. And there seems to be something strange about it."

"What?" he said.

"The city that we went over seems to me to be wise in its very being.[62] Because it is well-counseled, isn't it?"

"Yes."

"And surely it's clear that this very thing, good counsel, is a certain kind of knowledge, since it's presumably not by ignorance but by knowledge that people counsel well."

"That's clear."

"But many kinds of knowledge of all varieties are surely present in the city."

"How could there not be?"

"Then is it on account of the carpenters' knowledge that the city is called wise and well-counseled?"

"Not at all," he said; "on account of that it's called skilled in car-   C
pentry."

---

61   That complete human goodness must include the four virtues named would have been a prevalent opinion. That no fifth virtue was regarded as having that same "cardinal" status is less likely. In several of Plato's dialogues, Socrates lists piety along with these four, but in the *Euthyphro* (12D) he says that it is a part of justice. What Socrates is always emphatic about is that the primary virtues are inseparable from one another; in the *Protagoras* (349C) he compares them to the parts of a face. By logic alone, the most he could claim here is that, when three virtues had been found, the fourth would somehow be in what was left, rather than simply identical to it. Socrates' assumption of the fourfold character of human excellence is playful, like his discovery of the character of the guardians in a likeness to dogs in Bk. II. Whatever comes to light as a result of such an assumption stands or falls not as a logical deduction but on its merits as a way of making sense of human life. In fact, through the influence of this dialogue, the idea of these four cardinal virtues came to epitomize the classical understanding of the best life. In Dante's *Purgatory* (Canto I, lines 37-39), they are figured as the four stars that shine in Cato's face.

62   That is, the city is not just "really" wise, wise in fact or to a high degree, but wise by its very structure, to whatever extent the people in it are capable of wisdom. What makes it the city it is makes it wise, because it was designed to let any capacity for wisdom born in it have scope to develop and to act on its behalf.

"Then it's not on account of the knowledge that counsels about how wooden equipment would be best that a city is called wise."

"No indeed."

"Well then, is it the knowledge about things made of bronze or anything else of that sort?"

"None whatever of those," he said.

"And it's not the knowledge about growing the fruits of the earth; that makes it skilled in farming."

"It seems that way to me."

"What about it, then?" I said. "Is there any knowledge in the city just now founded by us, on the part of any of its citizens, by which it counsels not about things in the city pertaining to someone in particular, but about itself as a whole, and in what way it would interact best within itself and with other cities?"

"There certainly is."

"What is it," I said, "and in which of them?"

"It's guardianship," he said, "and it's in those rulers whom we were just now naming complete guardians."

"So on account of this sort of knowledge, what do you call the city?"

"Well-counseled," he said, "and wise in its very being."

"Now do you imagine," I said, "that there will be more metalworkers present in our city than these true guardians?"

"A lot more metalworkers," he said.

"And compared also to all the rest who are given names for having any particular kinds of knowledge, wouldn't these guardians be the fewest of them all?"

"By a lot."

"Therefore it's by means of the smallest group and part of itself, the part that directs and rules, and by the knowledge in it, that a whole city founded in accord with nature would be wise. And it seems likely that this turns out by nature to be the smallest class, the one that's appropriately allotted a share of that knowledge which, alone among the other kinds of knowledge, ought to be called wisdom."

"Very true, just as you say," he said.

"So we've discovered this one of the four—how we did it I don't know—both it and where in the city it's lodged."

"It seems to me at any rate," he said, "to have been discovered well enough."

"But as for courage, it and the part of the city it lies in, and through which the city is called courageous, are surely not very hard to see."

"How so?"

"Who," I said, "would say a city was cowardly or courageous by looking to anything other than that part of it which defends it and takes the field on its behalf?"

D

E

429A

B

wisdom

"No one," he said, "would look to anything else."

"Because I don't imagine," I said, "that whether the other people in it are cowards or courageous would be what determines it to be the one sort or the other."

"No."

"Then a city is also courageous by means of a certain part of itself, by its having in it a power such that it will safeguard through everything its opinion about what's to be feared, that it's the same things or the sorts of things that the lawgiver passed on to them in their education. Or isn't that what you call courage?"

C

"I haven't quite understood what you're saying," he said; "just say it again."

"I mean," I said, "that courage is a certain kind of preservation."

"What kind of preservation exactly?"

"Of the opinion instilled by law through education about what things and what sorts of things are to be feared. By preserving it through everything I meant keeping it intact when one is in the midst of pains and pleasures and desires and terrors and not dropping it. I'm willing to make an image of what it seems to me to be like if you want me to."

D

"I want you to."

"You know, don't you," I said, "that dyers, when they want to dye wool so it will be purple, first select, from among the many colors, wool of the single nature belonging to white things, and then prepare it in advance, taking care with no little preparation that it will accept the pigment as much as possible, and only so dip it in the dye? And what is dyed in this way becomes impervious to fading, and washing it, whether without soaps or with them, has no power to remove the color from it, but what is not done that way—well, you know what it comes out like, whether one dyes it with other colors or this one without having taken care in advance."

E

"I know," he said, "that it's washed out and laughable."

"Then understand," I said, "that we too were doing something like that to the extent of our power when we were selecting the soldiers and educating them with music and gymnastic training. Don't imagine that we devised that for any reason other than so they, persuaded by us, would take the laws into themselves like a dye in the most beautiful way possible, so that their opinion about what's to be feared, and about everything else, would become impervious to fading, because they'd had the appropriate nature and upbringing, and the dye couldn't be washed out of them by those soaps that are so formidable at scouring, either pleasure, which is more powerful at doing that than every sort of lye and alkaline ash, or pain, terror, and desire, more powerful than any other soaps. This sort of power and preservation through everything of a right and lawful opinion

430A

B

about what is and isn't to be feared, I for my part call courage, and I set it down as such unless you say otherwise."

"No," he said, "I don't say anything different, because it seems to me that you're considering the right opinion about these same things that comes about without education, as animal-like or slavish, and not entirely reliable, and that you'd call it something other than courage."

C

"Entirely true," I said, "as you say."

"Then I accept this as being courage," he said.

"Yes, do accept it," I said, "but as a citizen's courage,[63] and you'll be accepting it the right way. We'll go over something still more beautiful in connection with it later if you want, because what we've been looking for now is not that but justice. For the inquiry about that, I imagine this is sufficient."

"Yes," he said, "beautifully said."

"So two things are still left," I said, "that it's necessary to catch

D

sight of in the city, moderation, and the one for the sake of which we're looking for them all, justice."

"Quite so."

"How, then, might we discover justice so that we won't have to bother any more about moderation?"

"Well," he said, "I don't know and I wouldn't want it to come to light first anyway if we're no longer going to examine moderation. So if you want to gratify[64] me, consider this before that."

"I certainly do want to," I said; "unless I'd be doing an injustice."

"Consider it, then," he said.

E

"It's got to be considered," I said, "and as seen from where we are, it looks more like a sort of consonance and harmony than the ones before."

"How?"

"Presumably," I said, "moderation is a certain well-orderedness, and a mastery over certain pleasures and desires, as people say—being stronger than oneself—though in what way they mean that I don't know. And some other things of that sort are said that are like clues to it, aren't they?"

"They most of all," he said.

---

63   Glaucon saw correctly that some who appear brave have a merely natural, and unreliable, fearlessness. What Socrates has defined, as a courage sufficient for the present discussion, might be improved upon in at least two ways that would make it a more beautiful form of the virtue: it could be based on knowledge rather than right opinion, and it could be for its own sake rather than for the good sought by the city.

64   Glaucon speaks as though his desire to taste an understanding of all the virtues is immoderate, while Socrates replies as though indulging that desire is a just obligation. But it may seem that Socrates is immoderate in desiring to short-circuit the orderly discussion he had proposed. The question of the relation of moderation and justice is being playfully dramatized.

"But then isn't being stronger than oneself absurd? Because the one who's stronger than himself would presumably also be weaker than himself, and the weaker stronger, since the same person is referred   431A to in all these terms."

"How could it not be the same one?"

"But it appears to me," I said, "that this phrase intends to say that there's something to do with the soul within a human being himself that has something better and something worse in it, and whenever what's better by nature is master over what's worse, calling this 'being stronger than oneself' at least praises it. But whenever, from a bad upbringing or some sort of bad company, the better part that's smaller is mastered by the larger multitude of the worse part, this as   B a reproach is blamed and called 'being weaker than oneself,' and the person so disposed is called intemperate."

"That's likely it," he said.

"Then look over toward our new city," I said, "and you'll find one of these things present in it. Because you'll claim that it's justly referred to as stronger than itself, if in fact something in which the better rules over the worse ought to be called moderate and stronger than itself."

"I am looking over at it," he said, "and you're telling the truth."

"And surely one would find a multitude and variety of desires as   C well as pleasures and pains, in children especially, and in women and menial servants, and also in most of the lower sorts of people among those who are called free."

"Very much so."

"But you'll meet with simple and measured desires and pleasures, which are guided by reasoning with intelligence and right opinion, in few people, who are both best in nature and best educated."

"True," he said.

"Then don't you see that these too are present in your city, and that the desires in most people and those of the lower sorts are mastered there by the desires and intelligence of the lesser number of more   D decent people?"

"I do," he said.

"So if one ought to refer to any city as stronger than pleasures and desires, and than itself, that needs to be applied to this one."

"Absolutely so," he said.

"So then isn't it moderate too in all these respects?"

"Very much so," he said.

"And also, if in any city the same opinion is present in both the rulers and the ruled about who ought to rule, it would be present in   E this one. Doesn't that seem so?"

"Emphatically so," he said.

"Then as for being moderate, in which group of citizens will you say it's present when they're in this condition, in the rulers or in the ruled?"

"In both, presumably," he said.

"So do you see," I said, "that we had an appropriate premonition just now that moderation is like a certain harmony?"

"Why's that?"

"Because it's not like courage and wisdom, each of which by its presence in a certain part showed the city to be either wise or courageous. It doesn't act that way, but is in fact stretched through the whole across the scale, showing the weakest, the strongest, and those in between to be singing the same song together, whether you want to rank them in intelligence, or, if you want, in strength, or even by their number or their money or by anything whatever of that sort. So we'd be most correct in claiming that this like-mindedness is moderation, a concord of the naturally worse and better about which ought to rule, both in the city and in each one."

"The way it seems to me is completely in accord with that," he said.

"Well then," I said, "three of them have been spotted in our city—at least it seems that way. So what would be the remaining form by which the city would further partake in virtue? For it's clear that this is justice.

"That's clear."

"So now, Glaucon, don't we need to take up positions like hunters in a circle around a patch of woods and concentrate our attention, so that justice doesn't escape anywhere, disappear from our sight, and become obscure? Because it's evident that it's in there somewhere. So look and make a spirited effort to catch sight of it, in case you spot it in any way before I do, and you'll show it to me."

"If only I were able to," he said. "Instead, if you treat me as a follower who's capable of seeing what's pointed out to him, you'll be handling me in an entirely sensible way."

"Follow then," I said, "after offering up prayers along with me."

"I'll do that," he said; "just you lead."

"The place sure does look like an inaccessible and shadowy one," I said; "at any rate it's dark and hard to scout through. But still, one needs to go on."

"Yes, one does need to go on," he said.

And spotting something, I called, "Got it! Got it, Glaucon! We've probably got its trail, and I don't think it's going to get away from us at all."

"You bring good tidings," he said.

"But oh what a slug-like condition we were in," I said.

"In what sort of way?"

"All this time, you blessed fellow, and it seems it's been rolling around in front of our feet from the beginning, and we didn't see it for all that, but were utterly ridiculous; the way people holding something in their hands sometimes look for the things they're holding, we too weren't looking at the thing itself but were gazing off into the distance somewhere, which is probably the very reason it escaped our notice."

"How do you mean?" he said.

"Like this," I said: "it seems to me that although we've been saying it and hearing it all along, we haven't learned from our own selves that we were in a certain way saying it."

"That's a long prologue for someone who's eager to hear," he said.

"Well then, hear whether I mean anything after all," I said. "Because from the beginning the thing we've set down as what we needed to do all through everything when we were founding the city, this, it seems to me, or else some form of this, is justice. Surely we set down, and said often, if you remember, that each one person needed to pursue one of the tasks that are involved in the city, the one to which his nature would be naturally best adapted."

"We did say that."

"And surely we've heard it said by many others that doing what's properly one's own and not meddling in other people's business is justice, and we've said it often ourselves."

"We have said that."

"This, then, my friend," I said, "when it comes about in a certain way, is liable to be justice, this doing what's properly one's own. Do you know where I find an indication of this?"

"No, tell me," he said.

"It seems to me," I said, "that the thing that's left over in the city from the ones we've considered—moderation, courage, and wisdom—is what provided all of them with the power to come into being in it and provides their preservation once they've come into being, for as long as it's in it. And in fact we were claiming that justice would be what was left over from them if we were to find the three."

"And that is necessary," he said.

"And certainly," I said, "if one had to judge which of these would do our city the most good by coming to be present in it, it would be hard to decide whether it's the agreement of opinion of the rulers and ruled, or the preservation of a lawful opinion that arises in the soldiers about what things are and aren't to be feared, or the judgment and guardianship present in the rulers, or whether it's this that does it the most good by being in it, in a child and a woman and a slave and a free person and a craftsman and a ruler and one who's ruled, the fact that each of them, being one person, did what was properly his own and didn't meddle in other people's business."

"It's hard to decide," he said; "how could it not be?"

"Therefore, it seems that, with a view to a city's virtue, the power that comes from each person's doing what's properly his own in it is a match for its wisdom and moderation and courage."

433A

B

C

D

"Very much so," he said.

"And wouldn't you place justice as a match for these as to a city's virtue?"

"Absolutely so."

E   "Then consider whether it will seem that way in this respect too: will you assign the judging of lawsuits in the city to the rulers?"

"Certainly."

"And will they judge them with their sights on anything else besides this, that each party not have another's property or be deprived of his own?"

"No, only on that."

"Because it's the just thing?"

"Yes."

434A   "Then in this respect too, having and doing what's properly one's own would be agreed to be justice."

"That's so."

"Now see if the same thing seems so to you that does to me. If a carpenter tries to work at the job of a leatherworker, or a leather-worker at that of a carpenter, or if they trade their tools and honors with each other, or even if the same person tries to do both jobs, and everything else gets traded around, would it seem to you to do the city any great harm?"

"Not very great," he said.

"But I imagine when someone who's a craftsman by nature, or some other sort of moneymaker, but proud of his wealth or the mul-

B   titude of his household or his strength or anything else of the sort, tries to get in among the warrior kind, or one of the warriors into the deliberative and guardian kind when he doesn't merit it, and *they* trade their tools and honors with each other, or when the same person tries to do all these jobs at the same time, then I imagine it would seem to you too that this change and meddling among them would be the ruin of the city."

"Absolutely so."

"Therefore among the three classes there are, any meddling or

C   changing into one another is of the greatest harm to the city, and would most correctly be referred to as the greatest wrongdoing."

"Precisely so."

"And wouldn't you say the greatest wrongdoing toward one's own city is injustice?"

"How could it not be?"

"So this is injustice. And let's say this the other way around; the minding of their own business by the moneymaking, auxiliary, and guardian classes, when each of them does what properly belongs to it in a city, is the opposite of that and would be justice and would show the city to be just?"

"It doesn't seem to be any other way than that to me," he said.

"Let's not say it in quite so rigid a way yet, but if this form is   D
agreed by us to be present in each one of the people as well and to be
justice there, then we'll join in going along with it. What more would
there be to say? And if not, then we'll consider something else. But for
now let's complete the examination by which we imagined it would
be easier to catch sight of what sort of thing justice is in one human
being if we tried to see it first in some bigger thing that has justice in
it. And it seemed to us that a city is just that, and so we founded the   E
best one in our power, knowing well that it would be present in a
good one at least. So let's carry over what came to light for us there
to one person, and if they're in accord, it will turn out beautifully; but
if something different shows up in the single person, we'll go back to   435A
the city again and test *it*. And maybe, by examining them side by side
and rubbing them together like sticks, we could make justice flame
forth from them, and once it's become evident we could substantiate
it for ourselves."

"Then it's down the road you indicate," he said, "and it behooves
us to go there too."

"Well then," I said, "does the bigger or smaller thing that someone
refers to by the same name happen to be unlike the other one in the
respect in which it's called the same, or like it?"

"Like it," he said.

"Therefore a just man will not differ at all from a just city with   B
respect to the form of justice, but he'll be like it."

"He'll be like it," he said.

"But the city seemed to be just because each of the three classes of
natures present in it did what properly belonged to it, while it seemed
also to be moderate, courageous, and wise on account of certain other
attributes and characteristic activities of these same classes."

"True," he said.

"Therefore, my friend, we'll regard a single person in this way
too, as having these same forms in his soul, and as rightly deserving   C
to have the same names applied to them as in the city as a result of
the same attributes."

"There's every need to," he said.

"It's certainly a light question about the soul we've landed ourselves into now, you strange fellow," I said, "whether it has these
three forms in it or not."

"It's not quite such a light one we seem to me to be in," he said.
"It's probably because the saying is true, Socrates, that beautiful
things are difficult."

"So it appears," I said. "And know for sure, Glaucon, that it's my
opinion we'll never get hold of this in a precise way along the sorts   D
of paths we're now taking in our arguments, because there's another,
longer and more rigorous road that leads to it. Maybe, though, we can

get hold of it in a way worthy, at least, of the things that have already been said and considered."

"Isn't that something to be content with?" he said. "For me, at present anyway, it would be good enough."

"Yes, certainly," I said; "that will be quite sufficient for me too."

"Don't get tired, then," he said; "just examine it."

E   "Well then," I said, "isn't there a great necessity for us to agree that the same forms and states of character are present in each of us as are in the city? Because presumably they didn't get there from anywhere else. It would be ridiculous if anyone imagined the spirited character didn't come to be in the cities from particular people who also have this attribute, like those in Thrace and Scythia, and pretty generally in the northern region, or similarly with the love of learning, which

436A   one might attribute especially to the region round about us, or the love of money that one might claim to be not least round about the Phoenicians and those in Egypt."

"Very much so," he said.

"That's just the way it is," I said, "and it's not difficult to recognize."

"Certainly not."

"But this now is difficult: whether we act each way by means of the same thing, or in the different ways by means of different things, of which there are three—whether we learn by means of one of the things in us, become spirited by means of another, and feel desires in turn

B   by means of a third for the pleasures having to do with nourishment and procreation and as many things as are closely related to these, or whether we act by means of the whole soul in each of them, once we're aroused. These are the things that will be difficult to determine in a manner worthy of the discussion."[65]

"It seems that way to me too," he said.

"Then let's try to mark out whether they're the same as one another or different, in this way."

"How?"

"It's obvious that the same thing isn't going to put up with[66] doing or undergoing opposite things in the same respect and in relation to

C   the same thing at the same time, so presumably if we find that happening in the things in question, we'll know that they're not the same but more than one thing."

"Okay."

---

65   The argument, which Socrates will compare to swimming through difficult waters, lasts until 441C.

66   This clause is the first known articulation of what Aristotle later called the principle of contradiction. The verb Socrates uses here indicates an uncertainty about what the proposition rests on, though the statement is highly precise in other respects. As always, Socrates is offering a starting point for discussion. It should also be noted that he is not speaking about what can be said or thought, but making an observation about the way things are in fact.

"Then consider what I say."

"Say it," he said.

"Does the same thing have the power to stand still and move," I said, "at the same time in the same respect?"

"Not at all."

"Then let's agree about it in a still more precise way, so that we won't be quibbling as we go on. Because if anyone were to say of a person who was standing still but moving his hands and his head, that the same person was standing still and moving at the same time, I imagine we wouldn't consider that he ought to say it that way, but that some one thing about the person stands still while another moves. Isn't that so?"

D

"It's so."

"So if the one who said that were to get still more cute, making the subtle point that tops stand still as a whole and move at the same time, when they spin around with the point fixed in the same place, or that anything else going around in a circle on the same spot does that, we wouldn't accept it, since it's not with respect to the same things about themselves that such things are in that case staying in place and being carried around, but we'd claim that they have in them something straight and something surrounding it, and stand still with respect to the straight part, since they don't tilt in any direction, but move in a circle with respect to the surrounding part; and when the straight axis is leaning to the right or the left, or forward or back, at the same time it's spinning around, then it's not standing still in any way."

E

"You've got that right," he said.

"Therefore, when such things are said they won't knock us off course at all, any more than they'll persuade us that in any way, the same thing, at the same time, in the same respect, in relation to the same thing, could ever undergo, be, or do opposite things."

437A

"Not me at any rate," he said.

"Be that as it may," I said, "in order that we won't be forced to waste time going through all the objections of that sort and establishing that they aren't true, let's go forward on the assumption that this is how it is, having agreed that, if these things should ever appear otherwise than that, all our conclusions from it will have been refuted."

"That's what one ought to do," he said.

"Well then, would you place nodding 'yes' as compared to shaking one's head 'no' among things that are opposite to each other, and having a craving to get something as compared to rejecting it, and drawing something to oneself as compared to pushing it away, and everything of that sort? Whether they're things one does actively or experiences passively, there won't be any difference on that account."

B

"Sure," he said, "they're opposites."

"And what about thirst and hunger and the desires in general," I said, "as well as wishing and wanting? Wouldn't you place all these things somewhere in those forms just mentioned? For example, wouldn't you claim that the soul of someone who desires either has a craving for what it desires, or draws to itself what it wants to become its own, or, in turn, to the extent it wishes something to be provided to it, nods its assent to this to itself as though it had asked some question, stretching out toward its source?"

"I would indeed."

"And what about this? Won't we place not wanting and not wishing and not desiring in with pushing away and banishing from itself and in with all the opposites of the former things?"

"How could we not?"

"Now these things being so, are we going to claim that there's a form consisting of desires, and that among these themselves, the most conspicuous ones are what we call thirst and what we call hunger?"

"We're going to claim that," he said.

"And the one is for drink, the other for food?"

"Yes."

"Now to the extent that it's thirst, would it be a desire in the soul for anything beyond that of which we say it's a desire? For instance, is thirst a thirst for a hot drink or a cold one, or a big or a little one, or in a word, for any particular sort of drink? Or, if there's any heat present in addition to the thirst, wouldn't that produce an additional desire for cold, or if cold is present, a desire for heat? And if by the presence of magnitude the thirst is a big one, that will add a desire for a big drink, or of smallness, for a little one? But being thirsty itself will never turn into a desire for anything other than the very thing it's naturally for, for drink, or being hungry in turn for food?"

"It's like that," he said; "each desire itself is only for the very thing it's naturally for, while the things attached to it are for this or that sort."

"Then let's not be unprepared, and let someone get us confused, on the grounds that no one desires drink, but decent quality drink, and not food but decent quality food, since everyone, after all, desires good things. So if thirst is a desire, it would be for a decent quality of drink, or of whatever else it's a desire for, and the same way with the other desires."

"Well, maybe there could seem to be something in what he's saying," he said, "when he says that."

"But surely," I said, "with all such things that are related to something, the ones that are of particular kinds are related to something of a particular kind, as it seems to me, while the sorts that are just themselves are related only to something that's just itself."

"I don't understand," he said.

"Don't you understand," I said, "that what's greater is of such a sort as to be greater than something?"

"Certainly."

"Than a lesser thing?"

"Yes."

"And a much greater thing than one that's much less, right?"

"Yes."

"And also a thing that was greater than one that was less, and a thing that's going to be greater than one that's going to be less?"

"Yes, of course," he said.

"And something more numerous is related to something that's fewer, and something twice as many to something that's half as many, and all that sort of thing, and also something heavier to something lighter and faster to slower, and in addition, hot things are related to cold things, and isn't everything like that the same way?"

"Very much so."

"And what about the kinds of knowledge? Aren't they the same way? Knowledge just by itself is knowledge of what's learnable just by itself, or of whatever one ought to set down knowledge as being of, while a particular knowledge or a particular sort is of a particular thing or a particular sort of thing. I mean this sort of thing: when a knowledge of constructing houses came into being, didn't it differ from the other kinds of knowledge so that it got called housebuilding?"

"Certainly."

"And wasn't that because it's a particular kind of knowledge, and any of the others is a different sort?"

"Yes."

"And wasn't it because it was about a particular sort of thing that it too came to be of a particular sort, and the same way for the other arts and kinds of knowledge?"

"That's the way it is."

"Well then," I said, "if you've understood it now, call that what I meant to say then, that with all the things that are such as to be about something, the ones that are only themselves are about things that are only themselves, while the ones that are of particular kinds are about things of particular kinds. And I'm not saying at all that the sorts of things they're about are the same sorts they themselves are, as a result of which the knowledge of what's healthy and sick would be healthy and sickly, and the knowledge of bad and good things would be bad and good; instead, I'm saying that when a knowledge came into being that was not just about the very thing knowledge is about, but about a particular thing, and that was what's healthy and sick, it too as a result came to be of a particular sort. And this made it no longer be called simply knowledge, but, with the particular sort included, medicine."

"I've understood it," he said, "and it does seem that way to me."

439A   "So wouldn't you place thirst," I said, "among those things in which to be for something is exactly what they are? Thirst is, of course, for something."

"I would, yes," he said; "it's for drink anyway."

"And isn't a particular sort of thirst for a particular sort of drink, while thirst itself is not for a lot or a little, or for a good or a bad one, or, in a word, for any particular sort, but thirst itself is naturally just for drink itself?"

"Absolutely so."

"Therefore the soul of someone who's thirsty, to the extent he's thirsty, wants nothing other than to drink, and stretches out to this, and sets itself in motion toward it."

"Clearly so."

"So if anything ever pulls it back when it's thirsty, it would be some different thing in it from the very thing that's thirsty, and that tows it like an animal toward drinking? Because we claim that the same thing couldn't be doing opposite things in the same part of itself in relation to the same thing at the same time."

"No, it couldn't."

"In the same way, I imagine, one doesn't do well to say about an archer that his hands push and pull the bow at the same time, but rather that one hand is the one pushing it and the other the one pulling it."

"Absolutely so," he said.

"Now do we claim that there are some people who sometimes, while they're thirsty, aren't willing to drink?"

"Very much so," he said, "many people and often."

"Well what should one say about them?" I said. "Isn't there something in their soul telling them to drink and something preventing them from it that's different from and mastering what's telling them to?"

"It seems that way to me," he said.

"And doesn't the thing that prevents such things come about in it, when it does come about, from reasoning? But the things that tug and pull come to it from passions and disorders?"

"It looks that way."

"So not unreasonably will we regard them as being two things and different from each other, referring to that in the soul by which it reasons as its reasoning part, and that by which it feels erotic love, hunger, and thirst, and is stirred with the other desires, as its irrational and desiring part, associated with certain satisfactions and pleasures."

"No, we'd regard them that way quite reasonably," he said.

"So let these two forms be marked off in the soul," I said. "But is the part that has to do with spiritedness, and by which we're spirited, a third thing, or would it be of the same nature as one of these two?"

"Maybe the same as one of them," he said, "the desiring part."

"But I once heard something that I believe," I said, "about how Leontius, Aglaion's son, was going up from Piraeus along the outside of the north wall, and noticed dead bodies lying beside the executioner. He desired to see them, but at the same time felt disgust and turned himself away; for a while he struggled and covered his eyes, but then he was overcome by his desire, and running toward the bodies holding his eyes wide open, he said, 'See for yourselves, since you're possessed! Take your fill of the lovely sight.'"

440A

"I've heard that myself," he said.

"This story certainly indicates," I said, "that anger sometimes makes war against the desires as though it were one thing acting against another."

"It does indicate that," he said.

"And don't we often observe it in many other ways as well," I said, "when desires overpower someone contrary to his reasoning part, that he scolds himself and is aroused against the part in him that's overpowering him, and just as if there were a pair of warring factions, the spiritedness of such a person becomes allied with his reason? But as for its making a partnership with the desires to act in defiance when reason has decided what ought not to be done, I don't suppose you'd claim you'd ever noticed such a thing happening in yourself, or, I imagine, in anyone else."

B

"No, by Zeus!" he said.

"Then what about when someone thinks he's being unjust?" I said. "The more noble he is, won't he be that much less capable of getting angry at being hungry or cold or suffering anything else at all of the sort from the person he thinks is doing those things to him justly, and won't he be unwilling, as I'm saying, for his spirit to be aroused against that person?"

C

"That's true," he said.

"But what about when he regards himself as being treated unjustly? Doesn't the spirit in him seethe and harden and ally itself with what seems just, and submitting to suffering through hunger and cold and all such things, it prevails and doesn't stint its noble struggles until it gains its end or meets its death, or else, called back, like a dog by a herdsman, by the reason that stands by it, it becomes calm?"

D

"It is very much like what you describe," he said. "And certainly in our city we set up the auxiliaries like dogs obedient to the rulers, who were like shepherds of the city."

"You conceive what I want to say beautifully," I said. "especially if you've taken it to heart in this respect in addition to that one."

"In what sort of respect?"

"That it's looking the opposite of the way it did to us just now with the spirited part, because then we imagined it was something having to do with desire, but now we're claiming that far from that, it's much more inclined in the faction within the soul to take arms on the side of the reasoning part."

"Absolutely," he said.

"Then is it different from that too, or some form of the reasoning part, so that there aren't three but two forms in the soul, a reasoning one and a desiring one? Or just as, in the city, there were three classes that held it together, moneymaking, auxiliary, and deliberative, so too in the soul is there this third, spirited part, which is by nature an auxiliary to the reasoning part, unless it's corrupted by a bad upbringing?"

"It's necessarily a third part," he said.

"Yes," I said, "as long as it comes to light as something differing from the reasoning part, the same way it manifested itself as different from the desiring part."

"But it's not hard to make that evident," he said, "since one could see this even in small children, that they're full of spiritedness right from birth, while some of them seem to me never to get any share of reasoning, and most get one at a late time of life."

"Yes, by Zeus," I said, "you put it beautifully. And also in animals one could see that what you're describing is that way. And in addition to these things, what we cited from Homer in some earlier place in the conversation[67] will bear witness to it:

Striking his chest, he scolded his heart with words.

Here Homer has clearly depicted that which reflects on the better and the worse as one thing rebuking another, that which is irrationally spirited."

"You've said it exactly right," he said.

"Well, with a lot of effort we've managed to swim through these waters, and we're tolerably well agreed that the same classes in the city are present in the soul of each one person, and are equal in number."

"They are."

"Isn't it already a necessary consequence, then, that a private person is wise in the same manner and by the same means that a city was wise?"

"How else?"

"And the means by which and manner in which a private person is courageous is that by which and in which a city was courageous, and everything else related to virtue is the same way for both?"

"Necessarily."

"So, Glaucon, I imagine we'll claim also that a man is just in the very same manner in which a city too was just."

---

67   In 390D, *Odyssey* XX, 17 was cited as a depiction of a spirit of courageous endurance. Here it is more fully revealed as a reining in of spiritedness, in accord with the account of courage in 429B-430B as standing by an opinion, and as directed not only at external adversaries.

"This too is entirely necessary."

"But surely we haven't forgotten somewhere along the way that the city was just because each of the three classes that are in it do what properly belongs to them."

"We don't seem to me to have forgotten that," he said.

"Therefore we need to remember also that for each of us, that whoever has each of the things within him doing what properly belongs to it will be just himself and be someone who does what properly belongs to him."[68]   E

"It needs to be remembered very well indeed," he said.

"Then isn't it appropriate for the reasoning part to rule, since it's wise and has forethought on behalf of the whole soul, and for the spirited part to be obedient to it and allied with it?"

"Very much so."

"Then as we were saying, won't a blending of music with gymnastic exercise make them concordant, tightening up the one part and nourishing it with beautiful speeches and things to learn while   442A relaxing the other with soothing stories, taming it with harmony and rhythm?"

"Exactly so," he said.

"So once this pair have been nurtured in this way, and have learned and been educated in the things that truly belong to them, they need to be put in charge of the desiring part, which is certainly the largest part of the soul in each person and by nature the most insatiable for money. This part needs to be watched over so that it doesn't get filled with the so-called pleasures of the body and, when it becomes big and strong, not do the things that properly belong to it, but try to enslave   B and rule over things that are not of a kind suited to it, so that it turns the whole life of all the parts upside-down."

"Very much so," he said.

"And wouldn't this pair also stand guard on behalf of the whole soul and body against their external enemies in the most beautiful way," I said, "one part deliberating while the other goes to war, following its ruler and accomplishing with its courage the things that have been decided?"

"That's the way it is."

"And I imagine we call each one person courageous on account of this part, when the spirited part of him preserves through pains   C and pleasures what's been passed on to it by speeches as something to be feared or not."

"Rightly so," he said.

"And wise by that little part, the one that ruled in him and passed those things on, and it in turn has knowledge in it of what's advanta-

---

68   The reader should note that this last phrase has changed its meaning by passing to the other side of the analogy between city and soul. Here it no longer refers to limiting oneself to the particular job one is most suited for by nature. This is spelled out at 443C-D.

geous for each part and for the whole consisting of the three of them in common."

"Very much so."

"And what next? Isn't each person moderate by the friendship and concord among these same things, when the ruling part and the pair that are ruled are of the same opinion that the reasoning part ought to rule and aren't in revolt against it?"

D

"Moderation is certainly nothing other than that," he said, "in a city or a private person."

"But each person will be just on account of the thing we repeat so often, and in that manner."

"That's a big necessity."

"Then what about this?" I said. "Surely it hasn't gotten fuzzy around the edges for us in any way, has it, so it would seem to be some other sort of justice than the one that came to light in the city?"

"It doesn't seem to me it has," he said.

E

"Well," I said, "we could establish this beyond all doubt, if anything in our soul still stands unconvinced, by applying the commonplace standards to it."

"What sort of standards exactly?"

"For example, if we were asked to come to an agreement about that city and the man who's like that by nature and upbringing, as to whether it seemed such a man would steal a deposit of gold or silver he'd accepted in trust, do you think anyone would imagine he'd be more likely to do that than all those not of his sort?"

443A

"No one would," he said.

"And wouldn't temple robberies, frauds, and betrayals, either of friends in private or cities in public capacities, be out of the question for this person?"

"Out of the question."

"And in no way whatever would he be unfaithful to oaths or other agreements."

"How could he?"

"And surely adultery, neglect of parents, and lack of attentiveness to the gods belong more to any other sort of person than to this one."

"Any other sort for sure," he said.

B

"And isn't the thing responsible for all that the fact that each of the parts within him does what properly belongs to it in connection with ruling and being ruled?"

"That and nothing else."

"So are you still looking for justice to be anything other than the power that produces men and cities of that sort?"

"By Zeus," he said, "not I."

"So our dream has come to complete fulfillment; we said we suspected, right from when we started founding the city, that by

the favor of some god we were liable to've gotten to an origin and   C
outline of justice."

"Absolutely so."

"And what it was in fact, Glaucon—and this is why it was so
helpful—was an image of justice, that it was right for the natural
leatherworker to do leatherwork and not do anything else, and for
the carpenter to do carpentry, and the same way for the rest."

"So it appears."

"And the truth is, justice was something like that, as it seems, but
not anything connected with doing what properly belongs to oneself
externally, but with what's on the inside, that truly concerns oneself   D
and properly belongs to oneself, not allowing each thing in him to do
what's alien to it, or the classes of things in his soul to meddle with
one another, but setting his own house in order in his very being,
he himself ruling over and bringing order to himself and becoming
his own friend and harmonizing three things, exactly like the three
notes marking a musical scale at the low end, the high end, and the
middle; and if any other things happen to be between them, he binds   E
all of them together and becomes entirely one out of many, moderate
and harmonized. Only when he's in this condition does he act, if he
performs any action having to do with acquiring money, or taking
care of the body, as well as anything of a civic kind or having to do
with private transactions; in all these cases he regards an action that
preserves that condition and helps to complete it as a just and beautiful
act, and gives it that name, and regards as wisdom the knowledge that
directs that action. Anything that always breaks down that condition,   444A
he regards as an unjust action, and the opinion that directs *that*, he
regards as ignorance."

"You're absolutely telling the truth, Socrates," he said.

"Okay," I said. "if we were to claim that we've discovered the just
man and the just city, and exactly what justice is in them, I imagine
we wouldn't seem to be telling a total lie."

"By Zeus, certainly not," he said.

"Shall we claim that, then?"

"Let's claim it."

"So be it," I said. "What needs to be examined after this, I imagine,
is injustice."

"Clearly."

"Doesn't it in turn have to be some sort of faction among these   B
three things, a meddling and butting in and an uprising of a certain
part of the soul against the whole, in order to rule in it when that's not
appropriate, because it's of such a kind by nature that it's only fitting
for it to be a slave?[69] I imagine we'll claim something like that, and that

---

69   A few more words appear at the end of this sentence, but they vary among the manuscript
sources and no version of them quite makes sense to me or to any editor, one of whom (Adam)
suspects the problem started with "an illiterate scribe" who was trying to be helpful.

the disorder and going off course of these parts is injustice as well as intemperance, cowardice, foolishness, and all vice put together."

C   "Those are the very things it is," he said.

"Then as for doing unjust things and being unjust," I said, "and in turn doing just things, isn't it by now patently obvious exactly what all these are, if indeed that's so for both injustice and justice?"

"How so?"

"Because," I said, "they don't happen to be any different from what's healthy or diseased; what those are in a body, these are in a soul."

"In what way?" he said.

"Presumably, healthful things produce health and diseased things produce disease."

"Yes."

"Then is it also the case that doing just things produces justice,

D   while doing unjust things produces injustice?"

"Necessarily."

"And producing health is settling the things in the body into a condition of mastering and being mastered by one another in accord with nature, while producing disease is settling them into ruling and being ruled one by another contrary to nature."

"That's it."

"Then in turn, as for producing justice," I said, "isn't that settling the things in the soul into a condition of mastering and being mastered by one another in accord with nature, while producing injustice is settling them into ruling and being ruled one by another contrary to nature?"

"Exactly," he said.

"Therefore, it seems likely that virtue would be a certain health,

E   beauty, and good condition of the soul, while vice would be a disease, deformity, and weakness."

"That's what they are."

"And don't beautiful practices lead to the acquisition of virtue, and shameful ones to vice?"

"Necessarily."

"So what remains at this point, it seems, is for us to consider next

445A   whether it's profitable to perform just actions, pursue beautiful practices, and be just, whether or not it goes unnoticed that one is of that sort, or to do injustice and be unjust, so long as one doesn't pay the penalty or become better by being corrected."

"But Socrates," he said, "the question already appears to me to have become laughable, whether, when life doesn't seem worth living with the body's nature corrupted, even with all the foods and drinks and every sort of wealth and political rule, it will then be worth living

B   with the nature of that very thing by which we live disordered and corrupted, even if someone does whatever he wants, but not the thing by which he'll get rid of vice and injustice and acquire justice and virtue, seeing as how it's become obvious that each of them is of the sort we've gone over."

"It is laughable," I said. "Nevertheless, since we've come this far, far enough to be able to see clearly that this is the way it is, it wouldn't be right to get tired out."

"By Zeus," he said, "getting tired out is the last thing we ought to do."

"Come up to the mark now," I said, "so you too can see how many   C
forms vice has, the way it seems to me, at least the ones that are even worth looking at."

"I'm following," he said; "just speak."

"Well," I said, "as though from a lookout spot, since we've climbed up to this point in the discussion, there appears to me to be one look[70] that belongs to virtue and infinitely many to vice, but some four among them that are even worth mentioning."

"How do you mean?" he said.

"There are liable to be as many dispositions of a soul," I said, "as there are dispositions among polities that have looks to them."

"How many, exactly?"   D

"Five for polities," I said, "and five for a soul."

"Say which ones," he said.

"I say that one," I said, "would be this type of polity we've been going over, but it could be named in two ways, since if one exceptional man arose among the rulers it would be called kingship, but aristocracy if there were more than one."

"True," he said.

"This, then," I said, "is one form that I'm talking about, since whether one or more than one man arose, it wouldn't change any of the laws of the city worthy of mention, since the upbringing and   E
education they got would be the way we went over."

"Likely not," he said.

---

70   The word is *eidos*, translated most of the time as 'form'. Here, as in 402C, the context makes the word's primary meaning prominent and vivid. Socrates is using a live metaphor for the intelligible look of a thing.

BOOK V

Note

Socrates assumes the imagined city has served its purpose, and proceeds to use its results for an orderly examination of the kinds of bad
character in human beings. But there is an uprising within the community of listeners. Polemarchus is the first to state the grievance that
the commune approach to the sexual life of the guardians hasn't been
talked about in any detail. The desiring part of the listeners' souls is
asking for some attention, and it wins over both of Socrates' spirited
auxiliaries, Adeimantus first and then Glaucon too. The unanimity of the
community is both announced and displayed by Thrasymachus, in his
first words since the first book. He has been won over, at least on this
night, from competing with others for things like gold to join them in
hearing talk that has roused his interest. And the desire of the group to
lead that talk toward lighter topics should not mask the fact that they
have already forgotten their plan for the night, to go to a party. Socrates'
pretense of dragging his feet is his characteristic irony in its briar-patch
mode. He has brought a diverse group of souls into some harmony,
among themselves and within themselves, and uses the occasion to
challenge some of their strongest beliefs about the sexes, the family,
and what constitutes fitness to rule. The last of those topics leads to an
intellectually demanding examination of the possibility that there could
be knowledge and not merely opinions, and Glaucon shows himself well
able to make contributions to it.

449A   "Well, I call that kind of city and polity, and that kind of man, good
and right, and if this sort are right, the rest are bad and wrong, in the
ways the cities are managed and the way the soul's disposition is
constituted in private persons, and the badness takes four forms."

"What sorts are they?" he said.

And I was going on to describe them in order, the way it appeared
B   to me they change out of one another in each case, but Polemarchus,
who was sitting a little way from Adeimantus, reached out his hand
and grabbed him from above by his cloak at the shoulder, drew him
near, stretching himself forward, and was saying something while
stooping toward him, of which we heard nothing but this: "Shall we
let it go, then," he said, "or what shall we do?"

"Not in the least," said Adeimantus, now speaking loudly.

And I said, "What in particular won't you let go?"

"You," he said.

C   "Because of what in particular?" I said.

"You seem to us to be taking the lazy way out," he said, "and to be cheating us out of a whole form that belongs to the argument, and not the least important one, to avoid going over it, and you seem to've imagined you'd get away with speaking of it dismissively, saying it's obvious, about women and children, that what belongs to friends will be shared in common."

"And wasn't I right, Adeimantus?" I said.

"Yes," he said, "but this 'right' needs explanation, like the rest of it, about what the manner of the sharing would be, since there could be many. So don't pass over which of them you're talking about, since we've been waiting all this time imagining you'd make some mention somewhere about the procreation of children, how they'll be produced and once they're born how they'll be raised, and of this whole sharing of women and children you're talking about. Because we think it has a big bearing, in fact a total impact, on whether the polity comes into being in the right way or not. But now, since you're taking on another polity before you've determined these things sufficiently, it seemed right to us to do what you've heard, to refuse to let you go until you've gone over all these things just like the rest."

"Me too," said Glaucon; "put me down as a partner in this vote."

"Don't worry," said Thrasymachus, "consider these things as having seemed good to all of us, Socrates."

"Oh what you folks have done by ambushing me," I said. "So much discussion about the polity you're setting in motion again, as though from the beginning,[71] when I was rejoicing at having already gotten to the end of it, feeling content if anyone would leave these things alone and accept them the way they were stated then. You have no idea what a big swarm of arguments you've stirred up with the things you're now demanding; since I saw that at the time I passed it by, fearing it would cause a lot of trouble."

"What!" said Thrasymachus. "Do you imagine these people have come this far now to fritter away their time looking for gold rather than to listen to arguments?"

"All well and good," I said, "but within measure."

"The measure in hearing such arguments, Socrates," said **Glaucon**, "for anyone who has any sense, is a whole life. So give up on that as far as we're concerned; just see that you don't get tired in any way of going all through the way it seems to you about the things we're asking, what the sharing of children and women will be among our guardians, and about the rearing of those who are still young that takes place in the time between birth and education, which seems to

D

450A

B

C

---

71   This wonderful scene is full of resonant language. The discussion of the best polity may need to go back to its beginning in Bk. II, but the words of the participants hearken back to their first interactions in Bk. I, from the grabbing of a man's cloak to a majority decision stated in the form of a legislative enactment. See the footnote to 328B.

be the most troublesome time. So try to say in what way it needs to happen."

"It's not easy to go through, you happy fellow," I said, "because it has a lot of doubtful points, even more than the things we went through before. It could even be doubted that what's spoken of is possible, and even if it came about as much as it possibly could, there will also be doubts even in that case that this would be the best thing. That's why there was a certain reluctance to touch on these things, for fear, dear comrade, the argument would seem to be only a prayer."

D

"Don't be reluctant at all," he said, "since your listeners won't be unfair or disbelieving or ill-disposed."

And I said, "Most excellent fellow, I take it you're saying that to give me courage?"

"I am," he said.

"Well you're doing exactly the opposite," I said. "If I believed I knew what I was talking about, your pep talk would have been a beautiful one; to speak when one knows the truth, among people who are intelligent and friendly, about things that are of greatest importance and dear to us, is secure and encouraging, but to make one's arguments at the same time one is doubtful and searching, which is exactly what I'm doing, is a frightening and perilous thing. It's not because I'm liable to be laughed at—that's childish—but from fear that I'll not only tumble away myself from the truth, about things one least ought to fall down on, but that I'll also be lying in ruins with the friends I've dragged down with me. So instead I'll fall on my face in obeisance to Adrasteia,[72] Glaucon, for her favor for what I'm about to say. I hope it's a lesser sin to become an unwilling murderer of someone than a deceiver about what's beautiful and good and just and lawful. That's a risk it's better to run among enemies rather than friends, so it's a good thing you gave me encouragement."

E

451A

And Glaucon, with a laugh, said, "Okay, Socrates, if we experience anything discordant from what you say, we'll release you like someone purified from being a murderer and cleared as no deceiver of us. Just speak up boldly."

B

"Well, certainly someone who's released even in that situation is purified," I said, "as the law says, so it's likely that if it's that way there, it is here too."

"Speak, then," he said, "with that assurance."

"It's necessary to go back again now," I said, "and say what probably should have been said then in the proper place. And maybe this would be the right way, after the male drama has been completely finished, to finish the female drama in turn, especially since you're calling for it this way. To my way of thinking, for human beings born

C

---

72   Literally "She who can't be run away from," a name given by Aeschylus (*Prometheus Bound*, line 936) to the goddess who takes vengeance on proud speech.

and educated in the way we went over, there is no other right way
for them to get and treat children and women than to hasten down
that road on which we first started them. We tried, I presume, in the
argument, to set the men up like guardians of a herd."

"Yes."

"Then let's follow that up by giving them the sort of birth and   D
rearing that closely resemble that, and consider whether it suits us
or not."

"How?" he said.

"This way. Do we imagine that the females among the guard dogs
ought to join in guarding the things the males guard, and hunt with
them and do everything else in common, or should they stay inside
the house as though they were disabled by bearing and nursing the
puppies, while the males do the work and have all the tending of the
flock?"

"Everything in common," he said, "except that we'd treat the
females as weaker and the males as stronger."

"Is it possible, then," I said, "to use any animal for the same things   E
if you don't give it the same rearing and training?"

"It's not possible."

"So if you're going to make use of women at the same tasks as
men, they'll also have to be taught the same things."

"Yes."   452A

"Music and gymnastic exercise were given to the men."

"Yes."

"Therefore this pair of arts needs to be made available to the
women too, as well as the things connected with war, and they need
to be applied in the same manner."

"It's likely, based on what you're saying," he said.

"Probably," I said, "many of the things being talked about now
would look absurd if they're done the way they're being described,
just because they're contrary to custom."

"Very much so indeed," he said.

"Do you see which of them would be most absurd?" I said. "Isn't it
obvious that it would be for the women to be exercising naked in the
wrestling schools alongside the men, and not just the young ones but   B
also those who're already on the older side, like the old men who're
still devoted to exercising in the gyms when they're wrinkled and
not a pleasant sight."

"By Zeus," he said, "that would look absurd, at least the way
things are at present."

"But as long as we've got ourselves started talking about it, we
shouldn't be afraid, should we, of all the jokes of whatever sort from
witty people at the advent such a change in both gymnastic exercise
and music, and not least about having war 'tools' and 'mounting'   C
horses?"

"You've got that right," he said.

"Instead, since we *have* started to talk about it, we need to pass right to the tough part of the law, asking these guys *not* to do what properly belongs to them but to be serious, and to recall that it's not much time since it seemed to the Greeks the way it does now to many of the barbarians, that it's shameful and absurd to look at a naked man, and when the people of Crete first introduced gymnasiums, and then the Spartans, the fashionable people of the time took the opportunity to ridicule all that. Don't you imagine they did?"

"I do."

"But since it appeared to those who adopted the practice, I imagine, that it was better to uncover all such things than to hide them, what had been absurd in their eyes was stripped away by what was exposed as best in their reasoning. And this reveals that one who considers anything absurd other than what's bad is empty-headed, as is one who tries to get a laugh by looking at any other sight as laughable than one that's senseless and bad, or who takes seriously any mark of what's beautiful that he's set up other than what's good."

"Absolutely so," he said.

"Well then, isn't this the first thing that needs to be agreed about these things: whether they're possible or not? And shouldn't a chance for disputes be given to anyone who wants to dispute it, whether it's someone fun-loving or the serious type, as to whether female human nature is capable of sharing in all the work that belongs to the nature of the male kind, or not in any at all, or in some sorts and not others, and whether in particular this last applies to things connected with war? Wouldn't someone be likely to get to the end of the subject most beautifully by starting off the most beautifully in this way?"

"By far," he said.

"Then do you want us to carry on the dispute ourselves against ourselves, on behalf of the others," I said, "so that the opposing argument won't be under siege undefended?"

"There's no reason not to," he said.

"So let's say, on their behalf, 'Socrates and Glaucon, there's no need for anyone else to dispute with you, because you yourselves, at the beginning of the process of settling the city that you founded, agreed that each one person had to do the one thing that properly belonged to him by nature.'"

"Suppose we did agree to that; how could we not?"

"'Well is there any way that a woman isn't completely different from a man in her nature?'"

"How could she not be different?"

"'Then isn't it also appropriate to assign each of them different work that's in accord with their nature?'"

"Of course."

"'So why aren't you mistaken now and contradicting yourselves,   C
when you also declare that men and women ought to do the same
things, despite having the most diverse natures? Will you be able to
make any defense against this, you amazing fellow?'"

"Not very easily, just on the spur of the moment," he said; "but I'll
ask you, in fact I *am* asking you, to be the interpreter of the argument
on our side too, whatever it is."

"This is what I was afraid of a long time ago, Glaucon," I said,
"as well as many other things I foresaw, and I was reluctant to touch   D
on the law about the way of having and bringing up women and
children."

"No, by Zeus," he said, "it seems like it's no easy matter to
digest."

"No, it's not," I said. "But it's like this: whether one falls into a little
swimming tank or into the middle of the biggest sea, all the same one
just swims none the less."

"Quite so."

"Well then, don't we too have to swim and try to save ourselves
from the argument, and just hope for some dolphin to pick us up on
his back or for some other sort of rescue that's hard to count on?"

"It looks that way," he said.

"Come on then," I said, "let's find a way out somewhere if we can.   E
Because we're agreed that a different nature needs to follow a different pursuit, and that a woman and a man are different in nature; but
we're claiming now that these different natures need to follow the
same pursuits. Are these the things we're accused of?"

"Precisely."

"Oh Glaucon," I said, "what a noble power the debater's art   454A
has."

"Why in particular?"

"Because many people even seem to me to fall into it unwillingly,"
I said, "and imagine they're not being contentious but having a conversation, because they're not able to examine something that's being
said by making distinctions according to forms, but pounce on the
contradiction in what's been said according to a mere word, subject-
ing one another to contention and not conversation."

"That *is* exactly the experience of many people," he said, "but that
surely doesn't apply to us in the present circumstance, does it?"

"It does absolutely," I said. "At any rate, we're running the risk   B
of engaging in debate unintentionally."

"How?"

"We're pouncing, in an altogether bold and contentious manner,
on 'the nature that's not[73] the same' as a result of a word, because

---

73   The word "not" is not in any manuscript or other ancient source, but the sense seems to
require it, and most editors, though not the most recent and thorough one, have inserted it.

that's what's required not to have the same pursuits, but we didn't give any consideration whatever to what form of different or same nature we were marking off, and how far it extended, at the time when we delivered up different pursuits to a different nature and the same ones to the same nature."

"No, we didn't consider that," he said.

C "Well, according to that, then," I said, "it seems like we're entitled to ask ourselves whether it's the same nature that belongs to bald people as to longhaired ones, and not the opposite one, and whenever we agree that it's opposite, if bald people do leatherwork, not allow longhaired people to, or if the longhaired ones do, not allow the others."

"That would certainly be ridiculous," he said.

"Well is it ridiculous for any other reason," I said, "than because we weren't reckoning on every sort of same and different nature at D the time, but only watching out for that form of otherness and likeness that was relevant to the pursuits themselves? For example, with a male doctor and a female doctor, we meant that it's the soul that has the same nature. Don't you think so?"

"I do."

"But with a male doctor and a male carpenter, it's different?"

"Completely different, I presume."

"So," I said, "if the men's or women's kind is manifestly superior in relation to any art or other pursuit, won't we claim that this needs to be given over to that one of the two? But if they apparently differ E only in that the female bears the young and the male mounts the female, we'll claim instead that it hasn't yet been demonstrated in any way that a woman differs from a man in respect to what we're talking about, and we'll still believe that our guardians and the women with them ought to pursue the same activities."

"Rightly so," he said.

455A "Now after this, don't we invite the one who says the opposite to teach us this very thing, what art or what pursuit it is, among those involved in the setup of the city, for which the nature of a woman is not the same as but different from that of a man?"

"That's the just thing to do, anyway."

"And perhaps someone else as well might say the very thing you were saying a little while ago, that it's not easy to say anything adequate on the spot, but not hard if someone has been considering it."

"He would say that."

"Then do you want us to ask the person who contradicts this sort B of thing to follow us, if we somehow show him that no pursuit related to the running of a city is uniquely for a woman?"

"Certainly."

"'Come on then,' we'll say to him, 'answer: is this the way you meant that one person is naturally fitted for something and another isn't, that in it the one learns something easily, the other with difficulty? And that the one, on the basis of a brief study, would be apt to discover a lot about what he'd learned, while the other, even when he's gotten a lot of study and practice, couldn't even hang on to what he'd learned? And for the one, the aptitudes of his body would adequately serve the purposes of his thinking, while for the other it would be the opposite? Are there any other things than these by which you marked off the one naturally suited for each thing from the one who's not?'"

C

"No one's going to claim there're any others," he said.

"Then do you know of anything practiced by human beings in which the man's kind isn't of a condition that surpasses the woman's in all these respects? Or shall we make a long story out of it, talking about the art of weaving, and tending to things that are baked or boiled, the activities in which the female kind is held in high repute and for which it's most absurd of all for it to be outdone?"

D

"You're telling the truth," he said, "that the one kind is dominated by the other by far in everything, as one might put it. But many women are certainly better than many men at many things, though on the whole it's the way you say."

"Therefore, my friend, there isn't any pursuit of the people who run a city that belongs to a woman because she's a woman or to a man because he's a man, but the kinds of natures are spread around among both kinds of animal alike, and by nature a woman takes part in all pursuits and a man in them all, but in all of them a woman is weaker than a man."

E

"Quite so."

"So are we going to assign all of them to men and none to women?"

"Really, how could we?"

"But we'll claim, I imagine, that there's a woman with an aptitude for the medical art and another without it, and a woman with an aptitude for music and another who's unmusical by nature."

"Of course."

"Then isn't there a woman with an aptitude for gymnastic training and warfare, and one who's unwarlike and not fond of gymnastic exercise?"

456A

"I imagine so."

"What else? Is one woman philosophic and another antiphilosophic? Is one spirited and another lacking in spirit?"

"These things are possible too."

"Then it's also possible for there to be a woman with an aptitude as a guardian, and another without one. Wasn't it that sort of nature we also selected as belonging to the men with an aptitude for being guardians?"

"That very sort."

"And therefore the same nature for guardianship of a city belongs to a woman as to a man, except to the extent that one is weaker or stronger."

"So it appears."

B   "And so women of that sort need to be selected to live together and guard together with men of that sort, since they're competent and are akin to them in their nature."

"Entirely so."

"And don't the same pursuits need to be assigned to the same natures?"

"The same ones."

"Then we've come back around to what we said before, and we're agreed that it's not contrary to nature for the women among the guardians to be assigned to music and gymnastic training."

"Absolutely so."

C   "So we weren't legislating things that are impossible or like prayers, since we set down the law in accord with nature. But it seems instead that it's the things that're done now, contrary to these, that are done contrary to nature."

"So it seems."

"Wasn't our question whether the things we'd be talking about are possible and best?"

"It was indeed."

"And it's been agreed that they're possible?"

"Yes."

"And that they're best is the thing that needs to be agreed to next?"

"Clearly."

"Now as for turning out a woman skilled at guardianship, one education won't produce men for us and another one women, will it,
D   especially since it gets the same nature to work with?"

"No other one."

"Then what's the state of your opinion about this in particular?"

"About what exactly?"

"About assuming in your own estimation that one man is better and another worse. Or do you regard them as all alike?"

"Not at all."

"Then in the city we've been founding, which do you imagine would turn out as better men, the guardians, when they've gotten the education we went over, or the leatherworkers, educated in leathercraft?"

"You're asking a ridiculous question," he said.

"I understand," I said. "What about it then? Compared to the rest of the citizens, aren't these the best men?"

"By far."

"And what about the women? Won't these be the best among the   E
women?"

"They too, by far," he said.

"And is there anything better for a city than for the best possible
women and men to arise in it?"

"There isn't."

"And music and gymnastic training, when they come to their aid
in the way we've gone over, bring this about?"   457A

"How could they not?"

"Therefore the ordinance we set down for the city is not only
something possible but also the best thing."

"So it is."

"Then the women among the guardians need to take off their
clothes, since they're going to be clothed in virtue instead of a cloak,
and they need to share in war and the rest of the guardianship
connected with the city, and not engage in other activities, but less
arduous parts of these same activities need to be given to the women
than to the men because of the weakness of their kind. And a man
who laughs at naked women engaged in gymnastic exercise for the   B
sake of what's best 'plucks a laugh from his wisdom while it's still
an unripe fruit,'[74] having no idea, it seems, what he's laughing at or
what he's doing. For the most beautiful thing that's being said or will
have been said is this: that what's beneficial is beautiful and what's
harmful is ugly."

"Absolutely so."

"Then shall we claim that we're escaping from one wave,[75] so to
speak, by saying this about the law pertaining to women, so that we
don't get completely swamped when we set it down that our male
and female guardians must pursue all things in common, but that   C
in a way the argument that says that's possible and beneficial is in
agreement with itself?"

"And it's certainly no small wave you're escaping," he said.

"But you'll claim it's no big one either," I said, "when you see
what comes after this."

"Speak, then, and I'll see," he said.

"A law that goes along with this one," I said, "and with the others
that preceded it, is, as I imagine, the following."

"What?"

"That all these women are to be shared among all these men, and   D
none of the women is to live together privately with any of the men,

---

74   The line from Pindar is just "plucks his wisdom while it's still an unripe fruit," aimed at
philosophers. Socrates adds a word that makes the line turn back in its author's general direction, since Pindar too was making fun of the incongruities philosophic speculation presents to
conventional eyes.

75   In the sea of troubles they've landed in, as remarked at 453B, in which they still face the
danger of going under for the third time before the end of Bk. V.

and their children are to be shared too; a parent is not to know the offspring that are its own, or a child its parent."

"This is much bigger than the former one," he said, "in respect to doubtfulness about both what's possible and what's beneficial."

"About what's beneficial, anyway," I said, "I don't imagine there'd be any arguing that it's not the greatest good for the women to be shared or for the children to be shared, if possible, but about whether it's possible or not, I imagine there'd be a very great dispute."

E   "There could very well be dispute about both," he said.

"You're talking about a unified front among arguments," I said, "and here I was imagining I could run away from one of them, if it seemed to you to be beneficial, and I'd have the one about whether it's possible or not left."

"But you didn't get away with running away," he said, "so give an account of yourself on both counts."

"I'll have to stand trial," I said. "Do me this much of a favor though;
458A   let me go about it holiday-style, like dawdlers who're in the habit of feasting on their own thoughts when they're walking by themselves. People like that, you know, before finding out how there can be something they desire, put that aside so they won't wear themselves out pondering about what's possible or not, and taking it for granted that the thing they want is already there, they're already arranging the rest and enjoying going through the sorts of things they'll do when
B   it happens, and otherwise making a lazy soul even lazier. I've gotten soft myself by now, and on those questions I desire to put them off and consider later how they're possible, but now, taking it for granted that they're possible, if you let me, I'll consider how the rulers will organize them when they happen, and what would be the most advantageous way, for both the city and the guardians, for them to be done. I'll try together with you to consider these things first, and those later, if you give permission."

"I do give permission," he said; "go ahead and consider."

"I imagine, then," I said, "if in fact the rulers are going to be worthy
C   of that name, and their auxiliaries by the same token worthy of theirs, the ones will wish to follow orders and the others to give them, while the latter themselves obey the laws on some matters, but imitate the laws on all the other matters that we'll leave up to their judgment."

"That sounds right," he said.

"Then you," I said, "as their lawgiver, once you've selected the women in the same way you also selected the men, will distribute them as far as possible to those with similar natures; and they, since they have their houses and meals in common, and none of them
D   possesses any property of that sort privately, will be together, and while they're mingled together in the gyms and in the rest of their upbringing, they'll be led, I imagine, by an inborn necessity, toward

mingling with each other sexually. Or do the things I'm talking about not seem necessary to you?"

"Not in the geometrical sense anyway," he said, "but they seem to be necessities of an erotic sort, which are liable to be sharper than the former at persuading and attracting most of the populace."

"Very much so," I said. "But the next thing to consider, Glaucon, is that unregulated sexual contact with one another, or doing anything else at all of that sort, isn't pious in a city of people favored by destiny,[76] and the rulers aren't going to allow it."

"No, it wouldn't be just," he said.

"So it's clear that the next thing we'll do is make marriages sacred to the greatest extent possible, and it's the most beneficial ones that would be sacred."

"Absolutely so."

"So in what way will they be the most beneficial? Tell me this, Glaucon, because I see in your household both hunting dogs and true-bred birds in great numbers. Well, by Zeus, have you paid any attention to their matings and breeding?"

"To what sort of thing?" he said.

"First, among those of the same kind, even though they're true bred, aren't there some that also turn out best?"

"There are."

"Then do you breed from all of them alike, or are you eager to breed as much as possible from the best ones?"

"From the best ones."

"And then what? From the youngest, or from the oldest, or as much as possible from those in their prime?"

"From those in their prime."

"And if they weren't bred that way, do you expect the race of birds or of dogs would be much worse?"

"I do," he said.

"And what do you suppose about horses," I said, "and the rest of the animals? That it would be any different?"

"That would certainly be strange," he said.

"Ayayay, dear comrade," I said, "how greatly in need we are, then, of top-notch rulers if it's also the same way with the human race."

"Well it is the same way," he said, "but what does that have to do with the rulers?"

"There'll be a necessity," I said, "for them to use a lot of medicines. Presumably we believe that for bodies that don't need medicines, those of people willing to follow a prescribed way of life, even a rather

E

459A

B

C

---

76   The word Socrates uses ordinarily would mean "happy people." Socrates would certainly argue that lack of restraint in sexual indulgence couldn't make anyone happy, but since he links it here with piety rather than moderation, the root sense of the word "happy" is reinforced: having a good divinity or destiny.

ordinary doctor is sufficient; but when there's a need to use medicine, we know that a more courageous doctor is needed."

"True, but what point are you making?"

D "This one," I said: "our rulers are liable to need to use falsehood and deception in abundance for the benefit of those they rule. And we claimed, of course, that all that sort of thing is useful in the form of medicine."

"And rightly so," he said.

"Well, it seems like it's not least in the marriages and procreation that this rightness comes into play."

"How so?"

"It follows from the things that've been agreed to," I said, "that as often as possible the best men ought to have sex with the best women, and the worst on the contrary with the worst, and the offspring of
E the former ought to be reared, but not those of the latter, if the flock is going to be of top quality to the highest degree possible. And all these things ought to happen without the notice of anyone except the rulers themselves, if the guardians' herd is also going to be as free as possible of internal conflict."

"With the utmost rightness," he said.

"Then don't some sort of festivals and sacrifices need to be set up by law, in which we'll bring together the brides and grooms, and
460A suitable hymns need to be made by our poets for the marriages that take place? We'll make the number of marriages be up to the rulers, in order that they might preserve the same number of men as much as they can, having regard to wars, diseases, and everything of the sort, and in order that, as far as possible, our city might not become either big or little."

"Rightly," he said.

"I imagine some ingenious lotteries need to be made up, so that the ordinary man mentioned before will blame chance and not the rulers for each marriage pairing."

"Very much so," he said.

B "And presumably those among the young men who are good in war or anywhere else need to be given special honors and prizes, and among other things a more unrestricted privilege to sleep with the women,[77] so that on this pretext, as great a number of children as possible would also at the same time be begotten by such people."

"Rightly so."

"And won't the officials set up for this purpose take over the offspring born on each occasion, male or female officials or both, since, of course, the ruling offices are shared among the women and men?"

---

77   The balancing act going on in this passage is evident here in various ways. Sex among the guardians is not to be a right, unregulated (*ataktôs*, 458D), but a privilege more or less unrestricted (*aphthonestera*), and while the pairings are solemnized with all the trappings of marriages, they are apparently not meant to last beyond the festive occasions at which they are celebrated.

"Yes."

"So I expect they'll take those born to the good ones into the fold[78]   C
and turn them over to some sort of nurses who live separately in a
certain part of the city; but the offspring of the worse sort of people,
and any of the others that might have been born with defects, they'll
hide away in a place not spoken of and not seen, as is fitting."

"If indeed the race of the guardians is going to be pure," he said.

"Won't these officials also be in charge of the feeding, bringing the
mothers to the fold when they're swollen with milk, contriving every
sort of means so that none of them will recognize her own child, and   D
providing other women who have milk if they don't have enough,
and see to it that the mothers themselves suckle for a moderate time,
but turn over the watchfulness and other work to wet nurses and
nurses?"

"You're describing a great ease of childbearing," he said, "for the
women among the guardians."

"And it's appropriate," I said. "Let's go on to the next thing we
proposed, since we claimed that the offspring ought to be born particularly from those in their prime."

"True."

"Then do you share my opinion that twenty years is the average   E
time of the prime of life for a woman, and thirty for a man?"

"Which of the years?" he said.

"Starting from her twentieth and up to her fortieth, for a woman
to bear children for the city," I said, "and for a man, once he passes
his swiftest peak at running, to beget children for the city from then
until his fifty-fifth."

"For them both," he said, "that's certainly their prime both in body   461A
and in intelligence."

"Then if someone older or younger than that engages in generating offspring into the community, we'll claim it's a transgression
that's not pious or just, since it produces for the city a child that, if it
escapes notice, will have been brought forth without being born with
the sacrifices and prayers that would be offered at every marriage by
priestesses, priests, and the whole city together, that from good and
beneficial people better and more beneficial offspring might always
come forth; instead, it will have been born under cover of darkness   B
in the presence of terrible unrestraint."

"We'll rightly make that claim," he said.

"And the same law applies," I said, "if any of the men still propa-
gating has sexual contact with any of the women who are of childbearing age when a ruler hasn't joined him with her; we'll charge
him with bringing a bastard child into the city, unsanctioned and
unconsecrated."

---

78   The word refers to a pen for young livestock, but also to a special enclosed place within a
temple.

"Quite rightly," he said.

"But, I imagine, when both the women and the men get beyond the age to reproduce, we'll no doubt leave them free to have sex with anyone they want, except with a daughter, a mother, a daughter's children, a mother's parent, or the women with a son or his children or with a father or his parent, and all that only after it's been insisted that they take the most zealous care not to bring forth even a single fetus into the light of day, if one is conceived, and if any is forced on them, to handle it on the understanding that there's to be no raising of such a child."

"These things too are reasonably said," he said; "but how are they going to distinguish their fathers and daughters, and the others you just mentioned, one from another?"

"There's no way," I said. "But from that day on which any of them becomes a bridegroom, whatever offspring are born in the tenth month after that, or even the seventh, to all of these he'll apply the name sons to the males and daughters to the females, and they'll call him father, and in the same way he'll call their offspring his grandchildren, and they in turn will call people like him grandfathers and grandmothers, and they'll call those who were born at the same time their mothers and fathers were producing children sisters and brothers, so that, as we were just saying, they won't have sexual contact with one another. But the law will grant brothers and sisters permission to be joined together if the lottery falls out that way and the Pythia[79] confirms it."

"Quite rightly," he said.

"So, Glaucon, this or something like it is the way of sharing women and children among the guardians of your city. The next thing after this ought to be to have it established out of the argument that this goes along with the rest of the polity and is by far the best way. Or how should we proceed?"

"That way, by Zeus," he said.

"Well then, wouldn't this be a source from which an agreement might come, that we ask ourselves what's the greatest good we can state in the organization of a city, at which the lawgiver ought to aim in setting down the laws, and what's the greatest evil, and then consider on that basis whether the things we were just now going over fit into the footprint of the good while they don't fit into that of the evil?"

"That most of all would be the way," he said.

"Then can we have any greater evil in a city than that which tears it apart and makes it many instead of one? Or a greater good than that which binds it together and makes it one?"

"No we can't."

"And doesn't the sharing of pleasure and pain bind it together, when as much as possible all the citizens feel joy and pain in almost

---

79   The priestess of Apollo at Delphi. Presumably the rulers would know which cases involved actual incest and avoid them, and would take her into their confidence.

the same way at the coming into being and passing away of the same things?"

"Absolutely so," he said.

"But the private appropriation of such things dissolves it, when some people become overwhelmed with pain and others overcome with joy at the same experiences of the city and of the people in the city?"

"How could it not?"   C

"And doesn't that sort of thing come from this, that people in the city don't utter such words as *mine* and *not mine* at the same time, and the same with *somebody else's*?"

"Exactly so."

"So isn't that city governed best in which the most people say this *mine* and *not mine* on the same occasion about the same things?"

"Much the best."

"And this is precisely whichever city is in a condition closest to that of a single human being?[80] For instance, whenever a finger of any of us is wounded, presumably the whole community extending from the body to the soul in a single ordering under the ruler within it would   D
be aware of it, and it all would suffer pain as a whole together with the part that's afflicted, and is that the sense in which we mean that a human being has a pain in his finger? And is it the same story for any other part of a human being whatever, both for a part afflicted with pain and for one that's eased by pleasure?"

"It's the same," he said, "and as for what you're asking, the best constituted city is the one situated closest to such a condition."

"So I imagine that when one of its citizens undergoes anything at all, good or bad, such a city most of all will claim the thing that   E
happened to him as its own, and all of it will share the pleasure or share the pain."

"Necessarily," he said, "if it's one with good laws, anyway."

"This would be the time," I said, "for us to go back to our own city, and examine in it the things agreed in the discussion, to see whether it has them the most or some other city has them more."

"We need to, don't we?" he said.

"What about it, then? There are certainly both rulers and people   463A
in other cities as well as in this one, aren't there?"

"There are."

"And won't all of these call one another citizens?"

"How could they not?"

"And in addition to 'citizens', what name do the people in other cities call their rulers by?"

---

80   The discovery that the soul has parts justified the use of a city as an analogy to it. It is the listeners' insistence that Socrates look more closely within the city that leads to this hypothesis that the kind of unity necessary within each person is also the right standard for a city. The analogy that was operative in Bks. II-IV is now being applied in reverse.

"In most of them, despots,[81] but in those that are democratically ruled, this very name, rulers."

"And what about the people in our city? In addition to citizens, what will they say their rulers are?"

"Protectors and auxiliaries," he said.

B "And what will they call the people?"

"Givers of compensation and sustenance."

"And what do the rulers in other cities call the people?"

"Slaves," he said

"What do the rulers call one another?"

"Fellow rulers," he said.

"And what about ours?"

"Fellow guardians."

"And can you say whether any of the rulers in the other cities could refer to one of his fellow rulers as his kinsman and another as an outsider?"

"In fact many do."

"And does he consider his kinsman as one of his own people and speak of him that way, and of the outsider as not one of his own?"

"In that way."

C "But what about the guardians there with you? Is there anyone at all among them who could regard or speak of any of his fellow guardians as an outsider?"

"Not at all," he said; "any time he bumps into anyone, he'll regard himself as meeting up with a brother, a sister, a father, a mother, a son, a daughter, or descendants or ancestors of these."

"You put it most beautifully," I said, "but also tell me this. Are
D you legislating only the names of kinship for them, or also the performing of all the actions that follow from the names, all the things custom calls for about respect for fathers and about taking care of parents and needing to be obedient to them, to avoid being on bad terms with gods and human beings because anyone who'd act otherwise would be doing things that aren't pious or just? Will you have these things or other ones singing around their ears straight from childhood as the common sayings coming from all the citizens about
E fathers, whomever anyone points out to them as fathers, and about their other relatives?"

"These," he said; "it would be ridiculous if they only uttered the names of kinship with their mouths, without the deeds."

"Therefore in it most of all cities, when any one person is doing well or badly, people will sound out in harmony the word we were just speaking, that what's *mine* is going well or what's *mine* is going badly."

---

81   The word *despotês* literally meant slaveholder, and was sometimes used for tyrants. People who would use that word for their king or oligarchic rulers would be acknowledging that they themselves had no power.

"Most true," he said.

"And weren't we claiming that a sharing of pleasures and pains   464A
followed along with this opinion and this word?"

"And we were right in claiming it," he said.

"Then won't our citizens most of all share the same thing in
common, the very thing they name *mine*? And by sharing that in that
way, won't they most of all have a sharing of pain and pleasure?"

"By far."

"And isn't the cause of this, in addition to the rest of the set-up,
the sharing of women and children among the guardians?"

"Most of all by a long way," he said.

"But surely we agreed that was the greatest good for a city, liken-   B
ing a well-governed city to the way a body stands in relation to the
pain and pleasure of a part of it."

"And we were right in agreeing to that," he said.

"So the cause of the greatest good for the city has been revealed to
us as the sharing of children and women among the auxiliaries."

"Very much so," he said.

"And so we're also agreeing to the things prior to that, because we
claimed, no doubt, that there had to be no private houses for them, or
land, or any possession, but they were to get their sustenance from   C
the other people as recompense for guardianship, and all consume it
in common, if they were going to be guardians in their very being."

"Rightly," he said.

"Well then, what I mean is, don't the things said before as well as
the things being said now fashion them still more into true guardians
and make them not tear apart the city by giving the name *mine* not
to the same thing but each to something different, with one of them
dragging into his own house whatever he has the power to acquire
apart from the others, and another into his own house, which is a   D
different one, and having different women and children, bringing in
private pleasures and griefs for things that are private? But with one
opinion about what's their own as they all strain toward the same
goal to the limit of their power, won't they be affected alike by pain
and pleasure?"

"Exactly so," he said.

"And what about this? Won't lawsuits and accusations against
one another virtually vanish from among them because they possess
nothing private but the body and everything else in common? And
that's why it belongs to them from the start to be free of divisions,   E
all the ones human beings divide over on account of having money,
children, and relatives."

"It's a big necessity," he said, "that they'll be freed from that."

"And there couldn't justly be any lawsuits among them even for
battery or assaults, since presumably we'll claim it's a beautiful and
just thing for anyone to defend himself against someone his own

age, which will make it necessary for them to keep their bodies in shape."

"That's right," he said.

465A   "And this custom is also right in this respect," I said: "presumably if anyone gets his spiritedness aroused against someone, he'd be less likely to come to greater divisions if he gives his angry spirit its fill in such a way."

"Quite so."

"And surely an older person will be assigned to rule over all the younger ones and correct them."

"Obviously."

"And certainly it's likely a younger person will never raise his hand to hit or do any other violence to an older one, unless the rulers order him to, and I don't imagine he'll even do any other sort of dishonor
B   to someone older, since a pair of sufficient safeguards prevent it, fear and respect, respect on the grounds that it bars him from laying a hand on parents, and fear that others would come to the defense of the one who suffered it, some as sons, some as brothers, and some as fathers."

"It does turn out that way," he said.

"So will the men keep peace with one another in every way as a result of the laws?"

"Very much so."

"And if these guardians are not at faction among themselves, there'll be no dire peril that the rest of the city will ever split into factions against them or against one another."

"No there won't."

C   "I'm reluctant even to mention, on account of their tackiness, the most petty of the evils they'd be freed from, the flatteries of the rich by the poor, the strained circumstances and all the grief they have in raising children and getting money for the necessary subsistence of the household, making debts and repudiating them, making all sorts of shifts to save money for the women and domestic slaves, to turn over to them to manage, and all the things, dear friend, they go
D   through over these things and those like them, obvious and degrading and not worthy of talking about."

"They are obvious," he said, "even to a blind person."

"So they'll be free of all these things, and they'll live a more blessedly happy life than the most blessedly happy one the Olympic champions live."

"How so?"

"Presumably the latter are considered happy on account of a small part of what belongs to these people, because the victory these people win is a more beautiful one and the provision made for them by the public is more complete.[82] For the victory they win is the preservation of the whole city, and they're crowned with the provision of food and of everything else needed for life for themselves and their children, and they receive honors from their city while they live and share in a worthy burial when they die."

"And those are beautiful things," he said.

"And do you remember," I said, "that in the earlier discussion an argument—I don't know whose[83]—reprimanded us because we weren't making the guardians happy, who, though they'd be capable of having everything that belonged to the citizens, wouldn't have anything? I believe we said that if this fell in our way anywhere, we'd consider it at a later time, but for now we were making the guardians guardians and making the city as happy as we could, but we weren't looking to one group in it and fashioning that to be happy."

"I remember," he said.

"What about it, then? If indeed the life of our auxiliaries appears as much more beautiful and better than that of Olympic champions, is there any fear of how it appears next to the life of leatherworkers or any other craftsmen or the life of farmers?"

"It doesn't seem so to me," he said.

"However, the just thing is to say here what I also said there, that if the guardian is going to try to become happy in such a way that he won't even be a guardian, and a life so measured and steady, that's also, as we're claiming, best, won't satisfy him, but he falls into a senseless and juvenile opinion about happiness that will drive him to taking everything in the city for his own by means of his power, he'll know that Hesiod was wise in his being when he said that there's a way in which 'the half is more than the whole.'"[84]

"If he asks my advice," he said, "he'll stay in this life."

"Do you go along, then," I said, "with the partnership of the women with the men, which we've gone over, in their education, with their children, and in guarding the other citizens, and agree that, both when they're staying in the city and when they're going to war, they need to guard and hunt together the way dogs do, and share everything in common in every way as far as is in their power, and that in so doing they'll be acting in the best way and not contrary to the nature of the female in relation to the male, in the way the pair is naturally fitted to share things in common with each other?"

---

82 Athletes at the Olympic games represented their cities, and the winners were given meals at public expense all their lives.

83 This would direct everyone's attention to Adeimantus, but it also softens the blow when Socrates says what he thinks of such an opinion just below. To some degree, the reproach would probably be felt by all the listeners.

84 *Works and Days,* line 40. Socrates echoes the words of Glaucon in 362A. The word for "more" is also the one that Thrasymachus constantly used in Bk. I, when he was claiming that more is always better.

"I go along with that," he said.

"Then doesn't this remain to be determined," I said, "whether after all it's possible among human beings too, the way it is among other animals, for this partnership to come about, and in what way it's possible?"

"You beat me to it," he said, "by saying what I was just about to bring up."

E

"As for what's involved in war," I said, "I imagine the manner in which they'll go to war is obvious."

"How's that?" he said.

"They'll take the field in common, and besides, they'll bring as many of the children to the war as are tough, so that, just like the children of the other craftsmen, they'll see the things they'll need to

467A   do to work at the craft when they're grown up. And in addition to watching, they'll help out and take subordinate roles in all the things that have to do with war, and tend to the needs of their fathers and mothers. Or haven't you noticed what happens with the arts, for instance with the children of potters, how long a time they spend watching as helpers before taking a hand at making pots?"

"Very much so."

"Is it necessary for them to educate their children more carefully than the guardians do theirs by experience and observation of the things that concern them?"

"That would be totally ridiculous," he said.

B

"And certainly every animal fights in an exceptional way in the presence of its young."

"That is so, but Socrates, there's no small risk, for those who've been defeated, and that sort of thing is apt to happen in war, that they'll have lost the children in addition to themselves and make it impossible for the rest of the city to recover."

"What you say is true," I said; "but first of all, do you think one ought to arrange things so as never to run any risks?"

"By no means."

"Well what about it then? If it's necessary to take a risk, shouldn't it be one in which they'll be better off when they succeed?"

"Obviously."

C

"Well do you imagine it makes little difference, and isn't worth a risk, whether or not children who're going to be competent men at warfare watch the things involved in war?"

"No, it makes a difference for what you're talking about."

"Then this is the way one needs to start out, by making the children observers of war, and if some additional means of safety is devised for them, things will go well, won't they?"

"Yes."

"And first of all," I said, "their fathers won't be ignorant, will they, but knowledgeable in every way human beings can be about all the things on campaigns that are dangerous or not?"

"Likely so," he said.

"So they'll take them to the latter and be wary of the former."   D

"That's right."

"And presumably as rulers," I said, "they'll set over them people who are no slouches but are qualified by experience and age to be leaders and tutors."

"That's fitting."

"But, we'll claim, many things also turn out for many people contrary to expectation."

"Very much so."

"So with a view to such things, my friend, it behooves us to give them wings right away while they're little children, so that if there's any need they'll escape by flying away."

"How do you mean?" he said.

"They need to be mounted on horseback," I said, "as young as pos-   E sible, and once they've been taught to ride they need to be brought to the sight on horses, not on spirited or aggressive ones, but on horses as swift of foot and docile as possible. Thus, in the most beautiful way, they'll get a look at the work that belongs to them, and in the safest way, if there's any need, they'll save themselves by following after older leaders."

"You seem to me to be getting it right," he said.   468A

"And what about what's involved in war?" I said. "How should your soldiers bear themselves toward one another and toward enemies? Is the way that seems evident to me the right one or not?"

"Say what it's like," he said.

"If one of them leaves his post," I said, "or throws down his weapons or does anything of the sort out of cowardice, doesn't he need to be reassigned as some sort of craftsman or farmer?"

"Very much so."

"And if one of them is taken alive by the enemy, shouldn't he be given as a gift to his captors, to use their catch however they   B want?"

"Exactly."

"But if someone shows the highest distinction and gains a good reputation, doesn't it seem to you that first, on the campaign, he should be crowned with wreaths by his fellow soldiers, and by each of the youths and children in turn? Or not?"

"That seems good to me."

"And what about shaking his hand?"

"That too."

"But I don't imagine this too would seem good to you," I said.

"What's that?"

"That he kiss and be kissed by each."

"That most of all," he said. "And I have an addendum to the law,
C   that as long as they're on that campaign, no one he wants to kiss be
allowed to refuse him, so that if someone happens to be in love with
anyone, male or female, he'd be more zealous to carry off the highest
honors."

"Beautiful," I said. "Because it's already been said that marriages
will be more readily arranged for someone good than for others,
and selections of such people will be more frequent, beyond the
others, in order that the most children possible will be born of such
a person."

"We did say that," he said.

"And surely even according to Homer, it's just to do honor in
D   such ways to all those among the young who are good. For Homer
also said that, when he gained a good reputation in war, 'Ajax was
rewarded with the whole back of the ox,'[85] as if the appropriate honor
for someone bursting with youth and courage was that by which he'd
be honored and at the same time grow in strength."

"Most rightly," he said.

"So we'll be persuaded by Homer," I said, "at least about these
things. For we'll honor good people at the sacrifices and at all such
occasions, to the extent they've shown themselves good, both with
E   hymns and with the things we were just now speaking of, and on top
of that 'with choice seats and meats and full wine cups,' so that along
with honoring them we'll be forming good men and women."

"You're speaking most beautifully," he said.

"Okay. Now if any of those who die on the campaign meets his
death in a way that gains him a good reputation, won't we first declare
him to be of the golden race?"

"Most of all."

"And won't we be persuaded by Hesiod that when any people
469A   of such a race die,

> They become consecrated as holy divinities on earth,
> Good guardians, warding off evil from humans endowed
>   with speech?"[86]

"We'll be persuaded."

"Therefore, after finding out from the god[87] how one ought to bury
divinities and godlike people and with what mark of distinction, won't
we also bury them in whatever way that he prescribes?"

"Why wouldn't we?"

---

85   *Iliad* VII, 321. The quotation in Socrates' next speech is VIII, 162.

86   This is clearly a quotation of *Works and Days* 122-123, but Hesiod wrote (about people who
lived in a past golden age), "They are divinities by the will of great Zeus,/ Good guardians on
earth for mortal humans."

87   That is, by consulting the priestess of Apollo at Delphi. See 427B-C.

"And for the rest of time, won't we care for their tombs and wor- **B**
ship at them as at those of divinities? And won't we follow these same
observances when any of those judged to have been surpassingly good
in their lives die, of old age or in any other manner?"

"It would be just, at any rate," he said.

"And what about this? How will our soldiers deal with their
enemies?"

"In what respect in particular?"

"In the first place, in respect to taking slaves, does it seem just for
Greek cities to take Greeks as slaves, or as far as possible not even
to leave them for another city to take, but to get them in the habit of
sparing the Greek race as a precaution against enslavement by the **C**
barbarians?"

"Sparing them is wholly and totally better," he said.

"Therefore they won't possess a Greek slave themselves, and
they'll give that advice to the other Greeks?"

"Very much so," he said; "at least that way they'd turn against the
barbarians instead, and hold off from their own kind."

"And what about stripping the dead of anything except weapons?" I said. "When they win a victory, is that a desirable practice?
Or doesn't it offer a pretext for cowards not to go up against someone
who's fighting, on the grounds that they're performing one of their **D**
duties when they keep stooping down around a dead body, though
many an army has been destroyed before now by such rapacity?"

"Quite so."

"Doesn't it seem unbefitting a free person and a moneygrubbing
thing to strip a corpse, and a sign of a womanish and petty way of
thinking to consider as the enemy the body of a dead opponent who
has fluttered away, leaving behind that with which he made war? Or
do you suppose those who do this are behaving any differently from **E**
dogs that take out their anger on the rocks thrown at them but don't
touch the one throwing them?"

"Not even a little differently," he said.

"Therefore one should give up stripping corpses and preventing
their recovery?"

"One should certainly give it up, by Zeus," he said.

"And no doubt we won't bring the captured weapons, and especially not those of Greeks, to the temples as offerings, if we have any
consideration for the good will of the rest of the Greeks. Instead, we'd **470A**
be afraid it would be a pollution to bring such things to the temple
from our own people, unless the god particularly says something
different."

"Quite rightly," he said.

"And what about ravaging Greek land and setting fire to the
houses? Will your soldiers do anything of that sort to their enemies?"

"I'd listen with pleasure," he said, "if you revealed your opinion."

B   "Well, it seems good to me," I said, "for them to do neither of these things, but to take away the year's crops. Do you want me to tell you why?"

"Very much indeed."

"It appears to me that war and civil war are two different things, just like these two names they're called by, which apply to two kinds of division in two respective things. The two things I mean are, on the one hand, one's own kind and kin, and on the other, what's foreign and alien. Civil war is the name applied to hostility within one's own kind, and war applies to hostility between foreigners."

"And there's certainly nothing off course about what you're saying," he said.

C   "Then see if I'm also on course when I say this: I claim that the Greek race is itself with itself its own kind and kin, but alien and foreign to a barbarian race."

"Beautifully on course," he said.

"Therefore when Greeks fight with barbarians and barbarians with Greeks we'll claim they're at war and are natural enemies, and that this hostility of theirs should be called war, but whenever Greeks do

D   anything of the sort to Greeks we'll claim they're natural friends, but in such circumstances Greece is sick and divided, and that this sort of hostility should be called civil war."

"I go along with regarding it that way," he said.

"Consider, then," I said, "that in the sort of civil war now acknowledged as such, wherever any such thing happens and a city is split apart, if each of the two sides ravages the land and burns the houses of the other, civil war is held to be an abomination and neither of the sides is considered loyal to the city, or they would never have dared to devastate their nurse and mother. But it seems to be within measure

E   for those who prevail to take away the crops from those they defeat, and to think of themselves as people who are going to be reconciled and not always be at war."

"This way of thinking is far more civilized than that other," he said.

"What about it, then?" I said. "Won't the city you're founding[88] be Greek?"

"It's bound to be," he said.

"And won't the people be good and civilized?"

"Emphatically so."

---

88   At 461E Socrates called the city Glaucon's, and his wording here strengthens that way of speaking. It is as if the content of Bk. V has made Socrates less willing to claim the city as his own.

"But won't they be loyal to all things Greek? Won't they regard Greece as their own place and participate in religious observances in common with the rest of the Greeks?"

"Emphatically so on that point too."

"Then won't they regard a division with Greeks, since it's with their own people, as civil war and not even name it merely war?"

471A

"That's right."

"So they'll have their divisions in the spirit of people who're going to be reconciled?"

"Very much so."

"So they'll bring their opponents back to their senses and not punish them with slavery or destruction, not being enemies but people intent on inducing moderation."

"That's the way," he said.

"Therefore, being Greeks, they won't devastate Greece, or set fire to houses, and they won't agree with anyone who says that everyone in any city is their enemy—the men, women, and children—but hold that a few enemies are always the ones responsible for the division. For all these reasons they won't be willing to devastate their land, since most of them are friendly, or to knock down their houses, but they'll maintain the conflict up to that point at which the responsible parties are forced to pay the penalty by the guiltless people who're suffering from it."

B

"I agree," he said, "that this is how our citizens ought to conduct themselves toward their opponents, but toward the barbarians they should act the way Greeks do now toward one another."

"So shall we also impose this as a law on the guardians, not to ravage land or burn houses?"

C

"Let's impose it," he said, "and certainly these things and the ones that preceded them are all well and good, but it seems to me, Socrates, that if anyone left it to you to discuss this sort of thing you'd never remember what was pushed aside before you'd mentioned all this, the question of whether it's possible for this type of polity to come into being and in what way it would ever be possible. Because I certainly grant that if it were to come into being, everything in the city in which it came into being would be good, even things you're leaving out; I mean that they'd also fight their enemies best because they'd desert each other least, since they recognize their own troops as brothers, fathers, and sons and call to them by these names. And also if the female group were in combat along with them, either in the ranks themselves or drawn up in the rear, both to frighten the enemy and in case any need for assistance should arise, I know that with all this they'd be people no one could fight. And I see all the good things at home that would be to their benefit. But since I agree that there would be all these things and tens of thousands of others if this polity were to come into being, don't keep saying more about that, but let's try

D

E

from this point on to persuade ourselves of this very thing, that it's possible and in what way, and let the rest go with our blessings."

472A   "This is so sudden," I said. "It's as though you've launched an attack on my argument, and have no tolerance for me to squeeze out its last drops. Maybe you don't realize that when I've hardly escaped a pair of waves you're now bringing on the biggest and most crushing third wave; when you see and hear it, you'll have complete sympathy, understanding that it was fitting after all that I was hesitant and fearful to state and undertake the examination of an argument so contrary to general opinion."

B   "The more you say that sort of thing," he said, "the less you'll be let off by us from saying how it's possible for this polity to come into being. Just speak and don't waste any more time."

"Well then," I said, "isn't this the first thing that should be recalled, that it's because we were seeking what sorts of things justice and injustice are that we got to this point?"

"It should, but what about it?" he said.

"Nothing; except, if we find out what sort of thing justice is, will we also hold that the just man needs to be no different from that very thing, but be in every respect of the same sort that justice is? Or will we be satisfied if he's as close to it as possible and participates in it the most in comparison with other people?"

"The latter," he said. "We'll be satisfied."

"Then it was for the sake of a pattern," I said, "that we were seeking both what sort of thing justice itself is, and the completely just man, in case one could come into being, and what he'd be like if he were to come into being, as well as injustice and the most unjust man, so that by looking off toward them to see what they appear to us to be like in relation to happiness and its opposite, we'd be constrained to agree about our own selves as well, that whoever was most similar to them would have a lot in life most similar to theirs. But it wasn't for the sake of our demonstrating that it was possible for these things to come into being."

"That's true, as you say," he said.

"Do you imagine someone would be any less good a painter, who had painted a pattern of what the most beautiful human being would be like, and had rendered everything in the picture well enough, because he wasn't able to show that it was also possible for such a man to come into being?"

"Not I, by Zeus," he said.

"Well then, don't we claim that we too were making a pattern in speech of a good city?"

E   "Certainly."

"Then do you imagine we're describing it any less well on that account if we're not able to demonstrate that it's possible to found a city that's the way we were describing it?"

"Surely not," he said.

"So that's the way the truth of it is," I said; "but if it's also necessary for this effort to be made for your pleasure, to demonstrate in what way most of all and as a result of what it would be most possible, then you, the same as me, should make some concessions in return for such a demonstration."

"What sort of concessions?"

"Is it possible for anything to be done in practice the way it's described in speech, or does action have a nature to attain to truth less than speaking does, even if it doesn't seem that way to somebody? But do *you* agree or not that it's that way?"

473A

"I agree," he said.

"Then don't require this of me, to be obliged to represent the sorts of things we went through in speech as coming into being in every respect in deed as well, but if we turn out to be able to discover that a city could be founded that's closest to the things described, then declare that we've found out that it's possible for these things to come into being the way you ordered us to. Or will you not be satisfied if that happens? I'd be satisfied."

B

"I would too," he said.

"Then it looks like the next thing for us to do is try to search out and demonstrate whatever is now done badly in cities, on account of which they aren't managed this way, and what would be the smallest change by which a city could come into this mode of political association—preferably a change of one thing, or if not that, of two, and if not that, of as few things as possible in number and the smallest in strength."

"Absolutely so," he said.

C

"Well with one change," I said, "it seems to me we can show that it could be transformed, though it's not a small or easy one, but it is possible."

"What's that?" he said.

"I'm in for it now," I said, "up against what we likened to the biggest wave. But it's got to be said, even if, literally just like an uproarious wave, it's going to drown me in laughter and humiliation. Consider what I'm about to say."

"Say it," he said.

"Unless philosophers rule as kings in their cities," I said, "or those now called kings and supreme rulers genuinely and adequately engage in philosophy, and this combination of political power and philosophy joins together in the same position, while the many natures that are now carried away to one of the two in isolation are forcibly blocked off from that, there is no rest from evils for the cities, dear Glaucon, or, I think, for the human race, and this polity that we've now gone over in speech will never before that sprout as far as it can and see the light of the sun. This is what's been putting a reluctance

D

E

to speak in me all this time, my seeing that it would be proclaimed to be far beyond belief, because it's hard to see that in no other way would anyone be happy in private, or any city in public."

And he said, "Oh, Socrates, what a thing you've blurted out, both the words and the meaning! Now that you've said it, you can expect a great many people after you this very instant, and no slouches, flinging off their cloaks, stripped down, grabbing up whatever weapon happens to be near each one, running full speed, ready to do amazing things. If you don't fend them off with arguments and get away, you'll pay the penalty by being well and truly ridiculed."

474A

"And don't I have you to thank for this?" I said.

"And I'm doing a beautiful job of it," he said. "But I won't give you up for lost; I'll defend you with the means in my power. And I have the power to help out with good will and by cheering you on, and maybe I'd give you replies in a more harmonious spirit than someone else would. So since you have such help, try to show the doubters that things are the way you say."

B

"The attempt has to be made," I said, "especially since you offer so formidable an alliance. Now it seems necessary to me, if we're somehow going to dodge the people you speak of, to define for them what we mean by philosophers when we have the audacity to claim they ought to rule, so that once it becomes thoroughly clear, one will have the power to defend oneself by showing that it's fitting by nature for them both to engage in philosophy and to take the lead in a city, and for everyone else not to engage in it and to follow a leader."

C

"This would be the time to define them," he said.

"Come then, and follow me here, if we're somehow or other going to explain it fittingly."

"Lead on," he said.

"Then will it be necessary to remind you," I said, "or do you remember that when we claim someone loves something, if it's being said correctly, it has to be clear that he doesn't love part of it and part not, but is devoted to it all?"

"It's necessary to remind me, it seems," he said, "since I have no recollection of it at all."

D

"It would be fitting for someone else to say what you're saying, Glaucon," I said, "but it's not fitting for an erotic man to be unmindful of the fact that all those in their first flowering in one way or another sting and arouse an erotic lover of boys, and seem to be worth paying attention to and giving a warm welcome. Don't you people behave that way toward the beautiful? One, because he's snub-nosed, is praised by you by being called adorable, and the hooked nose of another you folks claim is kingly, while you claim the one in the middle compared to them has proportion; you claim the dark ones look manly and the pale ones are children of the gods, and do you imagine the name "honeychild" is anything but a product of a baby-talking lover who

E

finds a yellowish complexion easy to take if it's in the flowering of
youth? And in a word, you folks make every excuse and come out   475A
with any utterance so as not to reject anyone blossoming in the first
prime of life."

"If you want to pin it on me," he said, "to talk about the way erotic
people behave, I go along with it for the sake of the argument."

"And what about wine-lovers," I said; "don't you see them
doing these same things and welcoming every sort of wine on any
excuse?"

"Very much so."

"And surely you notice, I assume, that lovers of honor, if they
can't become generals, are lieutenants, and if they can't be honored
by grander and more prestigious people, are content with being
honored by lesser and more ordinary ones, since they're desirous of   B
honor as a whole."

"Exactly."

"Then affirm this or deny it: when we speak of someone as desiring something, will we claim he desires all of that form, or part of it
and part not?"

"All of it," he said.

"Then won't we claim the philosopher too is a desirer of wisdom,
not of part of it and part not, but of all of it?"

"That's true."

"Therefore if someone's picky about the things he learns, especially when he's young and doesn't yet have a rational account of   C
what is or isn't useful, we'll claim that he's no lover of learning and
not philosophic, just as we'd claim that someone who's picky about
his food isn't hungry, doesn't desire food, and isn't a food-lover but
a bad eater."

"And we'll be right in claiming it."

"But in justice, we'll claim that person who's readily willing to
taste everything learnable and goes toward learning gladly and in
an insatiable spirit is a philosopher, won't we?"

And Glaucon said, "Then many strange people will be like that   D
according to you. Because all those who love sights seem to me to be
that way, since they take delight in studying them, and those who
love listening are some of the strangest people to include among philosophers; they wouldn't be willing to go voluntarily to discussions or
any such way of passing the time, but just as if they'd hired out their
ears for listening, they run around to all the choruses at the festivals of
Dionysus,[89] not missing any of those in the cities or in the villages. Are

---

89   Festivals held throughout the winter and early spring in Athens and its environs at which
comedies and tragedies were staged. This reference might remind the reader that those passing
the time at this discussion will have already missed the torchlight spectacle at the festival of
Bendis.

E

we going to claim that all these and everyone else devoted to learning such things and to the superficial arts are philosophers?"

"Not at all," I said, "just that they're like philosophers."

"And who do you say are the true ones?" he said.

"The lovers of the sight of the truth," I said.

"And that would be right," he said, "but how do you mean it?"

"Not in any way that's easy to explain to someone else," I said; "but I imagine you'll grant me something like this."

"Like what?"

476A

"That since beautiful is the opposite of ugly, the pair of them[90] are two."

"How could that not be so?"

"And since they're two, each of them is also one?"

"That too."

"And it's the same story with just and unjust, and good and bad, and with all the forms:[91] each of them itself is one, but since they make their appearance everywhere in common with actions and bodies and one another, each appears to be many."

"You're putting it correctly," he said.

"That's the way I make the distinction, then," I said: "on one side the lovers of sights, the lovers of the arts, and the practical people you were just speaking of, and on the other side the people our discussion is about, the only ones anybody could rightly call philosophers."

B

"How do you mean?" he said.

"Presumably," I said, "the lovers of listening and of sights devote themselves to beautiful sounds and colors and shapes and everything crafted out of such things, but their thinking is incapable of seeing and devoting itself to the nature of the beautiful itself."

"That's exactly how it is," he said.

"But wouldn't those who are capable of getting to and seeing the beautiful itself, by itself, be rare?"

"Very much so."

C

"But if someone believes there are beautiful things, but doesn't believe in beauty itself, and isn't capable of following if anyone leads him up to the knowledge of it, does he seem to you to be living in a dream or awake? Just consider; isn't it dreaming when anyone,

---

90   This is the third person dual pronoun (*autô*). Formulations to the effect "each is one and both together (*amphoterô*) are two" occur repeatedly in Plato's dialogues, for example at *Theaetetus* 185B. There, as here, the context of the remark is an approach to the central presupposition that distinguishes philosophic learning from all other kinds, the conviction that knowledge and opinion are different in kind. The relevance to that distinction of knowing how to count up to two returns to the dialogue both playfully and seriously in 522C, where the following discussion uncovers a capacity of the soul higher than reasoning, much as a part of the soul between reasoning and desire was uncovered in Bk. IV.

91   The word form (*eidos*) is now used for the first time in the dialogue with the precise sense spelled out just below: the invisible look by which thinking can grasp an intelligible thing itself.

whether in sleep or waking, believes a likeness to something isn't a likeness but is the thing itself that it seems like?"

"I at least would claim that such a person is dreaming," he said.

"And what about the opposite of that, when someone believes there is a beautiful itself and is capable of catching sight of it as well as of the things that participate in it, and doesn't think it *is* the things that participate or that the things that participate are *it*—does *he* seem to you to be living a waking life or a dream?"

D

"Very much a waking life," he said.

"Then since he's discerning something, wouldn't we be right in claiming that this person's thinking is knowledge, while that of the other person is opinion, since he's accepting the seeming?"[92]

"Very much so."

"Then what if the latter, who we claim is accepting a seeming but not discerning anything, gets rough with us, and contends that we're not telling the truth? Will we be able to calm him down in any way and persuade him gently, concealing the fact that he's not in a healthy condition?"

E

"We'll certainly have to do exactly that," he said.

"Come on then, and consider what we're going to say to him. Or do you want us to do it this way, to ask him questions, telling him that no one will begrudge it if he does know anything, but we'd be glad to see that he knows something? But tell us this: does someone who does discern discern something or nothing? Let's have you answer me on his behalf."

"I'll answer that he discerns something," he said.

"Something that is or is not?"

"Something that is. For how could anything that *is not* be discerned?"

477A

"Then even if we might consider it in more ways, have we got this sufficiently, that what completely *is* is completely knowable, while what is not is unknowable in any way at all?"

"Quite sufficiently."

"Okay; now if there is a way for something both to be and not be, wouldn't it lie between what *is* purely and simply and what in no way is?"

"Between."

---

92   The word used here for knowledge (*gnômê*) is the root of the verb translated as "discern" (*gignôskein*), implying a grasping of something by evidence. The verb translated "accept the seeming" (*doxazein*) is built on the word for opinion (*doxa*) and related to the word used constantly to mean "it seems" (*dokein*). Discernment is what Socrates implied in Bk. I that Thrasymachus lacked (347D). It goes beyond a merely passive relation to appearances, and is a step toward knowing in the unqualified sense (*eidenai*), a verb Socrates will begin to use just below. None of this is technical jargon; it is vivid, shared, ordinary speech, evoking familiar experiences. For that reason, the precision in the intricate stretch of argument about to begin is not merely verbal or logical, but is itself a potential step toward knowing.

B

"Then since knowledge applied to what is, and what applied to what is not was by necessity ignorance, doesn't one need to look for something in between ignorance and knowledge, if there happens to be any such thing, to apply to this in-between kind?"

"Very much so."

"Don't we say opinion is something?"

"How could it not be?"

"A capacity different from knowledge, or the same?"

"Different."

"Therefore opinion is directed at one thing and knowledge at another, each in accord with its own capacity."

"That's the way it is."

"And doesn't knowledge naturally apply to what is, to discern the way what *is* is? But it seems to me to be necessary instead to make a distinction in this way first."

"How so?"

C

"We'll assert that capacities are a certain class of beings by which we, and everything else that might have any power, have the power to do what we're capable of; I'm speaking of sight and hearing, for example, as being among the capacities, if that lets you understand what the form is that I mean to describe."

"I do understand," he said.

"Then hear what appears to me about them. In a capacity I don't see any color or shape or any of the many other things of that sort that

D

I look to when I distinguish for myself that some are one thing and others another. In a capacity I look only at what it's directed to and what it accomplishes, and by that I call each of them a capacity, and that which is directed at the same thing and accomplishes the same thing I call the same capacity, while I call that which is directed at something different and accomplishes something different a different capacity. What about you? What do you do?"

"The same," he said.

"Then direct yourself here again, most excellent fellow," I said. "Do you claim that knowledge is some sort of capacity, or what class do you put it in?"

E

"In this one," he said, "as, in fact, the most potent of all capacities."

"And what about opinion? Is it in with capacities or shall we carry it over to another form?"

"Not at all," he said, "since opinion is nothing other than that by which we're capable of accepting a seeming."

"But just a little while ago you agreed that knowledge and opinion aren't the same."

"How could anyone with any sense," he said, "ever posit that something infallible is the same as something not infallible?"

"A beautiful point," I said, "and it's clear that it's agreed by us   478A
that opinion is something different from knowledge."

"It's a different thing."

"Therefore, since each of them is a different capacity, each is of
such a nature as to be directed at something different?"

"Necessarily."

"And knowledge is presumably directed at what is, to discern the
way what *is* is?"

"Yes."

"And we claim opinion accepts a seeming"

"Yes."

"Is that the same thing that knowledge discerns? And will the
same thing be both knowable and a matter of opinion? Or is that
impossible?"

"It's impossible," he said, "based on the things that have been
agreed; if indeed a different capacity is of such a nature as to be
directed at something different, and the pair of them together are
capacities, opinion and knowledge, and each of them a different   B
capacity, as we claim, then based on these things, there's no room for
what's knowable and what's a matter of opinion to be the same."

"Then if what's knowable is what is, what's a matter of opinion
would be something other than what is?"

"Something other."

"Then does one accept a seeming of what is not? Or is it impossible
at any rate for what is not even to have a seeming? Think about it.
Doesn't someone who accepts a seeming refer his opinion to something? Or is it possible to accept a seeming when there's nothing to
accept a seeming of?"

"It's impossible."

"But someone who accepts a seeming accepts a seeming of some
one thing?"

"Yes."

"But surely what is not would not be spoken of in the most correct
way as some one thing but as nothing?"   C

"Certainly."

"And by necessity, we assigned ignorance to what is not, and
knowledge to what is?"

"Rightly," he said.

"Therefore one doesn't accept a seeming of what is or of what is
not?"

"No."

"And therefore opinion would be neither ignorance nor knowledge?"

"It seems not."

"So then is it outside these, surpassing either knowledge in clarity
or ignorance in absence of clarity?"

"Neither."

"But then," I said, "does it appear to you that opinion is something darker than knowledge but brighter than ignorance?"

"Very much indeed," he said.

D   "And it lies inside the pair of them?"

"Yes."

"Therefore opinion would be in between this pair?"

"Exactly so."

"Well, weren't we claiming in the earlier discussion that if anything would come to light as a sort of thing that is and is not at the same time, such a thing would lie between what *is* purely and simply and what in every way *is not*, and that neither knowledge nor ignorance would be directed at it, but instead something that came to light as between ignorance and knowledge?"

"Rightly so."

"And now the very thing we call opinion has come to light in between this pair?"

"It has come to light."

E   "So what would be left, it seems, is for us to find that thing that participates in both being and not being, and isn't rightly referred to in either way purely and simply, so that if it comes to light, we could in justice refer to it as being what opinion is about, assigning the extremes to the extremes and the in-betweens to the in-betweens. Isn't that the way it is?"

"That's the way."

"So with these things as a foundation, let him tell me, I'll say, and 479A   let him give an answer, that good fellow who believes there isn't any beautiful itself or any sort of form of beauty itself that's always the same in the same respects, but does believe in the many beautiful things, that lover of sights who doesn't stand for it in any way when anyone claims that the beautiful is a single thing, or the just, or the other things like that. 'Now, most excellent fellow,' we'll say, 'is there any of these many beautiful things that won't also show itself to be ugly? Or any of the just things that's not unjust? Or any of the pious things that's not impious?'"

"No," he said, "it's necessary for them to show themselves as both B   beautiful and ugly in some way, and for all the other things you're asking about as well."

"And what about the many double-sized things? Do they show themselves any the less as halves than as doubles?"

"Not that either."

"And things that we'll claim are big or little, and light or heavy— will these names be applied to them any more than their opposites will?"

"No," he said, "but each of them will always have a share of both."

"So is each of the many things that which anyone claims it is more than it isn't that?"

"It's like the plays on words at dinner parties," he said, "and the children's riddle, the one about the eunuch, about throwing something at a bat, and they make a riddle out of what he threw and what it was on.[93] Because these many things too have double meanings, and it's not possible to think of any of them in a fixed way as being or not being, or as both or neither."

"Do you have any way you can handle them then," I said, "or any more beautiful place where you could put them than in between being, proper, and not being? Because presumably nothing will show itself to be darker than what *is not* in order to not-be more than it, or brighter than being in order to *be* more."

"Most true," he said.

"Then it seems we've made the discovery that the many things most people customarily believe about what's beautiful and the other things are rolling around between what *is not* and what *is* purely and simply."

"We've made that discovery."

"And we agreed beforehand that if any such thing would come to light, it would need to be said that it's what opinion is about but isn't knowable, a wandering, in-between thing captured by the in-between capacity."

"We are in agreement."

"Then as for those who gaze upon many beautiful things but don't see the beautiful itself, and aren't even capable of following someone else who leads them to it, and upon many just things but not the just itself, and all the things like that, we'll claim that they accept the seeming of everything but discern nothing of what they have opinions about."

"Necessarily," he said.

"And what in turn about those who gaze upon each of the things themselves, that are always the same in the same respects? Won't we claim that they discern them and don't have opinion about them?"

"That too is necessary."

"And won't we also claim that these people devote themselves to and love those things at which knowledge is directed, while the former devote themselves to and love those things at which opinion is directed? Or do we not recall that we claimed they love and gaze upon beautiful sounds and colors and that sort of thing, but can't stand for the beautiful itself to be anything?"

C

D

E

480A

---

93 "A man and not a man saw and didn't see a bird and not a bird on a stick and not a stick and threw and didn't throw at it a rock and not a rock." The eunuch had bad eyesight, the bat was on a reed, the rock was a piece of pumice, and the throw missed.

"We remember."

"So we won't be hitting any false note in calling them lovers of opinion rather than lovers of wisdom? And will they get violently angry with us if we speak of them that way?"

"Not if they're persuaded by me," he said, "since no one has a right to be angry with the truth."

"Therefore those who devote themselves to each thing itself that *is* ought to be called philosophers and not lovers of opinion?"

"Beyond a shadow of a doubt."

BOOK VI

Note

When Socrates and Glaucon have agreed that any genuine philosopher has all the virtues and is perfectly suited to rule a city, Adeimantus speaks up once again on behalf of popular opinion. Socrates gradually persuades Adeimantus that the popular prejudice against philosophy results from experience with two types of impostors, those who pretend to know how to manage political life without philosophy, and those who pretend to practice it. But the genuine philosopher must study something that transcends justice, by which it and all human life are governed and illuminated. Even an indirect approach to that study is demanding, and Glaucon returns to the discussion as Socrates offers two of the most famous images in the dialogue, inviting the use of two different kinds of imagination, the sun and the divided line. These two prepare the way for a third image that begins the following book, which will complete Socrates' central exposition of what philosophy is and why it is inescapably needed.

"So the philosophers, **Glaucon**," I said, "and those who aren't   484A
philosophers, have shown up in a certain respect for who they each
are, now that we've gone through some long discussion with a lot
of effort."

"Well," he said, "it probably wouldn't be easy to do with a short
one."

"It appears not," I said. "Anyway, it seems to me they could be
brought to light in a still better way if it were only about this that it
was necessary to speak, and one didn't need to go through the many   B
things that remain for someone who's going to get a clear sight of the
way a just life differs from an unjust one."

"What's after this for us, then?" he said.

"What else but what comes next?" I said. "Since those capable of
reaching what's always the same in the same respects are philosophers, while those who aren't, but are in a shifting condition as they
wander among the many things, are not philosophers, which of them
ought to be leaders of a city?"

"How should we state it," he said, "if we were to speak in a measured[94] way?"

---

94   Glaucon appears to want to hedge his answer the way a practical person would, rather
than displaying the erotic desire for truth that Socrates attributed to his nature (474C–475C).

"That whichever sort show themselves capable of safeguarding the laws and practices of cities," I said, "are the ones to appoint as guardians."

"That's right," he said.

C "And is this clear too," I said, "whether a blind person or one who has sharp sight ought to watch over anything as its guardian?"

"How could that not be clear?" he said.

"Well, do they seem any different from blind people, those who are lacking in knowledge of what each thing is in its being, who have no clear pattern in the soul and no capacity to look off, the way painters do, to what's truest, constantly referring back to there and contemplating it with as much precision as possible, so that here too D lawful practices involving what's beautiful and just and good may be established if they need to be established, while they also watch over the ones that are in place in order to preserve them?"

"No, by Zeus," he said, "they aren't much different at all."

"Then are those the people we're going to set up as guardians, rather than the ones who've discerned each thing that is, without being left behind them in experience either, or lagging in any other part of virtue?"

"It would surely be strange to choose other people," he said, "so long as these weren't left behind in the other respects, since they'd stand out in that very thing that's just about the most important one."

485A "Then shouldn't we explain this, the way in which the same people will be able to possess both the one and the other sort of attributes?"

"Very much so."

"What we were saying when we started this discussion is that it's necessary first to get a clear understanding of their nature, and I imagine that if we agree sufficiently about that, we'll also agree that it's possible for the same people to possess these attributes, and that nobody other than these people ought to be leaders of cities."

"How so?"

B "Let this be agreed to by us about the natures of philosophers, that they always have an erotic desire for what can be learned that reveals to them any of the being that always *is* and doesn't wander around under the sway of coming to be and passing away."

"Let it be agreed."

"And also," I said, "that they desire all of it, and don't willingly give up any part of it, small or larger, or more honored or less, just as we were going over before about lovers of honor and erotic lovers."

"You're putting it rightly," he said.

"Then consider after that, whether it's necessary for those who're C going to be the sort of people we were describing to have in their nature this attribute as well as that one."

"What's that?"

"An aversion to falsehood,[95] and never to be willing to accept what's false, but to hate it and love truth."

"Likely so," he said.

"It's not just likely, my friend, but entirely necessary for someone of an erotic nature to love everything akin to and at home with his beloved."

"That's right," he said.

"Well, could you find anything more at home with wisdom than truth?"

"How could that be?" he said.

"So is the same nature capable of being a lover of wisdom and a lover of falsehood?"   D

"By no means."

"Therefore the one who's a lover of learning in his very being has to stretch out toward all truth straight from youth as much as possible."

"In its entirety."

"But we're surely aware that for anyone whose desires incline strongly to one thing, they're no doubt weaker for things other than that, as if they were a stream that's been channeled off in that direction."

"Surely so."

"So in the person in whom they've flowed toward what's learnable and everything of that sort, I imagine they'd be concerned with the pleasure of the soul itself, by itself, and would pass by those that come through the body, if he's not pretending to be a philosopher   E
but truly is one."

"That's a big necessity."

"Then certainly such a person would be moderate and in no way a lover of money, because money and extravagant spending are taken seriously for the sake of things that it behooves anyone else but this person to be eager for."

"That's how it is."

"And here's something it's no doubt also necessary to consider   486A
when you're going to judge a nature as philosophic or not."

"What's that?"

"That you don't overlook whether it has its share of pettiness, since a focus on inconsequential things is presumably what's most contrary to a soul that's intent on constantly reaching out toward the whole that comprises all of what's divine and human together."

"Most true," he said.

---

95   Is this in conflict with the need to go along with the noble lie of 414B-C and the abundance of falsehoods and deceptions mentioned at 459C-D, or does it perhaps determine the difference between those things and the true lie described in 382A-B? This may not be easy to decide.

"When someone's thinking has a grandeur to it, and a contemplation of all time and of all being, do you imagine human life could possibly seem to be anything greatly important?"

"Impossible," he said.

B "Then such a person also won't regard death as a terrible thing?"

"Not in the least."

"Then in a cowardly and petty nature, the way it looks, there'd be no trace of genuine philosophy."

"It doesn't seem that way to me."

"What about it then? Is there any way an orderly person who's no lover of money and not petty and doesn't make pretenses and isn't a coward could become a hard bargainer or unjust?"

"There's none."

"So when you're considering whether a soul is philosophic or not straight from youth, you'll also take this into consideration, whether it's just and civilized or antisocial and fierce."

"Very much so."

C "And I don't imagine you're going to leave out this."

"What's that?"

"Whether learning is easy for it or hard. Or do you expect anyone would ever be sufficiently fond of anything that he did if he was doing it with pain and accomplishing little with a lot of effort?"

"That couldn't happen."

"And what if he was full of forgetfulness and couldn't retain anything he did learn? Would it be possible for him not to be empty of knowledge?"

"How could he not?"

"So if he worked with no profit, don't you imagine he'd necessarily end up hating both himself and that kind of activity?"

"How could he not?"

D "Then let's not ever accept a forgetful soul among those that are adequately philosophic, but let's look for one that needs to be good at remembering."

"Absolutely so."

"But we'd claim that anything of an unmusical and graceless nature would pull it in no other direction than into disproportion."

"What else?"

"And do you regard truth to be akin to disproportion or to being in proportion?"

"Being in proportion."

"Then in addition to the rest, let's seek out the kind of thinking that's in proportion and graceful by nature, that its own innate tendency will cause to be easily drawn to the look of each sort of being."

"How else?"

"What about it then? Do we seem to you to have gone through   E
things that are in any way not each necessary and attached to one
another for a soul that's going to get hold of what *is* in an adequate
and complete way?"

"Most necessary indeed," he said.   487A

"Then is there any way you could find fault with such a pursuit,
when no one could ever become able to pursue it adequately if he
were not by nature good at remembering, a quick learner, lofty in his
thinking, graceful, and a friend and kinsman of truth, justice, courage,
and moderation?"

"Not even the god of scorn could find fault with such a thing,"
he said.

"And when such people have been brought to complete fulfillment by education and age," I said, "wouldn't you turn over the city
to them alone?"

And **Adeimantus** said, "Socrates, no one could say a word against   B
you about these things, but every time people hear what you're saying
now, they have an experience something like this: they believe that
from inexperience in questioning and answering they're led a little off
course by the argument at each question, and when the little deflec-
tions have been added up at the end of the discussion, a big blunder
blazes up that's opposite to the things they said in the first place,
and like unskillful checker players who end up getting backed into
a corner by people who are skilled at it, and have no way to make a   C
move, they too end up backed into a corner and not having any way
to say anything in their turn by this other sort of checkers played not
with game pieces but with arguments.[96] But that certainly doesn't
make the truth be any the more that way, and I speak as one looking
at the present instance. Because someone might now claim he's not
able to oppose your statement on the grounds of any particular thing
you ask, but is able to see in fact that all those who get themselves
involved in philosophy, and don't drop it after dabbling in it while
young for the sake of education, but dwell on it longer, become for   D
the most part quite warped, not to say completely depraved, while
those who seem the most decent sort are still affected by the pursuit
you're recommending in this way at least, that they become useless
to their cities."

And when I heard this, I said, "But do you believe those who say
that are mistaken?"

"I don't know," he said, "but I'd be pleased to hear how it seems
to you."

"You'd hear that to me, at any rate, they appear to be telling the
truth."

---

96   This is a more civilized version of the complaint Thrasymachus made in anger in Bk. I,
when he claimed Socrates had to lie and twist the words of others to defeat them in arguments
(340D).

E   "Then how is it right to say" he said, "that cities will have no rest
from evils until philosophers rule in them, if we agree that they're
useless to the cities?"

           "You're asking a question," I said, "that needs an answer given
by way of an image."

           "And I guess you're not in the habit of speaking in images," he
said.

           "That's nice," I said. "You're mocking me after you've dropped me
488A   into an argument that's so resistant to demonstrations? Just listen to
the image, then, so you can see even better how tenaciously[97] I make
images. Because the experience that the most decent philosophers
undergo in relation to their cities is so hard to get at that there's not a
single other experience like it, but it's necessary to pull things together
from many places in order to give an image of it and a defense on their
behalf, the way painters depict goatstags and the like by amalgamating
things. Think of something like this as happening in connection with
either many ships or one: There's a shipowner of a size and strength
B   beyond all those on the ship, but a little deaf and likewise somewhat
shortsighted, and another problem like those is that his knowledge
of seafaring skills is a little short too. The sailors are divided against
one another over the steering, with each one imagining that he ought
to be at the helm, even though he's never learned the art and can't
point to a teacher he's had or a time when he was studying it, and on
top of that, they claim it's not even teachable, and they're ready to
C   cut someone to pieces for even saying it is. They're always pushed in
around the shipowner himself, begging and doing everything to get
him to turn over the helm to them, and sometimes, when they don't
persuade him but others do instead, they either kill the others or throw
them out of the ship. When they've put the gullible shipowner out
of action with mandrake[98] or liquor or something else, they rule the
ship and make their own use of what's in it, sailing it while drinking
D   and feasting the way such people are likely to. On top of that, they
show their approval for anyone who's clever at grasping a way for
them to rule, by using either persuasion or force on the shipowner,
by calling him skilled at sailing and at helmsmanship, and someone
who knows his stuff about a ship, while they revile anyone who's
not that sort as useless. As for the true helmsman, they don't even
understand that it's necessary for him to pay attention to times and
seasons, to the sky and the stars and winds and everything pertaining
to the art, if he's going to be a skilled ruler of a ship in his very being.

---

97   Literally "stickily." The point is generally missed in translations that take the word in the
sense of either of its common uses, to mean "eagerly" or "stingily," rather than as a live metaphor. The image Socrates is about to use was not new (see for example Sophocles' *Antigone*, lines
162-163), but it was probably never elaborated with so much painstakingly chosen detail as it is
here.

98   A narcotic plant.

They imagine that it's not possible to acquire the skill and practice of how one gets the helm whether anybody wants him to or not, and to acquire helmsmanship too at the same time. So with things like that going on around the ships, don't you think the one who's a skilled helmsman in the true sense, in his very being, would be called a stargazer and a windbag and useless to *them* by seafarers on ships that are operated in that way?"

"Very much so," said Adeimantus.

"Now I don't imagine you need the image to be analyzed to see that it resembles the condition of cities in relation to the true philosophers, but that you understand what I mean."

"Very much so," he said.

"Well first of all, then, teach the image to that fellow who's surprised that philosophers aren't honored in their cities and try to persuade him that it would be much more surprising if they were honored."

"I'll teach it," he said.

"Also that you're telling the truth that the most decent people engaged in philosophy are useless to most people; tell him, though, to blame their uselessness on those who have no use for them and not on the decent people. It's not natural for a helmsman to beg sailors to be ruled by him, or for the wise to go to the doors of the rich—the one who came up with that cute remark[99] told a lie; what's naturally true is that, whether it's a rich person or a poor one who's sick, it's necessary to go to the doors of the doctors, and necessary as well for everyone who needs to be ruled to go to the doors of someone capable of ruling, not for the ruler to beg the ruled to be ruled, if in truth they're to get any use out of him. But he won't be mistaken if he likens the politicians who now rule to the sailors we were just talking about, and likens those spoken of by these people as useless star-babblers to helmsmen in the true sense."

"Totally right," he said.

"As a result of these things, then, and in these circumstances, it's not easy for the best pursuit to be well thought of by people whose pursuits are its opposites, but the biggest and strongest slur on philosophy comes from people who claim to be pursuing it, the very ones the complainant against philosophy is talking about when you declare that he says most of those who go into it are completely depraved, while the most decent ones are useless; I admitted that what you said was true, didn't I?"

"Yes."

"And haven't we gone over the cause of the uselessness of the decent ones?"

"Thoroughly."

---

99   Reportedly the poet Simonides.

E

"So do you want the next thing we go over to be the inevitability of depravity in most of them, and for us to try to show, if we're able to, that philosophy is not the cause of that?"

"Very much so."

"Let's listen and speak, then, by casting our memories back to the point at which we were going over the sort of nature that has to be innate in someone who's to be a gentleman.[100] If you've got it in mind, the first point was that truth led him, and he needed to follow it completely in everything or else be a fraud who has no part in true philosophy in any way."

490A

"It was so stated."

"And isn't this one thing that's so violently contrary to popular opinion amongst the opinions now held about him?"

"Very much so," he said.

"So won't we be giving a defense that's tailor-made by saying the following? That someone who's a lover of learning in his very being would be of such a nature as to strive toward what *is*, and wouldn't linger with the many particular things that have a seeming of being, but would keep going and not blunt the edge of his erotic desire or let up from it until he gets hold of the nature of what each thing itself *is* with the capacity of the soul that's suited to get hold of such a thing, and is suited to it by its kinship with it, and once he's come near by means of that and joined with what *is* in its very being, and has given birth to intellectual insight and truth, he'd discern and be truly alive and be nourished, and in that way cease from his labor pains, but not before that."

B

"That's tailor-made in the utmost possible degree," he said.

"What about it then? Will this person have anything to do with loving falsehood, or just the opposite, hate it all?"

C

"Hate it," he said.

"And if truth leads the way, I don't imagine we'd ever claim that a chorus of evils could follow it."

"How could it?"

"But a healthy and just state of character would, with moderation also in attendance."

"That's right," he said.

"Then what need is there to force the rest of the chorus that belongs to the philosophic nature to line up again from the beginning? Because you remember, no doubt, that, as properly belonging with these things, courage, loftiness of mind, quickness at learning, and memory went along with them. And you objected that, while everyone would be obliged to agree with the things we were saying, if someone left the arguments aside and looked to the people them-

D

---

100   See the note to 409A on the force of this word. It is meant to sum up the qualities of character listed in 487A, when Adeimantus was moved to object.

selves that the discussion was about, he'd claim to see that some are useless and many are depraved with every sort of vice. In examining the cause of the slur, we've come now to this question: why in the world are most of them depraved? And for the sake of that, we took up again the nature of those who are philosophers in the true sense, and defined it from necessity."

"That's it," he said.

"So," I said, "what we need to do is look at the corruptions of this   E
nature, at how it's destroyed in most people while a small remnant escape, the ones who are not depraved and whom people call useless, and after that look at those who imitate this, and settle into the   491A
practice of it, to see what sort of natures souls have that go into a pursuit that's unfit for them and beyond them, so that they hit the wrong note often, so as to attach to philosophy everywhere and for everyone a reputation of the sort you describe."

"What corruptions do you mean?" he said.

"I'll try," I said, "to go through them for you if I'm able to. I imag-
ine everyone will agree with us about this, that such a nature, having all the attributes we assigned it just now if it was going to become a   B
philosopher in the full sense, springs up on few occasions and in few human beings—don't you think so?"

"Emphatically."

"And for these few, think how many and great the potential disasters are."

"What, exactly?"

"The most surprising thing of all to hear is that every one of the things we praised in the nature tends to ruin the soul that has it and tear it away from philosophy. I'm talking about courage, moderation, and everything we went through."

"That's a strange thing to hear," he said.

"And what's more," I said, "on top of these things, all the so-called   C
goods corrupt it and tear it away—beauty, riches, bodily strength, family connections with power in the city, and everything akin to these; you get the type of things I'm talking about."

"I get it," he said; "I'd also be glad to learn more precisely what you mean."

"Then grasp it as a whole in the right way," I said, "and it will appear very evident to you, and the things said about it before won't seem strange."

"How do you advise me to do that?" he said.

"With every seed or growing thing," I said, "whether in the ground   D
or among animals, we know that one that doesn't get the food or the climate or location suited to it in each case will be that much more lacking in what's proper to it, the more vigorous it is, since presumably what's bad is more antagonistic to something good than to something that's not good."

"How could it not be?"

"So I imagine it's reasonable for the best nature to come off worse than an inferior one from being in too unfavorable an environment."

"It is."

E

"Then, Adeimantus," I said, "won't we claim that with souls too, those with the greatest natural talents become exceptionally bad when they get bad guidance in youth? Or do you imagine that great injustices and undiluted vice come from an inferior nature rather than from one with youthful vigor ruined by its upbringing, and that a weak nature will never be the cause of great things either good or bad?"

"No," he said; "that's how it is."

492A

"Well then, I imagine that if the nature we set down as that of the philosopher meets up with suitable learning, it will necessarily come into every virtue as it grows, but if it's brought up without being seeded and planted in suitable soil, it will come instead into everything opposite, unless it happens to get the help of one of the gods. Or do you believe, the way most people do, that some young people are corrupted by sophists, and that any sophists in a private capacity cause any corruption even worth mentioning, and that it's not the very people who say that who are the greatest sophists and who educate in the most complete way and turn out young and old, men and women, as the sort of people they want them to be?"

B

"When, exactly?" he said.

"Whenever a multitude of them sits down together in one bunch," I said, "in assemblies or law courts or theaters or army camps or any other gathering in common of a crowd, and, with a lot of racket, blame some of the things that are said and done and praise others, excessively in both cases, shouting and clapping, and added to that, the rocks and the place in which they are, by echoing, make the racket of blame and praise double. In a situation like that, what do you imagine a young person, as the saying goes, has in his heart? Or what sort of private education will hold up against it for him, and not be inundated by that sort of blame and praise to be swept off and carried by the tide in whatever direction it takes, so that he'll claim the same things are beautiful and shameful as they do, and make a practice of doing the very things they do, and be like them?"

C

D

"That's a big necessity, Socrates," he said.

"And we haven't yet spoken of the biggest necessity," I said.

"What's that?" he said.

"What these educators and sophists impose by deed in addition to speech when they fail at persuasion. Or aren't you aware that they punish anyone who's not persuaded with penalties in dishonor, money, and death?"

"Yes, very harshly," he said.

"So what other sophist, or what sort of private discussion going in the opposite direction do you imagine will prevail over these?"

"None, I imagine," he said.   E

"No," I said, "and even to try is the height of folly. A state of character related to virtue in a different way, that runs counter to the education it's gotten from these people, doesn't happen, hasn't happened, and won't happen, my comrade—a human one, that is, though for the divine sort let's follow the proverb and make an exception from the statement, since it behooves us to be well aware that if anything whatever might be saved and become what it ought to be in such a state of political life, if you say   493A it was saved by divine dispensation you won't be speaking badly."

"It doesn't seem any different to me," he said.

"Then in addition to that," I said, "let this also seem so to you."

"What?"

"That none of the private professionals whom these people call sophists and regard as rival artisans teaches anything other than these opinions held by most people, the ones they give as opinions when they're assembled in groups, and he calls that wisdom. It's the very sort of thing someone would do if he was making a close study of the moods and desires of a big and strong beast he was fostering, to   B learn the way he ought to approach it and the way to get hold of it, and when it's hardest to handle or most gentle, and what makes it become that way, and on what particular occasions it's in the habit of uttering its vocal sounds, and what sounds in response calm it or make it fierce when they're uttered by someone else. And once having learned all that by being around it and spending time with it, he'd call it wisdom, and having systematized it like an art he'd turn to teaching, knowing nothing at all about what's in truth beautiful or shameful among these opinions and desires, or good or bad, or just or unjust,   C he'd name all these things after the opinions of the great animal, calling what delights it good and what annoys it bad, but he'd be calling necessary things just and beautiful; he'd have no other account to give of them, but as for the nature of the necessary and the good, and the great extent by which they differ in being, he'd neither have discerned it nor be able to show it to anyone else. Now before Zeus, wouldn't someone like that seem to you to be a bizarre teacher?"

"To me, yes," he said.

"And does there seem to be any difference between that fellow and the one who regards it as wisdom to have made a close observation of   D the mood and pleasures of the many and various assembled people, whether in painting or music or politics? Because if anyone consorts with them for showing off either poetry or any other craft or service to the city, making the masses his sovereigns over and above the ways they necessarily are, there'll be the proverbial Diomedean necessity[101]

---

101 This seems to mean you pay for your pleasures one way or another. Various attempts have been made to explain who the Diomedes in question was and whether he paid the price or forced others to.

for him to turn out what they applaud. But as for that stuff's being in truth good or beautiful, have you ever yet heard anyone give an argument on its behalf that wasn't ludicrous?"

E

"And I don't imagine I ever will either," he said.

"Now keeping all these things in mind, let that former point be brought back to mind: with respect to the beautiful itself, as distinct from the many beautiful things, or to any given thing itself, as distinct

494A

from its many particular instances, is there any way a multitude is going to stand for that or believe there is such a thing?"

"No way in the least," he said.

"Therefore," I said, "a multitude is incapable of being philosophic." [102]

"Incapable."

"And therefore, it's a necessity that people who do engage in philosophy will be criticized by them."

"A necessity."

"And also by all those private persons who attach themselves to the crowd and desire to gratify it."

"Clearly."

"So do you see any salvation from that for a philosophic nature, so that it will stick with its pursuit in order to get to its end? Keep in

B

mind the results of the things we went over earlier, since it was agreed by us that quickness at learning, memory, courage, and loftiness of mind belong to this nature."

"Yes."

"Then right away, such a person will be first among children in all things, especially if his body grows as a match for his soul."

"How could he fail to?" he said.

"So I imagine when he gets older, his family and fellow citizens will want to use him for their own interests."

"How could they not?"

C

"Then they'll be lying at his feet, begging and honoring, getting their hooks into him early by flattering in advance the power he's going to have."

"It does tend to happen that way," he said.

"So what do you imagine someone like that will do in such circumstances," I said, "especially if he happens to be from a big city, and rich and well born in it, and also good-looking and tall? Won't

D

he be brimming with unattainable hope, considering himself good enough to handle the affairs of the Greeks and the barbarians too, and

---

102 Notice that Socrates is not saying that most people are incapable of philosophy, but only that a large group of people has no such capacity when acting or thinking as one mass. Socrates would probably say that, given enough time in one-on-one discussion with someone who has begun to grasp philosophic possibilities, there would be hope for anyone. See Plato's *Gorgias*, 471E-472D.

won't he lift himself to a lofty height over these things, filled up with pretentious preening and a vapid, stupid, smugness?"[103]

"Will he ever," he said.

"Now if someone made a quiet approach to a person in that situation and told him the truth, that he had no sense in him and needed some, and that it's not obtainable unless one slaves over the acquisition of it, do you imagine it would be as easy as falling off a log to get him to hear that through so much interference?"

"Far from it," he said.

"But then if, due to being of a good nature and having an affinity for discussion," I said, "he somehow has an insight and is turned back and drawn toward philosophy, what do you imagine those people are going to do who believe they'll be losing the use of him and his company? Is there any length they won't go to, any word they won't utter, both about him, so that he won't be persuaded, and about the one doing the persuading, so that he won't be able to, as they plot against him in private and institute adversary proceedings in public?"

E

"That's a big necessity," he said.

495A

"So is there any way such a person is going to engage in philosophy?"

"Not at all."

"Do you see, then," I said, "that we weren't speaking badly in saying that, after all, even the very parts that go to make up a philosophic nature, when they turn up in a bad upbringing, are in a certain way the cause of one's falling away from the pursuit of it, as are the so-called goods, riches and all such trappings?"

"No indeed," he said; "it was rightly said."

"So, you strange fellow," I said, "this is the destruction and corruption, so great and of such a kind, of the best nature in relation to the best pursuit, and few of them come into being anyway, as we claim. And those who wreak the greatest havoc on their cities and on private people come particularly from among these men, and so do those who do the greatest good, if they happen to be drawn that way. A puny nature never does anything great, nothing at all, nothing for a private person and nothing for a city."

B

"Most true," he said.

---

103 Everyone who has been around the academic world has known some of these overgrown whiz kids whose careers reached their peaks before they actually happened, but the details of this passage point particularly to one young man named Alcibiades. Xenophon (*Memorabilia* I, ii, 39-46) displays Alcibiades' arrogance toward his guardian, Pericles. Almost half of Thucydides' *Peloponnesian War*, from Bk. V, Chap. 43 on, is dominated by an account of Alcibiades' ambitions, which successively destroyed chances for peace between Athens and Sparta, led Athens to a disastrous expedition that proved to be its downfall, and took Alcibiades himself over to the side of the Spartans and then to that of the King of Persia. Plato, in his *Symposium* (216D-219D), makes Alcibiades reveal his belief in his irresistible good looks. During Socrates' lifetime, Alcibiades was considered the most promising of his young associates, while a younger man named Plato went almost unnoticed in the background.

C

"So when these people, for whom she's most suited, desert her in this way, they leave philosophy abandoned and unfulfilled and they themselves live a life that's neither suited to them nor true, while she, like an orphan with no relatives, suffers disgrace when others, unworthy of her, come in their place; these others make her incur the sort of accusations you declare are hurled at her by her accusers, that some who hang around her are good for nothing while most are good for plenty of evil."

"Yes, those're the things that're said at any rate," he said.

D

"And it's fair to say them," I said. "Because other puny little people notice that this place has become vacant, but is chock-full of beautiful names and outward appearances, and like escapees from prisons who run off to temples, they too are well pleased to hot-foot it out of the arts into philosophy, whichever ones of them happen to be the most refined in the concerns of their own little arts. For even with philosophy in such a shape, it's still left with a more lofty status in comparison to the other arts, and many defective natures aspire to it, but just as their bodies are maimed by their arts and crafts, so too

E

their souls have gotten stunted and crushed by their menial occupations. Or is that not necessary?"

"It very much is," he said.

"Do you suppose it's any different to see them," I said, "than a short bald blacksmith who's come into some cash, newly let out of jail and cleaned up at the bathhouse, wearing a freshly made cloak, decked out as a bridegroom and about to marry the boss's daughter because she's poor and abandoned?"

496A

"Not much different," he said.

"Then what sort of offspring are such people likely to father? Won't they be illegitimate and mediocre?"

"That's a big necessity."

"So what about people unworthy of an education, when they come around and associate with philosophy in a way she doesn't deserve? What sort of thoughts and opinions will we claim they'll generate? Won't they be truly fit to be listened to as pseudo logic, nowhere near having in them anything true born or worth paying any mind to?"

"Completely and totally," he said.

B

"So, Adeimantus," I said, "there's a very tiny remnant left of people who associate with philosophy in a manner worthy of her, probably someone well-born and well-bred in character but held down in banishment, who stands by her in accord with his nature for lack of people to corrupt him, or a great soul, when he's born in a small city and disdains the city's concerns because he sees beyond them, and presumably also a slight few, naturally gifted, might come to her from another art they justly hold in low esteem. And there might also be the sort of curb that holds our companion Theages in check,

C

because all the other things designed to drive someone away from

philosophy are there for Theages too, but taking care of the sickliness of his body, by shutting him off from politics, restrains him. Our own case, the divine sign,[104] is not worth talking about, since it might have happened with one other person before, or none. Those who've come to be among these few, and gotten a taste of how sweet and blessed an attainment it is, have also seen well enough the insanity of most people, and that none of them, in minding the concerns of their cities, is doing anything wholesome, to put it in one word, and that there is no ally with whom one might go to the aid of justice and survive,   D
but instead is like a human being fallen in among wild animals if he's not willing to join the rest in doing injustice and not sufficient as one person to hold out against all the savage beasts. Before he could be of any benefit to the city or his friends, he'd get himself killed, and would be useless to himself as well as to everyone else. Taking all these things into account, he keeps quiet and minds his own business, like someone in a storm, standing out of the dust and spray carried on the wind under the shelter of a little wall. Seeing the others filled with lawlessness, he's content if he himself can live his life here clean of   E
injustice and impious deeds, and at his exit from it, make his departure in a gracious and benign manner, with beautiful hope."

"That's certainly not the smallest accomplishment he could leave   497A
with," he said.

"And not the biggest either," I said, "as long as he doesn't happen to have a suitable polity; in a suitable one he himself will grow more and he'll safeguard the things shared in common along with those kept in private. But the things on account of which the slur on philosophy has taken hold, and that it has done so unjustly, seem to me to have been stated in a measured way, unless *you* still have something else to say."

"I have nothing further to say about that," he said, "but which of the current polities do you say is suitable for it?"

"None whatsoever," I said, "but that's in fact the accusation I'm   B
making, that among the cities there are now there's none constituted in a way that's worthy of a philosophic nature, and that's why it gets twisted and altered, just as a foreign seed planted in alien ground has a tendency to be overwhelmed and fade into the native vegetation, so too this species doesn't now hold onto its own capacity but falls away into a character alien to it. But if it should catch on to the best polity, best in just the way it too is, then it will make it plain that the   C
rest of the natures and pursuits are merely human but this one was godlike all along in its very being. And it's obvious that you're going to ask next what this polity is."

---

104 In Plato's *Apology* (31C-32A), this is described as "something like a voice" that came to Socrates when he was about to make a bad choice, and always kept him out of ordinary political life. The following passage in the *Apology* describes the way he simply did his duty when the law gave him some public function, and refrained from doing things popular opinion or powerful leaders tried to force him into.

"You haven't quite got it," he said; "I wasn't going to ask that, but whether it was the one we went over in founding the city, or something else."

"In every other respect it's the same," I said, "and in respect to this very thing it was mentioned then too that there would be a need for someone always to be in the city who has a rational understanding of the polity, the very same understanding that you, the lawgiver, had in setting down the laws."

D

"That was mentioned," he said.

"But it wasn't made sufficiently clear," I said, "out of fear of what you folks have made all too clear by not taking no for an answer—that the demonstration of it would be long and difficult, since even the part that's left is not the easiest of all things to go through."

"What's that?"

"By what means a city will avoid being destroyed by taking philosophy in hand. Anything big risks a fall, and as the saying goes, beautiful things are hard by their very nature."

E

"Nevertheless," he said, "let the demonstration get its completion by having this become evident."

"That won't be prevented by a lack of willingness," I said, "but if anything, by a lack of ability. You'll be here to see my zealousness anyway. Watch now how enthusiastically and audaciously I'm going to argue that a city ought to take up this pursuit in just the opposite way it does now."

"How's that?"

498A

"Now," I said, "those who take it up are adolescents just out of childhood, and between that and running a household and making a living they get close to the hardest part of it and then give it up, because they're made out to be consummate philosophers; and by the hardest part, I mean what's implicit in speech.[105] Later on, if they're invited along while others are doing this, they consider it a big thing if they're even willing to be listeners, thinking one ought to do it as recreation. And nearing old age, outside of a certain few, they're snuffed out much more than Heracleitus's sun,[106] inasmuch as they don't get fired up again."

B

"How should it be?" he said.

"Completely opposite; as adolescents and children they should take in hand an adolescent-style education and age-appropriate philosophy, and take very good care of their bodies, at a time when they're growing and maturing into manhood, to secure an assistant for philosophy. And as the years go forward in which the soul begins to be full-grown, they ought to intensify the exercise of it; but when

---

105   See 507B.

106   Fragment 6 (Diels-Kranz numbering): "The sun is new each day." Fr. 30: "This cosmos...was, is, and always will be everliving fire, kindled in measures and quenched in measures."

bodily strength is declining and they get out of politics and armed   C
service, from then on they should be put out to pasture to range
unfettered and do nothing else, except as a recreation, those, that is,
who are going to live happily and, at death, round out the life they've
lived with a fitting destiny in that other place."

"It's true you seem to me to be speaking enthusiastically, Socrates,"
he said, "though I imagine most of the people listening to you are still
more enthusiastic about resisting and aren't going to be persuaded
by any means, starting from Thrasymachus."

"Don't stir up a fight between Thrasymachus and me," I said,   D
"now that we've just become friends, not that we were enemies before
that. Because we're not going to give up our efforts until we either
persuade both him and the others or make some headway into that
life, in case they meet up with such discussions when they've come
to life again."

"Oh, you're talking about a short time, then," he said.

"No time at all," I said, "as compared to the entirety of it, though
it's no wonder most people aren't persuaded by these arguments.
Because they've never seen in existence what we now insist is,[107]
though they have seen a lot more phrases like this purposely matched   E
up instead of falling together spontaneously the way they just did.
But a man completely measuring up to and matching up with virtue
in word and deed to the limit of what's possible, holding power in a
city that's another of his kind, *that* they've never seen, not even one,   499A
much less more than one. Or do you think so?"

"By no means."

"And they certainly haven't come to listen enough to beautiful,
liberating discussions either, my blessed friend, discussions of the sort
that strain by every means to seek the truth for the sake of knowing,
and keep their distance from the cute and contentious arguments that
strain toward nothing other than outward show and competition in
lawsuits as well as in private gatherings."

"That they haven't," he said.

"Well, it was for these reasons," I said, "and from foreseeing them   B
then, that we were frightened, but we kept speaking anyway, forced
into it by the truth, saying that no city or polity, and likewise no man
either, would ever reach fulfillment until by chance some necessity
possesses those few philosophers who aren't depraved, but are now
called useless, to take into their care the running of a city whether they
want to or not, and makes them pay heed to the city, or else until a true
erotic desire for true philosophy, by some divine inspiration, comes
over those who are now in power or hold kingships, or over their   C

---

107   The last eight words translate *eidon genomenon to nun legomenon* (lit. "seen in existence what's
now being spoken of"), a rhyming dactylic jingle. The translation is too contrived to convey the
unforced simplicity of the original, which is as natural as "I'm a poet but I don't know it." On
the meaning of the balanced phrases, see the Glossary entries for *becoming* and *being*.

sons. And I claim there's no reason at all to think it's impossible for either or both of these things to happen; if so, we'd justly be laughed at for idly saying things like mere prayers. Isn't that so?"

"It is."

"So if any necessity has come along for people who are first-rate in philosophy to take into their care the running of a city, either in the limitless time gone by, or even now in some barbaric land, somewhere far outside our view, or if it will happen hereafter, we're ready to contend in argument about this that the polity that's been described did, does, and will exist whenever this Muse comes into power in a city. Because it's not impossible and we're not talking impossibilities; it's difficult, and that's granted by us."

"That's how it seems to me too," he said.

"But would you also say that it doesn't seem that way to most people?" I said.

"Probably," he said.

"Blessed fellow," I said, "don't make a blanket accusation against the masses like that. They'd certainly have an opinion of a different sort if, by being encouraging instead of contentious, you dispelled the slander from the love of learning by displaying who the philosophers you're talking about are, and differentiated their nature and pursuit the way we just did, so they won't take you to be talking about the people they supposed. And if they look at it that way, you'll certainly admit that they'll take on an opinion of a different sort and give a different answer. Or do you imagine that anyone who's ungrudging and civilized is harsh with someone who's not harsh, or resentful of someone who's not resentful? I'll get in ahead of you and say that I believe such a harsh nature turns up in some few people but not in a multitude."

"Don't worry," he said; "I'm of the same opinion."

"And aren't you of the same opinion on this very point as well, that it's those outsiders who are to blame for the fact that most people are harshly disposed toward philosophy, because they barge in where they don't belong like a bunch of drunks, hurling abuse among themselves, being fond of squabbling, and always making arguments directed at persons, doing what's least appropriate to philosophy?"

"Very much so," he said.

"Doubtless, Adeimantus, there's no leisure for anyone who has his thinking truly directed toward the things that *are* to gaze down at the concerns of human beings and get filled up with resentment and malice over battling with them; instead, by gazing on and contemplating things in a regular arrangement and always in the same condition, that neither do nor suffer injustice among themselves, all disposed in order in accord with reason, they imitate these things and take on their likeness as much as possible. Or do you imagine there's any way for anyone not to imitate whatever he dwells with and admires?"

"No possible way," he said.

"So the philosopher who dwells with what's divine and orderly   D
becomes orderly and divine to the extent possible for human beings,
though a lot of slander is hurled at them all."

"Absolutely so."

"So," I said, "if some necessity arises for him to attend to instilling
what he sees there into the characters of human beings in both private
and public, and not just mold his own character, do you imagine he'd
turn out to be a bad workman of moderation and justice, and of all
virtue of the populace?"

"He least of all," he said.

"So if the masses were to perceive that what we're saying about
him is true, would they be harsh against the philosophers and distrust
us when we say that a city could never become happy unless artists   E
using the divine model draft its outline?"

"They wouldn't be harsh if they perceived that," he said, "but
exactly what type of outlining are you talking about?"   501A

"Taking a city and the character of its people like a tablet," I said,
"first they'd wipe it clean, which is not very easy; but then you can be
sure that in this respect they'd be different from the rest right from the
start, in being unwilling to put their hands to either a private person
or a city, or to draft laws, before they either receive them clean or
make them that way themselves."

"And rightly so," he said.

"Then after that, don't you imagine they'd sketch in the shape of
the polity?"

"Of course."

"Then, as they work out the details, I imagine they'd look in both   B
directions, toward what's just by nature, and beautiful and moderate and everything of the sort, and also toward that which they're
to introduce into human beings, mixing together and blending a
manlike image out of the various pursuits, judging it by what even
Homer called godlike, or bearing a god's image,[108] when it arises in
human beings."

"Right," he said.

"And I imagine they'd erase one thing and draw another in again   C
until, as much as they could, they fashioned human states of character
favored by the gods to the greatest possible degree."

"In that way the drawing would come to be the most beautiful at
any rate," he said.

---

108 In a handful of characters in both the *Iliad* and the *Odyssey* Homer labels certain qualities
theoeides or *theoeikelon*. Socrates and Homer agree that men and women are outstanding by the
presence of something godlike, but they don't necessarily find it in the same people. There is
no apparent irony when Homer uses the first of the two epithets for Paris (*Il.* 3.16), whom he
depicts as lacking most, if not all, of the virtues.

"Well then," I said, "are we in any way persuading those folks you claimed would be rushing at us full speed, that the artist of polities we were commending to them then is of this sort? They got riled up about him because we were turning the cities over to him, but have they gotten any more calm about hearing that now?"

"Much more," he said, "if they have any moderation."

D   "And on what basis would they have any grounds to dispute it? Will they claim philosophers *aren't* lovers of what is and of truth?"

"That would certainly be absurd," he said.

"Well then, that their nature, that we've gone through, *isn't* at home with what's best?"

"Not that either."

"Well what about this? That such a nature, when it happens upon suitable pursuits, *won't* be completely good and philosophic, if any is? Or will they claim the ones we ruled out are more so?"

"Of course not."

E   "So will they still get angry when we say that until the philosophic kind comes to power in a city, there will be no rest from evils for a city or its citizens, and the polity we're telling a story about in speech won't reach fulfillment in deed?"

"Less so, maybe," he said.

"Then," I said, "are you willing for us not to say they're less
502A   angry but that they've calmed down and been persuaded in every last detail, so that they'll consent, if for no other reason than from being ashamed?"

"Very willing indeed," he said.

"Well then," I said, "let these people have been persuaded of this. But is anyone going to argue over the following point, claiming there'd be no chance that offspring of kings or of those in power would be born philosophers in their natures?"

"Not a single person would," he said.

"And if they were born that way, can anyone say there's a great necessity for them to be corrupted? That it's hard for them to be kept safe, even we admit, but is there anyone who'd argue that in the whole
B   of time not even one could ever be kept safe?"

"How could he?"

"But surely," I said, "if one is born and has a city obeying him, that's sufficient to bring to fulfillment everything that's now in doubt."

"Quite sufficient," he said.

"Since presumably," I said, "once a ruler has set down the laws and practices we went over, it's certainly not impossible for the citizens to be willing to follow them."

"Not by any means."

"But then is it anything wondrous or impossible for the very things that seem good to us to seem that way to others as well?"

"I can't think why," he said.   C

"And that they're best, if they're possible, I imagine we went over sufficiently in the earlier discussion."

"Quite sufficiently."

"So now, our conclusion about lawgiving appears to be that the things we're saying are best if they could happen, and while it's difficult for them to happen it's certainly not impossible."

"That's the conclusion," he said.

"Then since, by effort, that's reached an end, don't the things that remain after it need to be spoken about: in what manner, by what kinds of things learned and pursued, the saviors of the polity will be   D
present among us, and at what ages each group of them will take up each activity?"

"That surely needs to be spoken about," he said.

"It didn't turn out to be a wise thing in the earlier discussion," I said, "for me to have left out the objectionable matter of possessing women, the propagation of children, and the instituting of the rulers, even though I knew that the complete truth would be offensive and a hard thing to bring about, because as it is, the need to go through   E
these things came along nonetheless. And while the particular things about women and children are finished, it's necessary to go into the ones about the rulers as if from the beginning. And we were saying, if you recall, that they must be seen to be passionately devoted to the   503A
city, standing the test amid pleasures and pains, and being seen not to drop this conviction through drudgery or terrors or any other vicissitude, or else the person who's incapable is to be rejected, while the one who comes through untarnished in every way, like gold tested in the fire, is to be established as a ruler and given honors and prizes both while living and at his death. Some such things as that were being said when the discussion slipped past them with its face covered, in fear of setting in motion what's now at hand."

"You're telling the exact truth," he said; "I do recall."   B

"I was reluctant, dear friend," I said, "to state what has now been daringly exposed, but now let it be boldly stated: it's imperative to put philosophers in place as guardians in the most precise sense."

"Let it be so stated," he said.

"Then consider it likely that you'll have few of them, since the nature we went through needs to belong to them, but its parts are rarely inclined to grow together in the same place, but in most cases grow as something severed."

"How do you mean?" he said.

"With natures that are good learners, have memories, are intel-   C
lectually flexible, are quick, and have everything else that goes with these things, and are youthfully spirited and lofty in their thinking as well, you know that they aren't willing at the same time to grow up being the sort of natures that want to live with calmness and

stability in an orderly way, but instead are the kind that are carried off wherever their quickness happens to take them, and everything stable goes right out of them."

"You're telling the truth," he said.

"But with those natures with stable characters, on the other hand, that are not easily changeable, those one would treat as more trustworthy and that would be unmoved confronting terrors in war, wouldn't they be the same way confronting things to be learned also? They're hard to move and slow to learn as though they'd been numbed, and they're full of sleepiness and yawning whenever anything of the sort needs to be worked at."

"That's how they are," he said.

"But we claimed it was necessary to have a good-sized and high-quality share of both, or else not be allowed to take part in the most precise sort of education or in honor or in ruling."

"Rightly," he said.

"And don't you imagine that will be rare?"

"How could it not be?"

"So not only does it need to be tested in the labors, terrors, and pleasures we spoke of then but also, something we passed over then and speak of now, one needs to give it exercise in many kinds of studies to examine whether it will be capable of holding up under the greatest studies, or whether it will shy away like people who show cowardice in other areas."

"It's certainly appropriate to examine it that way," he said, "but what sort of studies in particular are you saying are the greatest?"

"No doubt you remember," I said, "that we pieced together what justice, moderation, courage, and wisdom each would be by distinguishing three forms that belong to the soul."

"If I didn't remember that," he said, "it would be just for me not to hear the rest."

"And what about what was said by way of preface to that?"

"What was it?"

"We were saying something to the effect that getting the most beautiful possible look at these things would take another, longer way around, which would make them become evident to someone who traveled that road, though it would be possible to provide illustrations approximating to the things that had already been said earlier, and you folks declared that would be sufficient. And so the things said at that time, as far as precision goes, as it appeared to me, were deficient; as for whether they were satisfactory to you people, that's something you could say."

"To me? In a measured way," he said; "and it looked like they were to the others as well."

"My friend," I said, "measuredness in such matters that stops short in any respect whatever of what _is_ turns out not to measure anything at all, because nothing incomplete is a measure of anything. But sometimes it seems to some people that they're well enough off already and don't need to search any further."

"A great many people feel that way a lot," he said, "because of laziness."

"That feeling, anyway," I said, "is one there's the least need for in a guardian of a city and its laws."

"Likely so," he said.

"So, my comrade," I said, "it's necessary for such a person to go around by the longer road, and he needs to work as a learner no less   D
hard than at gymnastic training, or else, as we were just saying, he'll never get to the end of the greatest and most relevant study."

"So these aren't the greatest ones," he said, "but there's something still greater than justice and the things we've gone over?"

"Not only is there something greater," I said, "but even for those things themselves, it's necessary not just to look at a sketch, the way we've been doing now, but not to stop short of working them out to their utmost completion. Wouldn't it be ridiculous to make a concentrated effort in every way over other things of little worth, to have them be as precise and pure as possible, while not considering the   E
greatest things to be worthy of the greatest precision?"

"Very much so," he said, "and a creditable thought it is, but what you mean by the greatest study, and what it's about—do you imagine," he said, "that anyone's going to let you off without asking you what it is?"

"Not at all," I said. "Just you ask. For all that, you've heard it no few times, but now you're either not thinking of it or else, by latching onto me, you think you'll cause me trouble. But I imagine it's more   505A
the latter, since you've often heard that the greatest learnable thing is the look[109] of the good, which just things and everything else need in addition in order to become useful and beneficial. So now you know pretty well that I'm going to say that, and in addition to it that we don't know it well enough. But if we don't know it, and we do know everything else as much as possible without it, you can be sure that nothing is any benefit to us, just as there would be none if we possessed something without the good. Or do you imagine it's any use   B
to acquire any possession that's not good? Or to be intelligent about

---

109   The word is *idea*. It is a synonym for, and cognate with, *eidos*, usually translated here as form, but since it refers to an intelligible look it is easy to slide over to the English word "idea." That would be a mistake, since the visual metaphor is strongly at work in it. The word *idea* was used in 369A for the look of justice in a soul, in 380D-E for the look of a god, in 479A for the look of beauty itself, and in 486D for the look of each kind of thing that truly *is* and draws the receptive soul to discern it. Commentators seem to think that Plato is putting in Socrates' mouth an anachronistic piece of jargon from his own later school, but I suspect Socrates simply means that Adeimantus has often heard one needs to gain clarity about, and keep one's eye fixed on, the ultimate good sought in any practical endeavor.

everything else without the good, and have no intelligence where anything beautiful and good is concerned?"

"By Zeus, I don't!" he said.

"And surely you know this too, that to most people, the good seems to be pleasure, and to the more sophisticated ones, intelligence."

"How could I not?"

"And, my friend, that the ones who believe the latter can't specify what sort of intelligence, but are forced to end up claiming it's about the good."

"It's very ridiculous," he said.

C   "How could it be otherwise," I said, "if after reproaching us because we don't know what's good they turn around and speak to us as though we do know? Because they claim that it's intelligence about the good as though we for our part understand what they mean when they pronounce the name of the good."

"That's very true," he said.

"And what about the people who define the good as pleasure? Are they any less full of inconsistency than the others? Aren't they also forced to admit that there are bad pleasures?"

"Emphatically so."

"So I guess they turn out to be conceding that the same things that are good are also bad. Isn't that so?"

D   "Certainly."

"Then isn't it clear that the disagreements about it are vast and many?"

"How could it not be clear?"

"And what about this? Isn't it clear that many people would choose the things that seem to be just and beautiful, and even when they aren't, would still do them, possess them, and have the seeming, though no one is content to possess what seems good, but people seek the things that *are* good, and in that case everyone has contempt for the seeming?"

"Very much so," he said.

E   "So this is exactly what every soul pursues, for the sake of which it does everything, having a sense that it's something but at a loss and unable to get an adequate grasp of what it is, or even have the reliable sort of trust it has about other things; because of this it misses out even on any benefit there may have been in the other things. On

506A   such a matter, of such great importance, are we claiming that even the best people in the city, the ones in whose hands we're going to put everything, have to be in the dark in this way?"

"Not in the least," he said.

"I imagine anyway," I said, "that when there's ignorance of the way in which just and beautiful things are good, they won't have gotten a guardian for themselves who's worth much of anything, in someone who's ignorant of that, and I have a premonition that no one's going to discern them adequately before that."

"You're very good at premonitions," he said.

"Then won't our polity be perfectly ordered if that sort of guardian **B**
does watch over it, one who knows these things?"

"Necessarily," he said. "But you in particular, Socrates, do you
claim the good is knowledge or pleasure or some other thing besides
these?"

"That's a man for you," I said; "you've done a beautiful job of
making it plain all along that the way things seem to others about
these things won't be good enough for you."

"But it doesn't seem just to me either, Socrates," he said, "to be
able to state the opinions of others but not one's own, when one has   **C**
been concerned about these things for such a long time."

"Well does it seem to you to be just," I said, "to talk about things
one doesn't know as though one knew them?"

"Not by any means as though one knew them," he said, "but
certainly it's just to be willing to say what one thinks as something
one thinks."

"What?" I said, "Haven't you noticed about opinions without
knowledge that they're all ugly? The best of them are blind. Or do
people who hold any true opinion without insight seem to you to be
any different from blind people who travel along the right road?"

"No different," he said.

"Then do you want to gaze on ugly things, blind and crooked,
when you'll be able to hear bright and beautiful ones from others?"

"Before Zeus, Socrates," said **Glaucon**, "you're not going to stand   **D**
down as if you were at the end. It'll be good enough for us if, the same
way you went over what has to do with justice and moderation and
the other things, you also go over what has to do with the good."

"For me too, comrade," I said, "and more than good enough. But
I'm afraid I won't be capable of it, but I'll make a fool of myself in
my eagerness and pay for it in ridicule. But, you blessed fellows, let's
leave aside for the time being what the good itself is, since it appears
to me to be beyond the trajectory of the impulse we've got at present   **E**
to reach the things that now seem to me to be the case. But I'm willing
to speak about what appears to be an offspring of the good and most
like it, if that's also congenial to you folks, or if not, to let it go."

"Just speak," he said, "and some other time you'll pay off the balance with a description of the father."

"I'd like to have the power to pay it in full and for you folks to   **507A**
receive it, and not just the interest on it as you will now. Give a recep-
tion, then, to this dividend[110] and offspring of the good itself. Be on
your guard, though, in case I unintentionally deceive you by paying
my account with counterfeit interest."

---

110 The Greek word *tokos* means both child and monetary interest.

"We'll be on guard according to our power," he said, "so just speak."

"After I've gotten your agreement," I said, "and reminded you of things mentioned in the previous discussion and often spoken of before now elsewhere."

"What sort of things?" he said.

B   "We claim that there are many beautiful things," I said, "and many good things, and the same way for each kind, and we distinguish them in speech."

"We do."

"But also a beautiful itself, and a good itself, and the same way with everything we were then taking as many, we go back the other way and take according to a single look of each kind, as though there is only one, and we refer to it as what each kind is."

"That's it."

"And we claim that the former are seen but not thought, while the 'looks' in turn are thought but not seen."

"Completely and totally so."

C   "And by which of the things within ourselves do we see the ones that are seen?"

"By sight," he said.

"And perceive the things heard by hearing, and all the perceptible things by the other senses?" I said.

"Of course."

"Well," I said, "have you reflected about the craftsman of the senses, how he was by far the most bountiful in crafting the power of seeing and being seen?"

"Not at all," he said.

"Then look at it this way: for one thing to hear and another to be heard, is there any need for another kind of thing in addition to the
D   sense of hearing and a sound, such that, if that third thing isn't present, the first won't hear and the second won't be heard?"

"There's nothing like that," he said.

"And I don't imagine," I said, "that there are many others either, not to say none, that have any additional need for such a thing, or can you name any?"

"Not for my part," he said.

"But don't you realize that the power of sight and being seen does have an additional need?"

"How's that?"

"Presumably you're aware that when sight is present in eyes and the one who has it attempts to use it, and color is present there in things, unless there's also a third kind of thing present, of a nature
E   specifically for this very purpose, sight will see nothing and colors will be invisible."

"What's this thing you're speaking of?" he said.

"The one you call light," I said.

"It's true, as you say," he said.

"Then the sense of sight and the power of being seen have been bound together by a bond more precious, by no small look, than that uniting other pairs, unless light is something to be despised."

"Surely it's far from being despised," he said.

"And which of the divine beings in the heavens can you point out as the ruling power responsible for this, whose light makes our sight see and visible things be seen as beautifully as possible?"

"The same one you and everyone else would," he said, "since it's obvious you're asking about the sun."

"And is it this way that sight is by its nature related to this god?"

"How?"

"The sun is not sight itself, nor is it that in which sight is present, what we call an eye."

"No indeed."

"But I imagine that's the most sunlike of the sense organs."

"By far."

"And doesn't it acquire the power that it has as an overflow from that which is bestowed by the sun?"

"Very much so."

"So while the sun isn't sight, but is the thing responsible for it, isn't it seen by that very thing?"

"That's how it is," he said.

"Now then," I said, "say that this is what I'm calling the offspring of the good, which the good generated as something analogous to itself; the very thing the good itself is in the intelligible realm in relation to insight and the intelligible things, this is in the visible realm in relation to sight and the visible things."

"How so?" he said. "Go into it more for me."

"With eyes," I said, "do you know that when one no longer turns them on those things to whose colors the light of day extends, but on those on which nocturnal lights fall, they grow dim, and appear nearly blind, just as though no pure sight was present in them?"

"Very much so," he said.

"But I imagine that whenever one turns them to the things the sun illumines, they see them clearly, and pure sight is manifestly present in these very same eyes."

"Certainly."

"In this manner, think of the power of the soul too as being the same way. Whenever it becomes fixed on that which truth and being illumine, it has insight, discerns, and shows itself to have an intellect, but whenever it becomes fixed on something mixed with darkness, something that comes into and passes out of being, it deals in seeming and grows dim, changing its opinions up and down, and is like something that has no intellect."

"It does seem like that."

E

"Then say that what endows the things known with truth, and gives that which knows them its power, is the look of the good. Since it's the cause of knowledge and truth, think of it as something known, but though both of these, knowing and truth, are so beautiful, by regarding it as something else, still more beautiful than they are, you'll

509A

regard it rightly. And as far as knowledge and truth are concerned, just as it's right over there to consider light and sight sunlike, but isn't right to consider them to be the sun, so too here it's right to consider both of these as like the good, but not right to regard either of them as being the good; the condition of the good requires that it be held in still greater honor."

"You're talking about a beauty hard to conceive," he said, "if it endows things with knowledge and truth but is itself beyond these in beauty, because it's sure not pleasure you mean."

"Watch your mouth," I said; "but look into the image of it still more closely."

"In what way?"

B

"I imagine you'd claim that the sun not only endows the visible things with their power of being seen, but also with their coming into being, their growth, and their nurture, though it's not itself coming-into-being."

"How could it be?"

"Then claim as well that the things that are known not only get their being-known furnished by the good, but they're also endowed by that source with their very being and their being what they are, even though the good is not being, but something over and above being, beyond it in seniority and surpassing it in power."

C

And Glaucon, in a very comical manner, said "By Apollo, that's a stupendous stretcher."[111]

"You're to blame for it," I said, "for forcing me to tell the way things seem to me about it."

"And don't by any means stop," he said, "not if there are any other things for you to go over in the likeness to the sun, in case you're leaving something out anywhere."

"That's for sure," I said; "I'm leaving out scads of things."

"Well don't skip over any little bit," he said.

"I suspect I'll skip over a lot," I said, "but be that as it may, as far as it's possible at present, I won't willingly leave anything out."

---

111 Glaucon literally says "that's a preternatural exaggeration," but his words (*daimonias huperbolês*), as Reeve notes, play on the sound of Socrates' words "surpassing it in power" (*dunamei huperechontos*). This is not particularly funny, but Socrates may mean that Glaucon is clowning to soften the impact of an implicit criticism, one that some readers share, that to say anything *is* "over and above being" is nonsensical. But the careful reader will see that Socrates delineates the notion of "being" in his last speech in a twofold way, as *to einai* or *to on*, substantives that posit that something *is*, and as *ousia*, the being-what-it-is at the core of anything; neither of these is the same as the grammatical copula that merely serves to attach a predicate to a subject.

"See that you don't," he said.

"Well then, as we're saying," I said, "think of them as being a   **D**
pair, one ruling as king over the intelligible race and realm, and the
other, for its part, over the visible—note that I'm not saying 'over the
heavens,' so I won't seem to you to be playing verbal tricks with the
name.[112] But do you grasp these two forms, visible, intelligible?"

"I've got them."

"Then take them as being like a line divided into two unequal segments, one for the visible class and the other for the intelligible, and cut
each segment again in the same ratio, and you'll get the parts to one
another in their relation of clarity and obscurity;[113] in the visible section, one segment will be for images, and by images I mean first of all   **510A**
shadows, then semblances formed in water and on all dense, smooth,
bright surfaces, and everything of that sort, if you get the idea."

"I get it."

"Then in the other part, put what this one is likened to, the animals
around us, and every plant, and the whole class of artificial things."

"I'm putting them," he said.

"And would you also be willing to claim," I said, "that it's divided
with respect to truth and its lack, such that the copy is to the thing it's
copied from as a seeming is to something known?"

"I would," he said, "very much so."   **B**

"Then consider next the way the division of the intelligible part
needs to be made."

"What way is that?"

"Such that in one part of it a soul takes as images the things that
were imitated before, and is forced to inquire based on presuppositions, proceeding not to a beginning but to an end, while in the other
part it goes from a presupposition to a beginning free of presuppositions, without the images involved in the other part, making its
investigation into forms themselves and by means of them."

"I didn't sufficiently understand what you mean by these things,"
he said.

"Once more, then," I said; "since you'll understand more easily   **C**
after the following preface. Now I imagine you know that people
who concern themselves with matters of geometry and calculation
and such things presuppose in accord with each investigation the
odd and the even, the geometrical shapes, the three kinds of angles,
and other things related to these; treating these as known and making
them presuppositions, they don't think it's worth giving any further

---

112 In Plato's *Cratylus* (396C), Socrates pretends to derive the word for "heavens" from the
words for "looking up."

113 The first cut is ___visible ‖ intelligible___ and the intelligible realm must occupy the bigger
part if length is analogous to clarity. The re-division, keeping the scale determined by the first
ratio, gives the pattern __|___‖___|_____ . Visible images of visible things occupy the
first segment on the left.

D
account of them either to themselves or to anyone else, as though they were obvious to everyone, but starting from these things and going through the subsequent things from that point, they arrive at a conclusion in agreement with that from which they set their inquiry in motion."

"I do know that very well," he said.

"Then you also know that they make additional use of visible forms, and make their arguments about them, even though they're thinking not about these but about those things these are images of, since it's in regard to the square itself, and its diagonal itself, that

E
they're making those arguments, and not in regard to the one that they draw, and likewise in the other cases; these very things that they model and draw, which also have their own shadows and images in

511A
water, they are now using as images in their turn, in an attempt to see those things themselves that one could not see[114] in any other way than by the power of thinking."

"What you're saying is true," he said.

"The latter, then, is what I meant by the intelligible form, and it's for the inquiry about it that the soul is forced to make use of presuppositions, not going to the source, because it doesn't have the power to step off above its presuppositions, but using as images those things that are themselves imaged down below, in comparison with which these images are reputed to be of preeminent clarity and are treated with honor."[115]

"I understand," he said; "you're talking about the things dealt

B
with by geometrical studies and the arts akin to that."

"Then understand me to mean the following by the other segment of the intelligible part: what rational speech itself gets hold of by its power of dialectical motion, making its presuppositions not sources but genuinely standing places, like steppingstones and springboards, in order that, by going up to what is presuppositionless at the source of everything and coming into contact with this, by following back again the things that follow from it, rational speech may descend in

---

114 A geometrical line is understood as having no breadth, and a plane figure as having no depth. A drawing in the sand, a shape cut out of some flat material, or even any appearance in our pictorial imaginations must falsify what it images if it is to image it at all.

115 This is the most striking implication of the divided line, which is itself a mathematical image. If the pattern in footnote 113, now regarded as upright with its left end at the bottom, has the ratio of image to original represented as we have drawn it, as 1:2 (though it can be anything and need not be commensurable), the upper segment of the visible part will be 2/3 of 1/3 of the whole line, and the lower segment of the intelligible part will be 1/3 of 2/3 of it. That this equality of the two middle segments holds in all cases is proved algebraically in James Adam's commentary on the *Republic* (Vol. II, p. 64), and in the authentically ancient manner, in the same number of steps, in Jacob Klein's *A Commentary on Plato's* Meno (UNC Press, 1965, p. 119). That equality implies that mathematical precision gains nothing in clarity or truth over observation by the senses, but stands at the same level. Conversely, the same equality makes the claim that the visible, and tangible, things around us are images and not the original beings.

that way to a conclusion, making no more use in any way whatever   C
of anything perceptible, but dealing with forms themselves, arriving
at them by going through them, it ends at forms as well."

"I understand," he said, "though not sufficiently, because you
seem to me to be talking about a tremendous amount of work; however, I understand that you want to mark off that part of what is
and is intelligible that's contemplated by the knowledge that comes
from dialectical thinking as being clearer than what's contemplated
by what are called arts, which have presuppositions as their starting
points. Those who contemplate things by means of the arts *are* forced
to contemplate them by thinking and not by sense perception, but since
they examine things not by going up to the source but on the basis of   D
presuppositions, they seem to you to have no insight into them, even
though, by means of their starting point, they're dealing with things
that are intelligible. And you seem to me to be calling the activity of
geometers and such people thinking but not insight, on the grounds
that thinking is something in between opinion and insight."

"You took it in utterly sufficiently," I said. "Along with me, take
it too that for the four segments of the line there are these four kinds
of experiences that arise in the soul, active insight for the highest
and thinking for the second, and assign the names trust to the third   E
and imagination to the last, drawing them up as a proportion[116] and
holding that, in the same manner these experiences have their shares
of clarity, the things they're directed to have corresponding shares
of truth."

"I understand," he said, "and I go along with it and rank them
as you say."

[handwritten: 1) Active insight 2) thinking 3) trust 4) imagination]

---

116 This is the point at which professors go to blackboards, students fill notebooks, commentators pontificate about "the Platonic theory of forms," and translators resort to words like
"intellection." But there are no technical terms here to be memorized, no theory laid down, and
no language outside the scope of ordinary speech. The style of this passage is not casual but it
is conversational, and the words used remain fluid, offered for their usefulness and constantly
subject to revision, and not dictated to make a chorus of disciples. The divided line is itself
the best corrective for those who seek to make it a rigid theoretical structure, since that way of
thinking is represented in it as the lower of the two ways of dealing with intelligible things, the
one that adopts presuppositions, cancels the dialectical process, and cannot achieve full clarity or truth. Exploration of the details of the image is not an end but a beginning. The reader
may also find entries in the Glossary to get more of a sense for the Greek words used here, but
this passage is intended, like everything else in the dialogue, to invite and promote one's own
thinking.

BOOK VII

514A–541B Socrates and Glaucon

Note

> The conversation returns to the topic of education, first in an image that
> depicts it as a turning around of the whole soul from the things that
> inevitably absorb it and prevent it from developing the highest capacities
> of its nature. The earliest phases of education, beginning even before a
> child could talk, with the use of music in the widest sense, and continuing
> in later childhood with gymnastic training, were discussed in Books III
> and IV, and the ultimate goal of all education was described by Socrates
> in Book VI as a bringing to sight of the good that makes evident the
> origin and aim of all things. For the years corresponding to what we
> call secondary and higher education, Socrates now proposes a program
> devoted to mathematical studies of all kinds. Because of the limits of
> mathematical understanding dealt with in the discussion in Book VI of the
> divided line, these are still intended as preparatory studies, occupying,
> in the guiding image of the cave, the long road up to the sunlight, but
> not suitable in the full light of day. The advanced study of things as they
> are, to be undertaken by those who have shown themselves capable in
> all their earlier education, Socrates calls dialectic.

514A "Next," I said, "make an image of our nature as it involves education and the lack of it, by likening it to a condition such as the following: picture human beings in a cavelike dwelling underground, having a long pathway open to the light all across the cave. They're
B in it from childhood on with their legs and necks in restraints, so that they're held in place and look only to the front, restricted by the neck-restraint from twisting their heads around. For them, the light is from a fire burning up above and a long way behind them, and between the fire and the prisoners there's an upper road. Picture a little wall built along this road, like the low partitions puppeteers use to screen the humans who display the puppets above them."

"I see it," he said.

C "Then see the humans going along this little wall carrying all
515A sorts of articles that jut out over the wall, figurines of men and other animals fashioned out of stone and wood and materials of all kinds, with some of the people carrying them past making appropriate sounds and others silent."

"You're describing a bizarre image and bizarre prisoners," he said.

"Like us," I said. "First of all, do you imagine such people would have seen anything of themselves or one another other than the shadows cast by the fire onto the part of the cave right across from them?"

"How could they," he said, "if they were forced to keep their heads immobile throughout life?"

"And what would they have seen of the things carried past? Wouldn't that be the same thing?"

"What else?"

"So if they were able to converse with one another, don't you think they'd speak of these very things they see as the beings?"

"Necessarily."

"And what if their prison also had an echo from the side across from them? Any time any of the people carrying things past uttered a sound, do you imagine they'd believe anything other than the passing shadow had made the sound?"

"By Zeus, I don't," he said.

"So in every way," I said, "such people wouldn't consider anything to be the truth other than the shadows of artificial things."

"That's a great necessity," he said.

"Then consider," I said, "what their release would be like, and their recovery from their restraints and their delusion, if things like that were to happen to them by nature. Whenever one of them would be released, and suddenly required to stand up, and turn his neck around, and walk, and look up toward the light, he'd suffer pain from doing all these things, and because of the blazes of light, he wouldn't have the power to get a clear sight of the things whose shadows he'd seen before. What do you imagine he'd say if someone were to tell him that he'd been seeing rubbish then, but now, somewhat nearer to what *is* and turned toward the things that have more being, he was seeing more accurately? And especially if, pointing to each of the things passing by, one forced him to answer as he asked what they are, don't you imagine he'd be at a loss and believe the things he'd seen before were truer than the ones pointed out to him now?"

"Very much so," he said.

"And if one forced him to look at the light itself, wouldn't he have pain in his eyes and escape by turning back toward those things he was able to make out, and consider them clearer in their very being than the ones pointed out to him?"

"That's how it would be," he said.

"And if one were to drag him away from there by force," I said, "along the rough, steep road up, and didn't let go until he'd dragged him out into the light of the sun, wouldn't he be feeling pain and anger from being dragged, and when he came into the light and had his eyes filled with its dazzle, wouldn't he be unable to see even one of the things now said to be the true ones?"

"That's right," he said, "at least not right away."

"So I imagine he'd need to get accustomed to it, if he were going to have sight of the things above. At first, he'd most easily make out the shadows, and after that the images of human beings and other

B

C

D

E

516A

B   things in water, and only later the things themselves; and turning from those things, he'd gaze on the things in the heavens, and at the heavens themselves, more easily by night, looking at the starlight and moonlight, than by day, at the sun and its light."

"How could it be otherwise?"

"Then at last, I imagine, he'd gain sight of the sun, not its appearances in water or in any setting foreign to it, but he'd have the power to see it itself, by itself, in its own realm, and contemplate it the way it is."

"Necessarily," he said.

C   "And after that, he could now draw the conclusion about it that this is what provides the seasons and the years, and has the governance of all things in the visible realm, and is in a certain manner the cause of all those things they'd seen."

"It's clear that he'd come to these conclusions after those experiences," he said.

"And then what? When he recalled his first home and the wisdom there and the people he was imprisoned with then, don't you imagine he'd consider himself happy because of the change and pity the others?"

"Greatly so."

"And if there had been any honors and commendations and prizes for them then from one another for the person who had the sharpest sight of the things passing by and remembered best all the things that D   usually passed by before and after them and at the same time, and based on those things had greatest ability to predict what was going to come, do you think he'd be longing for those rewards and feel jealousy toward the ones honored by those people and in power among them, or would he feel what Homer depicts,[117] and wish powerfully

> To be a bond-servant to another, tilling the soil
> For a man without land of his own,

and submit to anything whatever rather than hold those opinions and live that way?"

E   "The latter, I imagine," he said; "he'd submit to enduring everything rather than live in that way."

"Then give this some thought too," I said. "If such a person were to go back down and sit in the same spot, wouldn't he get his eyes filled with darkness by coming suddenly out of the sun?"

"Indeed he would," he said.

"And if he had to compete with those who'd always been imprisoned, at passing judgments on those shadows, at a time when his 517A   sight was dim before his eyes settled back in, and if this period of adjustment was not very short, wouldn't he make a laughingstock

---

117 *Odyssey* XI, 489-490. These verses, cited at 386C for deletion, seem now to have been rehabilitated.

of himself, and wouldn't it be said about him that after having gone up above he returned with his eyes ruined, and that it's not worth it even to make the effort to go up? And as for anyone who attempted to release them and lead them up, if they had the power in any way to get him into their hands and kill him, wouldn't they kill him?"[118]

"Ferociously," he said.

"Now this image, dear Glaucon," I said, "needs to be connected as a whole with what was said before, by likening the realm disclosed by sight to the prison dwelling, and the light of the fire within it to the power of the sun; and if you take the upward journey and sight of the things above as the soul's road up into the intelligible region, you won't miss my intended meaning, since you have a desire to hear about that. No doubt a god knows whether it happens to be true. What appears true to me appears this way: in the knowable region, the last thing to be seen, with great effort, is the look of the good, but once it's been seen, it has to be concluded that it's the very cause, for all things, of all things right and beautiful, that it generates light and its source in the visible realm, and is itself the source that bestows truth and insight in the intelligible realm. Anyone who's going to act intelligently in private or in public needs to have sight of it."

"I too join in assuming that," he said, "at least in whatever way I'm able to."

"Come, then," I said, "and join in assuming the following as well, and don't be surprised that those who've come to this point aren't willing to do what belongs to human beings, but their souls are eager to spend all their time up above; presumably it's likely to be that way, if this also stands in accord with the image already described."

"It's certainly likely," he said.

"And what about this? Do you imagine it's anything surprising," I said, "if someone coming from contemplation of divine things to things of a human sort is awkward and looks extremely ridiculous while his sight is still dim and if, before he's become sufficiently accustomed to the darkness around him, he's forced, in law courts or anywhere else, to contend over the shadows of the just or the images they're the shadows of, and to compete about that in whatever way these things are understood by people who've never looked upon justice itself?"

B

C

D

E

118   On reaching this last sentence, many readers forget that this story is told as an image of human nature as it involves education and the lack of it, not as a realistic depiction of the consequences of that lack. Hannah Arendt, in a lecture, once called the sentence the beginning of political philosophy. But whatever truth there may be in that, the sentence and the cave allegory as a whole have implications that run deeper than any possible political interpretation. The fact that Socrates later suffered the fate he describes here may make it difficult to concentrate on the act of intellectual imagination his image calls for, which asks us to consider not external enemies of philosophic emancipation from ignorance, but those things within ourselves that can resist learning to the death of all hope for understanding. In particular, one needs to reflect on what the restraints on the necks of the prisoners in the cave might represent. The image tells us that nature, not other people, puts those restraints on us.

"It's not surprising in any way whatsoever," he said.

518A   "But if someone had any sense," I said, "he'd remember that two sorts of disturbances occur in the eyes from two causes, when they're removed from light into darkness as well as from darkness into light. If he regarded these same things as occurring also with the soul, when he saw one that was confused and unable to make anything out, he wouldn't react with irrational laughter but would consider whether it had come from a brighter life and was darkened by its unaccustomed

B   condition, or was coming out of a greater ignorance into a brighter place and was overwhelmed by the dazzle of a greater radiance. That way, he'd congratulate the one soul on the happiness of its experience and life and pity the other, and if he did want to laugh at that one, he'd be less laughable for laughing at it than someone who laughed at the one coming out of the light above."

"You're speaking in a very balanced way," he said.

"So," I said, "if those things are true, we ought to regard them in the following way: education is not the sort of thing certain people who claim to be professors of it claim that it is. Surely they claim they

C   put knowledge into a soul it wasn't present in, as though they were putting sight into blind eyes."

"Indeed they do claim that," he said.

"But the current discussion indicates," I said, "that this power is present in the soul of each person, and the instrument by which each one learns, as if it were an eye that's not able to turn away from darkness toward the light in any other way than along with the whole body, needs to be turned around along with the whole soul, away from what's fleeting, until it becomes able to endure gazing at what

D   *is* and at the brightest of what is, and this, we're claiming, is the good. Isn't that right?"

"Yes."

"Then there would be an art to this very thing," I said, "this turning around, having to do with the way the soul would be most easily and effectively redirected,[119] not an art of implanting sight in it, but of how to contrive that for someone who has sight, but doesn't have it turned the right way or looking at what it needs to."

"That seems likely," he said.

"Then the other virtues said to belong to a soul probably tend to be near the things belonging to the body, since they're not present in the being of the soul before they've been inculcated by habits and practice,

E   but the virtue involving understanding, more than all, attains to being something more divine, as it seems, which never loses its power, but

519A   by the way it's turned becomes either useful and beneficial or useless and harmful. Or haven't you ever reflected about the people said to

---

119 The two words used here for education, the turning-around (*periagôgê*) or redirecting (*metastrophê*) of the whole soul, also have the meanings, respectively, of revolution and conversion.

be depraved but wise, how penetrating a gaze their little souls have and how sharply they discern the things they're turned toward, since they don't have poor sight but force it to serve vice, so that the more sharply it sees, that much more evil it accomplishes?"

"Very much so," he said.

"But surely," I said, "if, straight from childhood, this tendency of such a nature had been curtailed by having the edges knocked off that have an affinity with becoming, like lead weights that, through eating and the pleasures and greediness involved in such things, get to be growths on the soul that turn its sight excessively downward, and if, freed from them, it was turned toward things that are true, this same power of these same people would have seen them too most sharply, just as it sees the ones it's now turned toward."

"Very likely," he said.

"And what about this?" I said. "Isn't it likely, even necessary from what's been said before, that those who are uneducated and lacking experience with truth could never adequately manage a city, and neither could those who've been allowed to devote all their time to education—the former because they don't have any one goal in life that they need to aim at in doing all the things they do in private and in public, and the latter because they wouldn't willingly engage in action, believing they'd taken up residence in the Isles of the Blessed[120] while still living?"

"True," he said.

"So our job as founders," I said, "is to require the best natures to get to the study we were claiming earlier is the greatest thing, to see the good as well as to climb the path up to it, and when, having climbed up, they've seen it sufficiently, not to allow what they're now permitted to do."

"What in particular?"

"To stay there," I said, "and not be willing to come back down among those prisoners or take part beside them in their labors and honors, the more frivolous ones or even the more serious."

"What?" he said. "Are we going to do them an injustice and make them live worse when it's possible for them to live better?"

"My friend," I said, "you let it slip back out of your memory[121] that this is no concern of the law, for some one class of people in a city to be exceptionally well off, but that it contrive things so that this arises in the city as a whole, by harmonizing the citizens through persuasion

---

120   A conception of the afterlife thought to stem from ancient Crete, not gloomy like the Hades depicted by Homer (see 386B-387C), or childish like that envisioned by Musaeus (363C-D). Later poets amalgamated it with Homer's Elysian Fields, where life was easiest for mortals on earth (*Odyssey* IV, 563-568).

121   See 465E-466A. Glaucon is experiencing what is also virtually impossible for readers to avoid, the loss of the perspective in which the image of the just city earlier, and of the cave now, is only for the sake of understanding the internal condition of each human soul.

520A   and compulsion and making them contribute to one another a share of the benefit with which each sort is capable of improving the community; the law doesn't produce men of this sort in the city to allow them to turn whichever way each one wants but so that it may make full use of them for the binding together of the city."

"That's true," he said; "that did slip my mind."

"Then consider, Glaucon," I said, "that we won't be doing any injustice anyway to the philosophers who arise among us, but we'll be asking just things of them in requiring them also to care for the

B   other people and watch over them. We'll tell them that when people of their sort come along in other cities, it's reasonable for them not to share the burdens in those cities, since they spring up spontaneously in each of them against the will of the polity, and something that grows up on its own, not owing its upbringing to anyone, has just cause not to be too keen on paying for its support. 'But we've bred you both for yourselves and for the rest of the city like the rulers and kings in beehives, to be educated in a better and more complete way

C   than the others and more capable of taking part in both ways of life. So it's necessary for each of you in turn to go down into the communal dwelling and to get used to gazing at dark objects with the others, because when you're used to it you'll see thousands of times better than the people there, and recognize each sort of image for what it is and what it's an image of, from having seen the truth about beautiful and just and good things. And so the city will be governed by you and by us wide awake, and not in a dream the way most are governed now by people who fight with each other over shadows and form factions over ruling, as though that were some great good.

D   But the truth is surely this: that city in which those who are going to rule are least eager to rule is necessarily governed best and with the least divisiveness, while the one that gets the opposite sort of rulers is governed in the opposite way.'"

"Quite so," he said.

"Then do you imagine those who've been brought up will be unpersuaded by us when they hear these things, and be unwilling to share, each in turn, in the labors of the city while dwelling among themselves a lot of the time in the pure region?"

E   "It's not possible," he said, "because we'll be giving just obligations to people who are just. More than anything, each of them will go into ruling as something unavoidable, which is opposite to what those who rule in each city now do."

"That's how it is, my comrade," I said; "if you find a way of life

521A   better than ruling for those who are going to rule, there's a possibility for a well-governed city to come into being for you, because only in it will the rulers be those who are rich in their very being, not in gold but in that in which someone who's happy needs to be rich: a good and intelligent life. But if beggars and people hungry for private goods go into public life imagining that's where they need to go to steal off with the good, there's no possibility, because when ruling becomes something that's fought over, since that sort of war, being domestic and internal, destroys them and the rest of the city."

"Very true," he said.

"Well," I said, "do you know of any way of life other than that of   **B** true philosophy that looks down on political offices?"

"No, by Zeus," he said.

"It's necessary, though, for people who aren't in love with ruling to go after it; if they don't, the rival lovers will do battle."

"Certainly."

"And who else are you going to require to go into guarding the city than the people who are most thoughtful about those things by which a city is governed best, and who have other honors and a better life than the political sort?"

"None other than they," he said.

"Then at this point do you want us to consider in what way such   **C** people will be bred into that, and how one would lead them up to the light, just as some people are said to have ascended from Hades to the gods?"

"How could I not want that?" he said.

"So this wouldn't appear to be a matter of flipping a coin,[122] but of turning around a soul out of a day more like night to a true day, namely an ascent to what *is*, which is exactly what we're going to claim true philosophy is."

"Very much so."

"Then isn't it necessary to consider what things, among those that   **D** can be learned, have that sort of power?"

"Certainly."

"So, Glaucon, what would be a study that would draw the soul from becoming to being? And this occurs to me as I speak: weren't we claiming that it's necessary for these people to be trained in war while they're young?"

"We were claiming that."

"Then the study we're looking for ought to have this feature as well as that one."

"What feature?"

"That it's not without use for men involved in war."

"It should certainly be that way if possible," he said.

"Now they were educated by us earlier in gymnastic exercise and music."

"That was done," he said.

---

122 Literally, "of flipping an oyster-shell," a form of child's play involved in a game something like tag, in which who was "it" was determined by tossing a shell which could land with its dark or light side up.

E   "And presumably gymnastic activity is wholly taken up with what's becoming and passing away, since it oversees a body's growth and decay."

"It appears so."

"So this wouldn't be the study we're looking for."

522A   "No."

"And would it be music, as much of it as we went over before?"

"But that, if you recall," he said, "was an exact counterpart to gymnastic training, educating the guardians by means of habits, and giving them a certain evenness of temper brought about by harmony rather than knowledge, and a sense of proportion brought about by rhythm, and bringing along in speeches certain other habits closely related to these, as far as storytelling speeches were concerned, and the truer sort as well; but as for a study leading toward anything of the sort you're now looking for, there was nothing like that in it."

B   "You're reminding me quite accurately," I said, "because by its very being it had nothing of the sort in it. But, my miraculous Glaucon, what would be of that sort? Because all the arts, presumably, would seem to be for practical utility."

"How could they be anything else? And what other study is still left when music, gymnastic training, and the arts have been put off to one side?"

"Come on, then," I said; "if we can't get any more outside of these, let's take something that extends through all of them."

"Such as?"

C   "Such as this common thing that every branch of art, thinking, and knowledge makes additional use of, and which is among the first things it's necessary for everyone to learn."

"Such as?" he said.

"This trivial matter," I said, "of telling apart one, two, and three. In sum, I mean that it's number and calculating. Or don't they have this feature about them, that every sort of art and knowledge is obliged to get involved with them?"

"Very much so," he said.

"Even the art of warfare?" I said.

"It has a big need of it," he said.

D   "In the tragedies, at any rate," I said, "Palamedes[123] shows up Agamemnon every time as a completely ridiculous general. Aren't you aware that he claims he invented number and set up the battle formations for the army at Troy and counted up the ships and all the rest, as if before that they were unnumbered, and Agamemnon, it seems, didn't even know how many feet he had, if he really didn't

---

123 A legendary hero credited with inventing weighing and measuring, among other things. He was a popular subject for tragedies, since his story included outsmarting Odysseus and being framed as a spy and killed in revenge for it. Surviving fragments indicate that Aeschylus, Sophocles, and Euripides wrote about him.

have the skill of counting? So what in the world sort of general do you imagine he was?"

"An absurd one, I'd say," he said, "if that was true."

"Shall we, then," I said, "set down being able to calculate and count as another thing it's necessary for a man skilled at warfare to learn?"

"Most of all," he said, "not only if he's to understand anything at all about battle formations, but even more if he's to be a human being."

"And do you notice what I do about this study?" I said.

"What?"

"It's liable to be one of the things we're looking for, that by their nature lead toward insight, though no one uses it rightly, as something suited in every way to draw someone toward being."

"How do you mean?" he said.

"I'll try to make clear at least how it seems to me," I said. "So I'll differentiate by myself what does and doesn't lead to what we're talking about, and having looked on beside me, you give your agreement or disagreement so we can see more clearly whether it's the sort of thing I suspect."

"Point them out," he said.

"Okay," I said, "I'm pointing, if you see them, to some among the perceptible things that don't call insight[124] into play to examine them, as though an adequate judgment was coming from sense-perception, and to others that in every way demand that it examine them because sense-perception is coming up with nothing reliable."

"It's obvious that you're talking about things appearing from far away," he said, "and optical illusions made by painters."

"You haven't caught on at all to what I'm talking about," I said.

"Well what sort of things do you mean?" he said.

"The ones that *don't* call for insight," I said, "are all those that don't pass over into an opposite perception at the same time; I'm taking the ones that do pass over as those that call it into play, when sense-perception doesn't show something to be one thing any more than its opposite, whether it comes across it from nearby or far away. You'll see what I mean more clearly this way: we'd say these were three fingers,[125] the smallest, the next, and the middle one."

"Quite so," he said.

---

124 The word is *noêsis*, the active exercise of the power belonging to the top section of the divided line. Socrates is specifically *not* using the word *dianoia* here to say that sense-perception sometimes needs the problem-solving activity of intellect to resolve difficulties. He implies instead that apparent contradictions in sense experience can be the springboards for a direct engagement with intelligible things themselves. In 524D below, in concluding this line of argument, he uses the word *dianoia* for the whole thinking power that includes insight as well as reasoning.

125 Socrates can be imagined as bending his index finger down to the thumb, leaving the other fingers extended.

"And understand me to be talking about them as seen from nearby; just consider the following about them with me."

"What's that?"

D   "Each of them appears alike as a finger, and in that respect at least, it makes no difference whether it's seen as intermediate or at one extreme, whether it's white or dark, whether it's thick or thin, or anything that's like that, because in all these cases, with most people, the soul isn't forced to ask for insight into what a finger is. That's because sight at no point indicates to it that the finger is at the same time the opposite of a finger."

"No indeed," he said.

"Then in all likelihood," I said, "that sort of thing wouldn't be apt to call into play or arouse insight."

"Likely not."

E   "But what about their largeness and smallness? Does sight see that adequately, and does it make no difference to it whether any of them is situated intermediate or at one extreme? And likewise for touch with thickness and thinness or softness and hardness? And do the other senses reveal things of that sort in a way that's not deficient? Doesn't

524A   each of them work like this: in the first place, the sense assigned to hardness is forced to be assigned to softness as well, and it passes along to the soul that the same thing is both hard and soft at the same time while it's perceiving it?"

"That's how it works," he said.

"Then isn't it necessary in such cases," I said, "for the soul, for its part, to be at a loss about what this sensation is indicating as hard if it's saying the same thing is also soft, and with the sensing of a light or heavy thing, to be at a loss about what's light and heavy, if the sensation indicates that the heavy thing is light and the light thing is heavy?"

B   "Those are certainly strange readings for the soul to get," he said, "and in need of scrutiny."

"Then most likely in such cases," I said, "a soul will try first, by calling calculation and insight into play, to examine whether each of the things passed on to it is one or two."

"Certainly."

"And if they appear to be two, won't each appear as something distinct and one?"

"Yes."

"So if each is one and both together are two, it will be thinking the

C   two as separate, because it wouldn't be thinking inseparable things as two but as one."

"That's right."

"But we're claiming that sight saw large and small not as separate but as something mixed together, aren't we?"

"Yes."

"And for clarity about this, insight was required in turn to see large and small, not as mixed together but as distinct, the opposite of sight."

"True."

"And isn't this where it first occurs to us to ask what large and small are?"

"Beyond a doubt."

"And just for this reason we were calling something intelligible in the one case and visible in the other."

"With utmost rightness," he said.

"Well these are also the things I was just now trying to talk about   D
in saying that some things are apt to call in the thinking power while others are not, when I marked off the ones that strike sense-perception together with their own opposites as apt to call it in, and all those that don't as not apt to arouse insight."

"And by now I understand," he said, "and it seems that way to me too."

"Well, then, in which of these groups do number and the one[126] seem to be?"

"I have no idea," he said.

"Just gather it up from what was said before," I said. "Because if   E
the one, itself by itself, is seen, or grasped by any other sense, in an adequate way, it wouldn't be something that draws someone toward being, as we described in the example of the finger. But if something opposite to it is always seen at the same time, so that nothing appears any more one than the opposite as well, then at that point there would be a need for something to make a judgment about it, and in that situation a soul would be forced to be at an impasse and search for a way out, which would set the thinking power in it in motion, and it would   525A
have to ask what the one itself is; and so the study having to do with the one would be among the things that lead up to the contemplation of what *is*, and redirect the soul to that."

"And really," he said, "the sight having to do with that same item is not the least among the things that have this tendency, since we see the same thing at the same time as both one and infinitely many."[127]

"And if that happens with the one," I said, "wouldn't it also happen with all number?"

"How could it not?"

---

126 *One* is not considered a number but as that by which numbering is possible. An egg is the one, or perceptible unit, by which a dozen eggs are counted, and the one itself is that intelligible unit by which counting itself takes place from a purely mathematical standpoint. To an ancient Greek ear, the word for number (*arithmos*) would call to mind first of all a multitude or collection of perceptible things, which may explain why Glaucon is at first unable to answer the question.

127 Not only is one human being many arms, legs, etc., but any visible thing is extended and can be *seen* by an intelligent look to be infinitely divisible.

"But surely number is what the arts of calculation[128] and arithmetic are all about."

"Quite so."

"And so these show themselves to be things that lead toward truth."

"Preternaturally so."

B   "Then it looks like they'd be among the studies we're looking for, because it's necessary for someone skilled at warfare to learn them for the sake of military formations, and also for a philosopher because someone rising up out of becoming needs to get hold of being, or else never become skilled at reasoning."

"It is those things," he said.

"And our guardian is both a warrior and a philosopher."

"He certainly is."

"So, Glaucon, it would be appropriate to make a law about the study of it, and to persuade those who'll take part in the most impor-
C   tant concerns in the city to go into the art of calculation, and to take it up not for private purposes, but all the way until they arrive at the contemplation of the nature of numbers through insight alone, not practicing it for the sake of buying or selling like merchants or trades-men, but for the sake of war and of ease in redirecting the soul itself from becoming to truth and being."

"You put it most beautifully," he said.

"And now that the study having to do with the kinds of calculation
D   has been mentioned," I said, "I realize how intricate it is, and in how many ways it's useful to us for what we want, if someone pursues it for the sake of knowing itself and not for trade."

"In what respect in particular?" he said.

"This one that we were just talking about, the way it leads the soul strongly in the upward direction and forces it to discuss what has to do with numbers themselves, and doesn't stand for it in any way if someone engages in discussion with it by pointing to numbers that have visible or tangible bodies. You're probably aware of people who are formidable in these matters, and how, if someone in a discussion
E   tries to divide the one itself, they ridicule him and won't stand for

---

128   This probably refers more to the study of numerical ratios than to operations like multiplication and division, and hence to properties of numbers that belong to them only in relations
to one another. The distinction was a subtle one, and the understanding of it varied from one
author to another. (See Jacob Klein, *Greek Mathematical Thought and the Origin of Algebra*, MIT
Press, 1968, chs. 2-3) At any rate, what we would call arithmetic was thought of as having two
branches, and the name of this one (*logistikê*) corresponds to the name Socrates gives at 440B to
the reasoning part of the soul (*logismos*). Hence, just below, he takes this sort of mathematical
study as a prerequisite for the reasoning power a philosopher needs to develop.

it; instead, if you chop it up, they multiply it, on guard that the one should never appear to be not one but many parts."[129]

"You're telling the exact truth," he said.

"Well, what do you imagine, Glaucon, if someone were to ask them 'What sort of numbers is your discussion about, you marvelous people, in which the one is the sort of thing you people require it to be, with each and every one equal to every one without even a tiny difference, and with none having any part within itself?' What do you imagine they'd reply?"   526A

"This, I'd say: that they're talking about those things that only admit of being thought, and that it's not possible to handle in any other way."

"Do you see, then, my friend," I said, "that the study of them is liable to be requisite for us by its very nature, since it obviously forces the soul to use insight itself directed at the truth itself?"   B

"It sure does," he said, "and powerfully so."

"And what about this? Have you observed up to now that people who are by nature skilled at calculation are naturally quick at virtually everything learnable, while those who are slow, if they are educated and given training in that, even if they get no other benefit, still all make progress toward becoming quicker than they were?"

"It is like that," he said.

"And surely I'd imagine you couldn't easily find many studies that provide more hard work for the person learning and practicing them than this one does."   C

"No indeed."

"Then for the sake of all these benefits, the study of it is not to be passed over, but the people with the best natures need to be educated in it."

"I fully agree," he said.

"So let this one stand approved by us," I said, "and for a second one, let's consider whether the one next after that is appropriate for us."

"What's that? Or do you mean geometry?" he said.

"That very thing," I said.

---

129 Any mathematical object capable of division would be an extended magnitude belonging to the domain of geometry. The two arithmetical arts study multitudes as such, the unit of which is the one itself, a purely intelligible entity that is one and nothing but one. Fractions arise from either confusing magnitude and multitude, or deliberately fusing them as Rene Descartes did in the 17th century, when he invented a new mathematical discipline he called geometrical algebra. The ancient art of *logistikê* would handle what we call fractions as numerical ratios. If you think you've produced 2/3 by thrusting into the one itself and dividing it, your formidable opponents parry by saying you've really multiplied the unit threefold and looked at two of them in relation to the whole three. Fractions can be added but ratios cannot. Operations with ratios, such as compounding, require a precise attention to purely intelligible relations, and can help loosen the intellect from reliance on visual images. Socrates' language contains a smile at these formidable students of the arithmetical arts, but an entirely benign one.

D   "It's clear that as much of it as extends to things involved in war is appropriate. For encampments and occupying territory, and for gathering armies together and putting them in formations, and all the other ways people arrange military units in their battles themselves and on marches, whether one is skilled at geometry or not would make him two different people."

E   "But for things like that," I said, "some trifling little bit of geometry, plus calculation, would be sufficient; it's necessary to consider whether the bulk of it, that's more far-reaching, extends in any way toward that other goal, toward making it easier to gain sight of the look of the good. And we claim that everything does extend in that direction that forces the soul to be redirected into that realm in which the most privileged[130] of what is resides, which it's necessary for it to use every means to see."

"You're speaking rightly," he said.

"So if it forces one to gaze upon being, it's appropriate, but if upon becoming, it's not appropriate."

"So we're claiming."

527A   "Well, then," I said, "no one who has even a slight experience of geometry is going to dispute *this* with us anyway, that this kind of knowledge is completely the opposite of the words that are spoken in it by those who practice it."

"How so?" he said.

"There's no doubt they speak in a very absurd way, with a poverty of vocabulary, because they talk as though they were engaged in practical activity, making all their arguments for the sake of action, uttering the words 'squaring' and 'setting up against' and 'joining together' and everything like that,[131] though the whole study is doubtless pursued for the sake of knowing."

B   "Absolutely so," he said.

"So don't we still need to come to agreement about this?"

"About what?"

"That it's for the sake of knowing what always is, and not what's coming into being or passing away at any time."

"That's easy to agree to," he said, "because geometry is a knowing of what always is."

"Therefore, you true-born man, it would be something that draws a soul toward truth and works up philosophic thinking to get onto an upward track what we now keep on a downward one where it doesn't belong."

---

130 Literally "happiest."

131 A major theme of the first book of Euclid's *Elements* culminates, in Propositions 44-46, in the power to take the area from any rectilinear figure and reshape it into a parallelogram with a given base or angle, and to construct a square on any line. It would be difficult, and sound artificial, to restate the acts of understanding involved in these propositions without the language of doing and making. (Euclid was active about a century after Socrates' death.)

"To the greatest possible extent," he said.

"Then to the greatest possible extent," I said, "instructions need to   C
be given so that the people in your city of beauty[132] won't avoid geometry in any way, since even its side-effects are no small things."

"What side-effects?" he said.

"The very ones you were mentioning," I said, "that have to do
with war, and what's more, for all studies, to be receptive to them in
a more beautiful way, presumably we know it will make a difference
to the whole and to every part whether someone's been engaged in
geometry or not."

"By all means in every way, by Zeus," he said.

"So we'll make this a second study for the young?"

"Let's make it that," he said.

"And what next? Shall we make astronomy a third, or doesn't   D
that seem right?"

"It does to me anyway," he said, "because for being more obser-
vant about seasons and months and years, it's just the thing, not only
in farming and navigation but no less so in the business of a general
as well."

"You're charming," I said; "you seem like someone who's playing
to the crowd, in fear of being thought to be assigning useless studies.
It's no slight thing, but a difficult matter, to begin to have confidence
that in these studies a certain faculty in the soul of each person is
purified and fired up again when it's been ruined and blinded by   E
other pursuits, something more worth saving than thousands of eyes,
because with it alone is truth seen. So to those who look at these things
the way you do, you'll seem to be speaking of something inexpress-
ibly good, while all those who aren't aware of this in any way will
likely regard you to be speaking of nothing at all, since they won't
see any other benefit worth mentioning from them. Just decide right   528A
now which of the two groups you'll talk to, or else don't make your
arguments for either sort, but for your own sake most of all, though
you wouldn't begrudge it to anyone else, if anybody was able to get
any benefit from them."

"That's the way I prefer to do it," he said, "to discuss it and to ask
and answer questions mostly for my own benefit."

"Well, back up then," I said, "to the last step, because the way we
took up what came next after geometry wasn't right."

"How were we taking it up?" he said.

"After a plane surface," I said, "we were taking up a solid that
was already in rotation, before taking it up by itself, but the right
way is to take up a third dimension next after a second. And this is   B
presumably concerned with the dimension belonging to cubes and
with what partakes of depth."

---

132 All one word (*kallipolis*), and one that was in fact used for some Greek cities, so that Socrates
has now in effect named the imagined city.

"Yes it is, Socrates," he said, "but these things don't seem to have been discovered yet."

"And the causes of that are twofold," I said. "Since not even one city holds them in honor, these things, which are difficult, are sought after in a feeble way, and also, those seeking them need someone to give them direction, and they couldn't make the discovery without such a person, who's first of all hard to come by, and then, once one

C   had come along, the way things are now, those who are capable of seeking these things out wouldn't be persuaded to, because they're so sure of themselves. But if a whole city were to join in sponsoring these things by bringing them into honor, they would be persuaded, and by being continuously and vigorously sought after, it would become manifest how it is with them. Even now, when they're disdained by most people and curtailed by the people who seek them without having an understanding of what they're useful for, still in the face of all these things they grow inexorably by their own elegance,[133] and it wouldn't be at all surprising if they came to light."

D   "Yes, they are in fact exceptionally elegant," he said. "But tell me more clearly what you meant just now. Apparently you were taking geometry as what treats the plane surface."

"Yes," I said.

"And then first," he said, "you put astronomy after that, but later you backtracked."

"Because I was in a hurry to get through everything quickly," I said, "I took even longer. While the investigation of the dimension of depth was the next one, I stepped past it, because it's in a laughable state as an inquiry, and I spoke of astronomy after geometry, although it's a motion of something with depth."

"What you're saying is correct," he said.

E   "Let's put astronomy as the fourth study, then," I said, "since the one now being neglected will be present if a city ever pursues it."

"Likely so," he said. "And as for the thing you just now berated me about, when I was praising astronomy in a low-class way, I'll

529A   now praise the way you go into it, because it seems to me to be clear to everyone that it forces a soul to look up and takes it up there from down here."

"Maybe it's clear to everyone except me," I said; "to me it doesn't seem that way."

"So how does it seem?" he said.

"That the way the people who lead the ascent to philosophy undertake it now, it makes one look entirely downward."

---

133 One lovely example out of many may be found in Euclid's Prop. XII, 7. There is something odd about Socrates' tirade as well as his pretence of having first forgotten the very thing he criticizes others for neglecting. Jacob Klein suggests that the dimension of depth political communities are being accused of neglecting is really the one within the soul. (See *A Commentary on Plato's Meno*, pages 191-192.)

"How do you mean?" he said.

"It looks to me as though you're taking the study of the things above your own way, in a not ungenerous spirit," I said, "since even if someone were to learn something by bending over backward, gazing at decorations on a ceiling, you'd probably consider him to be viewing them with insight and not eyes. And maybe you're thinking about it in a beautifully nuanced way and I'm being simplistic, but I'm just not capable of regarding any other study as making a soul look upward than one that's concerned with what *is* and is invisible; if someone attempts to learn anything from perceptible things, whether with wide-open eyes gazing up or with squinty eyes peering down, I'd never claim he was learning, because knowledge has nothing to do with things of that sort, or that his soul was looking up rather than down, even if he was learning while doing the backstroke on land or on sea."

B

C

"I'm getting what I deserve," he said, "and you were in the right to slap me around. But exactly how did you mean that people need to learn astronomy in a way that runs counter to what they learn now, if it's to be learned in a way that helps toward the things we're talking about?"

"Like this," I said: "these decorations on the heavens, even though they're embroidered on something visible, can be regarded as the most beautiful and precise things of their kind, but they're far short of the true ones, the motions by which swiftness that *is* swiftness and slowness that *is* slowness are moved relative to one another in true number on all their true figures, and cause the things occupying them to move, motions which are grasped by reasoning and thinking and not by sight.[134] Or do you imagine they are?"

D

"By no means," he said.

"Accordingly," I said, "one needs to use the decoration around the heavens for examples for the sake of learning that approaches those other things, just as if one were to stumble on diagrams drawn and elaborated in an extraordinary way by Daedalus[135] or some other workman or artist. No doubt someone experienced in geometry, on seeing such things, would regard them as being very beautiful in their workmanship, but consider it ridiculous to inspect them in earnest as though in them one could get hold of the truth about equals and doubles or any other proportions."

E

530A

"How's that not going to be ridiculous?" he said.

---

134 One of the high points of ancient astronomy is Ptolemy's demonstration in Bk. XII, Ch. 1 of the *Almagest*, of the conditions for retrogradation, by a common proof that applies to any planet on either of two assumptions about its orbit. Ptolemy, writing five or six centuries after Socrates' time, was entirely in sympathy with this view that the astronomer was contemplating intelligible patterns at the heart of the cosmos.

135 A legendary sculptor, mentioned in Plato's *Meno* (97D-E) and *Euthyphro* (11C), whose statues were so lifelike they moved their eyes and sometimes ran away.

"So don't you imagine," I said, "that someone who's an astronomer in his being is of the same persuasion when he looks at the motions of the stars? He'd regard the maker of the heavens as having organized them and the things in them as beautifully as it's possible for such works to be organized, but as for the proportioning of a night to a day, and of these to a month, and a month to a year, and of the other stars
B   to these and to one another, do you imagine he wouldn't consider it absurd for someone to regard these things as always coming about in the same way without varying at all in any respect, even though they involve bodies and are visible, and to seek in every way to get hold of the truth about them?"

"It does seem that way to me," he said, "at least now that I'm listening to you."

"Therefore," I said, "we'll approach astronomy in the same way as geometry, by using problems,[136] and leave the things in the heav-
C   ens behind, if, by taking up astronomy in its very being, we're going to make what's naturally intelligent in the soul be useful instead of useless."

"You're imposing a task many times greater than the way astronomy is done now," he said.

"Yes, and I imagine we'll impose the rest after the same fashion," I said, "if we're to be of any use as lawgivers. But do you have anything to suggest about appropriate studies?"

"I don't," he said, "at least not at the moment."

"But I imagine motion presents itself not in one but a number of
D   forms," I said. "Maybe some wise person will be able to say what all of them are, but two are apparent even to us."

"What sort, exactly?"

"Alongside this one," I said, "there's an exact counterpart to it."

"What is it?"

"The same way the attention of the eyes is caught in relation to astronomy," I said, "ears are liable to have their attention caught in relation to harmonic motion, and these two kinds of knowledge are in a certain way sisters,[137] as the Pythagoreans say, and we go along with that, Glaucon. Or how do we regard them?"

"That way," he said.

E   "Then since it's a big job," I said, "we'll ask those people what they say about these topics, and whether there's anything else in addition to them, but beyond all that we'll watch out for our own concern."

"What's that?"

---

136   R. Catesby Taliaferro reports (*The Timaeus and Critias of Plato*, Bollingen Books, Pantheon, 1944, p. 23) an ancient story that Plato gave all his best students a table of planetary data and asked them to come up with ways of saving the appearances.

137   If the striking visible motions in place lead to a discovery of underlying ratios of magnitudes, the striking audible motions in time lead to a discovery of underlying whole number ratios.

"That the people we'll be bringing up never try to learn any of these things that's incomplete from our point of view, and doesn't invariably get to the place that everything invariably ought to reach, as we were just saying about astronomy. Or aren't you aware that people do something else of that sort with harmony as well? Because even though they for their part take careful measurements of audible intervals and tones in relation to each other, they do their work to no effect, just like the astronomers." 531A

"By the gods, they do," he said, "and it's ridiculous. They use the name 'compressed' for certain things and strain their ears to catch a sound from their vicinity, and some say they hear a certain extra sound in between, and that this is the smallest interval for things to be measured by, while others contend that it's just like the ones already sounded; both sides put ears ahead of intelligence."[138] B

"You're talking about the worthy folks who cause their strings trouble by tormenting them," I said, "stretching them on the rack; but so my image won't become overextended, with their getting beatings with a plucking tool, or with accusation, denial, and bluster from the strings, I'll call a halt to the image and declare that I'm not talking about them but about the people we just said we were going to ask about harmony. Because they do the same thing as the astronomers; C they look for the numbers in these audible consonant intervals, but they don't rise to the level of problems, to examine which numbers are consonant and which aren't, and why in each case."

"You're talking about a prodigious undertaking," he said.

"About a useful one," I said, "for inquiring about the beautiful and good, which it's useless to pursue in any other way."

"Likely so," he said.

"And I imagine," I said, "that the route through all the things we've gone over, if it gets to what they have in common and in kin- D ship with one another, and gathers together the things by which they're at home in one another's company, then undertaking them will contribute something to what we want and not be wasted labor; otherwise, it's wasted."

"I have an inkling of that too," he said. "But you're talking about a mighty big job, Socrates."

"You mean the prelude," I said, "or what? Don't we know that all these things are a prelude to the song itself that one needs to learn? Because I'm sure you don't think people who are skillful in these things are inclined toward dialectic."

"No, by Zeus," he said, "except for some very few that I've run E across."

---

138 The dispute was over the use of quartertones. The last clause adopts an insult one side had used against the other.

"So," I said, "do you think any people who aren't capable of give and take in argument will ever know any of the things we claim they need to know?"

"Not that either," he said.

532A "Well then, Glaucon," I said, "isn't this now the very song that dialectic sings through to the end? And the power of sight may be an image of it, even though it's something intelligible. We were saying that sight at a certain point undertakes to look at the animals themselves, and at the stars themselves, and finally at the sun itself. In the same way too, when anyone undertakes, by means of dialectic without any of the senses, to push on by means of reasoning to each

B thing itself that *is*, and doesn't give up before it gets hold of the good itself by insight itself, he comes to the end of the intelligible realm just as that other person did then to the end of the visible."

"Completely and fully," he said.

"What about it? Don't you call this mode of passage dialectic?"

"What else?"

"And as for the release from restraints," I said, "and the turning around from the shadows to the images and the light, and the road

C up out of the cave into the sun, and still being unable there to look at the animals and plants and the light of the sun, but looking at the divine semblances in water and at shadows of the beings, rather than at shadows of images cast by a light of a sort that, as judged in comparison to the sun, is only a shadow itself, all this practice of the arts that we went over has this power and is a way of leading what's best in the soul to the contemplation of the best among the things that are,

D just as then what was clearest in the body was led to see the brightest thing in the bodily and visible realm."

"I do accept that," he said. "And even though it seems to me to be thoroughly difficult to accept, in another way it's also difficult not to accept. Still and all, since it not only needs to be listened to now at present, but also needs to be gone back into again often, let's grant that these things are the way they're now being stated and go on to the song itself, and go over it the same way we went over the prelude. Tell

E us, then, what manner of power dialectic has, and exactly what forms it's divided into, and what paths they take, because it looks already as though it would be these that lead to that place that would give the one who reached it a rest from the road and an end to his journey."

533A "My dear Glaucon," I said, "you'd no longer be able to follow, though there'd be no lack of willingness on my part. You could no longer see any image of what we were talking about, but only the truth itself, at least what's apparent of it to me. Whether it appears in its very being or not no longer deserves to be confidently asserted, but that there is some such thing to see is something one can be sure of. Isn't that so?"

"Yes indeed."

"And also that only the power of dialectic could reveal it, and only to someone with experience in the things we were just going over, and that it's possible in no other way?"

"That too deserves to be confidently asserted," he said.

"At least no one will argue with us when we say this much," I said, "that it takes a different mode of inquiring to attempt, for each thing itself, in a methodical way that involves everything, to get hold of what each is. But all the other kinds of arts are directed, all of them, either toward opinions and desires of human beings, or toward generating or constructing things, or toward caring for things that grow or have been constructed; as for the remaining ones, which we claimed do get some grasp of what is, namely geometry and the ones that go along with it, we see that they dream about being but it's not possible for them to see it wide awake so long as they use presuppositions and leave them inviolate, unable to give an account of them. Because in a situation in which the beginning is what's not known, and the end and intermediate parts are woven together out of what's not known, what ingenuity could ever turn such concurrence of opinion into knowledge?"

"None at all," he said.

"Then isn't it only the dialectical mode of inquiry," I said, "that passes on to that, abolishing the presuppositions, back to the beginning itself, in order that it might be secured, and when the eye of the soul is mired to the depths of its being in some inarticulate morass, tugs it gently and draws it up above, using the arts we went over to assist it and help in turning the eye of the soul around? We spoke of the latter a number of times, out of habit, as kinds of knowledge, but they need a different name, something brighter than opinion but dimmer than knowledge. We demarcated it somewhere in the earlier discussion as thinking, but there can be no quibbling about a name, it seems to me, for people who have a consideration in front of them of things as great as those facing us."

"No indeed," he said. "What it signifies only has meaning in reference to the state of clarity in the soul."

"Then it's satisfactory," I said, "just as before, to call the first portion knowledge, the second thinking, the third trust, and the fourth imagination, and the last two both together opinion, and the first two both together insight; and opinion is about becoming while insight is about being. And as being is to becoming, insight is to opinion, and as insight is to opinion, knowledge is to trust and thinking to imagination.[139]

B

C

D

E

534A

---

139 The last two ratios Socrates gives arise from alternating the ratios of the segments within the two main parts. This is a mathematically sound step, and has the effect of pointing the careful reader toward a certain interchangeability between mathematics and our trust in our senses. If that reader has some competence in the theory of ratios, the passage is a second and stronger invitation to demonstrate the exact equality, in clarity and truth, between those two relations of the soul to its experience. (See the note to 511A.) This gives the mathematically inclined reader an opportunity to use math as a stepping stone beyond math, a small reflection, in direct experience, of the educational role Socrates assigns to mathematical studies.

But as for the proportion of the things these are directed toward, and the division in two parts of each of the two, the objects of opinion and of insight, let's let them go, Glaucon, so that we don't get filled with many times as many arguments as the number of those that have been gone through."

B

"It does seem that way to me as well about the other things," he said, "at least as far as I'm able to follow."

"And do you also call someone who takes hold of the being of each thing dialectical? And as for someone who can't, would you claim that he has no insight into it to the same extent that he can't give an account to himself or to someone else?"

"How could I claim he did?" he said.

"And isn't it the same way with the good? If someone can't distinguish the look of the good in speech by separating it out from among all other things, and, as if in a battle, put it through every sort of cross-examination,[140] determined to cross-examine it not against opinion but up against being, and in all these tests bring it through with the account of it still on its feet, will you declare that someone in that condition doesn't know the good itself or any other good either, and if he does somehow get hold of some image of it, that he gets hold of it by opinion, not knowledge, and that he's living his present life in dreams and sleeping it away, and before he's ever been awake here, he'll arrive in Hades first and go to sleep terminally."

C

D

"By Zeus," he said, "I'll declare every bit of that vehemently."

"And as for those children of yours, the ones you're raising and educating in speech, if you were ever to raise them in fact, I don't imagine you'd allow them to be rulers, sovereign over the greatest things in the city, if they were as irrational as lines."[141]

"No indeed," he said.

"So will you make it a law that they should take part most of all in that education as a result of which they'll be able to ask and answer questions most knowledgeably?"

E

"I'll make it a law," he said, "along with you."

"Well does it seem to you," I said, "that dialectic has been established by us as a capstone atop the things to be learned, that no other study could any longer be rightly set up as higher than this one, and

535A

that our consideration of the studies has now reached its end?"

"To me it does," he said.

---

140 As Socrates uses it, this word (*elegchos*) does not refer to a refutation conducted on the assumption that the truth is otherwise, but to an effort to push back toward the assumptions implied within an assertion. As such, it is part of the natural dialectical process someone genuinely striving for understanding would go through within himself. Examples of this type of clarifying cross-examination may be seen in Socrates' questioning of Polemarchus and Thrasymachus in Bk. I.

141 An irrational line has no common measure with the unit line, and no numerical ratio with it.

"Then the distribution of them is left for you," I said, "what people we'll be assigning these studies to and in what manner."

"Evidently," he said.

"And do you remember the selection of the rulers from before, what sort of people we picked out?"

"How could I not," he said.

"Then for the rest of it," I said, "assume that those natures are to be selected, because the most steady and courageous people are to be preferred, and if possible, the best looking, but besides that, not only are those whose characters are noble and tough to be sought, but they also need to have in their natures the things that are conducive to this education."

B

"What sort of things exactly would you single out?"

"Sharpness at studies, you blessed one," I said; "that, and learning without difficulty, needs to be in them from the start. Because, I tell you, souls are much more cowardly in rigorous studies than in gymnastic training, because the labor involved is more intimate, since it's private and not shared in common with the body."

"That's true," he said.

"And one needs to look for someone with a good memory who's firm and in every way fond of hard work. How else do you imagine someone's going to be willing to work at labors of the body and also complete so much study and exertion?"

C

"No one would," he said, "if he's not naturally gifted in every possible way."

"The mistake that's now made, anyway," I said, "and the dishonor that has fallen on philosophy because of it, which I also mentioned earlier, is that it's not taken up according to merit; it would have to be taken up not by illegitimate candidates, but genuine ones."

"How so?"

"First of all," I said, "the person who's going to take it up can't be halfhearted in his dedication to hard work, loving work half the time and lazy the other half, but this is what happens when someone is devoted to gymnastic exercise and to hunting, and loves hard work at everything that makes use of the body, but is no lover of learning or of listening and not inquisitive, but hates the work involved in all those things; and someone whose love of hard work goes over to the opposite extreme is also handicapped."

D

"What you say is completely true," he said.

"And speaking of truth," I said, "doesn't this same thing apply? Won't we class a soul as crippled if it hates a willing lie, can hardly bear to tell a lie itself, and gets exceedingly distressed when others do, but takes it calmly when it harbors the unwilling sort, and feels no great distress when it's caught being ignorant in some area, but contentedly wallows in ignorance like an animal of the pig variety?"

E

"Absolutely so," he said.

536A

"And as far as moderation is concerned," I said, "and courage, and loftiness of mind, and all the other parts of virtue, it's necessary to watch out for what's illegitimate and what's genuine. This is no small matter, because when anyone, whether a private person or a city, doesn't know how to examine such things thoroughly, they unknowingly rely on lame or illegitimate specimens for what they happen to need, in the one case friends, in the other, rulers."

"That's very much how it is," he said.

B   "So there's a need for us to be especially cautious about all such things, because if we take care to educate people who are sound of limb and sound of mind in so great a study and so great a discipline, justice herself will have no fault to find with us, and we'll keep the city and polity safe; but by bringing people of a different sort into them, we'll be doing everything contrary to that, and drown philosophy in a still greater flood of ridicule."

"That would certainly be a shame," he said.

"Quite so," I said, "but it looks like I'm getting in a ridiculous position right now."

"In what way?" he said.

C   "I forgot that we were being playful," I said, "and I got too worked up as I spoke. Because I looked at philosophy while I was talking, and when I saw her spattered with mud undeservedly, I seem to have gotten excessively distressed, and said what I said too earnestly, as if I were venting a spirited anger against those who were responsible."

"No, by Zeus," he said, "it didn't seem that way at all to me as a listener."

"But it did to me as a speaker," I said. "And let's not overlook this point, that in the earlier selection we picked older people, but in this one that won't be possible. Because one shouldn't believe Solon,

D   that someone who gets old is capable of learning many things, but that he's less capable of that than of running; all great and numerous labors are for the young."

"Necessarily," he said.

"Then the things that have to do with calculation and geometry, and with every preparatory study that's needed as preparation for an education in dialectic, should be set before them while they're children, but not as compulsory learning done with the trappings of instruction."

"Why, exactly?"

"Because someone who's free ought not to learn any learnable

E   thing by slavery," I said. "The labors of the body that are labored at by force don't make the body any worse, but no forced study is enduring in a soul."

"True," he said.

"So, most excellent one," I said, "don't raise the children by means of force in the things they learn, but by playing, so you'll also be able to see what each of them is naturally inclined toward." 537A

"What you say makes sense," he said.

"And you remember, don't you," I said, "that we were claiming the children also were to be led into war on horses as spectators, and if there was any safe place, brought up close and given a taste of blood like puppies?"

"I remember," he said.

"Well, in all these things," I said, "the labors, the studies, and the terrors, whoever always displays the most agility is to be enrolled among a certain select number."

"At what age?" he said.

"The age at which they're allowed to give up compulsory gym- B nastic training," I said, "since that's a time, whether it goes on for two years or three, when it's impossible to do anything else, because fatigue and sleep are enemies of learning. And at the same time, one of their tests, and that not the least of them, is what each will show himself to be in gymnastic training."

"Of course," he said.

"So after that time," I said, "the select ones from among the twenty-year-olds will be given greater honors than the rest, and the things they learned as children that came up in a miscellaneous way need C to be brought together for these young people into an overview of the kinship of their studies with one another, and with the nature of what *is*."

"That's the only sort of learning that's firmly fixed, at any rate," he said, "in those who get it."

"It's also the greatest test," I said, "of whether a dialectical nature is or isn't present, since someone capable of an overview is dialectical, and someone who's not isn't."

"I think so too," he said.

"Well, these are the things you'll need to examine," I said, "to find the ones who are most capable at that, and steady in their studies, as D well as steady in war and the rest of the things required of them, and when they pass thirty years of age, you'll establish the select from among the select in greater honors, and examine *them*, testing by the power of dialectic who's capable of freeing himself from the eyes and the other senses to go on to the very thing that *is* in the realm of truth. And it's precisely here, my comrade, that the job involves a lot of watchfulness."

"For what especially?" he said.

"Aren't you aware," I said, "of how much harm now comes about E involving the activity of dialectic?"

"Of what sort?" he said.

"There's no doubt," I said, "that people get filled with behavior that's out of line."

"Very much so," he said.

"And is it any wonder that this happens to them, do you think," I said, "and don't you sympathize with them?"

"Why should I do that, particularly?" he said.

538A   "It's sort of as if some changeling child were raised amid great riches," I said, "in a big and powerful family, with many flatterers, and when he became a man, realized that he didn't belong to those who claimed to be his parents, but couldn't find the true sources of his being; can you form any notion of how this person would feel about the flatterers and the people who'd made the switch, both at the time when he didn't know about the switch, and then when he did know? Or do you want to hear my notion of it?"

"I want to," he said.

B   "Well," I said, "I have a notion he'd have more respect for his father and mother, and the rest of his apparent family, than for the flatterers, and be less apt to neglect the needy among them, less inclined to do or say anything out of line to them, and less likely to disobey them than the flatterers about anything major, at the time when he didn't know the truth."

"That's likely," he said.

"Then, when he'd realized how things are, I have a notion that he'd back off on respecting these people and taking them seriously, and step up those attitudes toward the flatterers, and be persuaded C   by them to a greater degree than before, and start to live by their standards, associating with them openly; but as for that father of his, and the others made out to be his family, unless he were thoroughly decent by nature, he wouldn't even care about them."

"Everything you say is just the sort of thing that would happen," he said. "But how does this image bear on people who engage in arguments?"

"Like this. Presumably there are convictions in us from childhood about what are just and beautiful ways to act, among which we're brought up in the same way as by parents, obeying their authority and respecting them."

"There are."

D   "Then too, there are other activities opposed to these convictions, having pleasures in them that flatter the soul and draw us toward them, but they're not persuasive to those who have any sense of proportion at all; they respect their parents' convictions and remain obedient to them."

"That's true as well."

"What about it, then?" I said. "When someone who's that way, in the course of things, is asked the question 'What is the beautiful?' and when he gives the answer he's heard from the lawgiver, the argument

refutes this, and refutes it on many occasions in many ways, it starts   E
to beat him down into the opinion that this is no more beautiful than
ugly, and likewise with the just and the good and the things he used
to hold most in honor, after that, what do you imagine it's going to
do to him about his respect for those things and his obedience to their
authority?"

"It would necessarily mean he wouldn't honor them or obey their
authority in the same way," he said.

"So when he doesn't regard these things as worthy of respect or
congenial to him the way he did before," I said, "and doesn't discover
the true ones, is there any other sort of life he's likely to go over to   539A
than the flatteringly seductive one?"

"There isn't," he said.

"Then I imagine he'll seem to have turned from a law-abiding
person into someone who's out of line."

"Necessarily."

"Well isn't it likely," I said, "that this will be the experience of those
who engage in that sort of arguments too, which I was just saying
deserves a lot of sympathy?"

"Even pity," he said.

"Then in order that those thirty-year-olds of yours don't incur
this pity, doesn't the approach to the arguments need to be made by
someone who takes every precaution?'

"Very much so," he said.

"And wouldn't this be one all-inclusive precaution, that people
not get a taste of them while they're young? Because I imagine it   B
hasn't escaped your notice that adolescents, when they get their
first taste of arguments, exploit them as play, always using them to
contradict; imitating those who engage in cross-examining people,
they themselves cross-examine others, taking delight like puppies in
dragging and tearing apart with the argument the people nearby on
each occasion."

"It's beyond anything in nature," he said.

"Then when they themselves have cross-examined many people
and been cross-examined by many, they fall heavily and rapidly into   C
not holding the beliefs they held before, and as a result of this, they and
the whole of philosophy come into disrepute with everyone else."

"So true," he said.

"But an older person wouldn't be willing to get mixed up in that
sort of lunacy," I said. "He'll imitate someone who wants to discuss
and examine the truth rather than someone who makes it a game
and contradicts for the fun of it; he himself will be more balanced,
and make it a pursuit more worthy of respect instead of more dis-   D
reputable."

"That's right," he said.

"And wasn't everything that was said before this spoken by way of precaution, so the natures that one gets involved in arguments will be orderly and stable, and not, as now, anyone who happens to come to it without being suited to it?"

"Very much so," he said.

"So is it sufficient if someone who's doing nothing else is going to take part in arguments constantly and intensely, but is in training in the counterpart to the gymnastic training for the body, to keep at it for twice as many years as that?"

E

"Do you mean six," he said, "or four?"

"Don't worry," I said; "make it five. Now after this, they'll need to go back down into that cave of yours, and be required to rule in matters having to do with war, and in all the offices that belong to the young, so they don't lag behind the others in experience. And they still need to be tested even in these tasks, for whether they'll hold steady when they're pulled in all directions, or be thrown off course in any way."

540A

"How much time are you putting down for this?" he said.

"Fifteen years," I said. "And when they've turned fifty, the ones who've come through intact and excelled in all areas in every respect, in deeds and in varieties of knowledge, are at that point to be led to the end, and required to lift up the brilliance in their souls to look off to the very thing that endows all things with light, and seeing the good itself, to use that as a pattern to bring order to the city, to private persons, and to themselves for the rest of their lives, each taking his turn. For the most part they'll devote their time to philosophy, but when their turns come, they'll put in more hard labor at political life, ruling each in turn for the city's sake, not as though they were doing some beautiful thing but something unavoidable, and in this way they'll always have educated others of the same kind, leaving them in their place as guardians of the city when they themselves go to dwell in the Isles of the Blessed. And the city is to make memorials to them, and sacrifices in public to them as divinities if the Pythian priestess gives her consent, and if not, as blessedly happy and godlike people."

B

C

"You've made the rulers consummately beautiful men, Socrates," he said, "just like a sculptor."

"And there are women rulers as well, Glaucon," I said; "don't imagine that I've said any of the things I've said about men any more than about women, all those that turn up among them with suitable natures."

"Rightly so," he said, "if indeed they're to share in all things on equal terms with men, as we went through."

D

"How about it then? Do you folks agree that the things we've said about the city and the polity are not totally prayers, that while they're difficult, there's a way in which they're possible, but no other way than the one described, when philosophers in the true sense, either

one or more of them, having come to power in a city, look down on the things now held in honor, considering them unfit for free people and worth nothing, and having the most regard for what's right and for honors based on that, take the greatest and most needed thing   E
to be what's just, so that by ministering to that and making it grow they'll set their own city in order?"

"How?" he said.

"Everybody in the city who's more than ten years old," I said,   541A
"they'll send out into the countryside, and taking over their children, they'll raise them in their own ways and customs, the sort we went over before, getting them out of the states of character that they and their parents now have; and once the city and polity that we've described have been established in this—the quickest and easiest—way, will it be happy itself and bring the greatest benefit to the people in whose environs it arises?"

"Very much so," he said. "And as for how it would come into being, if it ever did come into being, you seem to me to have described   B
it well, Socrates."

"Then have we now had our fill," I said, "of arguments about this city and the man who's like it? Because presumably it's clear for him too what sort of person one ought to say he is."[142]

"It is clear," he said, "and it seems to me that precisely what you're asking has reached its end."

---

142 The reader may not find it quite so clear how the last steps of the image apply to the soul of one person. If the city represents the soul, what in each of us would correspond to the people over ten who need to be deported from the city, but remain in the suburbs and live off the benefits generated from within?

BOOK VIII

543A–548D Socrates and Glaucon
548D–569C Socrates and Adeimantus

Note

> After the long detour through the depths and heights of Books V through VII, Socrates finally returns to the topic he had tried to bring up when the best city had been described sufficiently to show that the arguments in favor of injustice were groundless. He now sets the polity of the best city in motion, to watch it display a succession of necessary stages of decay. He argues that each new stage is inevitable, but while the first metamorphosis comes because the patterns involved in human nature are too complex for any human rulers to anticipate and control, each subsequent transition comes about when the principle adopted as highest by any other form of political association reaches its own logical conclusion. The patterns of political corruption, unlike those of natural equilibrium, are all too easy to discern, when one simply asks what would happen if each of the less-than-best polities got exactly what it wished for. Once the first of the lower polities has come to sight, Adeimantus returns to the conversation in place of Glaucon, who had been Socrates' partner in the dialectical ascent through the three great images at the center of the dialogue, and the plan for higher education that came out of them. Each of the defective polities has conspicuous illustrations in the world around the speakers, especially in the histories of Sparta and Athens. More importantly, each has its reflection in a type of character found in human souls. The book ends with a description of the last stage of political decomposition, which occurs when a democracy reaches for the ultimate freedom, as it understands freedom.

543A   "Very well. The following things are agreed, **Glaucon**: that in a city that's going to be managed to the ultimate degree, women are to be shared in common, children, and their whole education, are to be shared in common, and the tasks involved in both war and peace are likewise to be shared in common, and those among them who've turned out best in philosophy and in relation to war are to be kings."

"Agreed," he said.

B   "And in fact we also acknowledged this, that once the rulers are set in place, they'll lead the soldiers and quarter them in houses of the sort we spoke of before, having no private property in them for anyone but shared in common by them all; and if you recall, we came to agreement at some point about what sort of possessions they'd have in addition to houses of that kind."

"I do recall," he said, "that we assumed that none of them ought to possess any of the things other people do now, but like fighters in

war and guardians, they'd receive recompense from the others for   C
their guardianship as annual maintenance for these purposes, and be
obliged to take care of themselves and the rest of the city."

"You're recounting it correctly," I said. "But go on, since we finished that, and let's remember where we made the digression to here
from, so we can go back to the same point."

"That's not hard," he said, "because almost exactly like now, you
were acting as though you'd gone completely through the discussion
about the city, saying that you'd rate a city of the sort you'd gone
over at that point, and a man like it, as good, though for that matter   D
it seems as though you were able to describe a still more beautiful
city and man. So anyway, you were saying that the other cities were   544A
misguided if this one is right, and you claimed, as I recall, that there
were four forms among the remaining polities about which it would
be worth having an account, and worth seeing the ways they, and the
people like them, go astray, so that, when we'd seen them all and come
to agreement about the best and worst sort of man, we could consider
whether the best is the happiest and the worst the most miserable,
or whether it might be otherwise. And when I was asking what four
polities you meant, at that point Polemarchus and Adeimantus broke   B
in, and that's how you took up the discussion and got here."

"You're remembering with complete correctness," I said.

"Well then, like a wrestler, take the same hold again, and when
I ask the same question, try to state what you were about to say
then."

"If I have the power to," I said.

"And in fact," he said, "I'm eager myself to hear what four polities you meant."

"It won't be difficult for you to hear them," I said, "because the   C
ones I mean are the very ones that have names: the one approved by
most people, that type from Crete and Sparta, and second, the one with
the second approval rating and called oligarchy, a polity fraught with
loads of evils, and coming next, the antagonist of that one, democracy,
and of course, breaking out from the pack, the illustrious tyranny, the
fourth and last disease of a city. Or do you know of any other look
of a polity that's situated in any distinct form? Because hereditary   D
monarchies and those that can be bought and certain polities like that
are presumably between these in some way, and one can find them
among the barbarians[143] no less than among the Greeks."

"Many strange varieties are talked about, anyway," he said.

"So are you aware," I said, "that it's also necessary for there to be
as many forms of human dispositions as there are of polities? Or do
you imagine their polities come 'from oak or rock'[144] and not from the   E

143 Socrates seems to assume that political life in its full sense came onto the scene among the
Greeks. See the glossary note on the word "city."

144 *Odyssey* XIX, 163.

kinds of character that tip the balance, so to speak, among the people in the cities, and pull the rest with them?"

"By no means," he said, "do I imagine they come from anywhere else but there."

"So if the forms of cities are five, the arrangements of the soul in private persons would be five as well."

"What else?"

"And we've already gone over the person who's like aristocracy,[145] whom we rightly claim is good and just."

545A   "We have."

"And don't we need to go on next to the less good kinds, the one that loves victory and honor, standing with the Spartan polity, and then the oligarchic, democratic, and tyrannical types, so that when we see the most unjust person we can place him opposite the most just? Won't our examination then be complete, as to how unmixed

B   justice is related to unmixed injustice for the happiness or misery of its possessor, in order to be persuaded either by Thrasymachus, that we should pursue injustice, or by the argument now being brought to light in favor of justice?"

"That's absolutely the way it needs to be done," he said.

"Well then, the same way we began with the kinds of character in polities before examining them in private persons, since that's more illuminating, so too now don't we need to examine the honor-loving polity? I don't know a name that it goes by, but it ought to be called timocracy or timarchy; we'll examine that sort of man in relation to

C   it, and then oligarchy and an oligarchic man, and having looked in turn at democracy we'll view a democratic man, and going on to the fourth and looking at a city that's subject to tyranny, once we've taken a look this time into a tyrannical soul, we'll try to become competent judges of the things we set out to decide."

"That would certainly be a rational way," he said, "for the viewing and the deciding to be done."

"Come on then," I said, "let's try to say how a timocracy would

D   arise out of an aristocracy. Is it this simple, that every polity changes from within that part of it which holds the ruling offices, when conflict becomes present in that, but as long as it's of one mind, even if it's very small, it's impossible for the polity to be destabilized?"

"That's how it is."

"So, Glaucon," I said, "how is our city going to be made unstable and in what manner will the auxiliaries and rulers come into conflict

---

145 Aristocracy is the name Socrates gave to the best polity in 445D, except for the case in which only one person fit to rule is available. It is one of three kinds of rule by a small minority of citizens that he distinguishes here. It means rule by the best, which he takes to apply to merit and not family titles. Oligarchy, which means rule by few, he uses only for rule by the rich, and the word timocracy, coined here, means rule by those most honored or most devoted to honor.

with one another and among themselves? Or would you rather have us invoke the Muses the way Homer does, to tell us 'how division first befell them,'[146] and claim that they reply in pompous language, like a tragedy, as though speaking in all seriousness, when they're playing with us and teasing the way someone would with children?"

"How so?"

"They'll say something like this: A city organized in this way is hard to destabilize, but since everything that comes into being is destructible, even an organization like this one won't endure for all time, but will come undone. Its coming undone will be like this: fertility and barrenness of both soul and bodies come not only to the plants in the earth but also among the animals on the earth, as the periodic returns of the cycles for each kind turn back upon their revolving courses, which are short for the short-lived kinds and opposite for the opposite kinds. For your kind, as wise as they are, those whom you educated as leaders of the city, with their calculation combined with observation, will nonetheless fail to achieve favorable births and preventions of birth, which will elude them, and they'll produce children when they ought not. For the begetting of a divine being, there's a period encompassed by a perfect number, but for the human kind,[147] it's the first one in which three intervals of expansion in the duplicate ratio, yielding four terms, of ratios that produce similarity and dissimilarity when they augment and diminish, bring everything into mutual conformity and commensurability. Four-to-three, as a starting point among these ratios, when mated with a multitude of five, produces two harmonies when it's increased three times; one of them is equal-times-equal in multiples of a hundred, the other of equal opposite sides but oblong, one side a hundred times the square number from the rational approximation to the diagonal of the square on a five-unit side, minus one from each hundred, or minus two if the irrational diameter is used, and the other side a hundred times the cubic number from three. This whole geometrical number,[148] sovereign

E

546A

B

C

---

146   Modeled on *Iliad* XVI, 112-113, the point at which things are about to spin completely out of control.

147   The following passage, down to "the cubic number from three," is notoriously obscure, and has given rise to considerable speculation through the centuries. The present translator has no great confidence in his rendering, and refers the curious reader to the source on which it primarily relies, James Adam's commentary *The Republic of Plato*, Vol. II, pp. 205-208 and 264-312. Socrates has just warned us that this whole speech is playful mimicry of Homeric grandeur, but that alone is no reason not to take it seriously, since Socrates has also told us that much of the *Republic*, and of learning, consists of play (536C).

148   This phrase has the double sense that each of the numbers entering into the calculation has some geometrical look, of a square, cube, or 3:4:5 triangle, but also that the number measures continuous magnitudes, making them harmonious with one another and intelligible to us. The interplay of arithmetic and geometry makes each realm more amenable to form and intelligibility. The number calculated here is interpreted by some as the measure, in solar years, of what was called the Great Year, the shortest period that would contain the cycle of every celestial body an exact whole number of times.

D   among its kind, is what governs better and worse in procreation, and
when your guardians, from ignorance of it, join bridegrooms with
brides inopportunely in marriage, the children will not be favored by
either nature or fortune. Those who precede them will set in place the
best of these children, but because of their deficiency in merit, once
they've come into power in place of their fathers, although they're
our[149] guardians, they'll begin to be careless, paying less regard than
they should, first, to musical education, and second to gymnastic
training, and from that point on your young people will become
E   more uncivilized. And those from among them set up as rulers won't
547A   be entirely perceptive about assessing those races of Hesiod's[150] and
yours, the gold and silver and bronze and iron. And by the mingling
together of iron with silver and bronze with gold, a dissimilarity and
inharmonious irregularity will be introduced, which, when they come
along, always breed war and antagonism wherever they arise. One
must declare division 'to be verily of this descent'[151] always, wherever
it arises."

"And we'll claim they answered quite rightly," he said.

"Necessarily so," I said, "since they're Muses."

B   "So what's the next thing the Muses say?" he said.

"Once division had come on the scene," I said, "the two strains
of iron and bronze in their race each pulled them in the direction of
moneymaking and of acquiring land and houses and gold and silver,
while the other two strains of gold and silver, inasmuch as they weren't
needy but rich in their souls by nature, led them toward virtue and
the ancient order of things. When they came into violence and strife
against one another, they agreed to a compromise, for land and houses
C   to be divided up and be appropriated, and they made slaves of the
people who'd been guarded by them before[152] as free friends and
providers of sustenance, holding them now as serfs and domestic
servants, paying attention to war themselves and to guarding against
these very people."

"That seems to me to be where this transformation comes from,"
he said.

"And wouldn't this polity be something intermediate," I said,
"between aristocracy and oligarchy?"

"Very much so."

"That's how it will be transformed, then, but how will it be man-
D   aged once it's been transformed? Or is it obvious that it will imitate

---

149   The Muses, who preside over all the civilizing influences, are still speaking.

150   See 469A and note.

151   *Iliad* VI, 211.

152   Since there are well-known books that claim "Plato's ideal state" includes slavery, it may
be worth noticing this explicit statement of Socrates that the first enslavement within it destroys
the best city.

the previous polity in some respects, and oligarchy in others, since it's in between them, while it will also have something that belongs to it in particular?"

"That's how it is," he said.

"In honoring the rulers, in that the war-making part of it refrains from farming, from manual arts, and from other money-making activity, and in that common meals are provided and care is taken over gymnastic training and competition in war—in all things such as these won't it imitate the previous polity?"

"Yes."

"But in being fearful of bringing the wise into ruling offices, since the men of that sort it possesses are no longer without duplicity or intent on their tasks but of mixed character, so that they turn to spirited people of a simpler sort, who are by nature turned more toward war than toward peace, in holding the tricks and subterfuges involved in war in honor, and in devoting all their time to making war, in many things such as these won't it have its own particular features?"

"Yes."

"Such people will in fact be covetous of money,"[153] I said, "just like those in oligarchies, fiercely doing reverence to gold and silver under cover of darkness, since they're in possession of coffers and household treasuries where they can store away and hide them, and they'll have walls surrounding their houses, in effect private nests, in which they'll lavish money on women and whomever else they might desire to spend a lot on."

"Quite true," he said.

"And they'll be miserly about money, because they revere it and don't possess it openly, and they'll love spending other people's money, prompted by desire, enjoying the fruits of it in secret, sneaking away from the law like children from a father, since they've been educated not by persuasion but by force, on account of having neglected the true Muse with her discourses and philosophy, and having honored gymnastic training with greater reverence than music."

"You're describing a polity," he said, "that's a mixture through and through of bad and good."

"It's mixed," I said, "but since it's dominated by spiritedness, one thing alone is most conspicuous in it, a love of victories and honors."

E

548A

B

C

---

153 Socrates is arguing that these are universal patterns found in human souls and communities, but details of his account of the timocratic pattern match up with historical accounts of Sparta. Socrates was accused of being a Spartan sympathizer (as indicated in Plato's *Gorgias*, 515E), possibly, in part, because the polity he advocated resembled the Spartan one in some respects. It is therefore worth comparing the strong criticisms he makes here with the factual records of the time. For one spectacular instance of the corruption of a Spartan ruler, compare the descriptions of Pausanias in IX, 82 of Herodotus' *History* and I, 130 of Thucydides' *Peloponnesian War*. In the latter work, see I, 95 for Sparta's recognition that its leaders couldn't be trusted outside its borders, and IV, 80 for an extreme instance of its duplicity and brutality toward slaves.

"Emphatically so," he said.

"Well," I said, "this is the way this polity would have come into being and what it would be like, as a sketch in words that outlines the polity without working it out precisely, since even from a sketch there's enough to see the most just and most unjust person, and it's a task inconceivable in length to go through all the polities and all the states of character without leaving anything out."

"That's right," he said.

"So who's the man in accord with this polity? How does he come to be and what sort of person is he?"

"I imagine," said **Adeimantus**, "for his love of victory at least, he'd come pretty close to this fellow right here, Glaucon."

"Maybe in that respect," I said, "but it seems to me he'd have a nature unlike his in these ways."

"What ways?"

"He'd have to be more inflexible," I said, "fond of music but a little less open to its influence, and fond of hearing talk but by no means good at speaking. And toward slaves, someone such as he would be brutal, rather than disdainful of slaves the way someone adequately educated would be, but he'd be gentle with those who are free and extremely obedient to rulers. He'd be passionate about ruling and being honored, judging himself worthy to rule not for his speaking or for anything of the sort, but for deeds of a warlike or war-related kind. And he's a person devoted to gymnastic exercise and hunting."

"Yes," he said, "that's the type of character that belongs to this polity."

"And wouldn't such a person despise money when he was young," I said, "but be ever more appreciative of it as he grows older, from having a bit of the money-lover in his nature and not being pure in his relation to virtue, because he's been deprived of its best guardian?"

"What's that?" said Adeimantus.

"Rational discussion blended with music," I said, "the presence of which is the only preserver of virtue that abides throughout life in someone who has it."

"You put it beautifully," he said.

"And it is in fact this sort of timocratic youth," I said, "who's like that sort of city."

"Entirely so."

"And he comes into being in some such way as this," I said: "sometimes he's a young son of a good father who lives in a city that's not well governed, and his father avoids honors, offices, and lawsuits, and all such fondness for civic involvement, and is willing to forego advantages in order not to have the aggravation."

"So how does the son get the way he is?" he said.

"To start with," I said, "when he hears his mother complaining that her husband isn't one of the rulers, and that she gets the worst

of it among the other women for that; then too, she sees that he's not   D
greatly concerned about money, that he doesn't fight back and trade
insults in private or in the law courts and the public arena, but puts
up with all that sort of thing with a tranquil spirit, and her perception
of things is that he always has his mind on himself and doesn't pay
her enough regard, positive or negative. She complains about all these
things and tells her son his father is unmanly and too lackadaisical,
and all the other songs in that style that women like to sing on that
theme."

"They do have quite a lot like that," said Adeimantus.   E

"And you know," I said, "that sometimes even the servants of such
men, who are to all appearances favorably disposed, say things like
that behind their backs to their sons, and if they see someone who
owes the father money or does him some other injustice, but whom he
doesn't proceed against, they egg on the son so that he'll take revenge
on all such people when he becomes a man, and be more of a man than   550A
his father, and when he goes out, he hears and sees other things of that
kind, those who tend to their own business being called stupid and
held in low esteem, while those who don't are honored and praised by
the same people. So then a young person who hears and sees all that
sort of thing, and from the other side hears the things his father says
and sees his ways of doing things up close, as compared with those
of the others, he's pulled by both these influences, as his father waters   B
the reasoning part of his soul and makes it grow, and the others the
desiring and spirited parts. Since his nature isn't that of a bad man,
but he's been accustomed to bad company with other people, pulled
by both these influences, he ends up in the middle, and turns over
the ruling place in himself to the middle part, the victory-loving and
spirited one, and he becomes a haughty, honor-loving man."

"You seem to me," he said, "to have gone through this man's
genesis just right."

"Then we've got the second polity," I said, "and the second   C
man."

"We've got them."

"Then shall we speak next, with Aeschylus, of 'another man stationed by another city,'[154] or keep to our design instead and speak of
the city first?"

"Certainly that," he said.

"And the next polity after that sort, I imagine, would be oligarchy."

"And what sort of set-up do you mean by oligarchy?" he said.

"The polity that comes from a property qualification," I said, "in
which the rich rule and a poor person has no share in ruling."

"I understand," he said.   D

---

154 A conflation of lines 451 and 570 of the *Seven against Thebes*.

"Then isn't what needs to be stated the way it first transforms from timarchy into oligarchy?"

"Yes."

"And how it transforms is surely obvious even to a blind person," I said.

"How?"

"That strong room full of gold each one has destroys that sort of polity," I said. "First they come up with ways to spend it on themselves, and alter the laws to fit that when they and their wives disobey them."

"Likely so," he said.

E "Then, I imagine, when one sees another and gets into rivalry they end up making the bulk of people like themselves."

"Likely so."

"Then as they move from there to an advanced stage of money-making," I said, "to the extent they hold that in higher regard, to that same extent they hold virtue in lower regard. Or doesn't virtue stand divided against riches that way, as though each of the two were lying in the scale of a balance, always inclining opposite ways?"

"Very much so," he said.

551A "So when riches and the rich are honored in a city, virtue and the good are honored less."

"Clearly."

"And what comes into practice is always what's honored, while what's dishonored is neglected."

"That's the way of it."

"So in place of being men who love victory and honor, they end up becoming lovers of money-making and money, and they give praise and admiration to the rich person and bring him into the ruling offices, but treat the poor person with dishonor."

"Entirely so."

"So then don't they set down the definitive law of an oligarchic
B polity, fixing an amount of money such that, the more of an oligarchy it is, the greater the amount, and the less so the lesser, proclaiming that there's to be no share in ruling for someone without wealth up to the prescribed assessment? Don't they either put it into effect by force of arms, or else, even before that, settle such a polity in place by intimidating people? Isn't that how it is?"

"That's just how it is."

"So, as they say, that settles it."

"Yes," he said. "But what exactly is characteristic of the polity? And what are the sorts of failings we were claiming it has in it?"

C "First off," I said, "this very thing that defines it is of that sort. Consider a case in which someone made people helmsmen of ships that way, from property qualifications, and wouldn't entrust one to a poor person even if he was better at helmsmanship."

"They'd have lousy sailing on their voyage," he said.

"And wouldn't it also be that way with any other sort of ruling whatever?"

"I imagine so."

"Except in the case of a city," I said, "or for a city too?"

"That most by far," he said, "inasmuch as it's the most difficult and most important sort of ruling."

"So that's one pretty big failing oligarchy would have."   D

"So it appears."

"And how about this? Would it be a lesser one than that?"

"What is it?"

"That such a city isn't one but by necessity two,[155] one consisting of the poor, the other of the rich, living in the same place and always plotting against each other."

"By Zeus," he said, "that's not lesser at all."

"And this is certainly not a beautiful thing either, that it's incapable of fighting any war, because it's forced either, by making use of an armed multitude, to be more afraid of them than of the enemies, or by not using them, to show up as truly rulers of few in the fighting   E
itself, at the same time they're also unwilling to put money into it since they're money-lovers."

"Beautiful it's not."

"And what about the thing we were finding fault with long ago, the squandering of effort in many directions in such a polity when   552A
the same people are farmers and moneymakers and warriors at the same times, or does that seem to be the right way to go?"

"Not in any way whatsoever."

"Now see whether this is the first polity to make room for this greatest of all these evils."

"What's that?"

"The possibility of selling everything one owns, and of someone else's acquiring what belongs to him, and his living in the city after selling it without belonging to any of the parts of the city, not acknowledged as a moneymaker or craftsman, a cavalryman or infantryman,[156]   B
just as a poor person without means."

"It's the first," he said.

"There's nothing in oligarchies at any rate to prevent that sort of thing. Otherwise there wouldn't be some ultra-rich while others are utterly poor."

"That's right."

---

155 See 462A-B.

156 The last two roles would go to people who could afford a horse or armor. There were military opportunities for the poor at the time, as light infantry troops or rowers in warships, but these are just the options this sort of polity is reluctant to use.

"And consider this: when that sort of person was rich and spending money, was he of any more benefit to the city for the jobs we just mentioned? Or while he seemed to be one of the rulers was he in truth neither a ruler nor a servant of it, but a drain on the available resources?"

C

"Like that," he said; "he seemed to be something else, but was nothing other than a drain."

"Would you want us to declare, then," I said, "that the same way a drone is tucked away in its compartment, a sickness within a hive, this sort of person is also tucked away in his house as a drone, a sickness within a city?"

"Very much so, Socrates," he said.

"Well, Adeimantus, hasn't the god made all the winged drones without stingers, but as for these with feet, while some of them lack

D

stingers, some have ferocious stings? Don't the ones from the stingless variety end up as beggars in their old age, while all the type that're called criminals come from the ones equipped with stingers?"

"Very true," he said.

"It's clear, therefore," I said, "that in a city in which you see beggars, somewhere out of sight in that vicinity there are thieves, pickpockets, temple robbers, and workers at all such criminal trades."

"That's clear," he said.

"So what about it? Don't you see beggars in cities with oligarchies?"

"Little short of everybody," he said, "outside of the rulers."

E

"May we not then assume," I said, "that there are also a lot of criminals in them that have stingers, that the rulers vigilantly suppress by force?"

"We assume so," he said.

"Won't we claim that such people crop up there from lack of education, bad upbringing, and a bad arrangement of the polity?"

"We will claim that."

"But then that's exactly the way a city with an oligarchy would be, and it would have that many evils and probably more as well."

"Pretty much," he said.

553A

"So let this polity that people call oligarchy, that has rulers that come from a property qualification, be done with as far as we're concerned; let's consider next the person who resembles it, how he comes into being and what he's like when he does."

"Yes indeed," he said.

"Is it especially in this way that someone changes out of that timocratic mold into an oligarchic one?"

"How's that?"

"It's when a son born to one of them admires his father at first and

B

follows in his footsteps, then sees him suddenly come into collision with the city as if he'd run aground on a reef with the loss of his possessions and himself, when he'd either been a general or held some high ruling office and then fell into an entanglement in a law court at the hands of false accusers, and was either put to death, exiled, or stripped of his honors with the loss of all his property."

"Likely so," he said.

"But, dear fellow, when the son sees and suffers these things and loses his estate, I imagine he gets frightened, and immediately evicts that honor-loving and spirited part of himself headfirst out of its throne in his soul and, humiliated by his poverty, turns greedily to moneymaking, and little by little, by saving and working, he builds up wealth. Don't you imagine that such a person would then give the seat on that throne to his desiring and money-loving part and make it the Great King[157] in himself, festooning it with tiaras and neck bracelets and scimitars?"

"Indeed I do," he said.

"As for the reasoning and spirited parts, I imagine that, making them sit on the ground on one side and the other in subjection to it and enslaved, he doesn't allow the one to reason about or even consider anything else but where there'll be more money to get out of less, or the other for its part to admire or honor anything other than riches and rich people, or strive for honor on any single ground other than the possession of money and anything else that might contribute to that."

"There's no other change," he said, "so quick and forceful from a young honor-lover into a money-lover as that."

"So is this the oligarchic person?" I said.

"The change in him, at any rate, is from a man resembling the polity that oligarchy came from."

"So let's examine whether he resembles oligarchy."

"Let's examine it."

"In the first place, wouldn't he be like it by putting money highest?"

"Certainly."

"And surely also in being miserly and a drudge, satisfying only the necessary desires among those that belong to him, and not providing other expenses but holding down the rest of his desires in slavery, as frivolous things."

"Very much so."

"Since he's a grubby sort of person," I said, "getting an advantage out of everything, a man who builds up savings, just the type most people approve of, wouldn't he be like this sort of polity?"

"It seems that way to me anyway," he said. "At least money is the most honored thing for both the city and that sort of person."

C

D

E

554A

B

---

157   The phrase the Greeks used at the time for the king of Persia, indicating kingship to the ultimate degree.

"I don't imagine such a person has given a thought to education," I said.

"I doubt it," he said; "otherwise he wouldn't have set up a blind leader for his dance troop and honored him most."[158]

"Good point," I said. "And consider this: won't we claim that dronelike desires become lodged in him due to his lack of education, some of the beggar type and others of the criminal type, held down by force because he's paying attention to something else?"

C

"And how," he said.

"And do you know where to look," I said, "so you'll spot their crimes?"

"Where?" he said.

"To their actions as trustees for orphans, and to anything of that sort that might fall their way and let them get a lot of opportunity to do injustice."

"True."

"So isn't it evident from this that in other transactions, in which he's well regarded because he seems to be just, such a person is holding down other bad desires in him by exercising a quasi-decent constraint over himself, not by persuading them that what they want isn't for the better, or by civilizing them by argument, but by compulsion and fear, because he's fretting over the rest of his wealth?"

D

"Totally so," he said.

"And by Zeus, my friend," I said, "you'll find out about the desires in them that belong to the drone family, with most of them at least, when they need to spend other people's money."

"Oh yes," he said, "in a big way."

"Then such a person wouldn't be free of division within himself, or one person at all, but somehow double, though for the most part he'd have his better desires dominant over his worse desires."

E

"That's just how it is."

"So for these reasons, I imagine such a person would present a more respectable outward appearance than many, but the true virtue in a like-minded and harmonized soul would elude him somewhere far away."

"It seems so to me."

555A

"And certainly a miserly person is an ineffectual contender in a city for any sort of victory, or other ambition for beautiful things, that requires private means, since he's not willing to spend money for the sake of a good reputation or on competitions for things of that sort; afraid to wake up his desires for spending and invite them into battle in alliance with a love of victory, he deploys some few of his resources, fighting his wars in oligarchic style, is outdone in most of them, and keeps on being rich."

---

158 Plutus, the god of wealth, was regarded as blind because riches are distributed so arbitrarily.

"Very much so," he said.

"Then are we still in any doubt," I said, "that the miserly money-maker is, by likeness, stationed alongside the city with an oligarchy?"

B

"None whatever," he said.

"Then it seems democracy needs to be examined next, for the manner it comes into being and for what it's like once it has, so that when in turn we've recognized the disposition of a man of the same sort, we can make him stand for judgment."

"We'd at least be proceeding consistently with ourselves," he said.

"Well, doesn't it change into democracy from oligarchy as some sort of consequence of the insatiable desire for the good it sets for itself, to have to become as rich as possible?"

"How, exactly?"

"I imagine that, since the rulers in it rule thanks to having a lot of possessions, they're not willing to curb all the young people who get out of control by a law preventing them from spending and wasting their goods, so that, by buying up the property of such people or lending money on it, they can become even richer and more esteemed."

C

"They want that more than anything."

"Then isn't this already obvious, that it's impossible to honor wealth in a city and have moderation in its citizens at the same time in any adequate way, and necessary to forget about one or the other?"

D

"Tolerably obvious," he said.

"So by condoning and encouraging out-of-control behavior in oligarchies, their rulers have sometimes forced people who were not without noble qualities into poverty."

"Quite so."

"So I imagine these people sit around in the city, equipped with stingers and fully armed, some owing debts, some having been deprived of privileges, and some suffering both, hating those who possess their property and the others as well, and plotting against them, lusting for revolution."

E

"That's what happens."

"But the moneymakers, who appear not to see them because they're hunched over their own concerns, continue to poison any of the others who lets them by administering doses of silver, and as they carry off in interest a sum many times as large as the principal, they make the drone and beggar multiply in the city."

556A

"How could they fail to multiply?" he said.

"And not even at that point are they willing to snuff out this sort of evil when it's bursting into flame," I said, "by restricting anyone from turning his own property to whatever use he wants, or by this other means by which that sort of damage is undone as a result of a different law."

"As a result of what law exactly?"

B   "The one that's second best after that one, and forces the citizens to pay attention to virtue. Because if a law required that most voluntary contracts be entered into at one's own risk, people in the city would be less shameless about how they made their money,[159] and fewer evils of the sort we were just describing would grow in it."

"A lot fewer," he said.

"But the way it is now," I said, "for all the reasons of that kind, those who rule in the city do treat those they rule that way. And where they and theirs are concerned, don't their young live in luxury, not putting effort into anything involving the body or the soul, soft when it comes to standing up to pleasures and pains, and lazy?"

C

"What else?"

"Meanwhile, haven't they neglected everything except moneymaking and paid no more attention to virtue than the poor have?"

"They haven't paid any."

"So with this sort of backdrop, when the rulers and those they rule run across one another, either traveling on the roads or in any other common undertakings, at public spectacles or on military campaigns, or when they become shipmates or fellow soldiers, or even in the very midst of dangers, when they observe one another, the poor are by no means despised by the rich in that situation. Often instead, when a lean, suntanned poor man, stationed in battle beside a rich man who's been pampered in the shade and has a lot of surplus flesh, sees him wheezing and full of confusion, don't you imagine he'd believe it was their own apathy that let such people be rich, and that one poor man would pass the word to another, when they'd meet privately, that 'our guys are men; *they're* nothing'?"[160]

D

E

"I know very well they'd do that," he said.

"Then just as a sickly body only needs a little nudge from outside to make it take sick, and sometimes gets to be at odds with itself even without the external pressures, doesn't a city that's in the same condition as that also fall into division in that way on a slight pretext, when people are brought in from outside either from an oligarchic city that's allied with one group or from a democratic one that's allied with the other, and get sick and do battle with itself, and sometimes do that even without the outside pressures?"

557A   "And violently so."

---

159 That is, if the law didn't permit seizing the debtor's property when he defaulted on a loan, the lender would have to assess someone's character before making a loan, and there would be no financial incentive for some people to encourage the ruin of others. But Socrates says it would be even better for the law to restrict the kinds of expenditure that would lead someone into ruinous debt in the first place.

160 The message might mean "[those] men are ours [for the taking], because they're nothing." This is one of the rare places where the translation follows an alternate reading in the 2003 Oxford Classical Texts version, in this case one in which the particle *gar* is absent.

"So democracy comes into being, I imagine, when the poor have won, and they kill some of the others, exile some, and give those who are left an equal share in the polity and ruling offices, and for the most part, the ruling positions in it are determined by lot."[161]

"It is in that way that democracy is instituted," he said, "whether it happens by force of arms or because the others give up out of fear."

"So what's their manner of living?" I said. "And what's this next sort of polity like? Because it's clear that a man like that will show up as the democratic sort."

"That's clear," he said.

"Well, first of all aren't they free, and doesn't the city get filled with freedom and free speech, and isn't it permissible in it to do whatever anyone wants?"

"So it's said," he said.

"And in a place where it's permissible, it's obvious that each person would manage the arrangement of his own life in private however it pleased him."

"It's obvious."

"So I imagine that every variety of human being would turn up in this polity most of all."

"How could it be otherwise?"

"This is liable to be the most beautiful of the polities," I said; "like an ornate cloak with every color worked into it, it too, since it's ornamented that way with every type of character, might appear the most beautiful. And probably a lot of people," I said, "like children and women looking at gaudy things, would also judge it to be the most beautiful."

"Very much so," he said.

"It's also, you blessedly lucky fellow, a made-to-order place in which to look for a polity," I said.

"Why, exactly?"

"Because it has every kind of polity in it, thanks to its permissiveness, and it's liable to be necessary for someone who wants to make arrangements for a city, which we've just been doing, to go into a democratic city to pick out one of whatever style pleased him, as if he'd found his way into a polity-bazaar, and when he'd made his selection he could set one up that way."

"He probably wouldn't be at a loss for examples at any rate," he said.

"And as for the fact that there's no requirement to be a ruler in this city," I said, "even if you're competent to rule, or to be ruled either, if you don't want to be, or to go to war when the rest of the city's at war, or to stay at peace when everyone else is, if peace doesn't appeal

161 Elections were considered an aristocratic practice. In Plato's *Apology* (32B), Socrates mentions a day when he was president of the Athenian assembly, the position having come to his tribe by rotation and to him by lot.

558A to you, or the fact that, even if some law precludes you from being a ruler or a judge, you can be both a ruler and a judge nonetheless, if the impulse for it takes you, isn't that way of living in the moment godlike bliss?"

"Maybe so, at least in that moment," he said.

"And how about the calm demeanor of some who've been convicted of crimes? Isn't that pretty? Or haven't you ever seen people who've been condemned to death or exile in this sort of polity, who stay around nonetheless and go right back into the midst of things and stalk around as though no one cares or sees, like the spirits of dead heroes?"

"A lot of them, in fact," he said.

B "And there's also its broadmindedness and total lack of pettiness, and its contempt for the things we were saying so solemnly when we founded the city, that unless someone had an extraordinary nature, he'd never become a good man if he didn't play amid beautiful things right from childhood and come in contact with all that sort of thing; in what a magnificent style it tramples all these things underfoot, not a bit concerned about the sort of pursuits anyone has been involved in when he goes into politics. Instead, doesn't it pay him honor if he just claims to be in favor of the people?"

"It's very noble that way," he said.

C "So democracy would have these features," I said, "and others closely akin to these, and it seems it would be an agreeable polity, nonauthoritarian and diverse, spreading some sort of equality to equals and unequals alike."

"You're talking about things that are very well known," he said.

"So consider who'd be that way as a private person," I said. "Or is the first thing to be examined the manner in which he comes into being, the way we examined the polity?"

"Yes," he said.

D "Isn't it this way? Wouldn't a son of that miserly, oligarchic fellow come along, brought up by his father, I imagine, with his father's qualities of character?"

"How could he help it?"

"So he too would be someone who ruled over the pleasures in himself by force, all those that are wasteful and not conducive to moneymaking, the ones in fact that are called non-necessary."

"That's clear," he said.

"Well, so that we won't be having our discussion in the dark," I said, "do you want us first to define the necessary desires and those that aren't?"

"I do want that," he said.

E "Wouldn't the ones we're not able to turn away from be called necessary justly, as well as all those that benefit us when they're fulfilled? Because it's necessary for us to have a craving for both these sorts, isn't it?"

"Very much so."

"So we'll justly apply this word 'necessary' to them."

"Justly."

"And what about the ones someone could get rid of if he trained himself from youth, which also do no good by being present, and some of which even do the opposite? If we claimed all these are non-necessary, wouldn't we be putting it beautifully?"

"Beautifully indeed."

"So shall we choose an example for each sort of what they are, so we can get hold of them in general outline?"

"Why shouldn't we?"

"Then wouldn't the desire to eat, up to the point of health and fitness, and for bread and side dishes in and of themselves, be neces-   B
sary?"[162]

"I imagine so."

"Presumably the desire for bread, at least, is necessary on both counts, in that it's beneficial and also in that it's capable of causing living to cease."

"Yes."

"And so is that for the side items, if in any way they provide any benefit for fitness."

"Very much so."

"But what about the desire that exceeds these and is for foods of kinds other than these, but is capable of being eliminated from most people when it's curtailed and educated from youth, and is harmful for the body and harmful for the soul as well, for its judgment and exercise of moderation? Wouldn't it rightly be called non-necessary?"   C

"With utmost rightness."

"And won't we also claim the latter desires are wasteful, while the former ones are profitable,[163] because they're useful for work?"

"Certainly."

"And will we claim it's the same way with sexual desires and other ones?"

"The same way."

"Now didn't we also say, about the person we just now named a drone, that he's loaded with pleasures and desires of that sort, and ruled by the non-necessary ones, while the person who's ruled by the necessary ones is miserly and oligarchic?"

"We sure did."

---

162   The necessary desire to eat is doubly limited by Socrates, in its extent and object, but is not confined to bare subsistence. The word for side dishes was translated "delicacies" in Bk. II. See 372C-D and note.

163   Literally, "of a moneymaking sort." The word *chrêmatistikos* plays on the previous clause in meaning, having the sense of gaining rather than wasting, and on the following one in sound, since the word for useful is *chrêsimos*.

D   "Backing up, then," I said, "let's say how a democratic person comes about from an oligarchic one. It appears to me that most of the time it happens like this."

"How?"

"When a young person, brought up the way we were just talking about, without education and in miserly fashion, gets a taste of honey by being a drone, and comes in contact with fiery and cunning beasts who can set him up with pleasures of every kind in every variation enjoyed
E   in every manner, you might imagine that would be the start for him of a change of the polity in himself from oligarchic to democratic."

"That's a big necessity," he said.

"Then just as the city changed when an external alliance of like with like supported one of its two parts, doesn't the young person too change in that way when external desires of a form that's related to and like one of the two parts within himself support that as well?"

"Absolutely so."

"And I imagine that if some alliance with the oligarchic part of himself supports it in return, coming either from his father or from
560A   somewhere in the rest of his family, giving him advice and also giving him a hard time, then there's a faction and an opposite faction, and a battle breaks out within him against himself."

"What else?"

"And at times, I imagine, the democratic part gives up ground to the oligarchic part, and among certain of his desires, some are destroyed and others driven out, and when a certain feeling of shame has arisen in the young person's soul, order is imposed again."

"That does sometimes happen," he said.

"But then again, I imagine, other desires akin to the ones that were driven out, cultivated in secret, make a comeback in numbers and
B   strength due to the father's lack of skill in raising children."

"It's usual for it to happen that way anyhow," he said.

"And don't they drag him back to the same company, and by a covert intercourse among desires, breed a multitude?"

"What else?"

"So finally, I imagine, they capture the stronghold of the young person's soul, when they observe that it's devoid of beautiful studies and pursuits and true speeches, which are the best watchmen and guardians in the thinking of men loved by the gods."
C   "Very much so," he said.

"Then, I imagine, lying and swaggering speeches and opinions rush up and take occupation of the same location in such a person."

"Forcefully," he said.

"Then doesn't he go back again to those Lotus eaters[164] and openly take up residence among them, and if any help arrives from his family

---

164 *Odyssey* IX, 91-97.

for the miserly part of his soul, don't those swaggering speeches block
the gates in the walls around the royal chamber in him, and refuse   D
to let in the allied contingent itself or even grant entry to private del-
egations of speeches from elders? Once they've come out on top in
battle, don't they give shame the name simplemindedness, and push
it out, a refugee without honor; don't they call moderation unmanli-
ness, fling mud at it, and throw it out; and don't they persuade the
young person that a sense of proportion and orderliness in spending
money is unsophisticated and slavish and, with an assist from a lot
of unprofitable desires, drive it out?"

"Forcibly."

"And once, one way and another, they've emptied and cleansed
these elements from the soul of the person they've occupied and made   E
a devotee of their exalted ceremonies, the thing they do right after
that is escort insolence, anarchy, wastefulness, and shamelessness
back in, crowned with wreaths, in a torch-lit procession, accompanied
by a vast chorus singing their praises and giving them pretty names,
calling insolence high education, anarchy freedom, wastefulness   561A
flamboyant style, and shamelessness courage. Isn't that the way," I
said, "that someone changes while young from someone brought up
amid necessary desires into someone who turns loose his non-necessary and unprofitable pleasures and gives them free rein?"

"And you've put it very vividly," he said.

"So after that, I imagine, such a person goes through life spending
no more money, effort, or time on necessary pleasures than on non-
necessary ones. If he's lucky, and doesn't go overboard in his bac-   B
chanalian revels, and if, as he gets a bit older, most of the turbulence
has subsided, and he lets some parts of the exiled group back in, and
doesn't give himself wholly over to the group that replaced them,
then he lives on having settled his pleasures into a certain equality.
He always surrenders rule over himself, until he's had his fill, to the
one that falls his way, as if he'd drawn straws, and then to another
in turn, not discriminating against any of them but supporting them
equally."

"Entirely so."

"And he isn't open to true reasoning," I said, "and doesn't allow
it inside the guarded perimeter, if anyone says that some pleasures
come from beautiful and good desires and others from worthless ones,   C
and that one should engage in and honor the former but curb and
enslave the latter; he shakes his head at all these things and insists all
pleasures are alike and deserve to be honored equally."

"When someone's in that condition, he does that emphatically,"
he said.

"So he passes his life that way from day to day, gratifying the
desire that turns up; at one time he gets drunk and has flute music   D
played, but at another he drinks water and fasts; at one time he takes

up gymnastic exercise, but there comes a time when he's lazy and lets it all slide, and then he spends his time as though he's engaged in philosophy. Often he gets interested in politics, and jumps up and says and does random things; then if he feels envious of any military men, he gets carried away with that, or if he feels that way about moneymakers, he's carried in that direction instead. There's no order or necessity present in his life, but he calls this way of living sweet, free, and blessed, and lives it throughout."

E

"You've given a perfect exposition of a life of any man committed to equality of rights," he said.

"At any rate," I said, "I imagine he's multifaceted and filled with the most states of character, and that this man is beautiful and diverse in the same way that city is. Many men and many women would be envious of his life, that has in it the most models of polities and temperaments."

"That's how he is," he said.

562A

"What about it then? Will this sort of man be lined up by us next to democracy, as someone to whom the name democratic is rightly applied?"

"Let him be lined up," he said.

"So the most beautiful regime and the most beautiful man would be left for us to go over," I said, "tyranny and a tyrant."

"Exactly," he said.

"Come on then, dear comrade; what's the turn by which tyranny comes into being? Because it's pretty evident it changes out of democracy."

"It's evident."

"Well, doesn't tyranny come from democracy in something of the same manner that democracy comes from oligarchy?"

"How so?"

B

"The good set before it," I said, "on account of which oligarchy was established, was riches, isn't that right?"

"Yes."

"Then the insatiable desire for riches, and the neglect of everything else for the sake of moneymaking destroyed it."

"True," he said.

"And isn't the insatiable desire for that which democracy defines as good also it's undoing?"

"What are you saying it defines it as?"

C

"Freedom," I said. "Because doubtless in a democratic city you'd hear that this is the most beautiful thing it has, and is the reason it's the only place worth living for anyone who's free by nature."

"That's exactly the wording that's used," he said, "and it's said a lot."

"Then isn't it exactly as I was headed for saying just now?" I said. "Doesn't the insatiable desire for that sort of thing and the neglect of everything else alter this polity too, and prepare the way for it to need a tyranny?"

"How?" he said.

"I imagine that when a democratic city that has a thirst for freedom happens to get bad wine stewards as the people in charge of it,   D
and it gets more deeply drunk than it ought by drinking it unmixed, then if the rulers aren't completely lenient and don't provide loads of freedom, it punishes them, charging that they're tainted with oligarchic leanings."

"That they do," he said.

"But the people who obey the rulers get smeared with mud as willing slaves and nobodies, while the rulers who act like they're ruled and the ruled who act like rulers get praised and honored in private and in public. Isn't it a necessity in such a city for freedom to extend to everything?"

"How could it not?"   E

"And for it to insinuate itself, my friend," I said, "into private households, with anarchy finally taking root all the way down to the animals."

"What sort of thing are we talking about?" he said.

"The sort that happens," I said, "when a father gets used to being like a child and is afraid of his sons, and a son gets used to being like a father, and has no respect for or fear of his parents, so he can be free;   563A
and resident aliens are treated like townspeople and townspeople like resident aliens, and there's the same equality for foreigners."

"It does get to be that way," he said.

"It gets to be that way with these things," I said, "and also with other little things of just that kind. A teacher in such a situation is afraid of his students and fawns on them, and students have contempt for their teachers and tutors alike, and in general the young ape their elders and try to rival them in words and deeds, while the old stoop   B
to the level of the young, filled with sprightliness and jokes as they imitate the young so they won't seem to be disagreeable or bossy."

"Very much so," he said.

"But the extreme limit of the freedom of the masses, my friend," I said, "is the extent it reaches in such a city when men and women bought as slaves are no less free than those who've paid for them. And how far equal rights and freedom go in the behavior of women toward men and men toward women, we've almost forgotten to mention."

"Aren't we going to mention, like Aeschylus," he said, "the thing   C
that did 'just pop into your mouth'?"[165]

"By all means," I said; "I'll speak of that, because anyone who had no experience of it wouldn't believe how much more freedom there is in the animals belonging to people there than anyplace else. Bitches

---

165 The words quoted are from Aeschylus's excuse when he was accused of revealing details of secret religious rites.

literally take after the women who own them, as the proverb has it, and horses and asses get used to making their way quite freely and majestically down the roads, bumping into anyone who gets in their way if he doesn't step aside, and all the other things they do get filled with that sort of freedom."

D

"It's my own nightmare you're telling me about," he said, "because I experience it often myself on my way out to the country."

"So do you get the point about all these things put together," I said, "how touchy they make the souls of the citizens, so that when anyone brings in anything with the slightest hint of slavery about it, they get upset and can't stand it? Because, as you no doubt know, they end up paying no attention to the laws, written or unwritten, so that no one can be their boss in any way."

E

"I know it very well," he said.

"So that, my friend," I said, "so beautiful and brash, is the origin out of which tyranny grows, as it seems to me."

"It's certainly brash," he said; "but what's the next step?"

"Exactly the same disease that destroyed the oligarchy when it cropped up in it," I said, "comes along in this polity as well, only more so and with more strength owing to its permissiveness, and enslaves democracy. And in the very nature of things, doing anything to excess has a tendency to cause a great change to the opposite in return, in seasons as well as in plants and living bodies, and not least in polities in particular."

564A

"Likely so," he said.

"Because it looks like an excess of freedom changes into nothing other than an excess of slavery, both in private and in a city."

"That's likely."

"So in all likelihood," I said, "tyranny doesn't get established out of any other polity than democracy, the supreme and most savage type of slavery from what I imagine is the pinnacle of freedom."

"That does make sense," he said.

"But I imagine that's not what you were asking," I said, "but what sort of disease it is that's the same as one that grows in oligarchy, and enslaves democracy when it grows in it."

B

"True, as you say," he said.

"Well, I was talking about that tribe of lazy, big-spending men," I said, "with the boldest element leading them and the less manly group following; they're the ones we compared to drones, some having stingers, the others lacking them."

"Rightly so," he said.

"Well, these two kinds are trouble in every polity they turn up in," I said, "like phlegm and bile in a body, and it's against these in particular that a good doctor and lawmaker for a city needs to take precautions far ahead of time, no less so than a wise beekeeper, at best so they don't get to be there, but if they do, for them to be surgically

C

removed, and their compartments in the hive along with them, as quickly as possible."

"Yes, by Zeus," he said, "completely and totally."

"Well then," I said, "let's take it up in this way, so we can see what we want set out more distinctly."

"How?"

"Let's divide the democratic city into three parts in the discussion, the way it is in fact divided. Because, no doubt, one class of people of   D
the sort we're talking about grows up in it, due to its permissiveness, no less than in oligarchy."

"It's just that way."

"But it has a much sharper sting in this polity than in that one."

"How so?"

"There, because it's not in good repute and is excluded from the ruling offices, it gets out of training and isn't robust, but in a democracy, this is presumably the preeminent class, outside of a few exceptions, and the part of it with the sharpest sting does the talk-ing as well as the acting, while the rest sit by around the speakers'   E
platforms buzzing and not putting up with anyone's saying anything else; so apart from some few matters, everything in such a polity is run by this sort of people."

"Very much so," he said.

"Well, another group that always distinguishes itself from the masses is of this sort."

"What sort?"

"When everybody's trying to make money, presumably, for the most part, those who are most orderly by nature get the richest."

"That's likely."

"Then I imagine the most honey for the drones, and the easiest to get, is lifted from there."

"How could anybody lift it out of people who have little of it?" he said.

"So I imagine the rich are the sort of people referred to as the feed-ing ground of the drones."

"Pretty much," he said.

"And the third group would be the people, all those who work   565A
with their own hands, stay out of politics, and don't own very much; whenever they unite, they're the most numerous and authoritative part of a democracy."

"They are," he said, "but they're not willing to do that often unless they get a share of the honey."

"And don't they always get their share," I said, "as much as the leaders are able to spread out among the populace when they take away the wealth from those who have it, and still keep the most themselves?"

"That's the way they get their share," he said.   B

"So I imagine those from whom it's taken are forced to fight back, by speaking among the people and doing whatever they can."

"Of course."

"So even when they don't want to cause a change in government, they get accused by the others of plotting against the people and being oligarchs."

"What else?"

C

"Then when they see that the people, not willingly but from ignorance and from being misled by the slanderers, are getting ready to treat them unjustly, don't they end up at that point, whether they want to or not, by truly becoming oligarchs, not of their own will but because that drone who's stinging them is giving birth to this evil too?"

"That's it exactly."

"So impeachments come along, and convictions, and trials back and forth."

"And how."

"And aren't the people always in the habit of choosing some one person exclusively as their leader, supporting him and building him up as someone great?"

"That's their habit."

D

"This is evident, then," I said, "that whenever someone grows into a tyrant, the root he sprouts from is the people's choice, and he comes from no other source."[166]

"That's very evident."

"And what's the beginning of the change from chosen leader to tyrant? Or is it apparent that it comes when the leader starts to do the same thing as the person in the story that's told about the temple of Lycaean Zeus in Arcadia?"

"What?" he said.

E

"That when someone gets a single taste of human entrails cut up in among those of the other sacrificial animals, he necessarily turns into a wolf. Haven't you heard the story?"

"I have."

"Doesn't it happen the same way too with anyone who's a chosen leader of a people, when he gets an exceedingly tractable mob, and doesn't shy away from the blood of his own tribe, but makes unjust accusations, exactly the sort they tend to make, brings someone into court, and stains it with blood, blotting out a man's life, tasting with unholy tongue and mouth blood shed from his own kind? Doesn't

566A

he drive people out of house and home, kill people outright, and hint

---

166 The word *turannos* meant someone who takes over as sole ruler without any regular lawful authority to do so. Socrates has confined the word *basileus* to lawfully chosen non-hereditary kings, and he referred to hereditary monarchy (*dunasteia*) in 544D as something outside the pattern of legitimate polities. His claim here, then, is that the natural growth of tyranny in a community under the rule of law occurs only in a democracy, or at least where there is a strong popular party.

at cancellations of debts and a redistribution of land? After that, isn't such a person necessarily doomed either to be killed by his enemies or be a tyrant and turn from a human being into a wolf?"

"That's necessary in a big way," he said.

"So he," I said, "turns out to be the one who starts the rebellion against those who have wealth."

"He does."

"And if he's banished and comes back in defiance of his enemies, doesn't he come back as a consummate tyrant?"

"Clearly."

"But if they're unable to banish him or put him to death by slandering him to the city, they plot to kill him by a violent death in secret."   B

"It does tend to happen that way, at any rate," he said.

"So at this point, all those who've gotten this far come up with the oft-repeated tyrannical demand, to ask the people for some bodyguards, so the champion of the people's cause can be kept safe for them."

"Very true," he said.

"And I imagine they give it to him, fearful on his behalf, but over-confident on their own."

"Very true."

"And when a man who has money sees this, and who along with   C
his money has the accusation of being an enemy of the people, at that point, comrade, in accord with the oracle that came to Croesus,[167] he

> Flees along the pebbled banks of the Hermus,
> Doesn't waste any time, and isn't ashamed to be craven."

"He wouldn't get a second chance to be ashamed," he said.

"And I imagine someone who's caught is given death," I said.

"Necessarily."

"But as for that chosen leader himself, it's clear he isn't stretched   D
out on the ground 'great in his greatness'[168] but standing tall in the chariot of the city after knocking down many others, a tyrant instead of a leader, and a consummate one."

"He's not going to be anything else," he said.

"Shall we go into the happiness that belongs to the man," I said, "and to the city in which such a personage turns up?"

"Let's go into it thoroughly," he said.

"Well during the time of his first days," I said, "doesn't he have a smile and a greeting for everyone he comes across, and claim he's   E
not a tyrant, and make a lot of promises both privately and in public, and free people from debts, and distribute land to the people and to those close to him, and make a pretense of being benign and mild with everybody?"

---

167 The fabulously rich Asian king of Lydia. The oracle is given in Herodotus' *History*, I, 55.

168 *Iliad* XVI, 776 and XVIII, 26; *Odyssey* XXIV, 40.

"Necessarily," he said.

"But I imagine that when he comes to terms with some of the enemies he ousted, and has killed off the rest, and his problems with them quiet down, the first thing he does is always to stir up some wars so the people will be in need of a leader."

"Very likely."

567A "And isn't that also to make them become poor by paying their money in taxes so they'll be forced to turn toward day-by-day concerns and be less likely to plot against him?"

"Clearly."

"And, I imagine, if he suspects that some people with thoughts of freedom won't leave it up to him to rule, it's also to let him have a pretext for destroying them by giving them up to the enemies. Isn't it necessary for the sake of all these things for a tyrant always to be agitating for war?"

"It's necessary."

"And by doing that, he's bound to become more an object of hate to the citizens?"

"How could he not?"

B "And don't some of those who are in power, who helped set him up, speak frankly to him and among themselves, protesting at what's happening—those who happen to be the bravest, that is?"

"Likely so."

"So the tyrant has to eliminate all of them quietly, if he's going to rule, until no friends or enemies are left of any use whatever."

"Clearly."

C "So he has to be sharp-eyed about who's brave, who's highminded, who's intelligent, and who's rich, and he has the great happiness to be obliged to be an enemy to all these people and plot against them whether he wants to or not, until he cleans out the city."

"A beautiful way to clean it up," he said.

"Yes," I said, "it's the opposite of what doctors do with bodies, because they take away what's worst and leave what's best, but he does the reverse."

"And it seems like that's what he has to do," he said, "if he's going to rule."

D "As a result," I said, "he's bound up in a blessed necessity that requires him either to live among a mass of mediocrities and be hated by them, or not live."

"That's the situation he's in," he said.

"Well, to the degree that he's more an object of hate to the citizens by doing these things, won't that make him need more spear-carrying guards, and more trustworthy ones?"

"How could it not?"

"Who are the people he can trust? And where's he going to send for them from?"

"A lot will show up on their own, with wings," he said, "as long as he's giving cash."

"More drones, by the dog" I said. "You seem to me to be talking about an assortment of foreign ones."   E

"And your impression of my meaning is a true one," he said.

"And who's in that very spot? Won't he be willing to take their slaves away from the citizens somehow, free them, and make them part of the spear-carrying guard around himself?"

"Emphatically so," he said, "since they're certainly the people he can trust most."

"What a blessed thing it is for a tyrant if, as you say, he has that   568A
sort of men as his trusted friends after he's destroyed the ones he had before."

"Well, they're certainly the sort he's got," he said.

"And these companions and new citizens admire him," I said, "and consort with him, while decent people hate him and stay away."

"How are they going to do anything else?"

"It's not for nothing," I said, "that tragedy in general is thought to be a wise thing, and Euripides surpassingly so within it."

"Why, in particular?"

"Because he also uttered this piece of dense thinking, that 'tyrants   B
are wise by consorting with the wise.'[169] And it's obvious he meant that the people he does consort with are the wise ones."

"He also extols tyranny as being 'on the level of a god,'" he said, "and for many other things, and the other poets do too."

"Well surely, then," I said, "since they're wise, the tragic poets will be understanding toward us, and toward anyone else who looks at political life in a way close to ours, for the fact that we won't admit them into our polity, since they're singers of tyranny's praises."

"I imagine they'll be understanding," he said, "at least all the   C
sophisticated ones among them."

"And as they travel around to the other cities, I imagine they'll collect big crowds, hire beautiful, strong voices that carry conviction, and pull those polities in the direction of tyrannies and democracies."

"Very much so."

"And to top it off, don't they get paid for these things, in money and in honor as well, especially, as one would expect, by tyrants, but secondly by democracies? But the higher uphill they go among the polities, the more their honor fails, as if it couldn't go on from short-   D
ness of breath."

---

169   The line is found in a fragment by Sophocles, but was also widely attributed to Euripides by his contemporaries. Its meaning was obviously something along the lines of the "cute remark" of Simonides mentioned in 489B, that since tyrants are rich they have no shortage of wise advisors available, but Socrates inverts the logic of it to produce the cynical claim that those who know what side of their bread the butter is on are the truly wise. What Adeimantus quotes next is from Euripides' *Trojan Women*, 1169.

"Very much so."

"But we've gotten off the track here," I said. "Let's get back to talking about the tyrant's encampment, that beautiful, big, variegated, ever-changing thing, and say where its support will come from."

"It's obvious," he said, "that if there's a temple treasure in the city, he'll spend that for whatever period of time the yield from selling it lasts, so there'll be less taxes for him to force the people to pay."

E

"And what about when that runs out?"

"It's obvious," he said, "that he, his drinking partners, and his intimate male and female companions will be supported out of what he inherits from his father."

"I understand," I said, "because the people who gave birth to the tyrant will support him and his cohorts."

"A great necessity will be upon it," he said.

"But what do you say to this?" I said. "Suppose the people get annoyed and say it's unjust for a son in the prime of life to be supported by his father, that on the contrary a father should be supported by his son, and that it wasn't for this that they gave birth to him and set him up, so that when he became great they themselves, as slaves to their own slaves, would be supporting him and the slaves and the rest of the dregs, but so that, with him as their chosen leader, they'd be freed from the rich and the self-described gentlemen in the city, and now they're ordering him and his cohorts to get out of the city, the way a father would throw a son out of the house along with his rambunctious drinking buddies."

569A

B

"Then a populace like that will soon find out, by Zeus," he said, "exactly what sort of creature they've given birth to, welcomed, and allowed to grow, and that they'd be the weaker ones, tossing out the stronger."

"How do you mean that?" I said. "Will the tyrant dare to use force against his father, and even beat him, if he doesn't obey?"

"Yes," he said, "as soon as he's taken away his father's weapons."

"You're saying a tyrant is a parricide, a dangerous person to look after an old man," I said, "and it looks like this by now would be acknowledged tyranny; as the saying goes, the people, by fleeing the smoke of enslavement to free men, would have fallen into the fire of being mastered by slaves, in place of that great and mismanaged freedom, wrapping themselves in the cruelest and bitterest slavery to slaves."

C

"That's exactly what becomes of them," he said.

"What about it, then?" I said. "Won't we be hitting the right note if we claim we've gone over enough the way democracy changes into tyranny, and what sort of thing it is that comes of it?"

"Quite enough," he said.

BOOK IX

Note

> Socrates argues that a tyrannical ruler always has a tyrannic soul, in which all desires, including the disordered ones ordinarily present only in alcohol-soaked dreams, have been allowed to grow and to break free under the dominance of one strong erotic passion. He and Adeimantus conclude that such a person achieves his dream life only by cutting himself off from all bonds of friendship with other human beings. Once the orderly presentation of the stages of human decay is complete, Glaucon returns to the conversation and Socrates asks him to assess the happiness and misery contained in these configurations of the soul. One way of determining that is provided by a re-thinking of pleasure and pain; most of what is considered intense but fleeting pleasure is judged to be illusory, with the illusion resulting from a failure to experience the full range of kinds of pleasures and allow the soul to find its own desirable condition. Socrates introduces a new image of the three-part soul to show that this expanded view of pleasure gives a foundation to widespread conventional attitudes of praise and blame. The happiest human being is declared to be someone who always lives the life of the best city, outwardly as well as inwardly, whether or not that city is ever brought into existence.

"What's left to be considered now," I said, "is the tyrannic man himself, how he changes out of a democratic one, what he's like once he has, and what kind of life he lives, miserable or blessedly happy." **571A**

"He's the one that's left," he said.

"Do you know what I still have a craving for?" I said.

"What?"

"We don't seem to me have made enough distinctions on the subject of desires, about what sort and how many there are. By being deficient in this, the inquiry we're pursuing will be more unclear."

"Isn't this still a perfect time to remedy that?" he said. **B**

"Very much so. Consider the point I want to look into about them, which is this: of the non-necessary pleasures and desires, some seem to me to be disordered, and they're liable to be innate in everyone, but when they're curbed by the laws and by the best desires, joined with reason, they're either completely eliminated in some people or a few are left in a weakened condition, while in other people, more **C**
and stronger ones are left."

"Which are the ones you're talking about?" he said.

"The ones that are awakened during sleep," I said, "when the rest of the soul, all the reasoning, civilized, ruling part of it goes to sleep and the animal-like, wild part, gorged on food or strong drink, is restless, fighting off sleep, and seeks to go and gratify its characteristic impulses. You know that in such a state it has the audacity to do

D   anything, as if it had been set loose from and rid itself of all shame and good sense. It doesn't shrink from trying, as it imagines, to have sex with a mother or with anyone else at all—human, god, or beast—or from staining itself with the murder of anyone at all, or draw the line at any flesh it might feed on; in a word, there's nothing senseless or shameless it won't do."

"What you say is completely true," he said.

"But, I imagine, when someone keeps himself in a healthy and moderate condition in relation to himself, and goes to sleep after stimulating the reasoning part of himself, feasting it with beautiful

E   reasons and considerations and bringing himself into accord with himself, and after indulging the desiring part neither deficiently nor to repletion, so that it's quieted down and won't cause any disturbance to

572A the best part by its enjoyment or pain, but will leave it alone by itself in its purity to look to and stretch itself toward perceiving something it doesn't know, something that was or is or will be, and after soothing the spirited part the same way, he won't go off and lie down to sleep with his spirit stirred up into anger against anybody, but having calmed down these two forms and set the third in motion, the one in which the activity of mindfulness arises, and when he comes to rest that way, you know, he's in the kind of condition in which he's most in contact with the truth, and at such a time disordered visions show up least in his dreams."

B   "I imagine that's absolutely the way it is," he said.

"Well, we've gotten carried away to go on talking about these things, but what we want to recognize is this: that some terrible, wild, lawless form of desires is present in each person, even in some of us who seem to be entirely well-balanced, and this becomes manifest in dreams. See if I seem to be saying anything at all, and whether you go along with it."

"I do go along with it."

"Then recall what we were claiming the democratic-style person

C   was like. He was presumably brought about by being raised from youth by a miserly father who honored only the money-making desires and had contempt for the non-necessary ones that arise for the sake of amusement or ostentation, isn't that right?"

"Yes."

"But when he'd mingled with men who were more sophisticated and full of the desires we've just gone over, he went charging off into every sort of insolence and into the form of those men, from hatred of

D   his father's miserliness, but since he had a better nature than his corruptors and was pulled in both directions, he settled into the middle between the two ways, and enjoying each within measure, as he imagined, he lived a life neither inhibited nor out of control, having become a democratic-style person from an oligarchic one."

"That was our opinion about such a person," he said, "and still is."

"Then think of a young son of such a person next," I said, "brought up in turn in *his* characteristic ways now that he's gotten older."

"I'm thinking of him."

"Then go on thinking of those same things happening to him that also happened to his father, of his being drawn into every kind of disorderliness, though it's given the name 'total freedom' by the ones doing the drawing, while his father and the rest of his family come to the aid of those desires in the middle range and the others back up the other kind. And whenever the formidable enchanters and tyrant-makers in the latter group have no other hope of getting control of the young person, they find a way to implant some sort of erotic passion in him as a leader for the slothful desires that soak up his available resources, some sort of big winged drone. Or do you imagine erotic desire in such people is anything but that?"

"Not I," he said; "it's nothing but that."

"So whenever the other desires are buzzing around that one, full of incense, perfumes, wreaths, wine, and the pleasures that are turned loose in that sort of company, increasing it and feeding to the utmost, they inject a sting of longing in the drone, and then this leader of the soul has insanity for its bodyguard and is in a frenzy, and if it gets hold of any opinions or desires in it with decent reputations and still capable of shame, it kills them and pushes them out of itself until it's cleansed of moderation and filled with the insanity it brought in."

"You're describing perfectly the coming into being of a tyrannic man," he said.

"And is it for that sort of reason," I said, "that erotic passion has for so long been described as a tyrant?"

"It could be," he said.

"And, my friend," I said, "doesn't a drunken man have a certain tyrannical way of thinking?"

"He sure has."

"And in fact someone who's insane and unbalanced tries to rule not only human beings but gods as well, and thinks he can."

"Very much so," he said.

"And a man becomes precisely tyrannic, you uncanny fellow, when, by his nature or pursuits or both, he becomes drunken, lustful, and crazy."

"Completely so."

"And it looks like that's also the way this sort of man comes into being. So how does he live his life?"

"As the jokesters say," he said, "you'll tell me that too."

"I'll tell exactly that," I said, "because I imagine that what comes next in those in whom the tyrant of erotic passion, dwelling within, steers everything to do with the soul, are feasts, revelry, celebrations, prostitutes, and everything of the sort."

"Necessarily," he said.

"And don't a lot of alarming desires, demanding a lot of satisfactions, spring up around that one day and night?"

"A lot for sure."

"And whatever income there might be is quickly spent."

"How could it not be?"

E

"And after that loans that eat away at his estate."

"What else?"

"And when all that runs out, won't the packed crowd of vigorous newly hatched desires cry out, and won't those who have them be stung into a frenzy as if they were driven by cattle prods, both by the other desires and especially by erotic passion itself, leading all the rest as its spear-carrying guards? Then won't they look for anyone who has

574A   anything that they can take away by cheating them or using force?"

"Intensely so," he said.

"So it'll be necessary to plunder it from every source, or be caught up in great spasms of anguish."

"Necessarily."

"Then, just as the upstart desires in him got the better of the old ones and took away what they had, won't he too in the same way think that since he's younger he deserves to get the better of his father and mother, and if he's wasted his own share, that he deserves to take away his parents' property and help himself to that."

"What else could he think?" he said.

B

"And if they don't turn it over to him, wouldn't the first thing he'd try be to steal it from his parents furtively and cheat them out of it?"

"Out of everything."

"But if at any point he's unable to, wouldn't he next seize it openly and use force?"

"I imagine so," he said.

"Well then, you amazing fellow, if the old man and old woman resist him and fight back, would he be cautious or reluctant about doing anything of a tyrannical kind?"

"I don't hold out very much hope for the parents of such a person," he said.

"Really, Adeimantus, before Zeus, does it seem to you that for

C

the sake of a newcomer, a lady-friend and non-necessary female companion, such a person would give a beating to his longtime friend and indispensable mother, or to his original friend, his indispensable father, when he's past his prime and elderly, for the sake of a non-necessary newfound boyfriend just entering his prime? That he'd make his parents the slaves of these people if he brought them into the same house?"

"By Zeus, yes," he said.

"It's a potent blessing, it seems," I said, "to bring a tyrannical son into the world."

"Totally," he said.

"And what about when the resources of his father and mother run out for such a person, but the swarm of pleasures already gathered in him is large? Won't he first lay hands on the wall of someone's house, or on the cloak of someone out walking late at night, and after that won't he clean out a temple? And in the course of all this, the opinions that he had for so long about things that are beautiful or shameful, that he'd regarded as just since childhood, are overpowered by opinions that have been newly released from slavery to carry spears for erotic passion and have come into ascendancy along with it, the ones that were released before as dreams during sleep, when he himself was still subject to laws and to his father while democracy governed within him. But under the tyranny of erotic passion, now that he's come to be, all the time he's awake, the sort of person he used to become occasionally in dreams, he won't hold back from any terrible murder, any flesh to feed on, any deed; instead, with erotic passion living in him in tyrannical style in every sort of anarchy and lawlessness, since it's his supreme ruler and the thing that holds sway in him as in a city, it will lead him to dare any act by which he'll feed it and the chaos surrounding it, some of it brought in from outside from bad company and some raised up and set free from within out of his own tendencies. Isn't that the life lived by such a person?"

"That's it," he said.

"And if there are only a few such people in a city," I said, "and the rest, the majority, are moderate, they go off and serve as body-guards for some other tyrant, or as auxiliaries for pay if there's a war somewhere, but if they come along in a time of peace and quiet, they commit a lot of minor crimes right there in the city."

"What sort do you mean exactly?"

"This sort: they steal, break into houses, pick pockets, walk off with people's clothes, pilfer from temples, kidnap people, and there are times when they hire out as perjurers, if they're competent at speaking, and give false testimony in return for bribes."

"You're talking about minor crimes, at any rate," he said, "as long as such people are few."

"That's because minor things are minor in comparison to major ones," I said, "and for corruption and misery in a city, all these things aren't even in the ballpark, as the saying goes, with a tyrant. Because it's exactly when a lot of such people turn up in a city, with others following along with them, and they become aware of how numerous they are, that they, combined with the senselessness of the populace,

D

E

575A

B

C

bring the tyrant into being: whoever among them most of all, himself within himself, has the biggest and strongest tyrant in his soul."

D "Likely so," he said, "because he'd be the most tyrannic."

"Mind you, that's if they willingly submit; but if the city doesn't give way to him, then just as he once punished his mother and father, in the same way again he'll punish his fatherland if he can, and bringing in new companions, with his dear old motherland, as the Cretans call it, enslaved to them, he'll hold and keep his fatherland

E in that condition. That would be exactly the end sought by such a man's desire."

"That's it absolutely," he said.

"In private life, before they rule," I said, "isn't this what these people are like: first, as for those they associate with, don't they stick with their own flatterers, people ready to do them any service, but

576A if they need anything from anyone, don't they themselves become obsequious, stooping to any posture to act like servants, though when they've got what they want they're completely different?"

"Emphatically so."

"So they live their whole lives without ever being friends to anyone, always someone's master or someone else's slave, but of freedom or true friendship, a tyrannic nature never has a taste."

"None at all."

"Wouldn't such people rightly be called incapable of trust?"

"How could they not?"

"And certainly unjust, as much as it's possible to be, if we were

B right about the sort of thing we earlier agreed that justice is."

"And we were certainly right," he said.

"Well then, let's sum up the worst person. Presumably, it's whoever is the sort of person awake that we described someone being in dreams."

"Very much so."

"And whoever is the most tyrannic by nature and gets hold of a monarchy, gets to be this way, and the more time he spends living in tyranny, that much more is he this way."

"That's a necessity," said **Glaucon**, taking up the argument.

"Now won't someone who's manifestly the worst person also

C manifestly be the most miserable?" I said. "And won't someone who's most a tyrant for the longest time also have been in truth the most miserable person for the longest time, even though many people have many opinions about it?"

"It's a necessity that these things be this way even so," he said.

"And would the tyrannic person be in accord with anything else but a tyrannical city by likeness, and a democratic-style person with a democratic city, and so on with the others?"

"Of course not."

"So whatever the relation is of city to city in virtue and happiness, won't that also be the relation of man to man?"   D

"How could it not?"

"And what's the relation in respect to virtue of a city with a tyrant to one with a king of the sort we went over first?"

"Completely opposite," he said, "since one is the best and the other the worst."

"I won't ask which of the two you mean," I said, "since that's obvious. But for happiness and misery now, do you judge them the same way or differently? And let's not be bowled over by looking at the tyrant, who's one person, or at some few people who might be around him, but since one needs to go in and take a look at the whole   E
city, getting down close and peering into everything, let's declare our opinion that way."

"The way you propose is the right one," he said, "and it's obvious to everyone that there's no city more miserable than one with a tyrant and none happier than one with a king."

"And would my proposal for the same things about the men   575A
also be right," I said, "if I proposed considering as worthy to judge about them that person who in his thinking is able to get inside the character of a man and see discerningly, and isn't bowled over, like a child looking on from outside, by the ceremonial display of tyrannical trappings that they put up as a front for the outer world, but sees them for what they are? And would I be right if I imagined that all of us ought to listen to that person who, as well as being able to judge, has also lived in the same house as the tyrant, and been present amid his actions at home to see how he is with those close to him, actions in which he could be observed most unadorned by stage props fit for   B
a tragedy, and who has also been present amid hazardous situations in public? Would we be right to insist that only someone who's seen all that give the report on what condition the tyrant is in with regard to happiness and misery in comparison with other people?"

"You would be completely right in proposing these things too," he said.

"Then do you want us to make believe," I said, "that we belong to the class of people who are able to judge and who've already happened to be around such people, so we can have someone who can answer the questions we ask?"

"Very much so."

"Come on then," I said, "and consider it this way for me. Keeping in mind the likeness between the city and the man, and looking at each   C
in turn in that light, tell me the attributes of each of the two."

"What sorts?" he said.

"To speak of the city first," I said, "would you say that the one with a tyranny is free or enslaved?"

"Enslaved as much as it's possible to be," he said.

"Surely you also see slave masters and free people in it."

"I see a little bit of that," he said, "but the whole of it, so to speak, and the most decent element in it anyway, is enslaved in disgrace and misery."

D   "So if the man is like the city," I said, "isn't it necessary for the same setup to be present in him too, for his soul to be filled with a lot of slavery and repression, for those parts of it that are the most decent to be enslaved, and for a small element that's the most corrupt and insane to hold mastery?"

"It's necessary," he said.

"What about it, then? Are you going to claim that such a soul is enslaved or free?"

"I'll certainly claim it's enslaved."

"And for its part, doesn't the city that's enslaved and has a tyranny do what it wants least of all?"

"Very much so."

E   "So then the soul that has a tyranny will also do what it wants least of all, to speak of the soul as a whole; since it's always dragged along by force as a result of a maddening frenzy, it'll be full of confusion and regret."

"How could it not?"

"And is it necessary for the city with a tyranny to be rich or poor?"

"Poor."

578A   "So then it's also necessary for a soul with a tyranny always to be impoverished and insatiably needy."

"That's the way it is," he said.

"What about this? Isn't it necessary for such a city and such a man to be full of fear?"

"Greatly."

"Do you imagine you'll find more moans and groans and laments and sufferings in any other city?"

"Not at all."

"But in a man, do you believe that such things are more plentiful in anyone other than this tyrannic one crazed by desires and erotic passions?"

"How could they be?" he said.

B   "So I imagine it was with an eye to all these things and others like them that you judged the city the most miserable of cities."

"Wasn't that right?" he said.

"Very much so," I said. "But what do you say now about the tyrannic man when you look at these same things?"

"That he's by far the most miserable," he said, "compared to all the rest."

"As to that," I said, "you're no longer speaking rightly."

"How's that?" he said.

"I imagine that this sort of person," I said, "is not yet the most extreme."

"Who, then?"

"This one here will probably seem to you to be still more miserable than that one."

"Who's that?"

"Someone," I said, "who while being tyrannic, doesn't live out   C
his life in private, but is unlucky, and by some misfortune gets the chance to become a tyrant."

"I judge by indications from the things said before," he said, "that what you say is true."

"Ye-es," I said, "but it's not right to conjecture about such things; one ought to examine things very well in such a discussion, because the inquiry is surely about the most important thing, a good or bad life."

"Quite right," he said.

"Then consider whether I'm saying anything to the purpose: it   D
seems to me we have to get a notion of it by examining it from this standpoint."

"From what standpoint?"

"From that of each one of the private persons in cities who are rich and own a lot of slaves, because they have this point of resemblance to tyrants, the fact that they rule a lot of people, though the number belonging to the tyrant surpasses theirs."

"It certainly surpasses theirs."

"Well, you know, don't you, that they have a sense of security and aren't afraid of their servants?"

"What would they be afraid of?"

"Nothing," I said; "but do you understand the reason?"

"Yes; the fact that the whole city protects each one of the private citizens."

"You put it beautifully," I said. "But what if one of the gods spirited   E
away one man who had fifty slaves, or even more, out of the city, him and his wife and his children, and put them, along with his servants and the rest of his property, in an isolated place where none of the free citizens could have any way to protect him? What sort of fear, and how much fear do you imagine he'd land in for himself, his children, and his wife, that they might be killed by their servants?"

"In total fear, I imagine," he said.

"Wouldn't he now be forced to grovel to some of his own slaves,   579A
and make them a lot of promises, and set them free when he wants no such thing? Wouldn't he be revealing himself as a flatterer of servants?"

"There's a great necessity for him to," he said, "or else be killed."

"And what if the god were to settle a lot of other neighbors in a ring around him," I said, "who wouldn't stand for it if any one person claimed he was entitled to be master of another, and who, if they could get hold of any such person anywhere, would take extreme vengeance on him?"

"I imagine he'd be in an even more completely abysmal plight," he said, "when he's being watched over from a perimeter made up entirely of enemies."

"And isn't the tyrant confined in a prison of that sort, since by his nature he's the kind of person we've been going over, filled with lots of fears and erotic passions of all varieties? Even though his soul is eager to sop up sensations, isn't he the only one in the city who doesn't have the ability to go out anywhere or to see all the things that other free people are desirous of seeing, but who, ensconced in his house most of the time, lives like a housewife and envies the rest of the citizens when any of them get to go out and see anything good?"

"Absolutely so," he said.

"So when a man who's badly governed within himself, the tyrannic man you just now judged the most miserable, doesn't live out his life in private but is forced by some chance to become a tyrant and to try to rule others when he's powerless to rule himself, doesn't he end up worse by reaping that sort of rotten fruit? It's as if someone with a diseased body powerless to control itself was forced to pass through life not in private but competing and fighting with other bodies."

"It's completely and totally like that, Socrates," he said, "and you're telling the utmost truth."

"Well then, dear Glaucon," I said, "isn't this a perfectly miserable thing to suffer, and doesn't the person who puts tyranny into effect live an even harsher life than the person judged by you to live the harshest?"

"No question about it," he said.

"In truth, then, even if someone might not think so, a person who is in fact a tyrant is in fact a slave as far as the most extreme sort of groveling and slavishness is concerned, and a flatterer of the most worthless people, and when his desires don't get fulfilled in any way, he shows himself to be the most needy of the most things and truly poverty-stricken, if someone knows how to take in view a whole soul; he's burdened with fear all through life, and full of violent outbursts and agonies, if his condition is like that of the city he rules—and it is like it, isn't it?"

"Very much so," he said.

"And on top of those things, won't we also give the man the attributes we spoke of before, and note that it's necessary for him to be and, by ruling, to become even more so, envious, incapable of trust, unjust, friendless, impious, and someone who gives hospitality and sustenance to every vice? As a result of all this, isn't it necessary for him to be especially prone to misfortune, and consequently for those near him to end up that way too?"

"No one who has any sense will deny what you say," he said.

"So now at last come on," I said, "and just as the judge in the final   B
round declares the result, you decide the same way who in your
opinion is first in happiness, who second, and the rest in order, five in
all, a kingly person, a timocratic one, an oligarchic one, a democratic
one, and a tyrannic one."

"It's an easy decision," he said; "I judge that, exactly the way they,
like choruses, made their entrance for virtue and vice, they also rank
in happiness and its opposite."

"Then shall we hire a herald," I said, "or shall I myself announce
that the son of Ariston has adjudged the best and most just person   C
the happiest, and this is the one who's most kingly and is a king
within himself, while the worst and most unjust person is the most
miserable, and this in turn is exactly the one who's most tyrannic and
who, to the greatest possible extent, is a tyrant both within himself
and within his city?"

"Take it as having been announced by you," he said.

"Well," I said, "shall I proclaim as an addendum, 'whether or not
the sort of people they are goes undetected by all human beings and
gods'?"

"Proclaim it addendum and all," he said.

"Okay, then," I said; "that would be one demonstration for us,
but take a look at this second one to see if it seems to amount to
anything."

"What's that?"   D

"Since the same way a city is divided into three forms," I said, "the
soul of each one of us is also in three parts, it seems to me there's also
room for another demonstration."

"What would that be?"

"This: it appears to me that for these three parts there are also three
pleasures, each uniquely appropriate to one of them, and the same
way with desires and modes of rule."

"How do you mean?" he said.

"One part, we claim, is that by which a human being learns,
another the one by which his spiritedness is roused; as for the third,
we had no uniquely appropriate name[170] to apply to it, because of its   E
multiform character, but we took what it has the biggest and strongest instances of in it, and called it the desiring part, on account of
the forcefulness of the desires for food and drink and sex and all the
other things that go along with these. And because it's by means of
money most of all that such desires are fulfilled, we've also called it   581A
the money-loving part."

---

170 Naming it for desiring is too broad if the other parts of the soul also have desires, and
naming it 'money-loving' is too narrow if some people with strong desires have contempt for
money; it can't be called the irrational or passionate or impulsive part since all those things are
equally true of spiritedness.

"And rightly so," he said.

"So if we were to claim that what it has is a pleasure in, and a love for, gain, couldn't we settle on that as the most appropriate single heading for it in our discussion, to indicate some clear meaning for ourselves whenever we speak of this part of the soul? By calling it money-loving and gain-loving, would we be giving it the right name?"

"It seems so to me, at any rate," he said.

B
"And what about the spirited part? Surely we claim, don't we, that as a whole it's always spurring itself on toward mastering and winning and being well thought of?"

"Very much so."

"So if we refer to it as victory-loving and honor-loving, would that be in tune with it?"

"Perfectly in tune."

"And it's certainly obvious to everyone that the part by which we learn is always entirely directed toward knowing the truth as it is, and as for money and reputation, it has the least concern about that of any of them."

"Least by far."

"So in calling it learning-loving and wisdom-loving, would we be naming it in accord with its leanings?"

"Of course."

C
"And doesn't it also rule in the souls of some people," I said, "while in others another of the parts does, whichever it happens to be?"

"That's how it is," he said.

"And for that reason, we say there are also three primary kinds of human beings:[171] wisdom-loving, victory-loving, and gain-loving?"

"Exactly."

"And three forms of pleasures, one underlying each of these?"

"Quite so."

"Do you know, then," I said, "that if you cared to ask three such people, each in turn, which of these lives is most pleasant, each would
D
sing the praises of his own most of all, and the money-lover would claim that, compared to gaining something, the pleasures of being honored or of learning are worth nothing unless there's something about them that makes him money?"

"That's true," he said.

"And what about the honor-lover?" I said. "Doesn't he regard the pleasure that comes from money as something vulgar, and the one that comes from learning, whenever the thing learned brings no honor, as smoke and hot air?"

---

171 In Book IV, it took quite a bit of argument to establish that there are three distinct parts of the soul (435C and following) corresponding to the three functions required by a city, but there was an old Pythagorean parable to the effect that human lives reflect the differing reasons people go to the Olympic games: most go to buy and sell, a few to compete, and the smallest number just to see the contests.

"It's just that way," he said.

"And the wisdom-lover," I said, "what do you imagine he thinks of the other pleasures in comparison to that of knowing the truth as it is and always being in a condition like that while he's learning?[172] Won't he think they're very far beneath it, and say they're in fact matters of necessity, since he wouldn't want any of the others if they weren't necessary?"

"We ought to know that well," he said.

"So," I said, "seeing as how the pleasures and the very life belonging to each form are in disagreement, not over living more beautifully or shamefully, or worse or better, but more pleasantly and painlessly, how could we know which of them is speaking the most truthfully?"

"I have no way at all to say," he said.

"But consider it this way: by what should things be judged if the judging is to be done in a beautiful manner? Shouldn't it be by experience and understanding and reason? Or could anyone have a better standard than that?"

"How could anyone?" he said.

"So consider: of the men, of whom there are three, who's the most experienced in all the pleasures we're speaking of? Does the lover of gain seem to you to be more experienced in the pleasure that comes from knowing, because he learns the truth itself for what it is, or does the lover of wisdom seem more experienced in the pleasure that comes from gaining something?"

"There's a big difference," he said. "It's necessary for the one to taste the other pleasures starting from childhood, but for the other, the lover of gain, it's not necessary to taste or to get any experience of learning how things are in their nature, of the pleasure in that and how sweet it is; what's more, even if he were eager to, it wouldn't be so easy."

"So," I said, "the lover of wisdom greatly surpasses the lover of gain in his experience of both sorts of pleasure."

"Greatly indeed."

"And how about in relation to the lover of honor? Is the lover of wisdom more inexperienced in the pleasure that comes from being honored than that person is in the pleasure that comes from using intelligence?"

"On the contrary," he said; "honor is attached to them all, so long as each achieves what he sets out for. Even the rich person is honored by many people, as are the courageous and the wise. So all are experienced in what the pleasure is like that comes from being

E

582A

B

C

---

172 In 376B, Socrates said flatly that the love of wisdom and the love of learning are the same thing. He thus does not think of wisdom as something opposite to philosophy, which would cancel the need for the latter if it were attained. He implies that any experience of learning attains truth and that no knowledge puts an end to learning.

honored, but it's impossible for anyone except the lover of wisdom to get a taste of the what's involved in the sight of what *is*, or of the sort of pleasure it has in it."

D

"Therefore, as far as experience is concerned," I said, "he'd do the most beautiful job of judging among the men."

"By far."

"And he's surely the only one who'll have had his experience with any understanding of it."

"Of course."

"And surely too, the instrument by which it's necessary to do the judging is not the instrument possessed by the lover of gain or the lover of honor, but by the lover of wisdom."

"What's that?"

"Presumably we've been claiming that it needs to be judged by rational arguments, haven't we?"

"Yes."

"And rational arguments are an instrument possessed by that person most of all."

"How could it be otherwise?"

"So if the things being judged were best judged in terms of riches and gain, wouldn't those things the lover of gain said in praise and blame necessarily be the truest?"

E

"By a long way."

"And if they were best judged in terms of honor and victory and courage, wouldn't the truest things be the ones the lover of honor and the lover of victory said?"

"Clearly."

"But considering that it's in terms of experience and understanding and reason?"

"Of necessity," he said, "what the lover of wisdom and the lover of rational argument says in praise would be the truest."

583A

"So among the pleasures, of which there are three, the one belonging to that part of the soul by which we learn would be the most pleasant, and that person among us in whom this part rules would have the most pleasant life?"

"How's it going to be anything else?" he said. "Someone with understanding is authoritative in his praise, at least when he's praising his own life."

"And what does the judge claim is the second-best life," I said, "and the second-best pleasure?"

"Clearly, that it's the one belonging to the warlike and honor-loving person, since it's closer to his own than the one belonging to the money-maker is."

"So it looks like that of the lover of gain is in last place."

"What else?" he said.

"So that would be two in a row that way, and twice that the just   B
person has been victorious over the unjust; the third, as in the Olym-
pics, is dedicated to the Protector, Olympian Zeus.[173] Notice that the
pleasure belonging to those other than the person with understanding
is not wholly true or pure, but is a sort of surface illusion, as I seem
to have heard said by some wise person. Now that would certainly
be the greatest and most decisive of the three falls."

"Very much so; but how do you mean it?"

"In the way that I'll ascertain," I said, "if you keep answering   C
questions while I keep inquiring."

"Ask away," he said.

"Tell me then," I said, "don't we claim pain is the opposite of
pleasure?"

"Quite so."

"And also that there's something that's neither having enjoyment
nor being in pain?"

"Certainly there is."

"Is it a certain tranquillity of the soul about these things that's in the
middle between the two of them? Or is that not how you mean it?"

"That's how," he said.

"Well, do you recall the words of sick people," I said, "the things
they say while they're sick?"

"What sorts?"

"That there's really nothing more pleasant than being healthy, but
it had escaped their notice, until they were sick, that it was the most   D
pleasant thing."

"I do recall hearing that," he said.

"And don't you also hear people who have some overwhelming
pain saying that nothing could be more pleasant than to stop being
in pain?"

"I do hear that."

"And I imagine you observe people getting into many other situations of that kind, in which, when they're suffering them, they extol
the absence of pain and a respite from that sort of thing, and not
enjoyment, as the most pleasant thing."

"Maybe that's because, at such a time, this becomes pleasant and
satisfying, as a relief," he said.

"Then it's also the case that whenever anyone stopped enjoying   E
something, the respite from pleasure would be painful."

"Maybe so," he said.

"Therefore, the tranquility we were just claiming was between the
two will at times be both pain and pleasure."

---

173 Two allusions are combined here; a third fall was needed to complete an Olympic wrestling
victory, and three toasts were commonly drunk at a dinner party, the first to Olympian Zeus
and the third to Zeus the Protector.

"It looks like it."

"And is it possible for something that's neither of two things to become both?"

"It doesn't seem so to me."

"And in fact the pair of them, what's pleasant and what's painful, when they come into the soul, consist of some sort of motion, don't they?"

"Yes."

584A "But didn't the tranquility that's neither painful nor pleasant show up just now in the middle between the two?"

"It did show up that way."

"Then how is it right to consider being without pain pleasant and not being without enjoyment distressing?"

"It's not right at all."

"Then it isn't that way, but just appears to be," I said; "alongside something painful, tranquility appears pleasant, and alongside something pleasant it now appears painful. There's nothing sound in these appearances in relation to the truth about pleasure, but only a sort of trickery."

"That's the way the argument is pointing, anyway," he said.

B "Well," I said, "take a look at pleasures that aren't preceded by pains, so you won't by any chance imagine in the present discussion that it's natural for things to be that way, for pleasure to be a cessation of pain and pain a cessation of pleasure."

"Where are they?" he said. "What kind are you talking about?"

"There are many others as well," I said, "but especially, if you care to consider them, the pleasures involving smells. Without any pain being felt beforehand, they suddenly come into being with indescribable strength, and they leave no pain behind when they cease."

"That's very true," he said.

C "So let's not be persuaded that pure pleasure is the removal of pain, or pure pain the removal of pleasure."

"No, we won't."

"But certainly it's pretty much the case that most of what are called pleasures that get to the soul through the body, and the strongest ones, are of this form," I said, "some kind of removal of pain."

"They are."

"And don't the advance pleasures and advance pains fall into the same category, the ones that arise from the prior anticipation of these feelings when they're about to happen?"

"They're in the same category."

D "Do you know what they're like," I said, "and what they resemble most?"

"What?"

"Are you accustomed to thinking of there as being such a thing in nature as an upper, a lower, and a middle region?" I said.

"I am."

"Well, do you imagine someone who's been brought from the lower to the middle region will imagine he's been brought anywhere else but to the upper region? And standing in the middle, looking back at the place he was brought from, would he consider himself to be anywhere else but in the upper region, as long as he hasn't seen the truly upper region?"

"By Zeus," he said, "I don't imagine such a person could imagine anything else."

"But if he were brought back again," I said, "he'd imagine he'd been brought to the lower region, and be imagining something true?"   E

"What else?"

"And wouldn't he have all these things happen to him as a result of being without experience of what's truly upper, in the middle, and lower?"

"Obviously."

"Then would you be surprised if people also held unsound opinions about many other things in which they had no experience of the truth, and were disposed toward pleasure and pain and the state in between them in such a way that, when they're brought to something   585A painful, they imagine the truth and are genuinely in pain, but when they're brought from pain to the in-between state, they strongly imagine they've come to a state of fullness and pleasure? Isn't it as if, without experience of white, they were looking away at gray in comparison to black,[174] so they're misled when, without experience of pleasure, they go from looking at pain to something painless?"

"By Zeus," he said, "I wouldn't be surprised at all; I'd be much more surprised if it weren't that way."

"Anyway, think about it this way," I said: "aren't hunger and thirst and things like that certain kinds of emptiness in the condition   B that involves the body?"

"What else?"

"And isn't ignorance or lack of understanding an emptiness in the condition that involves the soul?"

"Very much so."

"And wouldn't someone get filled up who takes in food or gains insight?"

"How could he not?"

"And does the truer fullness belong to something with less or with more being?"

"Clearly to that with more."

---

174   This clause seems in the manuscripts to be out of parallel with the following one, but the verb and preposition in it may be elastic enough to bear the sense that seems called for, and is given here.

"Well then, which of the two kinds do you regard as having the greater share of pure being, that of things like bread, drink, meat,

C   and nourishment all together, or the form that includes true opinion, knowledge, insight, and in short, all virtue? Judge it like this: does it seem to you that something has more being that's always holding onto what's the same, immortal, and true, and is that way itself and comes to be present in something that's that way, or something that holds to what's never the same and is mortal, and is that way itself and comes to be present in something that's that way?"

"The one that holds onto what's always the same greatly surpasses the other," he said.

"And does the being of what's always the same have any greater share of being than of knowledge?"

"Not at all."

"And what about of truth?"

"Not of that either."

"But if something had a lesser share of truth, wouldn't it also have a lesser share of being?"

"Necessarily."

D   "And overall, don't the kinds of things involved in the care of the body have a lesser share of being and truth than the kinds involved in the care of the soul?"

"By far."

"And don't you imagine it's the same way with the body itself as compared to the soul?"

"I do."

"And isn't something that's full of things with more being, and itself has more being, in its very nature more full than something full of things with less being, that itself has less being?"

"How could it not be?"

"Therefore, if it's pleasant to become filled with the things that

E   are naturally fitting, something that, in its very nature, is more full of things that *are* more would also make someone enjoy true pleasure in a more genuine and truer sense; but something that has a lesser participation with things that *are* would also be less truly and stably full and would have a lesser participation in true pleasure."

"With the utmost necessity," he said.

586A   "Therefore, it appears that people who have no experience of understanding and virtue, but are always hanging around at parties and such, are carried downward and back up as far as the in-between region, and wander through life that way; but because they've never gotten beyond that, they haven't even looked upward toward what's truly above and haven't been carried up to it. They haven't been filled with what *is* in its very being, or tasted pleasure that's stable and pure; instead, after the manner of cattle, with their eyes always bent down, and heads stooped over the earth, or tables, they feed, getting fattened

up and breeding. On account of their greed for these things they kick **B**
and butt heads with one another with their iron horns and hooves, and
kill each other because of their insatiability, since they aren't filling,
with things that *are*, the part of themselves that *is* and doesn't leak."

"Like an oracle, Socrates," said Glaucon, "that's the life of most
people through and through."

"Then isn't it also a necessity for the pleasures they hang around
with, which are phantoms and optical illusions of true pleasure, to
be mixed with pains, and to take on coloring by their placement next **C**
to each other, so that each looks strong by comparison? Don't the
pleasures give birth to erotic desires for themselves that drive fools
into frenzy? Don't they get fought over like the phantom of Helen
that Stesichorus[175] claims was fought over by the people at Troy from
ignorance of the truth."

"There's a great necessity for it to be like that to some degree,"
he said.

"And what about the spirited part? Isn't it necessary for other
things of that kind to happen involving this part itself when someone
either uses envy to relieve a love of honor, or violence to relieve a
love of victory, or spirited anger to relieve an irritation, chasing after **D**
a fulfillment of honor, victory, and spiritedness without reasoning
or intelligence?"

"It's necessary for there to be things like that involving this part
too," he said.

"What about it then?" I said. "Shall we confidently say that even
for the desires that have to do with the gain-loving and victory-loving
parts, those that follow knowledge and reason, and pursue in company
with these the pleasures that the thoughtful part ordains, and get hold
of these, they'll be getting the truest pleasures, as true as it's possible
for them to get, because they're the pleasures that accompany truth, **E**
and the ones that are properly their own, if indeed that which is best
for each thing is also most its own?"

"That's certainly what's most something's own," he said.

"So when all the soul follows its wisdom-loving part, and isn't
divided against itself, it's possible for each part to do what properly
belongs to it and to be just, both in other respects and in particular
with regard to pleasures, so that each part enjoys those that are its **587A**
own, that are the best, and to the greatest possible extent those that
are the truest."

"Exactly so."

"Therefore, whenever one of the other parts takes over, it's not
even possible for it to discover its own pleasure, and it forces the other
parts to pursue pleasure that's alien and untrue."

175 A poet who had maligned Helen, and later recanted by saying she wasn't really at Troy.
That claim is mentioned in Plato's *Phaedrus* (243A-B); Herodotus thinks it likely to have been
true (*History* II, 120).

"That's how it is," he said.

"And aren't the things that stand at the greatest distance from philosophy and reason the ones that bring about results like that the most?"

"Very much so."

"Isn't what stands at the greatest distance from law and order also the very thing that's most distant from reason?"

"Clearly so."

B   "Wasn't it the erotic desires of the tyrannic sort that showed themselves to stand at the greatest distance?"

"Far and away."

"And the orderly ones of the kingly sort were least distant?"

"Yes."

"So I imagine the tyrant will stand at the greatest distance from true pleasure that's his own, and the other person at the least distance."

"Necessarily."

"And therefore the tyrant will live the most unpleasant life," I said, "and the king the most pleasant."

"There's a great necessity for it."

"And do you know how much more unpleasantly a tyrant will live than a king?" I said.

"If you tell me," he said.

"It looks like there are three kinds of pleasure, one true-born and two bastard kinds, and the tyrant, having gone over to the far side C   beyond the bastard ones, after he's escaped from law and reason, lives among a certain group of slave pleasures as his spear-carrying guards, and it's not very easy to say how far he's brought himself down, except maybe this way."

"How's that?" he said.

"Presumably the tyrant stands at the third remove, starting from the oligarchic person, because the democratic type was in the middle between them."

"Yes."

"Then wouldn't he live with a phantom of pleasure at the third remove, in relation to truth, from that one, if the things said before were true?"

"That's how it would be."

"But the oligarchic person is in turn at the third remove from the D   kingly one, if we put the aristocratic and kingly ones on the same step."

"He is at the third."

"Therefore," I said, "a tyrant stands at a remove triply tripled in number from true pleasure."

"So it appears."

"Therefore," I said, "it looks like the phantom that is tyrannic pleasure would be a plane number in length."

"Exactly so."

"So from an expansion by the square and cube, it becomes clear by how big an interval it's removed."

"Clear to someone skilled at calculation, anyway," he said.

"Accordingly, if by turning it the other way around, someone states by how great a removal the king is removed from the tyrant in truth of pleasure, when he completes the multiplication he'll find him living 729 times more pleasantly, and the tyrant more wretchedly by the same interval."

"That's an incredible calculation that's come gushing[176] out of you," he said, "of the difference between the two men, the just and the unjust, in respect to pleasure and pain."

"Nevertheless," I said, "it's a number that's both true and fitting to their lives, if indeed days, nights, months, and years are fitting terms to put them in."

"They're certainly fitting," he said.

"And if the good and just person is the winner over the bad and unjust person by so great a margin, won't he be the winner in the dignity, beauty, and virtue of his life by an incredibly greater margin?"

"Incredibly indeed, by Zeus," he said.

"Okay," I said, "now that we've come to this point in the discussion, let's take up again the things that were said first, on account of which we got here. What was said, I believe, was that for the completely unjust person, who's reputed to be just, it's profitable to do injustice. Isn't that the way it was put?"

"That's the way."

"So now let's talk it over with him," I said, "since we're in agreement about doing injustice and doing what's just, in regard to what power each has."

"How will we do that?" he said.

"By molding an image of the soul in speech, so the person who says those things can see what sort of things he's been talking about."

"What particular sort of image?" he said.

"One of those sorts of things people tell stories about," I said, "the kinds of natures they say used to come into being once upon a time, the Chimaera, Scylla, Cerberus, and a bunch of others in which the looks of many things are said to have come together, grown into one."[177]

E

588A

B

C

---

176 The number Socrates has uttered, probably without pausing for breath, is in Greek a single word of seventeen syllables. He has also finagled a simple list of five kinds of people into a three-by-three array, a "plane number," and cubed it for no apparent reason. The point of all this playfulness comes out in the next speech. The tyrant's wretchedness is measured not only by the pains he must feel by day, but also by the pleasures he chases after by night. By one ancient calculation of the period of the sun, that would total 729 alternations a year of the cycle in which he is caught. Near the beginning of Bk. VIII there was an elaborate mathematical excursus on the beginnings of the decay of political order; here near the end of Bk. IX, it is echoed in this numerical summation of the ultimate human result of that process.

177 The first monster named was a combination of lion, goat, and snake, the second of a woman, dogs, and snakes, and the third of dogs and snakes.

"Those things are spoken of," he said.

"Then mold into one look a polymorphous, many-headed beast that has a circle of heads of tame and wild animals and is able to transform and grow all of them out of itself."

"That's a job for a formidable molder," he said. "However, since it's easier to mold a description of things like that than to mold clay, take it as molded."

"Then mold another unitary look of a lion, and a unitary one of a human being; let the first one be by far the biggest, and the second one second in size."

"These are easier jobs; they're molded."

"Then join the three of them into one, so that in some fashion they're grown together with one another."

"They're joined," he said.

"Now plaster around the outside of them an image of one of them, that of the human being, so that to someone who can't see what's inside, but only sees the outer covering, it appears to be a single living thing, a human being."

"It's plastered over," he said.

"And let's tell the person who says it's profitable for this human being to do injustice, and not advantageous to do what's just, that he's claiming nothing other than that it's profitable for him to strengthen the polymorphous beast and the lion and the things associated with the lion by feasting them and to starve and weaken the human being, so he can be pulled whichever way either of them lead him, that it's profitable for him not to get each of them used to the other or make them friends, but to let them fight among themselves and bite and devour each other."

"That's absolutely what someone who approves of doing injustice would be saying," he said.

"On the other hand, wouldn't the person who says what's just is profitable be claiming that one ought to do and say those things as a result of which the human being inside will be most in control of the human being, and will take care of the many-headed beast like a farmer, feeding and nurturing its tame heads and preventing the wild ones from growing, making the lion's nature an ally, and looking after all of them in common, making them friends to each other and to him, and will bring them up that way?"

"That's exactly what someone who approves of what's just says in turn."

"So on every count, someone who extols what's just would be speaking the truth, and someone who extols what's unjust would be lying, because, whether someone is looking to pleasure or to a good reputation and benefit, the advocate of justice is truthful while as for the objector, he says nothing sound and objects without even knowing what he's objecting to."

"He doesn't seem to me to know anything about it at all," he said.

"Well, let's persuade him gently, because he isn't willingly mistaken, by asking him, 'Blessedly happy fellow, wouldn't we claim that what's customarily held to be beautiful or shameful comes from something like this too, that beautiful things bring the beast-like nature under the control of the human, or perhaps rather under the control of the divine, while shameful ones make the tame the slave of the wild?' Will he concede that, or how will he reply?" D

"He'll concede it if he's persuaded by me," he said.

"Then is there any way, based on this argument, for it to be profitable to get hold of gold unjustly," I said, "if something like this happens: by getting hold of the gold, at the same time he enslaves the best part of himself to the most vicious part? If, by his having carried off E the gold he'd enslaved a son or daughter, and to wild and evil men at that, it wouldn't have been of profit to him even if he'd gotten colossal wealth out of it, but if he makes the most divine part of himself a slave to the most godforsaken and polluted part, and has no mercy, is he 590A not a miserable wretch, and does he not get the gold as a payoff for a catastrophe much more horrific than Eriphyle's[178] when she accepted a necklace for her husband's life?"

"Much more indeed," said Glaucon; "I'll answer you on his behalf."

"Don't you imagine it's for reasons of that kind that being self-indulgent has from oldest times been condemned, because in such a person that horrible great multiform beast is let loose farther than is necessary?"

"Clearly," he said.

"And aren't self-will and bad temper condemned when they make the lion-like and snake-like part grow and intensify itself out of all B proportion?"

"Very much so."

"And aren't luxury and softness condemned for slackening and loosening this same part when they infect it with cowardice?"

"Of course."

"And flattery and slavishness when they bring this same part, the spirited one, under the control of that unruly mob of a beast, and make the former take abuse on account of the latter's insatiability and for the sake of money, training it from youth on to become not a lion but a monkey?"

"And how," he said.

---

178 A string of disasters followed when Eriphyle was bribed by Polyneices to persuade her husband to join the attack of the Seven against Thebes: her husband Amphiaraus was killed in the fighting, she was killed in retaliation by her son Alcmaeon, and he was killed in retribution for giving the same necklace to his wife after he'd sworn to dedicate it to the god at Delphi.

C

"And why do you imagine servile and menial occupations are held in low esteem? Will we claim it's for any reason other than this, that when the form of his best part is of such a weak nature in someone that he's unable to rule the beasts within him, but ministers to them instead, all he's able to learn are the things that gratify them?"

"It looks that way," he said.

"So in order that even someone of that kind might be ruled by something exactly like what the best person is ruled by, don't we

D

claim he ought to be a slave to that best person who has the godlike part ruling within himself? We're not imagining that it's for the slave's harm that he ought to be ruled, as Thrasymachus imagined was the case with those who are ruled, but because it's better for everyone to be ruled by something godlike and intelligent, best of all when he has it for his own within himself, but otherwise as something imposed from outside, so that as far as possible everyone might be like-minded and friends, guided by the same thing."

"And rightly so," he said.

E

"The law too, which is the ally of everyone in the city, makes it clear that it intends something of that kind," I said, "as does rule over children, who aren't allowed to be free until we set up a polity within

591A

them just as in a city, caring for what's best in them with what's like it in us until we can replace it with a similar guardian and ruler in the child and then set him free."

"They do make that clear," he said.

"So then, Glaucon, in what respect and according to what argument shall we claim that it's profitable to do injustice or be self-indulgent or do anything shameful, as a result of which someone will be worse, though he'll have gained more money or more of some other sort of power?"

"In no respect at all," he said.

"Well, in what respect is it profitable to go undetected in doing

B

injustice and not pay a penalty? Doesn't someone who goes undetected become even worse, while in someone who doesn't go undetected and is punished, the beast-like part is calmed and tamed, the tame part is set free, and the whole soul, when it's allowed to settle into its best nature, acquiring moderation and justice along with understanding, takes on a condition more to be prized than the one a body has by taking on strength and beauty along with health, to the degree that a soul is more honorable than a body?"

"Absolutely so," he said.

C

"Isn't anyone who has any sense going to live his life by straining all his powers to that end, first of all by honoring the kinds of studies that work up that sort of condition in his soul, and disregarding the rest?"

"Clearly," he said.

"And next," I said, "he's not only not going to live as if he'd entrusted the condition and sustenance of his body to irrational animal pleasure and let it be turned toward that, he's not even going to live with a view toward health or put that first, in order to be strong or healthy or beautiful, unless he's also going to be moderate as a result of those things; it will always be manifest that he's adjusting the attunement of his body in the service of the harmony in his soul."

D

"Absolutely so," he said, "if he's going to be musical in a true way."

"Won't he also be attuned to order and harmony in the acquisition of money?" I said. "And since he isn't knocked off course by what seems like bliss to most people, will he be increasing the mass of its quantity without limit and having unlimited troubles?"

"I imagine not," he said.

"But keeping his eye on the polity within him," I said, "and being on his guard so that he doesn't disturb any of the things he possesses *there* by an abundance or shortage of wealth, he'll add to or use up his wealth guided by that as far as is possible."

E

"Exactly so," he said.

"And with honors as well, with his eye on the same thing, he'll willingly partake of and taste the ones he believes will make him better, but as for the ones that would undermine his deep-seated condition, he'll keep away from those in private and in public."

592A

"Then he won't be willing to take part in political life," he said, "if that's what he's worried about."

"By the dog," I said, "he will in his own city, anyway, and in a big way, though maybe he won't in his fatherland, unless some divine luck comes his way."

"I understand," he said; "you mean he will in the city we've now gone through founding, the one set down in speeches, since I imagine it's nowhere on earth."

"But maybe it's a pattern laid up in heaven," I said, "for anyone who wants to see it and for the one who's seen to establish in himself. It makes no difference whether it is or will be present anywhere,[179] because his actions will be those that belong to this city alone, and to no other."

B

"Likely so," he said.

---

179 In the 16th century, Thomas More coined the word "utopia," a noplace, from the Greek words *ou* and *topos* for a community governed by reason and co-operation.

BOOK X

Note

> Socrates takes a step back from the portrait of the best city to revisit the topic of poetry. Within the city, the emphasis had been on its role in early education, with a view to permitting the formation of good character. It was argued that the seductive power of imitation over the imagination in youth can be impossible to overcome once the power of choice is present in adulthood. Now Socrates looks at poetry from the point of view of an adult who lives not in but in accord with the best city. The question he raises now is how seriously the works of Homer and the tragic poets should be taken, and this leads eventually to the question of whether the soul is immortal. The immortality of the soul, in turn, introduces a new look at what the soul might be. The three-part structure suggested by ordinary experience and suited to the analogy with a city now seems inadequate. Philosophy too appears now in a different light, not as the power that makes it possible to govern a complex community of desires, but as the central impulse that might determine a human being's destiny. Socrates ends the discussion with a story about the journey of a human soul, and the balance of chance, necessity, and choice that make it be what it is.

595A   "I think more than ever that we founded the city the right way," I said, "for many other things about it too, but I say it not least as I reflect on what has to do with poetry."

"What do you have in mind?" he said.

"Not allowing any of it that's imitative in at all. Because now more than ever it shows up even more clearly that it shouldn't be allowed
B   in, it seems to me, when each of the forms present in the soul has been separated out as distinct."

"How do you mean?"

"Speaking among you folks here, since you won't inform on me to the tragic poets and all the other imitators,[180] everything like that appears to be a corruption of the thinking of the people who hear it, all those who don't have the knowledge of how the things themselves are as an antidote."

"What in particular are you thinking of when you say that?" he said.

---

180   It is reported that Plato wrote tragedies in his youth (Diogenes Laertius, *Lives of the Philosophers*, III, 5).

"It has to be spoken," I said, "and yet a certain love and reverence for Homer, that's had me in its grip since I was a child, holds me back from speaking, because he appears to have been the first to educate and lead the way in all these beautiful tragic things. Still, a man shouldn't be honored above the truth, and, as I say, it has to be spoken."

"Very much so," he said.

"Listen, then, or better, answer."

"Ask."

"As for imitation as a whole, could you tell me what in the world it is? Because I myself certainly don't comprehend anything at all about what it's meant to be."

"Oh, well then, no doubt I'll understand it," he said.

"There wouldn't be anything strange about that," I said, "since people with dimmer sight surely see many things before those with sharper vision do."   596A

"It's possible for that to happen," he said, "but with you present, I couldn't be confident about speaking if anything does appear to me, so look yourself."

"Then do you want us to begin examining it from this starting point, following our usual approach? Presumably we're accustomed to take some one particular form for each group of many things to which we apply the same name, or do you not understand?"

"I understand."

"So now let's take whatever group of many things you want; for instance, if it's okay with you, there are no doubt many couches and tables."

"Of course."

"But presumably there are two looks to these artifacts, one for a couch and one for a table."   B

"Yes."

"And aren't we also accustomed to say that it's with his eye on the look of either artifact that a craftsman makes couches in one case and tables in the other, the ones we use, and the same way in other cases? Because presumably none of the craftsmen crafts the look itself."

"How could he?"

"In no way. But now see what you call *this* craftsman."

"What sort?"   C

"One who makes everything, all the things that every single artisan does."

"You're talking about some amazing and formidable man."

"Yet that's not all; you'll soon say so even more. Because this same artisan is not only able to make artifacts, but also makes all the things that grow out of the earth, and fashions all the animals, both the others and himself, and on top of these things, he fashions the earth and the heavens and the gods, and the things in the heavens and under the earth in Hades."

D   "You're talking about a totally amazing mastermind," he said.

"Are you skeptical?" I said. "And tell me, does it seem to you there's absolutely no such craftsman, or that in a certain way there could be a maker of all these things, but in a certain way not? Or don't you notice that you yourself would also be able to make all these things, in a certain way at least?"

"And what would that way be?" he said.

"It's not hard," I said, "and there's more than one way for you to craft them quickly, but no doubt the quickest, if you want that, is for

E   you to take a mirror and carry it around everywhere; you'll instantly make the sun and the things in the heavens, and instantly the earth, and instantly yourself and the rest of the animals and artifacts and plants and all the things we were just talking about."

"Sure," he said, "appearances of them, but they're certainly not things that are that way in truth."

"A beautiful point," I said, "and you're getting at something essential to the discussion, because I imagine a painter is one of the craftsmen of this kind, isn't he?"

"Of course."

"But I imagine you'll claim he doesn't make the things he makes as true things, even though in a certain manner the painter too makes a couch, doesn't he?"

"Yes," he said, "he too makes an appearance of one."

597A   "But what about the couchmaker? You were surely saying just now that he doesn't make the form, weren't you? Isn't that precisely what we're claiming *is* the couch? Isn't what he makes just a particular couch?"

"I was saying that."

"Well, if he doesn't make the one that *is* a couch, he wouldn't be making something that *is*, would he, but something that's like a thing that *is* without being that? And if anyone were to claim that the work produced by the couch-workman or by any other artisan is something that *is* in the full sense, he's liable to be saying something that's not true."

"Not as it would seem to people who spend their time involved in discussions like these," he said.

"So let's not be surprised if that couch too is something pale in comparison to the truth."

"No."

B   "Then do you want us to inquire on the basis of these very things what in the world that imitator is?" I said.

"If that's what you want," he said.

"Don't there turn out to be three varieties of couch, one being the one in nature,[181] which I imagine we'd claim a god fashioned—who else?"

"No one, I imagine."

"And one that the carpenter did."

"Yes," he said.

"And one that the painter did. Isn't that how it is?"

"Let it be that way."

"So a painter, a couchmaker, a god—these three—are in charge of three forms of couches."

"Three, yes."

"Now the god, whether he didn't want to, or whether there was   C
some necessity on him not to turn out more than one couch in nature, made only one, that very one that *is* a couch; two of that sort, or more, were not generated by the god and could not be brought into being."

"How's that?" he said.

"Because," I said, "if he were to make only two, one would show up again and both of the others would have *its* form, and that, not those two, would be what *is* a couch."

"That's right," he said.

"So I imagine the god, knowing these things and wanting to be in his very being a maker of a couch that *is* in its very being, not just   D
some particular couchmaker or the maker of some particular couch, brought it into being as one by nature."

"It looks that way."

"Then do you want us to call him its nature-crafter or something like that?"

"That would be a just title anyway," he said, "seeing as how by nature he's made that and everything else."

"And what about the carpenter? Isn't he a craftsman of a couch?"

"Yes."

"And is the painter a craftsman and maker of such a thing?"

"By no means."

"But what will you claim he is in relation to a couch?"

"This seems to me the most even-handed thing to call him," he   E
said: "an imitator of that of which those others are craftsmen."

---

181 This is a puzzling phrase, since products of human art would ordinarily be thought of as opposed to natural things. If there is a couch in nature, it would perhaps be of the sort used by the people in the first city Socrates envisioned (372B). The look, not a visible shape but an intelligible design, that the many couches share, is dependent upon the nature of the human body. It is the latter that is something in nature in the sense that all instances of it participate in the same form, which makes them be what they are. There is something off-kilter about the whole use of couches and tables as an approach to the topic of imitation, and this is reflected in Glaucon's reluctant responses. The verbs used just below for generating and bringing into being have the same root as the word for nature (*phusis*), while the verbs for making and producing have the same root as the word for poetry (*poiêsis*).

"Okay," I said; "you're calling the person involved with the third generation starting from nature an imitator?"

"Quite so," he said.

"Therefore the maker of tragedies will be in that position too, if in fact he's an imitator; he and all other imitators are by nature third from a king, so to speak, that is, third from the truth."

"They may well be."

598A   "So we're in agreement about imitators. And tell me this about the painter: does it seem to you he tries to imitate each thing itself in nature, or the works of craftsmen?"

"The works of craftsmen," he said.

"The way they are, or the way they appear? Make that further distinction."

"How do you mean it?" he said.

"Like this: whether you look at it from the side or straight on or from anywhere at all, is a couch itself any different from itself? Or, the same way as everything else, does it look different while it's no different at all?"

"That's how it is," he said; "it looks that way, but isn't any different at all."

B   "Then consider that very point: in relation to which of them does painting make each thing it's about? Is that thing imitated from its being as it is or from its appearing as it appears? Is it an imitation of an appearance or of truth?"

"Of an appearance," he said.

"Therefore imitative art is somewhere far removed from what's true, and it looks like that's why it can produce everything, because it gets hold of some little piece of each thing, and a phantom at that. We're claiming, for instance, that a painter will paint us a leather-crafter, a carpenter, the other craftsmen, without understanding anything about any of these arts, but still, if he happens to be a good painter, and paints a carpenter by showing him from far removed, he might mislead children and foolish people into thinking it's truly a carpenter."

"Certainly."

"But, my friend, I imagine that this is what ought to be thought about everything of that sort: whenever anyone declares to us, about anyone, that he has come across a human being who knows every D   craft and everything else every single person knows, and that there's nothing he doesn't know more precisely than anyone, one ought to reply to the maker of such a declaration that he's some gullible fellow, and it appears he's met up with some trickster of an imitator and been fooled. So, since he himself is unable to assess the difference between knowledge, ignorance, and imitation, the trickster seemed to him to be all-wise."

"Very true," he said.

"Next," I said, "doesn't tragedy, along with its leader Homer, need to be examined, since we hear it said by some[182] that these people know all the arts and all human matters that have to do with virtue and vice, and all divine matters as well? They say it's necessary for a good poet, if he's going to do a beautiful job of composing poetry about the things he's writing about, to write with knowledge or not be able to write. So there's a need to consider whether they ran across those imitators and got tricked by seeing their works and not perceiving that they're at a third remove from what *is*, and easy to make for someone who doesn't know the truth, since they're making appearances and not beings, or whether there's something in what they say, and good poets genuinely know what they're talking about when they seem to most people to speak well."

"There's a very great need for that to be assessed," he said.

"Do you imagine, then, that if someone was capable of making both the thing that's going to be imitated and the phantom, he'd allow himself to take the crafting of phantoms seriously, and give that the primary place in his life as the best thing he has?"

"I don't."

"But if he was in fact knowledgeable about the truth of those things that he imitates, I imagine he'd give far greater precedence in seriousness to deeds than to imitations, and he'd strive to leave behind many beautiful deeds as memorials of himself, and be more eager to be the one praised than the one doing the praising."

"I imagine so," he said, "since there's no comparison in terms of the honor or the benefit."

"Well then, let's not demand an account about anything else from Homer or any of the other poets by asking, in case any of them was a doctor and not just an imitator of medical talk, what people any of the old or new poets is reported to have made healthy the way Asclepius did, or what students of medical art he left behind the way the latter left his offspring; let's not ask them about the other arts either—let's set that aside. But about the most important and most beautiful things Homer undertakes to speak of, about wars and commanding armies and running cities, and about the education of a human being, it would surely be a just thing to ask, in order to find it out from him, 'Dear Homer, if you're not in fact third from the truth about virtue, a craftsman of a phantom exactly the way we defined an imitator, but even second, and capable of discerning what activities make human beings better or worse in private and public life, tell us, which one of the cities was better governed on account of you the way Sparta was on account of Lycurgus, and many cities large and small on account of many other people? What city credits you with having been a good

E

599A

B

C

D

E

---

182   An extreme example may be found in Plato's *Ion*, but the general belief that profundity in poetry indicates wisdom about all aspects of life was, and is, widely shared.

lawgiver and having been of benefit to them? Italy and Sicily credit Charondas, and we credit Solon, but who credits you?' Will he have any to mention?"

"I don't imagine so," said Glaucon; "none is spoken of by Homer's own followers anyway."

600A   "But then is any war in Homer's time remembered for being well conducted with his leadership or advice?"

"None."

"But then are a lot of ingenious ideas for the useful arts or for any other practical endeavors reported of him, the sorts of things involved in the actions of a wise man, the way they're reported about Thales the Milesian or Anacharsis the Scythian?"[183]

"Nothing of the kind at all."

"But then if not in public life, is Homer reported to have been a guide in education for any people in private when he was alive, people who loved him for his company and passed down to later generations a certain Homeric way of life, as Pythagoras was himself exceptionally beloved for, so that later generations that still give his name even now to a Pythagorean manner of living seem in some way to be distinguished from everyone else?"

B

"Nothing like that is spoken of either," he said. "Because, Socrates, Homer's comrade Creophylus would probably seem even more preposterous for his education than for his name[184] if the things said about Homer are true, since it's reported that there was great neglect of him by that friend of his when he was alive."

C

"That is what's reported," I said. "But do you imagine, Glaucon, that if Homer was genuinely able to educate people and make them better because he had the capacity not to make imitations of those things but to know about them, he wouldn't have made comrades of many people and been honored and loved by them? After all, Protagoras the Abderite and Prodicus the Cean and a great many others are able to get the idea across to those around them, when they associate with them in private, that they won't be capable of managing either their household or their city if they themselves don't take charge of their education, and for this wisdom they're loved so ardently that the only thing their comrades don't do is carry them around above their heads. So if Homer had really been able to help people toward virtue, would the people of his time have allowed him or Hesiod to be itinerant reciters of poetry, and not have hung onto them more tightly than to gold, and made them stay in their homes with them, or, if they

D

E

---

183   Thales predicted a solar eclipse, and found a way to corner the market on olive oil; Anacharsis was credited with inventing the anchor and the potter's wheel.

184   The name means something like "one of the meat people."

couldn't persuade them to, have shadowed them like tutors[185] wherever they might be until they'd gotten an adequate education?"

"You seem to me, Socrates," he said, "to be telling the absolute truth."

"Then shouldn't we take it that all those skilled at poetry, starting from Homer, are imitators of phantoms of virtue and of the other things they write about, and don't get hold of the truth? Isn't it the same with them as what we were just saying, that a painter will make what seems to be a leathercrafter, when he himself understands nothing about leathercraft, for people who understand nothing about it but take their view of it from colors and shapes?"   601A

"Very much so."

"So I imagine we'll claim someone skilled at poetry also colors in the arts with certain colors that belong to each of them, by the use of words and phrases, though he himself understands nothing other than how to imitate in a way that makes it seem, to others like him who look at things through his words, that a character speaking metrically, rhythmically, and melodically seems to be speaking very well, whether he's talking about leathercraft, about commanding an army, or about anything else whatever. Thus these things by themselves have in them   B by nature some great enchantment, because, when the words of the poets are stripped of their musical colorings and they themselves are spoken by *them*selves, I imagine you know what sort of appearance that makes, since no doubt you've observed it."[186]

"I have," he said.

"Aren't they like the faces of people in their prime who aren't beautiful," I said, "the way they start to look when the glow of youth leaves them?"

"Absolutely," he said.

"Keep on going then and consider this: we're claiming that the poet, the imitator who makes the phantom, understands nothing about   C what *is* but its appearance, isn't that so?"

"Yes."

"Well, let's not leave it half-spoken; let's get an adequate view of it."

"Speak on," he said.

"Do we claim that a painter will paint reins and a bridle?"

"Yes."

"But a leathercrafter and a blacksmith will make them?"

"Quite so."

---

185 The passage rings the changes on various ways potential learners are pursued and pursuers. A tutor was a slave or servant who took a child to its lessons and never let it out of his sight, so the relation is reversed here for an adult so desirous of learning that he follows the wise poet from city to city. Protagoras and Prodicus were traveling teachers who went to the homes of the rich to train their sons for distinction in life.

186 Socrates gave one example earlier at 393D-394A.

"Well, does the painter understand how reins and a bridle need to be? Or is that something that not even the maker understands, the blacksmith or leatherworker, but only the person who knows how to use them, the horseman?"

"Very true."

"And won't we claim it's that way with everything?"

"What way?"

D "For each thing there are these three particular arts, of using, of making, and of imitating?"

"Yes."

"And isn't it the case that the excellence, beauty, and rightness of each implement, animal, and action is related to no other thing than the use for which each has either been made or been naturally adapted?"

"That's how it is."

"Therefore it's utterly necessary for the one who uses each thing to be the most experienced with it, and to be the one who reports to the maker what good or bad features the thing he uses has in its

E use; a fluteplayer, for instance, presumably reports to the flutemaker about which of his flutes are serviceable in his fluteplaying, and he'll prescribe what sorts of flutes he needs to make, while the other does his bidding."

"How could it be otherwise?"

"So the one reports about worthy and worthless flutes because he has knowledge, and the other will make them because he has trust?"

"Yes."

"Therefore, for the same implement, the one who makes it will have rightful trust about its beauty or worthlessness by being around

602A someone who knows and being obliged to listen to the knower, while the one who uses it will have knowledge."

"Entirely so."

"And will the imitator, by using them, have knowledge about whether the things he depicts are beautiful or right or not, or will he have right opinion from being obliged to be around someone who knows and being given directions about the sorts of things he ought to depict?"

"Neither."

"So the imitator will have neither knowledge nor right opinion about the things he imitates as to their beauty or worthlessness."

"It looks like he won't."

"Someone whose skill in making is imitative would be a highly accomplished fellow when it comes to wisdom about the things he makes."

"Not quite."

"But he'll imitate nonetheless, without knowing what makes each   B
thing worthless or worthy; it seems likely what he'll imitate will be
the sort of thing that appears to be beautiful to most people, who have
no knowledge at all."

"What else could it be?"

"So it appears that we're tolerably well agreed on these points: that
the skilled imitator knows nothing worth mentioning about the things
he imitates, that imitation is a kind of amusement and not serious,
and that those who dabble in tragic poetry, whether in iambic or epic
verse, are all imitators as much as it's possible to be."

"Very much so."

"Before Zeus," I said, "this imitating just deals with something   C
third from the truth, doesn't it?"

"Yes."

"So what sort of thing in a human being is it on which it has the
power that it has?"

"What sort of thing are you talking about?"

"This sort of thing: presumably the same magnitude doesn't appear
equal to us by sight from nearby and far off."

"No, it doesn't."

"And the same things appear bent and straight to those looking at
them in water and out of it, and also concave and convex by an optical
illusion having to do with colors, and every sort of confusion like this   D
is manifestly present in our soul; it's by exploiting this susceptibility of
our nature that perspective painting, and puppetry, and many other
ingenious contrivances like that are nothing short of witchcraft."

"True."

"And haven't measuring and counting and weighing shown
themselves to be most gracious helpers with these things, so that
something's appearing larger or smaller or more in number or heavier
doesn't hold sway in us, but what has calculated and measured or
even weighed does?"

"Certainly."

"But this would surely be the work of the reasoning part in a   E
soul."

"Of that, for sure."

"And when it has measured and indicated that certain things are
larger or smaller than others or equal to them, there are often contrary
things appearing to it at the same time about the same things."

"Yes."

"Weren't we claiming that it's impossible for the same thing to
hold contrary opinions about the same things at the same time?"

"And we were right in claiming it."

"Therefore the part of the soul that holds opinions contrary to   603A
the measures couldn't be the same as the part that holds opinions in
accord with the measures."

"No, it couldn't."

"But surely the part that puts its trust in measure and calculation would be the best part of the soul."

"What else?"

"So the part that opposes this would be one of the inferior things in us."

"Necessarily."

B "Well that's what I wanted to get agreement about when I was saying that painting and imitative art in general are far removed from the truth as they carry out their work, and they're also joined with the part in us that's far removed from thoughtfulness, and is a companion and friend that can lead to nothing healthy or true."

"Absolutely," he said.

"So imitative art, an inferior thing consorting with an inferior thing, gives birth to inferior progeny."

"It looks that way."

"Only the kind that pertains to sight," I said, "or also the kind that pertains to hearing, to which we give the name poetry?"

"Very likely that too," he said.

C "Well let's not just put our trust in a likelihood based on painting," I said; "let's also go up to that part of our thinking with which the imitative art of poetry is joined and see whether it's a trifling or serious thing."

"We should."

"Let's set it out like this: we're claiming that imitative art imitates human beings in action, engaged in forced or willing acts and imagining they've come out well or badly from doing so, and feeling pain or joy in all this. There's nothing else besides that, is there?"

"Nothing."

D "Well is a human being in a consistent state of mind through all these things? Or, the same way he was divided about what came from sight, and held opposite opinions within himself at the same time about the same things, is he divided in that way and at war himself with himself in his actions as well? But I'm recollecting that there's no need for us to come to agreement about that now, because we agreed well enough about all those things in the earlier discussion, that our soul is filled with tens of thousands of oppositions of that kind that arise at the same time."

"That's right," he said.

E "Yes, it's right," I said, "but it seems to me that it's necessary now to go through something we skipped over then."

"What's that?" he said.

"We had also said then, presumably, that a decent man will bear it more easily than others when he gets a share of some such misfortune as losing a son, or anything else he holds dear."

"Quite so."

"But now let's examine this point: whether he won't feel any grief at all, or whether that's impossible, but he'll somehow keep his balance about his pain."

"The truth is more like that," he said.

"Now tell me this about him: do you imagine he'll fight down   604A
the pain and resist it more when he's seen by his peers, or when he's alone by himself in solitude?"

"No doubt he'll bear up under it much more when he's seen," he said.

"But I imagine that when he's left alone he'll allow himself to utter many things he'd be ashamed of if anyone were to hear him, and he'll do many things that he wouldn't let anyone see him doing."

"That's how it is," he said.

"Aren't reason and law the things that encourage him to resist, while the suffering itself is what draws him to the pains?"

"That's true."

"But when a pull in opposite directions arises in a human being   B
about the same thing at the same time, we're claiming there are necessarily two things in him."

"How could there not be?"

"Isn't one of them ready to be persuaded by the law, the way the law leads it?"

"How so?"

"No doubt the law says that the most beautiful thing is to keep calm as much as is possible in misfortunes and not get worked up, since the good and bad in such things aren't obvious, and there's nothing that gets anyone forward when he takes it hard, and because nothing among human things is worthy of great seriousness, and being   C
in pain becomes an obstacle to that very thing we need to come to us as quickly as possible in these circumstances."

"What are you referring to?" he said.

"Deliberating with oneself," I said, "about what's happened, and, as in the fall of dice, arranging one's affairs to suit the way things have fallen out, in whatever way reason decides it would be best, and not to go on like children who've stumbled, holding the place that was bumped and wasting time in howling, but to get the soul accustomed always, as quickly as possible, to get on toward healing and righting what's fallen and sick, doing away with lamentation by the use of medical art."   D

"That's certainly the way anyone could deal with misfortunes most rightly," he said.

"Aren't we claiming the best part is willing to follow this reasoning?"

"Clearly so."

"And won't we claim the part that leads to memories of the suffering and to laments and is insatiable for them is irrational and lazy, and beloved by cowardice?"

"We'll claim that for sure."

"Doesn't the petulant part of us have a lot of variety in it for imitation, while the thoughtful and calm state of character, which is always much the same as itself, is neither easy to imitate nor readily understood when it is imitated, especially by a festive crowd with all the assortment of people gathered together in a theater? Because, no doubt, the imitation is of something that comes as foreign to them."

"Absolutely so."

"So it's obvious that the imitative poet isn't naturally drawn toward a part of the soul such as that, and his wisdom isn't built for pleasing it, if he intends to get a good reputation among most people; he's drawn instead toward the petulant and variable character because it's easy to imitate."

"Obviously."

"So at this point couldn't we justly take hold of him and set him out as a counterpart to the painter? Because he's like him in making things that are trifles in comparison to the truth, and they're also alike in consorting with a part of the soul that's another trifling thing, rather than with the best part. Thus, at this point, we'd be in the right in not admitting him into a city that's going to have good laws, because he stirs up this part of the soul and feeds it, and by making it strong he destroys the reasoning part; that's what happens in a city when, by making worthless people powerful, one turns the city over to them and ruins the more refined people. In the same way, shall we claim the imitative poet also introduces a bad polity in the soul of each person in private, by gratifying the foolish part of it that can't distinguish the greater from the lesser but regards the same things as now great, now small—that he's a phantom-maker making phantoms very far removed from the truth?"

"Very much so."

"But we haven't yet made the most important charge against imitative poetry. Because the fact that it's strong enough to corrupt even decent people, outside of some slight few, is surely wholly appalling."

"How's it not going to be, if it really does that?"

"Listen on and consider. Presumably, when the best of us hear Homer or any of the others, the tragic poets, imitating one of the heroes when he's in grief and indulging in a long extended speech of lamentations, or even singing a lament and beating his chest, you know that we enjoy it, give ourselves up to it, and follow along in empathy, taking it seriously, and we praise as a good poet whoever puts us in this condition the most."

"I do know that; how could I not?"

"But whenever sorrow comes to any of us personally, you realize that we pride ourselves, on the contrary, if we're able to stay calm

and bear it, feeling this to be what belongs to a man, while the other
response, which we were praising before, is that of a woman."   E

"I realize that," he said.

"Well that's a beautiful sort of praise, isn't it," I said, "for anyone
not to be disgusted but to enjoy it and praise it when he sees a man
of that sort, when he'd consider it unworthy of himself to be like such
a person but would be ashamed?"

"No, by Zeus," he said; "it doesn't seem to make sense."

"It does, though," I said, "if you look at it another way."   606A

"How?"

"If you take to heart the fact that the part that's held down by
force at the time of our personal misfortunes and has been hungering
to shed tears and get enough of lamenting and be satisfied, being by
nature of such a kind as to crave these things, is the part that's now
being given its fill by the poets and enjoying it; but the part of us that's
by nature best, not having been adequately educated by reason or by
habit, lets down its guard over this doleful part because it's watching   B
someone else's suffering and there's no shame to itself, if some other
person who purports to be a good man grieves inappropriately, in
praising and pitying that person. Instead, it considers its other part as
gaining in pleasure, and wouldn't accept its being deprived of that as
the price of holding the whole poem in contempt. I imagine only some
few people have it in them to reason out that the enjoying necessarily
moves from the realm of other people to that of oneself, because the
part that feels pity is not easy to hold down during one's own sufferings when it's strong from feeding on those of others."

"Very true," he said.   C

"Doesn't the same argument also apply to the part that laughs?
Because, if there are jokes you'd be ashamed to make yourself, but
that you greatly enjoy hearing in comic imitation or in private, and
don't detest as vile, aren't you doing exactly the same thing as with
the pitiable things? Because you held down by reasoning the part of
yourself that wanted to make the jokes, fearing a reputation for buf-
foonery, but now you let it loose, and don't realize that once you've
made it vigorous in one place you often get so carried away that you
become a comedian among your friends and family."

"Very much so," he said.

"And the same argument also applies to sexual desires and spirited   D
anger, and to all the feelings of desire as well as pains and pleasures in
the soul that we claim accompany us in every action, because poetic
imitation works up things of those sorts in us. It nourishes them,
watering what needs to be made more dry, and sets up as ruling in
us the very things that need to be ruled if we're to become better and
happier instead of worse and more wretched."

"I can't say any different," he said.

E   "Well then, Glaucon," I said, "whenever you run into admirers of
Homer saying that this poet has educated Greece and that, for managing human affairs and becoming educated about them, this poet is
worthy for someone to take up to learn from and to live by organizing

607A   his whole life in accordance with, shouldn't you be kind to them and
be glad they're being the best they can possibly be, and agree with
them that Homer is the most poetic of tragic poets and first among
them, while you still know that only as much poetry as consists of
hymns to the gods and praise of good people is to be admitted into
a city? But if you're going to let in the pleasure-laden Muse in lyric
or epic poetry, pleasure and pain as a pair will hold the kingship in
your city instead of law and the reasoning that seems best in each
case to all in common."

B   "Very true," he said.
       "So let that be our justification, now that we've brought back to
mind the things having to do with poetry, that since it's like that, it
was appropriate after all for us to turn it away from our city; the argument won us over. And let's explain to her, so she won't be able to
blame us for any insensitivity or incivility, that the quarrel between
philosophy and poetry is an ancient one. There's a lot of evidence[186] of
the old opposition between them: 'that yelping bitch, howling at her

C   master,' and 'great in the empty assemblies of fools,' and 'the prevail-
ing crowd of the oh-so-wise,' and 'those who come to the subtle conclusion that they're poor,' and tens of thousands more. Nevertheless,
let it be said that if poetic imitation aiming at pleasure should have
any argument to make to the effect that she should be present in a city
with good laws, we'd gladly take her back in, since we're well aware
that we ourselves are enchanted by her; but it's not a pious thing to

D   betray what seems true. Aren't you too enchanted by her, my friend,
especially when you look at her through Homer's eyes?"
       "Very."
       "Wouldn't it be a just thing for her to come back in that way, when
she's made her defense in lyric verse or in some other meter?"
       "Very much so."
       "And surely we'd also allow her champions, all those who aren't
poets but lovers of poetry, to make an argument in her defense without meter, to the effect that she's not only pleasant but also beneficial

E   to polities and to human life,[187] and we'll listen in a favorable spirit,
because assuredly we'll be the ones to gain if she's shown to be not
only pleasant but beneficial as well."
       "How could we not come out the gainers?" he said.
       "But if not, dear comrade, then the same way people who once
fell in love with someone, if they come to regard their love as not

---

186   The following anti-philosophic quotations are all in verse; none of the sources is known.

187   Aristotle's *Poetics* might be regarded as an acceptance of this invitation.

being beneficial, keep away from it even if that takes force, we too, on account of the love for such poetry that's arisen in us from our rearing at the hands of our lovely polities, we'll be rooting for her to be shown to be best and truest, but as long as she's not able to give her defense, we'll listen to her while chanting to ourselves this argument that we're making; that will be our counter-charm to ward off our falling back again under the spell of the love that's childish and belongs among the masses. We recognize that it's necessary for anyone who listens to this sort of poetry not to take it seriously as a serious effort to reach the truth, but to be cautious, fearing for the polity within himself, and to believe the things we've said about poetry."

608A

B

"I absolutely agree," he said.

"Because it's a great struggle, dear Glaucon," I said, "though it doesn't seem as great as it is, to become a reliable or worthless person, so it's not worth it to be enticed by honor or money or any ruling power or even by poetry into being careless about justice and the rest of virtue."

"I agree with you," he said, "based on the things we've gone through, and I imagine anyone else at all would too."

C

"And we haven't even gotten to the greatest rewards and prizes that lie ahead for virtue," I said.

"That's some incredible greatness you're talking about," he said, "if there are others greater than the ones mentioned."

"What great thing could come about in a little stretch of time?" I said. "Because this whole time from childhood to old age would surely be a little one compared to all time."

"No time at all," he said.

"What about an immortal thing, then? Do you imagine it needs to be seriously concerned about that amount of time and not about the whole of it?"

"I imagine you're right," he said; "but what's this thing you're talking about?"

D

"Haven't you noticed that our soul is immortal and never perishes?" I said.

And he stared at me and said in astonishment, "No, by Zeus, I haven't; can you explain that?"

"If not I'd be doing an injustice," I said. "And I imagine you can too, since there's nothing difficult about it."

"For me there is," he said, "but I'd be delighted if I could hear this undifficult thing from you."

"You could hear it," I said.

"Just speak," he said.

"Do you call anything good or bad?"

"I do."

E

"And do you think about them the same way I do?"

"How's that?"

"Everything that destroys or corrupts something is bad and everything that preserves or benefits it is good."

"That's what I think," he said.

"And what about this? Do you say there's something bad and something good for each thing, such as inflammation for eyes, and disease for the body as a whole, blight for grain, rot for wood, corrosion for bronze and iron, and, as I'm saying, for pretty much everything, something that's innately bad and a disease for each?"

"I'd say so," he said.

"And whenever any of these attacks anything, doesn't it make the thing it attacks bad, and finally dissolve and destroy the whole thing?"

"How could it not?"

"Therefore, what's innately bad for each thing and is its particular badness is what destroys each thing, or if that doesn't destroy it, there's no other thing that could still corrupt it. Certainly what's good could never destroy it, and neither could something that's neither bad nor good."

"How could they?" he said.

"So if we can find anything there is such that what's bad for it makes it defective but can't dissolve and destroy it, won't we know already that there *is* no destruction for anything of that nature?"

"Most likely that's how it would be," he said.

"What about the soul, then?" I said. "Doesn't it have something that makes it bad?"

"And how," he said; "all the things we've just been going over— injustice, intemperance, cowardice, and ignorance."

"And does any of these dissolve and destroy it? And think carefully so we don't get misled into imagining that an unjust, foolish person, when he's caught committing an injustice, has then been destroyed by his injustice, which is a badness of the soul. Go about it this way instead: just as the body's badness, which is disease, makes a body waste away and utterly destroys it and brings it to the point of not even being a body, all the things we were just speaking of also get to the point, each by the action of its own particular badness, by the settling in and presence of what corrupts it, of not being. Isn't that so?"

"Yes."

"Keep going, then, and examine soul in the same way. When injustice, or other badness, is present in it, does it, by its presence and by settling in, corrupt the soul and make it wither until, by bringing it to its death, it takes it away from the body?"

"Not at all," he said; "not that anyway."

"But surely the other possibility is illogical," I said, "that the badness of something else could destroy it in any way when it's own badness can't."

"That is illogical."

"Consider, Glaucon," I said, "that we don't imagine a body has to   E
be destroyed by the badness of foods, or by anything that belongs to
the foods themselves, whether it's staleness or rancidness or whatever
it might be; but if the badness of the foods themselves instills in the
body a badness of a body, we'll claim it gets destroyed by those other
things through the action of its own badness, which is disease. We'd
never think it right to say that the body, which is a different thing,   610A
is corrupted by the action of the badness of foods, which differ from
it, unless its innate evil is instilled by the action of the extraneous
evil."

"You're speaking quite correctly," he said.

"By the same argument, then," I said, "if the badness of a body
doesn't instill badness in a soul, we'd never think it right to say a soul
is destroyed by the action of an extraneous evil in the absence of its
own particular badness, one thing by the evil of another."

"That does make sense," he said.

"Well then, let's either prove that we aren't saying these things in
a beautiful way, or until they're refuted, let's not claim that by a fever   B
or by any other disease, or by cutting a throat or even if someone cuts
a whole body up into the tiniest possible pieces, a soul is any more
subject to being destroyed on account of these things, until someone
proves that by these things that are done to the body, a soul itself
becomes more unjust or more impious. But if an extraneous evil comes
into a different thing, while a particular thing's own particular evil
doesn't arise in it, let's not allow anyone to claim that either a soul or   C
anything else is destroyed."

"Well it's for sure," he said, "that no one's ever going to show
that the souls of dying people become more unjust on account of
death."

"But if anyone has the nerve to tackle the argument," I said, "just
so he won't be forced to agree that souls are immortal, and says that
a dying person does become worse and more unjust, we'll no doubt
think it right to point out that if the one who says that is telling the
truth, injustice would be fatal to anyone who has it, just like a disease,
and those who catch it would be killed by it, since it's a killer by its   D
nature. Those who get it most would die quickly, and those who get it
less would die at a more leisurely rate, but unjust people wouldn't die
of it the way they do now, at the hands of other people who impose
it as a penalty."

"By Zeus," he said, "injustice doesn't look all that terrible in that
case, if it's going to be fatal to someone who takes it up, since it would
be a release from troubles. But I imagine instead it's going to look
exactly the opposite, like something that kills other people if it can   E
but leaves the one who has it very much alive, and still more than
alive, unable to get any sleep. That's how far away it's located from
being fatal, as it seems anyway."

"You're putting it beautifully," I said. "When its own particular badness and its own particular evil aren't enough to kill and destroy a soul, an evil designed for the destruction of something else is hardly going to destroy a soul or anything else except the thing it's designed to destroy."

"It seems hardly likely, anyway," he said.

611A   "So when something isn't destroyed by any single evil, either its own or an extraneous one, isn't it clearly necessary that it always *is*, and if it always is, it's immortal?"

"It's necessary," he said.

"Well then, let that be how it stands," I said. "And if it is that way, you understand that there would always be the same souls. Because there certainly couldn't get to be any fewer if none is destroyed, and there couldn't get to be any more either, since if there got to be any more of any immortal things whatever, you know they'd be coming from something mortal, and everything would finally be immortal."

"What you say is true."

B   "But let's not imagine that either," I said, "since the argument doesn't allow it, and let's certainly not imagine that in its truest nature a soul is the sort of thing that's filled with lots of variety, non-uniformity, and difference within itself."

"How do you mean?" he said.

"It's not easy for something to be everlasting," I said, "if it's composed of many parts, as the soul now appears to us to be, and doesn't have a perfectly beautiful composition."[188]

"Likely not."

"Well now, the present argument and others as well would force us to the conclusion that the soul is immortal, but it has to be seen C   the way it is in truth, not deformed by its association with the body and other evils, the way we see it now; the way it is when it becomes pure has to be looked into adequately by reasoning. One will find it a far more beautiful thing, and will see through the various conceptions of justice and injustice, and all the things we've gone over now, to something more clear. We were telling the truth about it now as it appears at present; with the condition it's in, however, we've been looking at it like people who, when they catch sight of Glaucus[189] at D   sea, can't easily see his original nature any more, because some of the old parts of his body have been broken off by the waves, and others

---

188   The image Socrates made at 588B-589B was the most recent and most extreme picture of disunity in the soul, but his reference may be to its having three parts at all. The dialogue as a whole has taken the soul as analogous to a city, where the task is to find a polity that will succeed best at making one community out of many distinct members, but the current argument about immortality points to an abiding simplicity at the core of the soul. Even a perfectly harmonized three-part soul may only be an imitation of a higher unity.

189   A patron god of fishermen who lived in the sea.

worn down and completely deformed, while other things have grown on him, shells and seaweed and rocks, so that he looks more like any sea-monster than what he was by nature. And we too are looking at the soul when it's in a condition like that, as a result of myriads of evils. But, Glaucon, one needs to look in a different place."

"Where?" he said.

"At its philosophic desire, to get an idea of what it reaches for and what sorts of things it strives to be in company with, since it's akin to what's divine, immortal, and always in being, and to consider what would become of it if the whole of it pursued that sort of thing, and it was lifted by that impulse out of the sea it now inhabits and had the rocks and shells that are now on it knocked off, the many encrustations of earth and rock that grow wild all over it as a result of its allegedly happy feasts, since what it feasts itself on is earth. Then one could see its true nature, whether its form is multiple or single, or in what respect and what manner it is that way, but for now, as I imagine, we've done a decent job of going through the attributes and forms it has in its human life."

"Absolutely so," he said.

"And as for the other things in our discussion," I said, "didn't we rescue justice without bringing up the wages or reputations for it the way you folks claimed Hesiod and Homer do? Instead, didn't we find justice itself to be best for the soul itself, and that just things need to be done by it whether it has Gyges' ring or not, and besides such a ring, Hades' cap[190] too?"

"What you say is entirely true," he said.

"Well then, Glaucon, isn't it now at this point unobjectionable, in addition to that, to give back to justice and the rest of virtue all the wages of all the kinds that they secure for the soul from humans and gods, both while a human being is still living and when he's dead?"

"Absolutely so," he said.

"And will you folks give me back what you borrowed in the discussion?"

"What in particular?"

"I granted you the just person's seeming to be unjust and the unjust person's seeming to be just, because you two asked for it. Even if it wouldn't be possible for these things to go undetected by gods and human beings, it still had to be granted for the sake of argument, so justice itself could be judged in comparison with injustice itself. Or don't you remember?"

"I'd surely be doing an injustice if I didn't," he said.

"Now since they have been judged," I said, "I'm asking on justice's behalf for its reputation back again, and for you folks to agree that

E

612A

B

C

D

---

190 Another legendary source of invisibility. In this case the name is a pun on the object's power, "the cap of invisibility," since Hades is the invisible one (*a-eidês*).

the reputation it has is exactly the one it does have with gods and human beings, so that it may carry off the prizes it gains and confers on those who have it for the way it seems, since it has also made it obvious that it confers the good things that come from what it *is* and doesn't deceive those who take into their very being."

E

"The things you're asking for are just," he said.

"So will you give this back first," I said, "that it doesn't escape the notice of the gods, at least, that each of them is the sort of person he is?"

"We'll give it back," he said.

"And if it's not something that escapes their notice, the one would be loved by the gods and the other hated, just as we agreed at the start."

"There is that."

613A

"And won't we agree that everything that comes to someone loved by the gods is the best possible, at least with everything that comes from the gods, unless there was already some necessary evil for him stemming from an earlier mistaken choice?"

"Very much so."

"Therefore, in accord with that, the assumption that has to be made about a just man, if he falls into poverty or diseases or any other apparent evils, is that these things will finally turn into something good for him while he lives or even when he dies. Because someone is certainly never going to be neglected by the gods when he's willing

B

to put his heart into becoming just and pursuing virtue to the extent of becoming like a god as much as is possible for a human being."

"It's not likely anyway," he said, "that someone like that would by neglected by his own kind."

"And shouldn't we think the opposite of that about an unjust person?"

"Emphatically so."

"So the prizes from the gods for a just person would be something of that sort."

"To my way of thinking at any rate," he said.

"And what about from human beings?" I said. "Isn't it like this, if one ought to tell it the way it is? Don't clever unjust people do exactly the same thing as people who run well up the track but not

C

back down it? They go leaping off sharply at first, but become comical when they're finishing, wearing their ears on their shoulders as they run off uncrowned. But those who are truly skilled at running get to the end, take the prizes, and wear the crowns. Doesn't it most often turn out that way with just people too? Toward the end of each action and interaction, and of life, aren't they well regarded and don't they carry away the prizes given by human beings?"

"Very much so."

"So will you put up with it if I say the very things about them that you said about unjust people? Because I'm going to say that just **D** people, when they get older, are rulers in their cities if they want the offices, and take wives from wherever they want, and give their daughters in marriage to whomever they wish; and everything you said about the others, I now say about these. And about unjust people in turn, I'll say that most of them, even if they get away with it when they're young, are comical figures when they get caught at the last stage of the race, and when they come to a miserable old age they're treated with abuse by foreigners and townspeople, whipped, and as for the things you called crude—and you were telling the truth—imag- **E** ine you've also heard me say that they suffer all those things. But as I say, see if you'll put up with that."

"Completely so," he said, "since you're saying just things."

"These, then, would be the sorts of prizes and wages and gifts that come to a just person during his life from gods and human beings," I **614A** said, "in addition to the good things that justice itself provided."

"And very beautiful and reliable they are," he said.

"Well, these are nothing," I said, "in multitude or magnitude, compared to those that are in store for each sort of person after death. It would be right to hear them, so that in the hearing each of them may be paid in full the debt he's owed by the argument."

"You should tell them," he said, "since there aren't many other **B** things anyone could hear with more pleasure."

"I'm not going to tell you a tale of Alcinous, though," I said, "but it is a tale of a stalwart man, Er, son of Armenius, of the Pamphylian race.[191] At the time he was killed in a war, when the bodies gathered up on the tenth day were already decaying, his was taken up in sound condition; when he was brought home, and was about to be cremated on the twelfth day, while he was lying on the funeral pyre he came back to life, and once he'd revived he told what he saw in the other place.

"When the soul went out of him, he said, it traveled with many **C** others, and they reached a certain mysterious place where there were two chasms in the earth bordering on each other, and two others in the heavens directly above them. There were judges seated between them, who, once they'd passed judgment, told the just to proceed to

---

191   The story Odysseus tells about his wanderings in Bks. IX-XII of the *Odyssey* was addressed to Alcinous, the king of the Phaiakians. The phrase "tale of Alcinous" became a common expression for a story of tedious length, not as a comment on the original story but as a way of chiding someone by saying, in effect, "you're no Odysseus." Socrates is thus apologizing in advance for his own weakness as a storyteller. The word translated "stalwart" is almost the same as Alcinous's name, with a mu instead of a nu; the play on words suggests that the strength needed to secure a happy life, and even to engage in philosophy in a healthy way (619E), does not depend on having the luck to possess a powerful intellect (*alki-nous*). The story, though it incorporates and adapts details from various legends, is pure invention. The name Er is Hebrew, his father's name is spelled like that of Armenia in Asia Minor, and Pamphylia means "Everytribe."

the right and up through the heavens, and hung signs on them in front indicating their judgments; but the unjust they told to go to the left and down, and these too were wearing signs, in back, indicating all

D   the things they'd done. But when he himself came forward, they said he had to become a messenger to human beings about the things over there, and told him to listen to and look at everything in the place.

"There he saw souls going out at each chasm, one in the heavens and one in the earth, when judgment was passed on them, and at the other pair, from one of them souls coming up out of the earth full of dirt and dust, and from the other, others coming down from the

E   heavens clean. Those that were constantly arriving looked like they were returning from a long journey, and went off with relief into the meadow to rest the way they would at a festival; all those that were acquainted greeted one another and the ones returning out of the earth asked the others about the things in the other place while those coming from the heavens asked them about the things that happened to them. And they told their stories to each other, the ones lament-

615A   ing and weeping as they recollected all the things of all the sorts that they experienced and saw in their journey under the earth, which is a journey of a thousand years, and those from the heavens in their turn described delights and sights of beauty beyond belief.

"The many things they told would take a long time to repeat, Glaucon, but he said the chief point was this: for all the injustices they'd ever done in any way, and all the people they'd done them to, each of them had paid the penalty for all of them in turn, tenfold for each. That is, for every hundred year period, taking a human life to

B   last that long in order to make it be ten times over, they paid the price for each injustice, and if, for example, any were responsible for the deaths of many people, by betraying either cities or armies and plunging people into slavery, or had any part of the responsibility for any other evildoing, for all those things they'd get back sufferings ten times over for each one. On the other hand, if they'd been just and pious and had done any good deeds, they got the rewards they deserved

C   at the same rate. About those who died right at birth or lived a short time, he said other things not worth remembering. But for impiety and piety toward gods and parents, and for murder committed by one's own hand, he recounted still greater repayments.

"For instance, he said he was present when one person was asked by another where Ardiaeus the Great was. This Ardiaeus had become tyrant of a certain city in Pamphylia just a thousand years before that

D   time, and it was said he'd killed his aged father and older brother, and done many other impious things. He said the person who was asked replied, saying 'He hasn't arrived, and he won't be coming up here, because that was one of the horrible sights we saw; when we had undergone everything else and were near the mouth of the chasm, about to go up, we suddenly caught sight of him and others—most of

them tyrants, just about all, but there were some among them who'd
been guilty of great transgressions as private citizens. At the point   E
when they were imagining they'd be going up, the mouth didn't let
them through, but roared whenever anyone in such an incurable state
of depravity, or who hadn't paid a sufficient penalty, tried to go up.
There were men there,' he went on, 'savage and all fiery to look at,
standing by and paying close attention to the sound, who grabbed
some and led them off, but Ardiaeus and others they roped, hands,   616A
feet, and head, threw them down and skinned them, and dragged
them beside the outer road, scraping them on thornbushes, always
telling people who passed by why they were taking them away and
that they'd be thrown into Tartarus.'[192] And he said that though many
fears of all sorts had come over them there, the fear of each that this
roaring might come for him when he came up surpassed them all,
and when it was silent each one went up with the greatest relief. So
some of the penalties and punishments were of these kinds, and the
rewards were their corresponding opposites.   B

"And when those of each kind had been in the meadow seven
days, they had to get up and go out of there on the eighth day, and
reach a place after four days where they could see a straight shaft
of light, like a pillar, stretching from above through all the heavens
and earth, most nearly resembling a rainbow, but of greater bright-
ness and clarity. They reached it when they'd gone forward a day's
march, and at that spot they saw in the middle of the light the ends of   C
binding cords that stretched from the heavens to hold them, because
that light is what binds the heavens, like the ropes under a warship,
holding their whole circumference together in that way. Between the
ends of the cords stretched the spindle of Necessity, by which all the
revolutions are turned; its shaft and hook were diamond-hard, and
its knob was a mixture of that and other materials.[193]

"The nature of the knob is of the following sort. The shape is like   D
that of one here, but from what he said, it's necessary to think of it as
being this way: as if in one big hollow knob, completely emptied out,
another smaller one was inserted, fitted in just like bowls nested into

---

192   According to *Iliad* VIII, 13-16, Tartarus is the deepest pit in the universe, as far below Hades
as the heavens are above earth.

193   The spot the souls have reached represents the center of the spherical cosmos. The pillar of
light is the axial part of an encircling band. The warships to which this structure is compared
were triremes, large fast galleys that came into use during Socrates' lifetime. They got their
speed from three banks of oars, one above the other; apparently the large hulls this required
were held intact by encircling ropes with their ends joined inside the ship. As the winch of the
cosmos, around which the ends of the encircling cords within the light are twisted, Socrates
places a spindle. This was the ancient forerunner of the spinning wheel, a shaft with hooks to
which natural fibers were attached, and a weighted knob which was turned to twist them into
elongated threads. Thus the mechanism for holding the cosmos together becomes the control
knob for revolving the celestial spheres, and at the same time is the weaving instrument used
by the three Fates, the goddesses who wove the destinies of human beings.

E

one another, with another, third one the same way, and a fourth, and four more. Because there are eight knobs in all, inserted one within the next, with their rims showing as circles from above, ending in back in a continuous surface of a single knob around the shaft, which was driven all through them through the center of the eighth.

"The first and outermost knob has the widest edge on the circle of its rim, the second widest is that of the sixth, third that of the fourth, fourth that of the eighth, fifth that of the seventh, sixth that of the fifth, seventh that of the third, and eighth that of the second. The rim of the largest knob is speckled, that of the seventh is the brightest, that

617A

of the eighth gets its color from the seventh, which shines on it, those of the second and fifth are about the same as each other, yellower than the others, the third has the whitest color, the fourth is a little reddish, and the sixth is second in whiteness.[194] The whole spindle turns in a circle with the same rotation, but within the whole as it goes around, the seven inner circles go around gently in the direction opposite to the whole. In these latter motions the eighth goes at

B

the fastest rate among them, and the seventh, sixth, and fifth, at the same rate as one another, are second fastest; coming third in the rate at which it was circling back, as it appeared to them, was the fourth rim, fourth fastest the third, and fifth the second.[195] And it turns in the lap of Necessity.[196]

C

"On its circles, one standing atop each, a Siren is carried around with it, each emanating one sound, a single tone, and from all eight sounding together there is one harmonious sound. And three others are seated at equal intervals around it, each on a throne, three daughters of Necessity robed in white and wearing garlands on their heads,

194   The visible differences the bodies in the heavens present to the bodily eye are seen by the souls in the nested knobs that turn their spheres. From the outermost rim inward, they are (1) the fixed stars, (2) Saturn, (3) Jupiter, (4) Mars, (5) Venus, (6) Mercury, (7) the sun, and (8) the moon. The widths of the rims would correspond to the thicknesses of the spheres, which must accommodate the greatest and least distances of the bodies from the center. In the case of the sun, for example, that variation produces the inequality in the length of the seasons. The relative thicknesses given are not entirely accounted for by that, though, and may also suggest radial distances at intervals like those between strings tuned to a diatonic scale.

195   The spindle as a whole gives everything in the heavens a daily motion westward, but each of the bodies in the inner spheres has a slower eastward revolution as well, the moon completing a cycle fastest, in a month, the sun, Mercury, and Venus next at the same average angular rate, and Mars, Jupiter, and Saturn progressively slower.

196   Necessity may have two senses here. The spindle imparts necessity to the cosmos by determining a fixed order of motions, which may have consequences in all other motions. But the spindle's action is itself in some way subject to necessity, because its workings could not produce the celestial appearances alluded to in this paragraph. Either the bodies in spheres 2-8 must wander, on eccentric paths or epicycles not controlled by the spheres' own motions, or the knobs must be turned at non-uniform rates. Also, the spindle could not account for the fact that the seven wandering stars travel through the Zodiac, around an axis different from that of the daily motion. In its second sense, necessity is called "the wandering cause" in Plato's *Timaeus* (48A), the source of the discrepancy between the rational patterns of the cosmos and the workings of the perceptible world.

the Fates, Lachesis, Clotho, and Atropos, singing in harmony with
the Sirens, Lachesis of what was, Clotho of what is, and Atropos of
what is to be. And Clotho helps to turn the outer shell of the spindle
by putting her right hand to it from time to time, while Atropos does
the same to the inner ones with her left, and Lachesis puts each hand   D
to each in turn.

"When the souls got there, they were required to go directly to
Lachesis. A certain attendant first lined them up in rows and then
withdrew lots, and patterns of lives, from Lachesis' lap, went up on a
high platform, and spoke. 'The word of Lachesis, maiden daughter of
Necessity: Souls, creatures of a day, at the beginning of another death-
bearing cycle for a mortal race, no guardian deity will be assigned   E
to you by lot; you will choose a guardian deity. He who draws the
first lot, let him be first to choose a life to which he will be bound by
necessity. Virtue has no master; each will have more or less of it by
honoring or dishonoring it. The blame belongs to the one who chooses;
the god is blameless.'

"When he'd spoken these words, he flung the lots at them, and
each picked up one that fell beside him except Er himself, who wasn't
allowed to. And that made clear to each one who picked one up where   618A
in numerical order he would make his choice. After that, he next put
the patterns of lives on the ground in front of them, far more than
the souls who were present. And they were of all sorts, because there
were lives of all the animals as well as every human kind. There were
tyrannies among them, some fully realized and others wiped out
midway, ending in poverty and exile or in begging; and there were
lives of men with good reputations, some for looks and beauty and
strength, in athletic contests and otherwise, others for their birth and   B
the virtues of their ancestors, and lives of men disreputable on the
same grounds, and of women in like manner. An ordering of the soul
was not present in them, because it's necessary for the soul doing the
choosing to become different when a different life is chosen, but all
other attributes were, mixed with one another in lives both rich and
poor, some with sick ones and others with healthy ones, and still
others in between these.

"So, dear Glaucon, it looks like everything is at stake for a human
being here, and for that reason each of us needs to pay the utmost
attention, neglecting all other studies so that he may be a seeker and   C
student of this study, if there's anywhere it's possible for him to learn
and find out what will make him capable and knowledgeable for
distinguishing a worthwhile life from a worthless one, in order at all
times and places to choose the life that's better from among those that
are possible. When anyone reckons up all the things just mentioned,
both in combination with one another and separately, for how they
stand in relation to the virtue in a life, in order to know what harm
or good beauty will do when it's blended with poverty or wealth and

D   accompanied by any particular condition of the soul, and what high and low births will do, and private lives and ruling offices, and bodily strengths and weaknesses, and capacities to learn easily and difficulties in learning, and everything of the sort that has to do with a soul by nature as well as the things that are acquired, and what they'll do when blended together with one another—from all these things, one will be capable of coming to a conclusion in order to make a choice,

E   with a view to the nature of the soul, between a worse and a better life, and he'll call a life worse that will lead the soul to the point of its becoming more unjust, and call better one that will lead to its being more just. He'll let everything else go, because we've seen that, for

619A   the living and for the dead, this choice is the most powerful one. So he needs to go off to Hades holding adamantly to this opinion, so that even there he won't be knocked off course by riches and other evils of that kind, and fall into tyrannies and other actions like it so that he'll do many evils that can't be undone, and suffer even greater ones himself. He'll know instead always to choose the life at the mean between those things and avoid the extremes on either side, both in

B   this life, as far as possible, and in all the next life. That's the way a human being becomes happiest.

"So then the messenger from that place reported that the attendant spoke as follows: 'Even for the one who comes up last, if he chooses with intelligence, there's a life to be satisfied with, not a bad one, lying here for someone who'll put effort into living it. Let the one who's first to choose not be hasty, and let the one who's last not be dispirited.'

"As soon as these words were spoken, he said, the one who drew the first lot immediately came up and chose the biggest tyranny, choos-

C   ing out of thoughtlessness and gluttony without looking everything over carefully enough, but he failed to notice that eating his own children was included in what was allotted, as were other evils. And when he'd looked over it at leisure, he beat his breast and lamented his choice; but he didn't stick to the advice the attendant had given beforehand, because he didn't blame himself for the evils, but luck and divine beings and everything else but himself. He was one of those who'd come from the heavens, after he'd lived in an orderly polity in

D   his previous life, participating in virtue by habit, without philosophy. And one might well say it wasn't the lesser number of those caught in such a situation who'd come from the heavens, because they were out of training for taking pains; most of those who came out of the earth didn't make their choices right off the bat, because they'd suffered themselves and seen others suffer. For this reason, as well as from the luck of the draw, there was an exchange of evils and goods for most of the souls. It's always the case, though, whenever anyone

E   arrives at the life here, that if he engages in philosophy in a healthy way and the lot for his choice doesn't fall among the last ones, he stands a good chance, based on the reports from the other place, not only of being happy here but also that his journey from here to there and back again will not be traveled underground on a rough road but on a smooth one through the heavens.

"He said this in particular was a sight worth seeing, how the different souls each chose their lives, because it was pitiful and funny and wondrous to see.[197] Mostly they chose according to what they were accustomed to in the previous life. He said he saw a soul that had once been Orpheus choose the life of a swan out of hatred of womankind, since because of his death at their hands he was unwilling to be born by being conceived in a woman. And he saw the soul of Thamyris choose the life of a nightingale. And he saw a swan changing over into a choice of a human life, and other musical animals doing the same. The soul that drew the twentieth lot chose the life of a lion; it was that of Ajax, son of Telamon, who rejected becoming a human being, because he held in memory the judgment over the armor. The next soul was that of Agamemnon; in hatred of the human race on account of its sufferings, it too changed to another life, of an eagle. Having drawn a lot in the middle range, the soul of Atalanta, catching sight of great honors belonging to an athletic man, was unable to pass them by and took them. Next he saw the soul of Epeius, son of Panopeus, going into the nature of an artistic woman. And far back among those bringing up the rear he saw the soul of Thersites, who'd do anything for a laugh, slipping into a monkey. By chance the soul of Odysseus went to make its choice after drawing the last of all the lots; it had found relief from its love of honor by the memory of its earlier labors, and went around for a long time looking for a quiet life of a private man, and with some trouble it found one lying somewhere that had been ignored by everyone else. And it said when it saw it that it was delighted to choose it, and would have done the same even if it had drawn the first lot. And from the other animals, souls passed in the same way into human beings and into one another, unjust ones changing into wild animals and just ones into tame, and they got mixed in every sort of mixture.

"Now when all the souls had chosen lives, in the same order they'd drawn their lots, they went up to Lachesis, and she sent along with

620A

B

C

D

---

197   The people named are all from around the time of the Trojan war, about a thousand years before Socrates' time. The first two were poet-singers. Orpheus, who'd been taught by the Muses, died torn apart by frenzied Thracian women; Thamyris challenged the Muses, who deprived him of the power to sing. Ajax, the most powerful Greek warrior at Troy after Achilles' death, was enraged when Achilles' armor was awarded to Odysseus. Agamemnon, returning home in triumph from that war, was ambushed and killed by his wife and her lover. Atalanta was a young woman who could run faster than men, and said she would marry any man who could outrun her, if he was willing to be killed if he lost; she lost to a man who, with the connivance of Aphrodite, distracted her by dropping golden apples. Epeius built the Trojan horse. Thersites was a foot-soldier at Troy, a smart aleck who challenged his commanders in council, and he was definitely a cause of wit in others. The *Odyssey* presents Odysseus as a man willing to risk everything to test himself against every challenge the world might offer a human being, until he nearly loses everything and discovers what matters to him in finite human life.

E   each the deity it had chosen, as a guardian of its life and to fulfill what it had chosen. It led the soul to Clotho first, under her hand as it was turning the whirl of the spindle, to ratify the destiny it had chosen after it drew its lot; when it had been touched by her, it was led next to the spinning of Atropos, to make the thread that was spun irrevers-

621A   ible. From that point on it didn't turn around, and passed beneath the throne of Necessity. And once they'd come out through there, when the others had come out too, they all made their way into the plain of Lethe through terrible, scorching, stifling heat, since it was barren of trees and of everything else that grows in the earth.[198] Then, since evening was already coming on, they made camp beside the river of Heedlessness, whose waters no container can hold. It was necessary for them all to drink a certain amount of the water, and those who

B   were not saved from it by good sense drank more than that amount, but in each case, the one who drank it forgot everything. When they'd fallen asleep and midnight came, there came thunder and an earthquake, and suddenly each was borne away from there in a different direction, up to its birth, darting like shooting stars. Er himself had been prevented from drinking any of the water, but by what means and in what manner he got back into his body, he didn't know; he just suddenly had his sight again and saw himself lying at dawn on his funeral pyre.

C   "And so, Glaucon, the tale was saved and didn't die; it could save us too, if we're persuaded by it, and we'll get past the river Lethe in good shape without a stain on our soul. If we're persuaded by me and believe the soul is immortal and able to keep itself intact in the face of every evil, and every good as well, we'll always keep to the higher road and pursue justice with good sense in every way, so that we might be friends to ourselves and to the gods, both while we remain here

D   in this place and when we carry off the rewards for it like athletes on their victory laps. Both here and in the thousand-year journey we've been going through, we will do well."

---

198   The plain is beside the river Lethe, which brings forgetfulness of past lives. The word for truth (*alêtheia*) is formed as a negation of the root that signifies forgetfulness. In Plato's *Phaedrus* (248B), Socrates refers to a plain of truth, a fertile place where the soul, figured as two horses and a charioteer, can be nourished by the food it needs. Hence the plain of Lethe is a sterile place where the soul would wither in the absence of truth.

AFTERWORD

IMITATION
by John White

Note: This paper was given as a lecture at St. John's College and I have kept that form. This is not a scholarly paper, and there are no footnotes. I have taken two examples of imitation from Lessing (the scepter and Helen), and this is not stated within the body of the paper. Quotations from the *Republic* are from Allan Bloom's translation.

Since I want to talk about imitation, I must talk about two extraordinary books, the *Iliad* and the *Republic*. The *Iliad* uses "imitation" as a way to understand painting or sculpting (on Achilles' shield "the earth looked like earth that had been plowed though it was made of gold"). The *Republic* uses "imitation" to understand poetry.

Both the *Iliad* and the *Republic* are difficult to grasp, but the *Republic* has a special kind of difficulty. It is full of questions that turn back upon themselves and answers that somehow cancel or contradict themselves. For example, when Socrates throws out passages of Homer and also quotes him at great length, does he want us to hear Homer or not? Or when Socrates founds the "best city" on a noble lie and also tells us that the lie is a lie, does he want to fool us or not? And in what the *Republic* talks about—justice—we can see this odd "canceling" or "ambiguity" from the beginning. A discussion of justice draws attention to the actions of the discussion, as well as its explicit content and opinions. The "what" and the "how" of the discussion sometimes support each other—e.g., in Book I, where Socrates is a shepherd guarding his flock against a wolf. But sometimes they seem to "cancel" each other. "Doing good to friends and harm to enemies" is a definition that Socrates rejects in Book I. But when he talks to Thrasymachus and considers the claim that justice is the interest of the stronger, he treats him harshly. Finally, Socrates claims that he knows nothing and he begins to leave (end of Book I, beginning of Book II). When Glaucon and Adeimantus ask him to discuss that same opinion, Socrates says that he sees something wonderful in their nature, and he stays and talks for a long time. Has Socrates' action shown that, at some level, he believes that it is right to treat friends well and enemies harshly?

This same kind of difficulty or ambiguity appears in other ways, too. The style of the *Republic* is "decadent." It is a jumble of other styles—narrative, lyric and mimetic; it is both comic and tragic. The style is "realistic" to the point of obscuring the difference between history and fiction, real and ideal. No one style is employed in its purity. Poetry and the criticism of poetry are combined in an artful form.

These difficulties about style are not only present as questions *about* the dialogue; they are present *within* the dialogue also. When Glaucon and Adeimantus enter the conversation (in Book II), they are as much concerned with the proper way to praise justice as with justice itself. Glaucon (358a) thinks that Socrates has not refuted those who praise injustice; while Socrates may have punished Thrasymachus—pushed him around in speech, humiliated him—Socrates has not convincingly refuted injustice. Glaucon thinks that no one has ever praised justice competently, so he will praise injustice to give Socrates a pattern for the praise of justice. And for Adeimantus the greatest difficulty with justice is what happens when anyone tries to praise it. Parents, lawgivers, and poets contradict themselves when they talk about justice. They try to praise justice, but the style of their praise, the stories of rewards and the afterlife, really praises the seeming, the appearance, of justice. We should seem just to our judges. This style of praise (justice in an afterlife) conceals envy. It "exhorts one to be unjust and get away with it" in this life (367b). Adeimantus says that "of all those who claim to be praisers of justice—beginning with those who have left speeches—there is not one who has ever praised justice other than for the reputation and honors.... But as to what [justice] itself does with its own power..., no one has ever, in poetry or prose" adequately praised it (366c). Glaucon and Adeimantus think that Socrates understands this kind of difficulty and can give them the proper praise of justice. Do they want to hear poetry (praise of justice) or its criticism? Do they want poetry or philosophy? They want both.

So Socrates must do both: He must criticize poetry and be a kind of poet. Socrates does both of these things in the *Republic*. And Book X in particular is the most compact expression of the ambiguity and difficulty of what he tries to do—of looking at questions that turn back on themselves and answers that somehow cancel themselves. In Book X Socrates both gives his most radical criticism of poetry and also becomes explicitly "poetic," by telling tales of the afterlife (in the myth of Er).

Socrates gives three arguments against imitation in Book X. In this essay I will present them briefly and then examine them by looking at their underpinnings, their assumptions. The result of this examination turns out to be ambiguous: If Socrates' criticism of imitation succeeds, it succeeds in a perverse way, for it attacks not only the *Iliad* but also much that was said in the first nine books of the *Republic*. Book X turns against and "cancels" the unity and coherence of the *Republic* itself. Why is Book X there at all? Book IX ends so beautifully, with the best city a "pattern laid up in heaven;" it is uplifting. Why ruin this ending with the cranky, contradictory character of Book X? While I can't argue for the unity of the *Republic* on the level of an opinion—for example, that it is for or against poetry, for or against some particular definition of justice—I think I can give an image of its unity, an image that is able to guide us to the interpretation of some of Socrates' own poetry, the images he makes and the myth he tells.

I. Imitation and the Mirror

In Books II and III of the *Republic* Socrates gave long, sober arguments against imitative poetry: As far as content goes, poetry tells lies about gods and heroes; it talks of Hades and the afterlife, thereby undermining courage; its talk is neither "holy nor true" (377b-386b). And finally (397b ff.) tragedy, imitation without narration, was exiled for its imitative character: Imitation, where one has to jumble together "all modes and rhythms," encourages a doubleness or ambiguity in the character of the citizens; it violates the principle of the city, "one man, one job."

Now in Book X Socrates returns to the topic of poetry. His criticism of imitation this time is both more fierce and more respectful, for while he says that poets "maim the thought of those who hear them," he also says that "a certain friendship for Homer, and shame before him, which has possessed me since childhood, prevents me from speaking." (595b) This time when he criticizes poetry, unlike his earlier criticism, Socrates begins with an *image* of the imitative artist, a "wonderful and clever craftsman," and this image rules and guides the arguments that follow.

> For this same manual artisan is not only able to make all implements but also makes everything that grows naturally from the earth, and he produces all animals— the others and himself too—and, in addition to that, produces earth and heaven and gods and everything in heaven and everything in Hades under the earth. (596c)

Socrates tells Glaucon that this is not so wonderful, for he too could make all these things, in a certain way.

> You could fabricate them quickly in many ways and most quickly, of course, if you are willing to take a mirror [not a glass mirror; their mirrors were sheets of polished bronze] and carry it around everywhere; quickly you will make the sun and the things in the heavens; quickly, the earth; and quickly yourself and the other animals and implements and plants and everything else that was just now mentioned. (596d-e)

In Socrates' image of the mirror, who is the "clever man" and what is his mirror? I cannot answer these questions now, but I will return to them.

After making this image, Socrates gives three arguments against imitation. The first concerns the being of a work of art (596a-598b). The second concerns the knowledge which the imitator has (601b-602b). The third concerns virtue (598e-601b; 603e-606d). The conclusion of these arguments is that poetry needs an apology in its ancient quarrel with philosophy (607b). Within Book X this restatement of the exile of poetry forms a transition to the discussion of the immortality of the soul (608e ff.) and the myth of Er.

Here I will present Socrates' first two arguments—the being of an art work and the knowledge it contains. These arguments belong together because they both rely on the same assumptions and they both draw out the consequences of the image of the mirror. The third argument does not rely on the mirror, so I will consider it later.

The first argument is about being. In the case of a bed, there are three artisans concerned with it and there are three kinds of beds. First, there is one bed "by nature," produced by god. (Notice the oddity of this phrase: "the bed by nature.") The god makes only one bed; if he made two beds, it would come to light that they shared the same "Form." The god is called the "nature-begetter." Second, there is the bed we sleep on, made by a craftsman. He doesn't make the "Form" of a bed, but he does make a particular bed. He is both imitative and productive. Socrates says, "If he doesn't make what is, he wouldn't make the being but something that is like the being." (597a) Third, there is the bed that appears in the painting of an imitator. He is third because he does not imitate the "Form" of the one bed, as does the craftsman; instead he imitates what the craftsman has made. Socrates says (598b) that the painter imitates not the "being as it is" but the "looking as it looks" of a thing. He concludes that imitation is three removes from the truth about being.

Socrates' second argument concerns knowledge. For each thing, there are three arts concerned with it: the art of its use, the art of its making, and the art of its imitation. In the case of a bridle, Socrates asks who understands it best, who knows what he is talking about when he talks about bridles. In this case first place goes to the user because "the virtue, beauty and rightness of each implement, animal, and action [are] related to nothing but the use for which each was made, or grew naturally." Second place goes to the craftsman, who will have "right trust concerning its beauty or its badness" (601e). The imitator has neither knowledge nor right opinion about the bridle; no one can tell him how to paint it because there is no clear-cut use for a painting. The painter has neither knowledge nor right opinion with respect to the beauty or badness in anything. He can only paint what looks fair to the many (602b).

The painter, the imitative artist, gets third place in both of these arguments. Socrates concludes the arguments this way:

> Then it looks like we are pretty well agreed on these things: the imitator knows nothing worth mentioning about what he imitates; imitation is a kind of play and not serious; and those who take up tragic poetry in iambics and epics are all imitators in the highest possible degree. (602b)

These two arguments have some assumptions as their underpinnings. The first hypothesis is that "god made only one bed by nature." Socrates says:

> Do you want us to make our consideration according to our customary
> procedure, beginning from the following point? For we are, presum-
> ably, accustomed to set down some one particular form for each of the
> particular 'manys' to which we apply the same name. (596a)

Only with this assumption can Socrates give his analysis of the being of an
artwork (the three craftsmen) and its knowledge (the three arts). These "Forms"
help his argument in another way: Each argument analyzed an implement
or tool (bed and bridle), a work of craft or *technê designed for use* rather than
a natural being. The analysis is impossible if there is an important difference
between nature and art with respect to either being or our understanding of
being. For example, if use is the test of our knowledge, who is the user of a
giraffe or an ostrich such that he understands them for what they are? This
difference (between natural and artful being) is not a serious problem if we
follow Socrates' image of the mirror (which imitates implements and animals
and gods equally well) or if a thing is what it is by "participation" in a "Form."
Both "theories" (the poetic image and the philosophical distinction) allow us
to understand the being of a thing without reference to its coming-to-be, the
path by which it arrived. I.e., the understanding of being is as self-contained
as being seems to be. We can ignore the distinction between nature and art
because the distinction rests on the importance of becoming, motion.

The second assumption needed for these two arguments against imitation
is that the poet is similar to the painter (596e, 603c, 605a). Both arguments and
the image of the "mirror" concern painting directly, and we have to trust that
painting and poetry do the same kind of imitating in order to apply Socrates'
two arguments to poetry.

II. Poetry and Painting; *Laokoon*

Here I want to examine the second assumption that Socrates makes, the
similarity of poetry and painting. The best examination of the relation of poetry
to painting (and sculpture, too—the plastic arts) is Lessing's *Laokoon*. Laokoon
was a Trojan priest who told the Trojans not to bring a piece of sculpture into
their city, a wooden sculpture of a horse. Two serpents attacked Laokoon and
his sons for making this warning. Lessing uses the Laokoon theme because
it exists in two treatments, as an incident in the *Aeneid* and as a sculpture. In
the treatment in the *Aeneid*, Laokoon is bitten by a serpent.

> All the while his appalling cries go up to heaven—A bellowing, such
> as you hear when a wounded bull escapes from the altar, after it's
> shrugged off an ill-aimed blow at its neck.   (II, 223 ff.)

In the Laokoon statue, Laokoon is being bitten by a serpent and he is crying
out—or perhaps he is calling out, calling on some god, or saying something.
The statue is wordless, so we cannot tell. Laokoon's posture and the shape
of his mouth give this moment of pain a serene greatness and noble simplicity—a timelessness, a strange and wonderful presence. The wordless cry of
the statue (possibly wordless—we cannot tell) is not the awful bellowing of
which the poem speaks. This difference shows Lessing that the way to focus

an examination of the similarity of poetry and painting is to focus on how they express emotions—in particular, how they portray the experience of pain.

This difference in expression is striking and consistent: If one looks at Greek poets, there are many examples of heroes and gods expressing pain with a violence that ruins their "serene greatness" and beauty. When Achilles first hears of the death of Patroklus, he pours dust and ashes on his face and "fouls his handsome countenance" (XVIII, 24). Or in one of the two most terrible and wonderful moments in the book, when Zeus is finally faced with the death of his son, Sarpedon, and he cannot save him even though he has the power (Zeus has already saved his life twice), Zeus stops arguing with Hera and sits, wordless; Homer says "the father of gods and men wept tears of blood" (XVI, 459).

In general, if one listens to screams of pain in the *Iliad*, one can see a progression. Early in the book, the usual way of dying is that a spear is thrown and it "drives inward through the bone, and a mist of darkness clouded both eyes and he fell as a tower falls" (IV, 460). As the book goes on, screams of pain are mentioned as part of the dying. In Book XIII, when Zeus looks away from the battle, there is more boasting over fallen enemies, one man cries out in pain (393), and another "cried out then a great cry... and the spear in his breast was stuck fast but the heart was beating still and beating to shake the butt end of the spear" (441). A man is struck between the navel and genitals "where beyond all places death in battle comes most painfully to pitiful mortals" (568). Another man is struck in the eye; then his head is cut off, but the eyeball sticks to the point of the spear and is "lifted high like the head of a poppy" (XIV, 499).

The culmination of this progression of the violent expression of pain is in Book XVIII, the moment that answers and balances the silent, bloody tears of Zeus. After the death of Patroklus, Hera sends Achilles to the wall around the ships. He has no armor. He stands there on the wall, then goes to the ditch. He is caught between anger and grief. He cries out, a great brazen scream, and Athena makes the "unwearied dangerous fire" of heaven blaze from his head. The cry he gives is "wordless," a piercing utterance (without any possibility of becoming "winged").

The Greeks were immoderate in their poetry because moderation is not dramatic. The reason for the serenity of the statue is not the "moderation" of the Greeks, as some have theorized; the statue is "moderate" because it is a statue, because of the limitation of plastic art. The limit and goal of plastic art is physical beauty and beauty of expression: What is ugly must be veiled and transformed, and expressions of emotion must be moderated (if we are to feel something like pity and fear rather than disgust). Since the plastic arts can portray only one moment in time, they must choose a moment that most implies the wholeness of an action, and not a moment that expresses it. There is no one moment of expression, for an action is a temporal whole that needs a "before" and an "after," motivation and suffering, to be complete. The last moment, the suffering and the bellow of pain, is for plastic art the least useful: The eyeball on the spear becomes disgusting or funny after a while. So plastic art, when considering an action and its suffering, must choose the beginning, a moment of transition or choice—the moment where the soul has decided and is just about to move the body. It may choose the "last" moment of Laokoon's struggle only if the struggle is not quite over: We know Laokoon is doomed, while Laokoon is about to know and is about to bellow. (Of course, plastic art could choose a moment that is eternal, a moment of contemplation or a moment that expresses the serene self-sufficiency of the gods.)

Poetry does not have these limits. In it we can have wordless screams (which will stand out as wordless) and tears of blood because we do not see the ugly gaping mouth, and the moment is quickly left behind. In dramatic imitation, the ugly and disfiguring, the natural display of emotion, may and must be shown.

Poetry has a wider range than painting; much that it imitates can't be given in a painting. For example, consider the gods. To the painter they are "personified abstractions" who must remain the same, doing the one thing that is typical of them, if they are to be identified. To the poet these "personified abstractions," these timeless entities, must act, must enter time, and therefore they must have various passions and deeds. (Poetry violates the god's simplicity, 508d.) In poetry there are many moments when Aphrodite does not act like the abstraction of love, but the painter can't portray her then unless he adds some kind of label or sign, a non-visual element that is a substitute for a name.

If painters try to use Homer's "pictures" as a model, they will face impossible problems. For example. Homer treats of two kinds of beings, visible and invisible: men and gods. Painters can't do this. When a painting portrays gods and men together, it ignores the distinction between the visible and the invisible—a distinction that for Homer is not a matter of sight. Painting lowers the invisible. For example, if one wishes to paint the battle of the gods and men in Book XXI of the *Iliad*, one needs some visual scale of distinction between gods and men—a scale that tells you *this* figure is a god and *that* one is not because (perhaps) one figure is ten times as large as the other (XVIII, 518). Homer does say that the gods are "huge." But for Homer this "size" is not physical; the gods have stature, greatness. A painting would ignore this difference between gods and men by being so literal-minded about the word "huge."

What the visibility of the gods means for Homer is that they are only visible to men by an increased power of mortal vision, such as Athene grants to Diomedes. The gods are not invisible because of mists or clouds. Although Homer mentions them, in a painting clouds and mists would cease being a physical presence and would become a "sign." The gods are visible only to the greatest of the Greeks, and they are never visible to someone like Thersites. Visibility has little to do with vision, but a lot to do with the distinction between the great and the ordinary, the serious and the superficial. Homer's gods are related to men, and distinct from men, in this way: The gods reveal human life by showing its possibilities and limits. They are a kind of skepticism and self-consciousness. The gods are limits for us that are not merely "other," as are cats and crocodiles or stars or any of the many things that different people see as divine. The gods don't "exist" in the literal-minded sense of a painting that has both gods and men in it. The idea of human life is beautiful and real, and actual human life is incomplete without these ideas—even if they are "mere possibilities"—and without this kind of greatness. Only poetry can give us this kind of limit, one that "cancels" and affirms at the same time. These gods are "other," but their otherness has a human form. Painting has trouble showing us the otherness of the gods—this unique combination of same and other.

Poetry and painting are different because they imitate different things: Painting imitates bodies, silent presences whose parts co-exist in time, and poetry imitates wholes that unfold and complete themselves in time. When Homer describes an object, he usually gives it only one characteristic (the hollow ship, the black ship), but he describes actions in greater detail. When Homer does describe an object, the description is not visual and it serves other purposes. Let's consider three examples of Homer's kind of description, Homer's "pictures," to see how they work and what they are describing.

The first example is the description of a scepter. Homer gives two descriptions of it, and we have to look at them together to understand what he is describing and how he is doing it. When Agamemnon holds the scepter, this is what Homer says:

> Powerful Agamemnon
> stood up holding the scepter Hephaistos has wrought him carefully.
> Hephaistos gave it to Zeus the king, the son of Chronos,
> and Zeus in turn gave it to the courier Argeïphontes,
> and Lord Hermes gave it to Pelops, driver of horses,
> and Pelops gave it to Atreus, the shepherd of the people.
> Atreus dying left it to Thyestes of the rich flocks,
> and Thyestes in turn left it to Agamemnon to carry
> and to be lord of many islands and over all Argos.

Here is the second description. It is given by Achilles when he holds the scepter.

> This scepter, which never again will bear leaf nor
> branch, now that it has left behind the cut stump in the mountains,
> nor shall it blossom again, since the bronze blade stripped
> bark and leafage, and now at last the sons of the Achaians
> carry it in their hands in state when they administer the justice of Zeus.

$$(I, 234-239)$$

And then Achilles dashes the scepter to the ground. Neither description gives any visual information; they give a history. But they *are* descriptions of a sort if we look at the two descriptions together. One description calls the scepter the work of Hephaistos; the other describes the scepter as cut from the mountainside by unknown hand. The one talks of an ancient possession of a noble house; the other talks of a scepter destined to fit the hand of anyone who might chance to grab it. The one talks of a scepter held by one who rules over many islands and over all of Argos; the other talks of justice, then throws the scepter down. What is being described is not the scepter; the descriptions are giving us the difference between Agamemnon and Achilles.

Second, when Homer doesn't match up two descriptions of an object to give us something else, when he does want to describe something that demands a picture, what does he do? After all, the symbols of poetry are arbitrary and can be made to represent a body coexistent in space. How do bodies, whose parts coexist in space, lend themselves to a description? Here is the problem for a poet: since the description is in words and sentences, the description itself must be sequential. The temporal sequence obscures the co-existence of the parts; by the end of the description, the beginning is forgotten. The statue or painting, as a physical object, is experiences in time, just like any object. But its "image" character appears and is present all at once, as a whole—similar to what happens with a mirror. Speech never achieves the wholeness or "direct presence" of a painting. So when Homer is forced to enter the special province of plastic art, physical beauty and unmediated presence, what does he do? How does he describe Helen? A direct, "mirror-like" description, which considers her features one by one, can't help but be a kind of arbitrary jumble, a mere sequence—why talk of eyes first? How does Homer give us the experience of her beauty? He gives a mediate description of her beauty by describing an action: He has Helen come to the wall, and he describes how the sight of her affects old men (not young ones).

> They were seated by the gates, elders of the people.
> Now through old age they fought no longer, yet they were excellent
> speakers still, and clear, as cicadas who through the forest
> settle on trees, to issue the delicate voice of their singing.
> Such were they who sat on the tower, chief men of the Trojans.
> And these, as they saw Helen along the tower approaching,
> murmuring softly to each other uttered their winged words:
> 'Surely there is no blame on Trojans and strong-greaved Achaians
> if for long time they suffer hardship for a woman like this one.
> Terrible is the likeness of her face to immortal goddesses.
> Still, though she be such, let her go away with the ships, lest
> she be left behind, a grief to us and our children.

We don't know what she looks like. When Zeuxis made a painting of this scene, he did give a direct, mirror-like presentation of Helen's beauty. Helen was the only figure in the painting—no old men who have "winged words" and wrinkles. (Which is more beautiful: the looks of Helen or the looking of the old men?)

The third example of Homer's descriptions is the most complex and revealing: What does Homer do when he invades plastic art itself, when he goes behind and beneath the overwhelming presence of the beautiful object? What does he do when he describes both the presence of beautiful object and the context of this unmediated presence? What does he do when he describes both the being and the becoming of the object, both the image and the imitating?

> Thetis of the silver feet came to the house of Hephaistos.
> She found him sweating as he turned here and there to his bellows
> busily since he was working on twenty tripods....
> [Hephaistos] took the huge blower off from the block of anvil limp-
> ing.... He...gathered and put away

all the tools with which he worked in a silver strong box.
Then with a sponge he wiped clean his forehead, and both hands
and his massive neck and hairy chest....
[Hephaistos then] went to his bellows He turned those toward the
    fire...
And the bellows...blew on the crucibles,
from all directions blasting forth wind to blow the flames high,
now as he hurried from one place to another.
He cast on the fire bronze which is weariless... and gripped in one
    hand
the ponderous hammer, while in the other he grasped the pincers.

And then all this labor and sweat just disappear.

First of all he forged a shield that was huge and heavy.
Hephaistos made the earth upon it, and sky, and the sea's water,
and the tireless sun, and the moon waxing into her fullness,
and on it all the constellations that adorn the heavens....
On it he wrought in all their beauty two cities of mortal men.
And there were marriages in one, and festivals.
The people were assembled in the market place. Around the other
    city were lying
two forces of armed men shining in their war gear. He made upon it
    a soft field,
the pride of tilled land, wide and triple-ploughed, with many plow
    men upon it.
And as these making their turn would reach the end-strip of a field
a man would come up to them at this point and hand them a flagon
of honey-sweet wine, and they would turn again to the furrow.
The earth darkened behind them and looked like earth that has
    been ploughed
though it was made of gold. Such was the wonder of the shield's
    forging.

(XVIII, 369-549, selected)

Homer shows the labor of the imitating; he shows the making of the shield, its coming-to-be. But then the sweat and labor disappear. The ability to see this "disappearing" is what poetry can see about sculpting that sculpting can't see about itself—what sculpting 'forgets' about itself. I.e., poetry is able to see and understand the coming-to-be of images despite the nondynamic co-existence of their being. Visual images have a being that points away from itself to the imaged thing, where wonder overcomes and denies its own forging. But the "disappearing" is not just the secret that poetry knows about visual art. The disappearing—the disappearing, not the disappearance—is also the essential gesture that poetry imitates and repeats when it tries to give its own becoming. The invocation is both the appearing of the poem and the disappearing of the poet. With the invocation a poet disappears into the divine, which is a style and a rhythm ("Sing, goddess, of wrath...."). Poetry tries to hide its own becoming.

The shield is the greatest "presence" in the poem. The shield is a visual presence that is impossible to see because the looking has overcome the object and its looks.

> Thetis came to the ships and carried with her the gifts of Hephaistos.
> She found her beloved son lying in the arms of Patroklus crying
>   shrill....
> She clung to her son's hand and called him by name and spoke to
>   him:
> "My child, we must let this man lie dead,
> in the way he first was killed through the gods' designing.
> Accept rather from me the glorious arms of Hephaistos,
> so splendid, and such as no man has ever worn."
> The goddess spoke, and set down the armor on the ground
> before Achilleus, and all its elaboration clashed loudly.
> Trembling took hold of all the Myrmidons. None had the courage to
>   look straight at it.
> They were afraid of it. Only Achilleus looked, and as he looked
> the anger came harder upon him and his eyes glittered terribly, like
>   sunflare.
> He was glad, holding the shining gifts of Hephaistos.
> But when he had satisfied his heart with looking,
> he spoke to his mother and addressed her in winged words:
> "Mother, the god has given me these weapons; they are the work of
>   immortals.
> No mortal man could have made them."

Many have been tempted to draw this shield, but they can't. The things on the shield are in motion, and no human painting or sculpture could show that. But there is a divine kind of painting that can show things in motion, in their life.

Hephaistos is an unusual god, not a god of "serene greatness," for he limps and sweats and has a hairy chest. He was important to Achilles at another time, too. When the river Xanthos attacked Achilles and tried to give him an anonymous death—to bury him in mud, bodies, and watery blood— Hephaistos saved Achilles with his fire. Now, too, with the shield, Hephaistos says that he wishes he could hide Achilles from death and its sorrow; he wishes it as surely as there will be a shield to wonder at (XVIII, 467). Again Hephaistos uses his fire for Achilles: He makes a "shield of wonder" to replace Achilles' lost armor, his Uranian armor, taken by Hector (XVII, 195). This new *Olympian* armor is forged by a divine art that shows things in motion, in their life. The divine art that shows things in winged motion, the art the forges Olympian armor, is poetry.

III. The Third Argument and its Difficulties

Socrates gives a third argument against mimetic poetry in Book X. This argument both sums up the earlier criticisms (about being and knowledge) and goes beyond them. It has two parts; both parts concern "virtue." I'll look at the two parts separately and make some observations.

The first part of the argument (598e-601b) says that Homer must not himself have been virtuous because he did no "deeds." Homer founded no cities, conducted no wars, and is not credited with any inventions or devices; he is not famous for a way of life, as was Pythagoras, nor was he a teacher of virtue. If one has knowledge about virtue, one is more serious about deeds than speeches and imitations; one would be "more eager to be the one who is praised than the one who praises" (599b). Homer's art produced only a song, so he produced nothing serious, only an imitation of what is serious.

Either to defend Homer or to understand him better, we have to answer these questions: What was Homer's deed and what "invention or device" can we credit him with? Herodotus (II, 50-53) says that while Homer (and Hesiod) didn't invent the gods, he was the first to give them special honors, arts, names, and genealogies—a "theogony," a coming-to-be. Homer, by giving deeds, histories, and preferences to the gods, made them into characters. No longer are the gods merely the subject for statues and lyric poems, "timeless" hymns to Apollo or Zeus (Socrates allows this kind of poetry in his "healthy" city—372b). Now the gods are fit subjects for epic poetry, the kind of poetry that uses "winged words." But the gods and the *Iliad*, the book where the gods become characters, were not Homer's deed; they were the "devices" he needed to perform his deed. Homer devised Olympian armor, the *Iliad*, for the Greeks to look at, and this kind of *looking* produced the Greeks—they were Homer's deed. The Greeks were the kind of people they were because they had these gods and the *Iliad*, instead of cats or crocodiles or statues of Uranian gods.

Homer's deed, this bringing into being of a certain kind of person, has an odd timelessness for a deed; it is not over yet; it can still occur. When we read the *Iliad* attentively, we sit, unmoving and wordless, as if chained to a chair in a cave; we are aware only of the images before us. We are not aware of them as images. Instead, the images convince us that they are real, that our emotions are only reflections of Achilles' wrath and grief.

Socrates is aware of this kind of cave and this kind of defense of Homer: "Praisers of Homer say that this poet educated Greece" (606e). Socrates is aware that the Greeks have a "noble lie" in their souls, where they confuse nature and education: "The *inborn* love of such poetry we owe to our *rearing* in these fine regimes" (608a).

So far, in this "ancient quarrel of poetry and philosophy," I see no decisive advantage for either side. Homer is beautiful if bloody; the images of philosophy ("patterns laid up in heaven") are uplifting, if a little cold. But in most ways the quarrel remains a mere quarrel; no new understanding has been opened up by either side, nor have new possibilities come into view for either side. Philosophy sees through this poetic "disappearing" and the false objectivity of "forgetting." But, as poetry repeated the forgetting and the unself-conscious knowing of "disappearing," so may philosophy with its "pattern laid up in heaven (end of Book IX).

But now, when Socrates turns to the second part of this argument against Homer, he turns away from the "mirror" image and its emphasis on the imitation of objects: "Imitation imitates forced and voluntary actions" (603c). He goes beyond the limit and assumption of the first two arguments, the similarity of poetry and painting: "Let's not just trust the likelihood based on painting; but let's go directly to the very part of thought with which poetry's imitation keeps company and see whether it is ordinary or *serious*" (603c). We are no longer arguing about "truth" or "being," questions that can become the province of philosophy in a narrowly technical way—a kind of thinking that is "true" but has no greatness, a thinking that is hard for us to take seriously because it doesn't take seriously human life in its naive, non-technical immediacy.

With this new beginning, Socrates turns to the deepest criticism of poetry: Mimetic poetry does not produce "seriousness" about virtue in the soul of the spectator. He says that poetry cannot imitate a serious soul, a soul that is restrained, one that is "self-same." Poetry must imitate a soul in conflict. When we see tragic suffering, the best part of the soul, the measuring and calculating part, relaxes its rule over the other parts. Here Socrates says that he makes the "greatest charge" (605b) against mimetic poetry. This charge is more serious than those "third remove" criticisms in the first two arguments (about being and knowledge), technical arguments that relied on an image, the "mirror." Socrates says that mimetic poetry "fosters and waters desires, pains, pleasures, sex and spiritedness—things which ought to be dried up" (606d). Spiritedness, *thumos*, ought to be dried up.

Whatever else one might say about this criticism of poetry, one can't simply disagree with it: After looking at the *Iliad* with Lessing's help, we have to agree that the soul without conflict is not dramatic; it belongs on a pedestal, not in a poem. But, on the other hand, we also have to remember that if we are going to "dry up" *thumos*, that it was *thumos*, spiritedness, that made possible the *Republic* and its three-part soul by mediating between reason and appetite. This part of the soul, which conflicts with natural desires and goes beyond them in wanting relishes, made "guardianship" possible, with its dog-like combination of the qualities of "being gentle to friends and cruel to enemies" (375b ff.). The "measuring and calculating" part of the soul, reason, needs a force naturally allied to it, a guardian, if it is to rule the soul or the city. And if reason can't rule *both* soul and city, the image that rules and unifies the first nine books of the *Republic* is lost: the image where "the city is the soul 'writ large.'"

This new attack on mimetic poetry involves another surprise for us, as Socrates explores the restrained self-sameness of soul which poetry cannot imitate. The surprise is the immortality of the soul. When Socrates mentions immortality, Glaucon "looks him in the face with wonder" (608d). The immortality of the soul depends on the soul's simplicity and unity, its radical self-sameness. If the soul is "simple," how can it have three parts?

When Socrates tries to explain this difficulty about the parts of the soul (611c), that up until now the soul had three parts, he says that, so far, he has been talking about the "looks" of the soul only. All right, but that was his criticism of mimetic poetry in the first two arguments against it, the ones based on painting and the "mirror" (that poetry talks about "looks" instead of being). Whatever else we may think about this third attack on mimetic poetry, these arguments of Book X are also a kind of "canceling" and "turning against" much that was said in the first nine books—the most extreme form of the canceling I mentioned at the beginning (the special difficulty of the *Republic*).

Why is Book X there at all? Book IX ends so nicely, with the best city as a city in speech, a "pattern laid up in heaven," and there is a review of actual cities, cities "in deed." The tyrant has been "stripped of his tragic gear" (577a), which allows Socrates to answer the original question about the relation of justice and happiness: The just man is 729 times as happy as the tyrant (587e).

I think we can see the reason for including Book X if we look a little more closely at the "degeneration" of the cities in Books VIII and IX, because there we can see the return of mimetic poetry despite its exile in Book III, and we can see the emergence of a special concern with poetry in one of the cities, a democracy.

Before the "degeneration" begins, Book VII ends with the description of the best city and the education of the philosopher-kings. Glaucon recognizes the completion of the discussion when he says, "just like a sculptor, Socrates, you have produced men who are wholly fair" (540a). Then the "degeneration" begins as Socrates makes the gesture characteristic of poetry—an invocation: "How will our city be moved? Do you want us, as does Homer, to pray to the Muses to tell us how 'faction first attacked,' and shall we say they speak to us with high, tragic talk, as though they were speaking seriously?" (545d). So the sculptural climax of Book VII is insufficient; poetry has returned after its exile.

The "degeneration" must bring back mimetic poetry because the degeneration involves choices and actions. And conversely, the presentation of a variety of cities demands something like a "degeneration." If one is going to describe various cities, which city does one start with? Without a principle of order, the cities are a jumble and the description would be a jumble (as in the problem of describing Helen; eyes or teeth first?). And not only does the "degeneration" involve a return to mimetic poetry in its Homeric beginning, but poetry itself enters at one stage of the degeneration, a democracy.

Democracy enters with a kind of flourish because the transition from oligarchy to democracy echoes the transition from the first city, Socrates' "city of utmost necessity" (369d), to the "feverish city" in Book II. In Book II, Glaucon had objected to the simple, unified "pig city" because it had no relishes, nothing beyond the necessary—not even sexual desire goes beyond what is economically feasible ("They will have sweet intercourse with one another, and not produce children beyond their means"—372b). Now, in Book IX, in the degeneration from oligarchy to democracy, an oligarchic father satisfies only necessary desires; he holds down other desires by force (554a); he is unable to compete for "noble objects" (555a). The son feels that this is petty, that his father has no generosity or magnificence or freedom. The son hears "boasting speeches...persuading [him] that measure and orderly expenditure are rustic and illiberal" (560c). He has a desire for relishes (559a-b). Again, with democracy as with the fall of the "pig city," many kinds of relishes and imitators are added to the son's life, but now there is no desire for a *katharsis* or purging, as there was in Book II. So the democratic man becomes overwhelmed by his possibilities, his freedom and his choices.

For this democratic man, freedom of choice depends on the fact that no particular choice is serious. No choice is serious because no choice closes off other possibilities; no choice makes him this rather than that. At his best, he is intrepid and daring—capable of both action and deliberation: He can love beauty without softness, and he "needs no lying poet" to make monuments for him; he will make his own (I am thinking of Pericles' praise of the Athenians in the funeral oration). But at his worst, this is his attitude toward a choice: He says, "Some say it's good, some say it's bad—everyone has his own opinion. We won't *know* until we try it. If it doesn't work, we'll change it back. Why not? After all, it's not written in stone." He can experiment with anything because no choice has serious consequences; there is *nothing* written in stone for him. The democratic man is a soldier one day, a flute-player the next, a philosopher the next (561c). With these superficial choices, choices that don't touch him deeply, he never actually becomes anything. For example, he doesn't become a soldier; he becomes an *imitation* of a soldier. He does something for a while—he is even serious for a while—but then he turns away and forgets. He turns to another kind of life; but he is always trapped by the ordinary.

When the democratic man looks at people and tries to understand them and their choices, their justice—when he looks for some kind of brotherhood or a sameness beneath human differences—he discovers that all human differences and choices are superficial; no choice is serious. Living in a democratic city, he confronts the variety of human differences and the jumble of choices every day. He sees that people follow their strongest inclination or ruling passion as long as it is strongest, and then they change. When he looks at the cities of the world, he sees the same thing: Democratic cities have democratic laws, oligarchic cities have oligarchic laws, etc. In each case the strongest faction makes the rules and defines justice, as long as it is strongest. What universal justice does he see? What truth is hidden beneath the overwhelming variety? In each case, universally and without exception, justice is the interest of the stronger.

Thrasymachus knows this hidden truth, and he reveals the cynicism and tyranny beneath the surface. No mere "refutation in words" can succeed in dealing with what Thrasymachus says. For while Socrates may be able to tie him in knots and make him look foolish, that might only be a sign of Socrates' superior strength and skill in arguments and thereby a sign of Socrates' superficiality (that he accepts the "truth in speech" and ignores the truth revealed by deeds—that he is "more serious about speeches and imitations than deeds"—Socrates' criticism of Homer, 599b). The victory would be only one more self-contradictory praising of justice; it would confirm the truth "in deeds" of what Thrasymachus says about the role of strength. Socrates' victory would be a mere "victory in speech." While a "city in speech," a "pattern laid up in heaven," might seem to be an uplifting possibility, a mere "victory in speech" for Socrates here is an ugly, fearful possibility. Glaucon and Adeimantus know this: Despite Socrates' victory "in speech" in Book I, our souls may harbor a "secret lawlessness," an imperviousness to speech: No speech may touch us deeply. We don't need to know the soul's opinion about the truth of justice. Its opinion about whether the armor should be returned or not (for example); we aren't even sure that the "truth in speech" matters in the depths of the soul. But the soul *must* act—must either return the armor or not. There is no third possibility. Only an impossible experiment could help us see this truth about the soul. We would have to know what the soul would *choose* if it had perfect freedom and invisibility. Glaucon proposes this: We need a "ring of Gyges," a magical freedom and invisibility for the soul, to discover the truth about the soul's choosing.

Glaucon and Adeimantus and the democratic man himself need more protection than has been offered in the first nine books. A democratic man needs to be protected not just from making the wrong choice about "returning the armor," for example; he needs to be protected from cynicism and superficiality. Can mimetic poetry do this? Is it "ordinary or serious" (603c)?

And not only does the democratic man need to be protected from the possibility of degeneration, philosophy also needs to be protected from this possibility. Is *it* "ordinary or serious?" (Most of the world thinks philosophy to be trivial, as Socrates knows.) Is philosophy only "victories in speech," a continuation of the struggle for victory on a different playing field with words as weapons? Is it a non-serious possibility thrown onto the world's stage by democracy and its tolerance for non-serious choices? Is philosophy only a continuation of the democratic style, a jumbled and decadent style (debate, oration, and argument; both comic and tragic) with a new content, where only the novelty of its content distracts one from its inability to see deeply into the soul? This is Socrates' question; this is the greatest challenge to mimetic poetry and to philosophy's "city in speech." This is why Book X is there.

Let's look again at the result of this third argument against imitation. What Socrates now says in criticism of mimetic poetry is a criticism of *thumos* and the three-part soul, and thereby it reveals difficulties in much of what was said and constructed in the first nine books: the unity of the soul and of the city, and the unity of the guiding image of the first nine books (the city is the soul "writ large"). The unity and coherence of the book is in doubt. Book X is the most compact expression of this kind of "cancellation" and turning against itself, because it contains both the most austere criticism of poetry and the myth of Er.

IV. *Katharsis* and the Silver Soul

When we read the *Iliad* or watch a tragedy, we sit absorbed, as if chained to a chair in a cave. Socrates says we are to leave that cave in order to see the sun and the world in its light. Education and its canceling, its "purging" (*katharsis* is the word Book III uses to describe education), are to take the place of poetry and its *katharsis*. We are to give up our Homeric, Olympian armor, even though it has somehow made us what we are.

But in this replacement of one *katharsis* by another, we must first ask why we are in the position of having to choose between poetry and philosophy. Why do we need any *katharsis* at all? What in our souls finds purification, resolution, unification in response to speeches about deeds? Socrates has criticized Homer as one who is more serious about speeches than about the deeds with which they deal. This understanding of "seriousness" makes us ask why we want to hear speeches about deeds; why do we want to hear praise of deeds? Why do Glaucon and Adeimantus want to hear the correct praise of justice from Socrates? Why does the incorrect praise bother them so much?

To answer these questions we need to look at the 'silver' soul (*thumos*), the kind of soul that Book X wants to "dry up," not the gold or bronze soul. The *Republic* asks us to see the limits of this kind of soul, how it begins in the desire for relishes and ends in the acceptance of a noble lie.

How can we understand the beginning of the silver soul, the desire for relishes? At the beginning of Book II Socrates constructs a simple, unified city, a "true and healthy" city. Glaucon says that it has no relishes; it is a "city fit for pigs"; it is contemptible. What this city needs is a large dose of luxury, fever. The occupations that are added to this city when it attempts to become worthy of honor are suggestive: hunters, imitators concerned with figure and color and music, poets, rhapsodes, actors, craftsmen for feminine adornment, servants, teachers, beauticians, barbers and cooks. Imitators and poets have been added, along with cosmeticians and barbers.

The silver in our soul asserts itself and becomes visible by having a certain contempt for mere nature; it does not begin in simple greed or lust. It does not want two pieces of meat; it wants one piece with relish. It does not want two coats; it wants one coat with a gold braid on it. It does not sexually desire two women rather than one, or two men rather than one; it wants a sexual object that is "improved": lipstick, jewelry, perfume, or a bone in the nose and tattoos—anything, it seems, as long as mere nature is gone beyond, adorned, transformed. The silver soul is willing to pervert even the apparent naturalness of erotic attraction. The silver soul is angry at the pig city and "mere nature." It wants a kind of revenge, because the soul and its terrible beauty are invisible and unrecognized. There is no friendship in the pig city, no relation of souls; there is only an economic partnership (371e). The justice of the artisan (paying debts and telling the truth, the first definition of justice in Book I) is contemptible. "Paying debts" is an economic exchange based on bodily needs; it is not a relation of souls.

So the idea of "paying debts" must get some relish; it must be adorned and transformed by the silver soul, not just "refuted" or thrown out. "Doing good to friends and evil to enemies" adds relish to "paying debts." This is the second definition of justice in Book I; the definition comes up when a friend gives you his weapons, then asks for them back when he has gone mad. The mere idea of "paying debts" can't handle this situation because it is an economic definition that does not recognize "friendship." Honor is the just recognition for this doing of good and evil (to friends and enemies) because honor is payment adorned with relish, praise (as the "good and the evil" adorn the idea of "debts").

But there is a difficulty with honor as a kind of payment. Although honor is a reward for the silver soul, how can the soul arrange things so that honor does not become a mere payment for services rendered? If honor becomes a payment, the silver soul falls back to the level of a bronze soul. And a bronze soul can't give honor; it can only give payment, large as that payment might be. For example, would you return to the risks of war if you were offered "seven unfired tripods, ten talents of gold, twenty shining cauldrons, twelve horses, seven women of Lesbos, twenty Trojan women, Agamemnon's daughter in marriage and seven citadels"? Achilles rejects this offer; it is offered in the spirit of payment; Agamemnon is incapable of saying "I'm sorry—we were friends and I violated it." (Later, when Achilles wants to re-enter battle, Agamemnon (and Odysseus) insists that he first take the payment: Achilles is desperate for battle in his rage and grief, and he is supposed to sit down, admire the presents and eat a meal. He begins to get angry again.) This payment is an insult. "Friendship" is a relation of souls that replaces the impersonality of an economic transaction.

"Friendship" and its recognition are meant to solve this problem of "honor as a payment." But the silver soul is caught by envy, by the clash of honor and friendship: He believes in friendship and is capable of it, but honor continually tempts him to stand out alone. (Achilles says to Patroklus, when honor prevents his return to battle but allows Patroklus to enter wearing his armor, "O that you and I could storm Troy together, by ourselves," hoping for a union of honor and friendship.)

How can the silver soul avoid this clash of honor and friendship and solve the problem of honor as a payment; the payment will become large and thereby confuse size with greatness? The silver soul can get the recognition he deserves only if he elevates another soul above himself, one who is beyond competing with him, one who is "friendly" but not a friend, one who is "objective," one who offers nothing useful, nothing with cash value. Thus the one who gives recognition, speeches of praise, is elevated above the doer of the deeds. And the one who praises but is not a "friend" needs knowledge of what is praiseworthy—knowledge of justice, souls, and speeches. The silver soul, the doer, must elevate the one who recognizes him— the one who praises, the imitator in speech—above himself in order to recognize himself as elevated above the bronze. So only a gold soul can understand the silver, giving him the recognition in speech or song that he deserves. But now the silver soul, besides being caught on the point of difference of deeds and speeches, is caught in another clash: What kind of praise? A speech or song? Poetry or philosophy?

Now let's look at the end of the silver soul; he begins in the desire for relishes and ends in the acceptance of a noble lie. This is the last and the highest thing the silver soul does: He takes the first definition of justice, "paying debts and telling the truth," and now he adorns the last part, the "telling the truth" part; he decorates it in the same way he adorned "paying debts." He doesn't take "the truth" to be justice. Instead, he believes a lie, but it is a noble lie, a lie with relish on it. He believes that his education was a dream and that all men are brothers, having Earth as mother. He believes in the brotherhood of man despite metallic differences (gold, silver, bronze) that are of special concern to him. So when the silver soul believes the noble lie, he is not merely taken in and fooled by it; he believes it in part *because* it is a lie, a lie (brotherhood, friendship without its passion and particularity) that demands nobility of soul in one who would believe it. The lie is "noble" in another sense also: It ennobles the soul that believes it (brotherhood) because it takes the viciousness from his anger, his criticism of "mere nature." The silver soul does these two things at once—he believes and he overcomes the belief—in the way that Socrates both censors Homer and quotes him at length—because the silver soul knows that the unadorned truth is not worth having.

These are the limits of the silver soul: Because he loves nature, truth, and justice only when they are adorned and transformed, he must be transformed, "purged," given a *katharsis*. But we can't merely do away with him when we purge the city, for this part of the soul binds together the other parts, reason and appetite. If we just "subtracted" him from the city, we might return to the pig city. The silver soul not only makes necessary another city, a "best" city, but it also makes possible the coming-to-be of that city or any city beyond the pig city. (The best city could not have come into being in the way taken by the pig city, simple addition without subtraction or *katharsis*; the standard of "usefulness" in the pig city prevents this—e.g., "To have a city we need a farmer, a carpenter, and we'll add a philosopher.") In particular, he makes possible the "best city" by his capacity for the kind of transformation called *katharsis*. For him, "subtraction" is addition and transformation.

The silver soul is not only capable of this kind of transformation and recognition, *katharsis*, he also demands it. But the recognition that poetry offers is, Socrates says, "a hymn to tyranny" (586b), for the songs of poetry reveal only the terrible beauty of the soul; they do not recognize its monstrosity. For example, Oedipus, at the end of the play, asks to be brought on stage after putting out his eyes. He won't get off the stage despite Creon's urging, and he says, "Apollo did this to me, but I put out my eyes." This line gathers and repeats what we have felt about him throughout the play, an alternation of "He is sinned against" (Apollo does these things and Oedipus suffers them) and "He is sinning" (Oedipus is bringing this upon himself). And then Oedipus says, "Only I can bear this suffering." The alternation of pity and fear—pity for him insofar as he suffers and fear of him insofar as he acts to bring these events upon himself—that we have felt is collected together: In claiming as his own the suffering that Apollo inflicts on him, is he active or passive? This deed, turning suffering into an action and action into a suffering, transcends the alternatives of pity and fear; Instead, Oedipus becomes an object of wonder. Whether he is right or wrong, good or evil, in what he did is no longer important. He has a greatness that goes beyond these questions of right and wrong. He is the object of our looking, our regard, in a new way, and a new kind of looking is called for. The play is a hymn to this greatness.

Since poetry grasps the greatness of Oedipus' soul but doesn't see its monstrosity, the play is a "hymn to tyranny." So philosophy and its understanding of greatness (491a ff.) —not just its understanding of good and evil—must take the place of mimetic poetry and its understanding of human greatness. Somehow the *Republic* must take the place of the *Iliad*.

V. Images

Now we can turn to the unity of the *Republic*. I promised to make or discover an image of it. Let me return to two passages I referred to at the beginning of this essay, the passages from Book X where Socrates made an image that guided his criticism of mimetic poetry:

> For this same manual artisan is not only able to make all implements but also makes everything that grows naturally from the earth, and he produces all animals—the others and himself too—and, in addition to that, produces earth and heaven and gods and everything in heaven and everything in Hades under the earth. (596c)

> You could fabricate them quickly in many ways and most quickly, of course, if you are willing to take a mirror and carry it around everywhere [not a glass mirror; their mirrors were sheets of polished bronze]; quickly you will make the sun and the things in the heavens; quickly, the earth; and quickly yourself and the other animals and implements and plants and everything else that was just now mentioned. (596d)

Who is this craftsman? It must be Homer. And the other question: What is that mirror? Look again at the *Iliad*.

> So [Hephaistos] spoke, and left [Thetis] there.
> He cast on the fire bronze which is weariless, and tin with it
> and valuable gold, and silver.
> First of all, he forged a shield that was huge and heavy,
> elaborating it about, and threw around it a shining triple rim that
>   glittered.
> He made the earth upon it, and the sky, and the sea's
> water and the tireless sun, and the moon...,
> and on it all the constellations that adorn the heavens....
> On it he wrought in all their beauty two cities of mortal men.

So what happens in the *Republic* is this: Socrates goes to the house of Cephalus, a prosperous manufacturer of armor, and there he forges a new shield from men with souls of gold, silver, and bronze. The *Republic* is that shield, that mirror, that will replace our Homeric, Olympian armor.

Could anyone really make such a shield in "deeds"? Is such a city possible? This best city is not possible in "deed" partly because it is a "pattern laid up in heaven," something like a "Form"—something unique which can't be imitated without distortion. To found the city, one would need to have gold separate from bronze or silver, silver separate from gold or bronze. But in so far as the best city is an image of the soul, all of the metals are present in each of us. No one could fully enter one of the classes without doing damage to the wholeness, the tri-partness, of his soul.

And even if the best city were to exist, it would degenerate (and this means that it would inevitably lead to a democracy and its problems) because of the impossible marriage number (546a), a number that Socrates constructs and the best city must solve if it is to endure without change. The impossibility of the marriage number means that the riddle of generation can't be solved: The city can't just continue after its founding. The city will degenerate without the founder and his ability to see the quality of our souls. But the founder cannot be "imitated;" he is not a "type;" he is original.

This inevitable degeneration means, on the one hand, that no kind of soul will be pure; all souls will be at least a bit of a mixture, a jumble. Even in the best soul there is mixed a deep secret lawlessness, as Glaucon suspected when he wished for a ring of Gyges. For Socrates says that there is some "terrible, savage, and lawless form of desire" in every man if only in dreams (572b); even the philosopher might dream of incest (571c).

On the other hand, the necessity for the presence of the founder, the original, means that the philosopher cannot just "disappear," cannot return to looking at the sun, once he has come on the scene; he cannot disappear behind a noble lie that attempts to hide the origin of the city. (i.e., he cannot become an "ideal," a noble lie, for the rest of human beings in the way that Homer, with the invocation of his poem, disappears into his style, leaving us with the song of a Goddess, the "noble lie" of epic poetry).

Who or what is this new shield designed to protect? What needs and can use the protection of the impossible city, a city in speech? In general, the city in speech will try to protect young gold and silver souls from being corrupted, being made cynical and vicious like Thrasymachus, by an uncritical look at the diverse opinions of the city (491a-495b). The shield will also work in the opposite direction: It will try to protect the city from the innocent savagery of unformed philosophic souls (491e) and from the corrupt savagery of the badly raised golden soul. Socrates points to this danger most clearly in the *Apology*, when he makes this prophecy:

> For now you have done this to me because you hoped that you would be relieved from rendering an account of your lives, but I say that you will find the result far different. Those who will force you to give an account will be more numerous than before; men whom I restrained, though you knew it not; and they will be harsher. Inasmuch as they are younger, and you will be more annoyed. (39c)

This new kind of "shielding" is not equally necessary in all cities: A golden soul is not the same danger to all cities nor are all cities equally dangerous to golden souls (some cities are contemptible—496b; usually the city ignores philosophers totally). Nor is poetry the same danger to all cities. Poetry is a particular danger to a democracy because it exaggerates democracy's tendency to tyranny and cynicism; it encourages the *eros* that takes over the soul with its "hymns to tyranny." Poetry is not said to be a danger to any city other than a democracy. So the shield is designed to protect the soul and the democratic city from each other.

This connection between the new shield and the democratic city allows us to interpret one final, baffling image of Socrates, and then to look at the myth of Er. Socrates makes a strange and monstrous image of the soul in Book IX (588c), an "image of the soul in speech." There is a man outside; inside there is a many-headed beast, a lion, and another man. In this image of the soul, which man, outside or inside, is the image and which the original? What unity does this image have, and what does it mean to make an image of man that includes two images of man, one being a reflection and purification of the other?

We can understand this image if we think of the relation of the "best city" and democracy. First, other cities may reflect more correctly than democracy particular features of the soul and particular understandings of justice, but only democracy and the "best city" have all the parts of the soul imaged in some way— for example, democracy is the only degenerate city that has philosophy (561d), even if the philosophy is not serious. And both democracy and the "best city" degenerate because of *eros*: A democracy succumbs to *eros* through the tyrannical hymns of poetry, while the "best city" cannot understand the marriage number and declines. Finally, for someone who wants to found a city or to understand human beings, a democracy is the best place to look, for there one will find all kinds of regimes and all kinds of souls on display (557d). Of all regimes, on the surface and from the outside, democracy is the most beautiful.

A democracy images the soul, but the parts are all jumbled up. It is like the "man on the outside," in Socrates' image of the soul. Because of that jumble, even if democracy is somehow the best city to live in, it is not the best city to have living in your soul. The "best city," the "man inside" in Socrates' image of the soul, is Socrates' "pattern laid up in heaven" (592b).

So now, at the end, in the myth of Er, after the return to the criticism of poetry, Socrates can try to satisfy Glaucon and Adeimantus. When they began this long conversation, they were suspicious of those who praise justice—poetry "cancels" itself when it tries to praise justice—and they wanted to hear the correct praise from Socrates. Socrates is ready to give it to them. He says that "we haven't yet gone through the greatest rewards for virtue" (608b), and now he will do so, with the immortality of the soul and the myth of Er. But first he checks with Glaucon: "Will you, then, stand for me saying about [the just man] what you yourself said about the unjust?" (613d). Now justice will get back what the argument owes it, a speech of praise; the argument is now able to "pay its debts and tell the truth"; it can even "do good to friends" while harming no one. Glaucon and Adeimantus are able to hear a kind of poetry praising justice without being pulled in two directions by it.

The myth of Er has a harmony of philosophy and myth, of *thumos* and mind, but the harmony is not complete or "simple." Immortality has been connected to the soul by the "desire to know" and the unity of soul that this desire indicates. But the myth of Er cannot be about this simplicity or this immortality; it cannot be an "uplifting" presentation of philosophy, an ideal harmony of knowledge and action, deeds and speeches, where poetry takes the place of philosophy and offers "patterns laid up in heaven." The myth emphasizes the soul and its choices, its doings and sufferings, as all myths and mimetic images must. And so the myth introduces faction into the soul, because there is faction in the soul whenever it comes to deeds, choices (603d). The myth, because it is a myth, talks about something that *may* be deeper than knowing, a choice. And thereby the myth is about another kind of immortality.

This other kind of immortality is a sign and expression of the soul's ambiguity, its monstrosity, its "un-naturalness." The soul's transcendence is not unambiguously a heavenly possibility. And so there is another argument for the soul's immortality in Book X (609a ff.), given just before the argument about the soul's simplicity. The soul is the only thing in nature that is not destroyed by its "specific evil," injustice (610e). So the soul has a strength beyond the natural, a greatness beneath the right and wrong of its ordinary choices, in its capacity to survive injustice and evil.

The myth is another look at the range of human possibilities and the spectacle of choice, a look that complements and echoes the first presentation of that spectacle, the democratic man and his possibilities. In the myth, however, unlike democratic life, choice doesn't occur in the ordinary course of our lives. Choice takes place in an interval between the time of rewards and the time of ordinary choices, between a time of immortality (relief from the burden of choosing) and the time of mortal life (the time of confusing choices). In this odd interval between two kinds of life, the soul come to a place where all kinds of lives are scattered about, with no rank or order, in a democratic jumble. And then the soul is asked to choose. The soul is alone—no teachers, no parents, no law-givers, no poets, no philosophers. The soul has put on the ring of Gyges.

The first man to choose (619b) was a virtuous man in his previous life. He comes from heaven to make his choice, but he chooses from habit, not "philosophy." He chooses a tyranny that involves eating his children. Then he complains about fate, and he blames everything but himself. He probably says "I didn't mean it," and he wishes that this choice were an ordinary choice, one that he could take back. But—and here we start to see the soul's monstrosity—he doesn't blame himself. When he blames circumstances, what he is saying is, "If the same circumstances came up, I would do the same thing again." Despite his tragic lamentation, he is accepting his choice and his suffering. ("Apollo did this to me, but I put out my eyes. Only I can bear this suffering.") There is something not serious about his tragic suffering; there is acceptance and even a kind of *joy* ("I would do it again, in the same circumstances").

The last one to choose is Odysseus. There aren't many lives left, but he makes a good choice because he has been cured of his love of honor, a cure in which philosophy was not needed. (The goal of philosophy is such a cure—521a, 540b, 592a.) The myth again points to a choice that might be deeper than knowledge. In the way that Socrates has said that the soul may include some "terrible, savage lawlessness" (572b), the soul may also have some "deep, secret attraction" to virtue. After all, Glaucon and Adeimantus in Book I say that they *choose* justice over injustice (347e), but they do not choose from knowledge or philosophy; they are very aware of the lack of a ground for their choice. There is something about their nature that strikes Socrates with wonder (368a).

The choice in the myth is a special kind of choice. It is very serious, because it determines all our other choices: Ordinary choices, the choices that we make in the course of our ordinary, mortal lives, are *imitations* of this one deep choice. We become what we choose here. This choice is always there, always made again and again, but it is somehow hidden and forgotten and covered by our ordinary choices. The danger for us that this kind of choice reveals is not so much that we will make the wrong choice—the first man to choose in the myth of Er, who chose tyranny, once before had made a good choice, a life of virtue and decency that took him to heaven, but he chose a life without "philosophy." (Glaucon and Adeimantus may have made this very choice.) The danger is that we will choose superficially, out of habit or honor. Our love for these images of glorious choice might betray us.

The myth ends with the waters of Lethe and forgetting; the deep choice and its moment are overcome by forgetting, the triumph of the ordinary over the serious. And thereby the myth points to something that is more mysteriousness than knowing: forgetting, Lethe, and ordinariness. Socrates says that we should spend our lives trying to be capable of making that special choice, trying to be "serious" and awake. Only philosophy and its peculiar call to a kind of human greatness can save us from superficiality, can hold together *thumos* and *nous*, poetry and thinking, the transcendence of the soul in its beauty and its monstrosity. This impossible shield holds apart, and binds together, the democratic city and the "best city"; it gives the soul a "pattern laid up in heaven" and allows philosophy to "come on the scene," stepping out of a mythical past and artfully arranging its own entrance. The *Republic* tries to hold together and see in one glance the desire for greatness and the love of truth.

GLOSSARY

Aristocracy (*aristokratia*) Rule by those few who are best qualified, by natural abilities, character, and education, to be rulers. Never used in this dialogue for rule by those who inherit wealth or honored names.

Art (*technê*) A combination of universal knowledge, particular experience, and practice at a skill that permits someone to produce a result in a reliable way. The word "science" would miss the point on one side, the word "craft" on the other. Though the examples in the dialogue range from a knowledge of medicine to an ability to ride a horse, an art is never mere book learning or mere manual skill. Any artful pursuit involves a range of capacities including some theory, an acquired recognition of how the theory applies to particulars, and sufficient adroitness to carry out that application. Socrates introduces the example of art in 332C as an uncontroversial instance of a power to do good.

Becoming (*to gignesthai, genesis, to gignomenon*) Existence in time and place as a changing and perishable thing. In 508D, Socrates says that there can be no knowledge of anything in the state of becoming, but only fluctuating opinion.

Being (*to einai, ousia, to on*) Refers not to existence but to stable identity. In the dative (*tô onti*) the participle may mean "in its being" as opposed to seeming, or "in its very being," that aspect or part of anything that makes it what it is. In the plural (*ta onta*) it refers to the things that *are* in the most emphatic sense, including whatever is always exactly what it is.

Character (*êthos*) A deep and stable tendency in a human being that has a natural basis but needs to be formed by education and built by thinking (400E). What Cephalus speaks of in 329D as the condition for a good old age is merely the natural disposition (*tropos*). It is the need to provide trustworthy guardians for a city that leads Socrates to introduce the notion of character in 375C; at the same time he displays what he is talking about by his efforts to help change the *tropos* of Glaucon and Adeimantus to respect justice (368B) into a state of character that could adhere to it.

City (*polis*) The sovereign and self-sufficient political community, limited in size by the capacity of people to work in association toward common ends. The principal alternative form of rule in Plato's time was an empire such as that of Persia; to link the two under a single name such as "state" would be contrary to Greek usage and to the nature of the things themselves. The Persian Wars of the 6th century BC provided an occasion for Greeks to discover what was distinctive in their political ways when the survival of those ways was threatened. The realization that the city is not land and buildings is displayed by Herodotus in Bk. VIII, Chap. 61 of his *History*, and made explicit by Thucydides in Bk. I, Chap. 10 of *The Peloponnesian War*. Thrasymachus turns to the city in 338D as the arena in which justice can be seen for what it is. Socrates takes that examination a step further, beginning in 369A, by turning from the haphazard array of actual cities to an attempt to see the city for what it is by tracing it to its origins.

Contemplation (*theôria*) The direct and calm beholding of anything visible or intelligible, that takes it in whole and simply as it is.

Courage (*andreia*) The virtue that permits someone to persevere in a freely chosen course of action in the face of frightening obstacles. It is not the natural fearlessness that might be found in animals as well as human beings, but a capacity that can be developed only by education.

Cross-examination (*elegchos*) The word comes from a verb that orignally means to expose someone to disgrace, and comes to apply to refutation of an adversarial kind. Socrates transforms the word to mean the testing of an assertion or opinion by tracing its implications and assumptions, and throughout Plato's dialogues he encourages others to welcome the experience and invites them to subject him to it as well. It is what people are referring to when they speak pedantically of the Socratic elenchus or vaguely of the Socratic method. In Bk. I of this dialogue, Cephalus walks away from it, Polemarchus accepts it gracefully, and Thrasymachus fights it tooth and nail. Someone who welcomes it, applies it to his own opinions, and presses it as far as it can go, Socrates calls dialectical (534B-C); only such a person does he regard as capable of becoming fully educated.

Democracy (*demokratia*) Rule by the mass of the population, understood in this dialogue as animated by the desire for the greatest possible freedom from restraint.

Dialectic (*dialektikê*) Thinking or inquiry that proceeds the way a constructive conversation does, from opinions through the testing of opinions, to more well-founded opinions. As part of the whole education of the whole human being, Socrates claims (533C-D), dialectical inquiry can lead beyond opinion to knowledge, but dialectic is also the humble approach to other people that allows discussion to be shared learning and not competitive debate (348A-B).

Socrates understands it to be a power inherent in rational speech itself, driving it to move beyond the assumptions it rests on at any time (511B).

Education (*paideia*) In Plato's *Sophist* (229D) this is distinguished from training in particular skills and said to have been recognized and named by the Athenians. There the Eleatic Stranger says that its traditional form is a combination of stern discipline and gentle encouragement. In 376E Socrates particularizes its two components as gymnastic exercise and music. The latter involves all the influences that refine and civilize the soul, the Muse-inspired arts of poetry, pictorial representation, and especially storytelling, in addition to melody, harmony, and song. Much of the *Republic* examines music in its broad sense as the first and most far-reaching aspect of education. And since Socrates says here that the true Muse educates by means of philosophy (548B-C), and in the *Phaedo* (61A) that the greatest form of music is philosophy, all of the *Republic* can be seen as a musical education aimed at spirited young souls.

Freedom (*eleutheria*) First of all, the condition of anyone who is not a slave, and of any city not under foreign domination. Conventionally, the condition of assumed superiority among those born rich enough not to need to earn a living. More deeply, the condition of anyone who gains any degree of leisure by participating in a political partnership. Less deeply, the mere absence of restraint prized in democracies; the argument to show the slavery inherent in this kind of freedom is made at 577D-E. Ultimately, the aim of the whole discussion in the *Republic* is to display freedom as the self-rule of a properly educated soul (590D-591C), capable of choosing its own life.

Imagination (*eikasia*) The power of perceiving the likeness of an absent or invisible thing in some other thing. That other thing may be anything: a three-dimensional object, a pattern of colors, a vocal utterance, or a description in words. Imagination in this sense has an active character, and is not the mere having of mental pictures, which would be *phantasia*. Socrates' image of the divided line (509D-511E) is founded throughout on the relation between image and original, and suggests that active imagination is the power that holds together all thought and perception to make our experience one and whole.

Imitation (*mimêsis*) The production of a likeness recognizable by an active imagination. The image produced is always perceptible to the senses or imagination, but the thing likened and revealed in the image need not be: at 375C and following, Socrates discovers a type of human character that is at once gentle and fierce in the image of a dog, and the resemblance points to a philosophic nature in the original not possible in the image. The effect of the imitation of human character in stories becomes a major theme of the *Republic*.

Insight (*nous*) The kind of thinking that beholds the things it thinks. The active exercise of this power (*noêsis*) is taken by Socrates to be the highest activity of the soul (511D), attaining truth and clarity to the greatest extent.

Justice (*dikaiosunê*) The virtue that governs actions and speech involving other human beings, only in an organized city, according to Thrasymachus (338D-339A), or in human society at large, according to an argument given by Glaucon (358E-359B), or in any group of people, according to Socrates (351C). That last way of thinking about what justice is has the surprising consequence that justice may be present within one person, as the power that permits any of us to be one source of action rather than many impulses; that possibility in turn leads to the analogy between a city and a soul that drives the whole inquiry in the *Republic*. The polity within a human soul, as the root of all human life, is what the title of the dialogue primarily refers to.

King (*basileus*) In this dialogue, always a sole ruler whose title to rule comes from merit and who rules by and is subject to laws.

Moderation (*sôphrosunê*) The virtue that permits the human response to desires, as for food, drink, or sex, or to aversions, as to authority, to be results of choice rather than of irrational impulse. The word is used in a broad, conversational way in Plato's dialogues, where there is no consistent distinction made between the settled state of character and the self-control (*en-krateia*) that needs to be exerted anew on each occasion. Aristotle, in the *Nicomachean Ethics*, does distinguish those two things, as well as a general capacity to recognize and adhere to a mean that belongs to all virtues of character; in such a context, the word moderation would not adequately convey the meaning of *sôphrosunê*.

Music (*mousikê*) See Education.

Oligarchy (*oligarchia*) Literally rule by a few, but used in this dialogue only for a polity animated by the love of money, in which the sole qualification to rule is ownership of some amount of property.

Polity (*politeia*) The title of the dialogue, meaning a political community or association, or the arrangement of functions and responsibilities among the people who belong to it. It is what makes a city one, and not merely many people living near each other, or subjected in common to force. It is a richer and more flexible word in this dialogue than "regime" or "constitution," and provides its central and governing metaphor of an arrangement of parts or powers within each human soul that leads to happiness or misery. See, for example, its use at 605B and 608B.

Presupposition (*hupothesis*) Anything taken as known and clear without examination. The English cognate "hypothesis" would be a perfectly good translation of the word, except that it refers to something deliberately adopted, while Socrates leaves open the possibility that it may be merely an unexamined assumption (510C-D). Something like "underpinning" or "underprop" might get at its literal sense of something set down underneath, which Socrates plays on at 511B.

Speech (*logos*) The intelligible content of language that is neither Greek nor English, spoken nor written. In particular, a *logos* can be any unity in the medium of speech: a word, a meaning, a sentence, a statement, a story, an argument, a discourse, a description, an explanation. In mathematics, a *logos* is a ratio, an intelligible pattern of relation in size. The city repeatedly built and rebuilt through the *Republic* is frequently referred to as having its being in speech.

Spiritedness (*thumos*) Passionate exuberance on behalf of anything to which one feels an attachment or in opposition to anything one feels as threatening or demeaning to one's attachments. It is the source of the craving for honor, but also the source of the feeling of respect. Socrates argues (439E-441C) that spiritedness is the middle part of the soul that can harness the desires to the intellect or vice versa. Glaucon displays spiritedness in an exemplary way when he objects in 372D to Socrates' portrait of a healthy city in which all natural appetites are satisfied and all rational necessities are provided for; he pronounces such a life unfit for human beings, feeling it as an insult to our dignity and insulting it in turn as fit only for pigs. The word has no connection with anything "spiritual" but names the same quality evident in a spirited horse or aroused by a pep talk (375A-B).

Thinking (*dianoia*) The way of dealing with intelligible things that moves from presuppositions to conclusions, contrasted by Socrates with insight (510B-511C). He uses first the former (at 524D), and later the latter (at 534A), in a wider sense for the whole thinking power.

Timocracy, timarchy (*timokratia, timarchia*) Words coined in this dialogue (545B) for a polity like that of Sparta, animated by the love of honor, and in which those who earn the most honor also earn the right to rule.

Trust (*pistis*) The attitude of the soul toward the things perceived by the senses, taking them uncritically as the true, original, or only beings.

Tyrant (*turannos*) A sole ruler who takes over a political community previously ruled in some other fashion, or a monarchy in which the succession prescribed by law would go to someone else. Socrates argues (565D) that the natural way for a tyrant to come to power is within a democracy, after being chosen as leader of the popular faction.

Virtue (*aretê*) The excellence of anything as an instance of its kind. The virtue of a jug would be to hold liquids without leaking, sit on a surface without tipping over, and have a handle for easy carrying. Liddell and Scott's lexicon derives the word from the name of Ares, the war god, but it is more likely to come from the verb *arariskô*, meaning to fit or be fitting. The virtue of anything is to be well fitted to its ends. But the word had a special application to human beings, referring to any quality of character that makes someone outstanding and admired, and to four such qualities as the primary or cardinal virtues: wisdom, courage, moderation, and justice. When Thrasymachus denies that justice is a virtue (348C), he is challenging the conventional opinion that there is anything moral about human excellence, which he regards instead as excelling others in getting the things one wants. Socrates responds by arguing that all successful activities depend on a knowledge of exactly what a situation calls for. Human virtue, then, would not be a comparative or competitive superiority, but the same in kind as the virtue of anything else.

Wisdom (*sophia*) The directing knowledge by which anyone can assess the best way to do or make anything. Hence its first and most widespread application is to those who possess arts. But then it becomes identified primarily with the intelligent judgment that can direct the whole life of a human being or community (429A), and the word for intelligence, *phronêsis*, is then used interchangeably with it (433B). But all these uses presuppose an ability to assess evidence of things that are true in themselves, and this is made explicit in the account of a presuppositionless, and therefore contemplative, knowing of unchanging being (511B-E). The gradual deepening of the meaning of *sophia* through the dialogue supersedes any verbal distinction between practical and theoretical wisdom, and Socrates denies that the two are separable.

INDEX